THE BOOK OF HOME RESTORATION

THE BOOK OF HOME RESTORATION

Traditional skills and techniques to restore and improve your home

· CONSULTANT EDITORS ·
John McGowan and Roger DuBern

SIDGWICK & JACKSON
LONDON

First published in hardback by Ebury Press
First published in paperback in 1988 by
Sidgwick & Jackson Ltd
1 Tavistock Chambers
Bloomsbury Way
London WC1A 2SG

Conceived and produced by
Swallow Publishing Limited
Swallow House, 11-21 Northdown Street
London N1 9BN

Editor Loulou Brown
Assistant Editor Angie Doran
Editorial Consultants Nick Carter, Michael Crossman
Art Director David Young
Designer Glynis Edwards
Assistant Designer Florrie Pinnock
Studio Del & Co
Illustrators Steve Cross, Hussein Hussein, Aziz Khan
Picture Research Liz Eddison

ISBN 0 283 99706 0

Typeset in Bembo by Dorchester Typesetting Group

Printed and bound in Spain by Imago

Contents

Introduction

Quality of workmanship is not the hallmark of our times; nevertheless, many of us live in homes that were built when craftsmanship was still considered to be an important virtue.

The Book of Home Restoration sets out to help you restore, renovate and enhance all parts of your home, whether it was built this century or some time before. It is first and foremost a practical book, written to convey the skills and knowledge of former craftsmen to the intelligent and enthusiastic amateur of today. But it is much more than just a practical manual: it shows how to achieve long-lasting and good quality results by employing the proper methods and materials.

The advice offered in this book, which has been provided by a team of specialists, will help you to achieve three objectives. Firstly, if you carefully follow the instructions given you will be able to do each job properly. Secondly, good workmanship is immensely satisfying to achieve. You will experience real pride and personal fulfilment from a job well done, using good quality materials. Thirdly, the end product will be compatible with the original work around it. Only by using the appropriate methods and materials can new and old look and feel comfortable together.

As well as outlining methods of working and correct materials, the book provides something of the historical background of the various crafts and shows how they evolved. Traditional tools, no longer used, are mentioned and, where space permits, the book gives details of skills and ways of working that are now only of historical interest.

Sometimes, original methods and materials have been superseded by other, better, modern equivalents. Also, it is very often difficult, or even impossible, to obtain the original tool or raw materials. When it is impractical to do a job using traditional materials, or where new methods and materials are preferable, this is clearly stated.

Whether you are tackling a whole room or just one part of it, thorough preparation and planning are essential if the best possible results are to be achieved.

Inevitably, not every job can be tackled by the amateur. Where a task is very difficult or dangerous, professional help is recommended. And if you discover you are unwittingly the owner of an antique or some other piece of fine workmanship, it is suggested you entrust its repair and renovation to a specialist.

Each chapter deals with a specific area of restoration and a combination of step-by-step illustrations and photographs will help you to understand the advice given in the text.

The book begins with Woodworking which gives details of techniques and skills which are employed in the following two chapters on Restoring Furniture and Wood Finishing. The chapter on Painting and Wallcovering considers both straightforward aspects of the work and time honoured and now fashionable techniques such as graining and trompe l'oeil.

Much of the advice and many of the methods described in Metalwork and Metalware link closely with those in the chapter on Glasswork. Similarly, the techniques and information given in Tiles and Tiling connect with the chapter on Flooring.

Plasterwork outlines one of the most difficult skills to master. Much of the information is set out here for the first time. The chapter on Brickwork and Stonework relates to work both within and outside your home, while Roofing and Garden Crafts are almost exclusively external tasks.

Whatever job you undertake, remember that to achieve the standards of quality worthy of a craftsman is not easy. Bear in mind the three 'Ps'- Patience, Practice and Perseverance - as relevant today as they were in the past.

Woodworking

Wood is both one of the most widespread and most versatile of building materials. Its easy accessibility, coupled with its strength and durability, have meant that it has been used from earliest times for constructing homes. Many houses are still made primarily of wood, but even those built of brick use large amounts of the material in joists, beams, floorboards and window frames.

Those qualities which have made wood so suitable for houses have been even more important in the manufacture of furniture. Before the use of metal and plastics earlier in this century, wood was the dominant element in all furniture-making, and it is still the most commonly used material for tables, chairs, chests and shelves. Its advantages are many: it can be shaped, jointed, carved, polished and stained – and it is fairly tough and hard-wearing. It is also one of the most satisfying materials to work with, calling for precision and patience, but no very difficult or highly specialized skills.

Few samples of the work of craftsmen living five or six hundred years ago remain; only the breathtaking beauty of the great cathedral roofs endures to remind us of their great skills.

Medieval carpenters' tools were crude and simple. Beams and boards were split from trees with mallets and wedges and then made smooth with an adze, a type of axe. With small items, the crudity of the tools and techniques was very apparent. Heavy chests, made from oak boards, were nailed or pegged together and wrapped with thick, iron bands.

The need for precision woodwork was met by the joiners. Instead of using thick planks of newly felled wood, they discovered how to fix together small pieces of wood. The framed and panelled doors and simple furniture that this new technology produced was lighter and better proportioned than anything that preceded it.

During the sixteenth and seventeenth centuries, attention focused on the comfort and beauty of domestic interiors. The simple chest was put up onto legs and the need to store linens and clothes securely and conveniently produced the chest-of-drawers. The stool and box seat gradually gave way to more comfortable chairs, with carved decoration and cushioned seats.

Many styles in furniture-making which emanated in one country were copied throughout the European continent. The Baroque style, for instance, influenced the whole of Europe. British furniture carried designs that originated from France and the Netherlands. It was imported into Denmark in the seventeenth century and had a marked influence on Danish taste.

American woodworking, although rooted in European traditions, soon developed its own unique features. New York became the centre for the manufacture of fine furniture. Woods of many varieties were abundant in the United States and wooden houses were built to rival the finest European stone houses in elegance and proportion. Techniques were European but the results subtly American. Noticeable features are the comparative scarcity of plasterwork and the abundance of fine joinery, seen in even the simplest of homes.

Many of the hand tools used today have been little changed for centuries, and some of the methods used are really ancient. We can help to preserve the legacy of skill and beauty left to us by former craftsmen by using their methods to produce beautiful workmanship.

Woodworking is a traditional craft which employs many skills. A lot of tools are required, and a number of those commonly used are shown here.

Tools and equipment

The tools described below are presented in the order in which they are usually used. This is logical, even though the items, which to the casual eye are identical, are not placed together in the text.

Carpenters used to prepare wood for use by splitting it from the log. As these splits always follow the direction of the grain, the wood was tough and had attractive markings or figuring. This technique is still used when so-called riven oak is required for restoration work.

Commercial wood now comes ready-sawn to size and is often planed to the required thickness. Modern quality saws are very expensive, but with care they should last a lifetime.

Cutting tools

Maul

This implement, made from solid elm and banded with iron, was used to drive wedges into felled wood.

Iron wedges

Wedges about 250mm (10in) long were usual in the past.

Two-handed cross-cut saw

A heavy implement designed to speedily cut lengths from large boards. This tool comes in one or two versions and in lengths of 1 to 1.9m (3 to 6ft).

Frame saws

Frame saws are useful for cutting small pieces of wood. Modern types have a light steel tube frame and disposable hardened steel sawblades. (Not available in the US.)

Drawknife

The drawknife is available from specialized tool merchants. It is best for shaving off pieces of wood up to 75mm (3in) wide. A 250mm (10in) blade is best. In use, the tool is pulled towards the user by the two side handles. For safety in use the blade must be kept very sharp with an oilstone (whetstone), as a blunt blade is liable to skip off the wood with serious results.

Adze

The adze is a rare type of cross-headed axe. Old tool dealers occasionally locate these tools – and they fetch a high price. Skilled hands used to be able to level and shape wood with amazing speed using a 1m (3ft) shipwright's adze. The wood was laid on the floor while the craftsman stood over it, swinging the adze between his feet. Adzed wood has a faint surface ripple which looks beautiful when it is polished.

Rip saw

This very handy tool has about five tooth points per 25mm (1in) and is designed for speedy cutting along the grain only. It has the usual handsaw shape and is available in lengths of up to 650mm (26in).

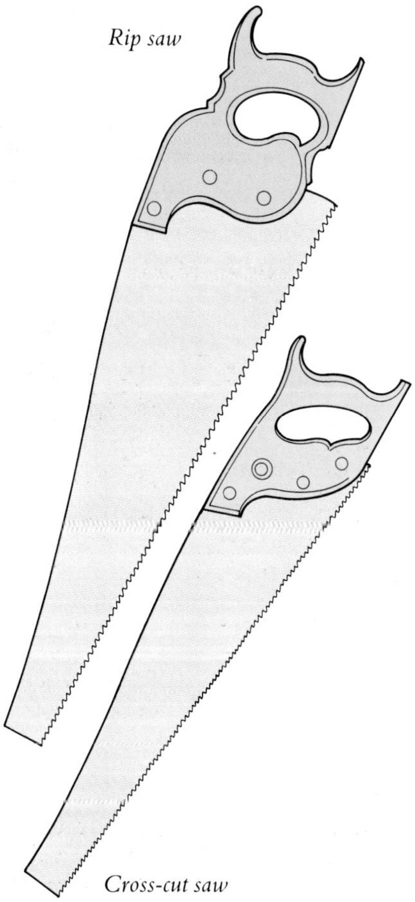

Rip saw

Cross-cut saw

Cross-cut saw

A cross-cut saw usually has seven teeth per 25mm (1in) and works well cutting across the grain. This is because the teeth of the saw are differently shaped.

Panel (hand) saw

A panel (hand) saw rips and cross-cuts fairly efficiently. A 530mm (22in) size with 10 points per 25mm (1in) serves well for most tasks, including sawing plywood and blockboard.

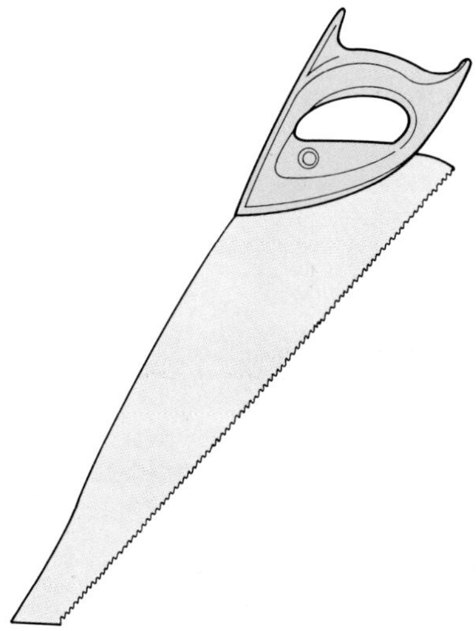

Sawing and marking

The fine jointing of parts before assembly demands precision and therefore more carefully made tools than those used for preparation.

Tenon (back) saw

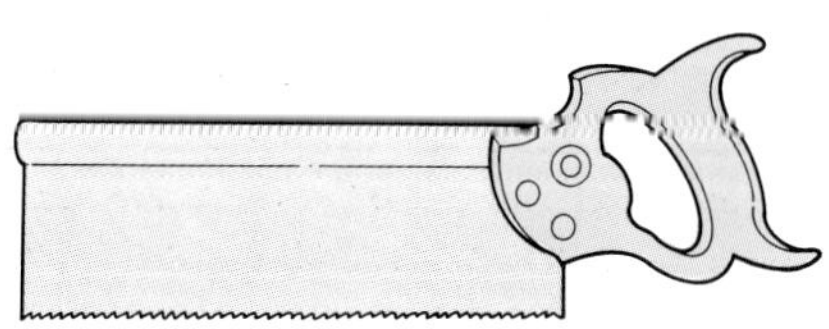

This is a compact, useful tool, used to cut large joints. A good size for general workshop duty is a 300mm (12in) 15-point saw. Try to find one with a non-slip wooden handle. The brass spine along the top of the saw helps accurate work by stiffening the blade.

Dovetail saw

A dovetail saw deals with most fine jointing jobs. Smaller than a tenon (back) saw, it cuts a thinner line. One with about 20 tooth points per 25mm (1in), and a 200mm (8in) blade dees for most difficult jobs.

Coping saw

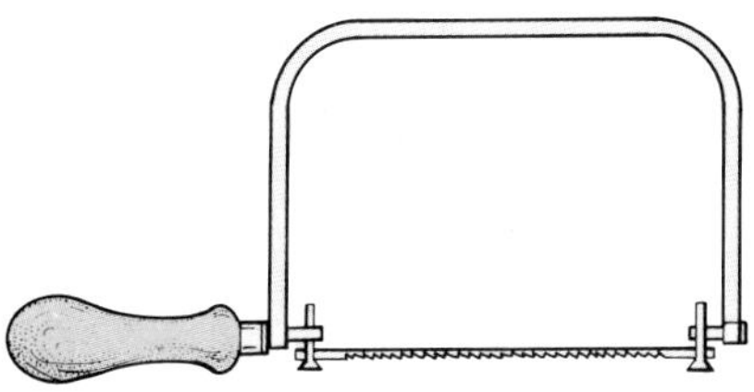

A coping saw is used for cutting out curved parts in thin wood. Mouldings and plywood can be trimmed easily too. The coping saw is a good investment, since the hard blades supplied will easily cut soft metals if required.

Marking knife
A marking knife is the professional's pencil. A fine knife cut across the wood is more precise than a thick pencil line and provides a start groove for a chisel or saw.

Marking gauge
This tool is used to mark lines parallel to the surface of the wood. It enables a precise measurement to be repeated exactly. Tricky to handle, the gauge is easier to control if the point is kept sharp.

Grooving and mortizing tools

Grooving (combination) plane
A grooving (combination) plane is the customary tool used for grooving. Quick to set up, it can be hard work to use, especially if the groove is large, but the job will be smooth and satisfying if the tool is sharp.

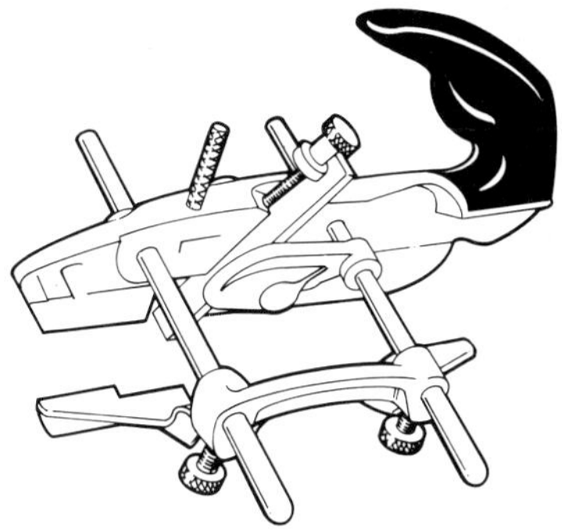

Router

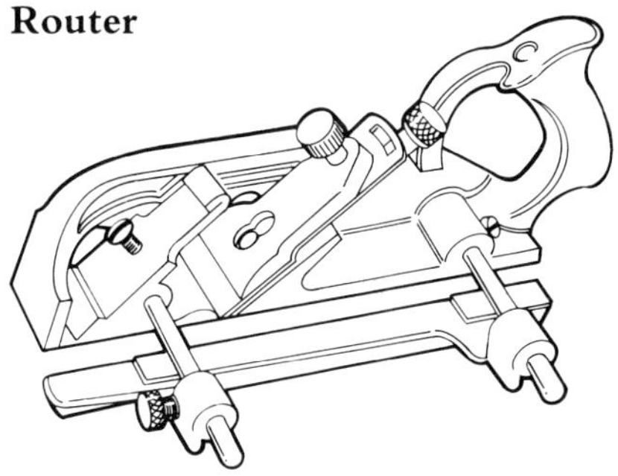

The hand router is a quick and efficient tool for cleaning and levelling the bottom of grooves and housing joints (dados).

Rebate (rabbet) plane

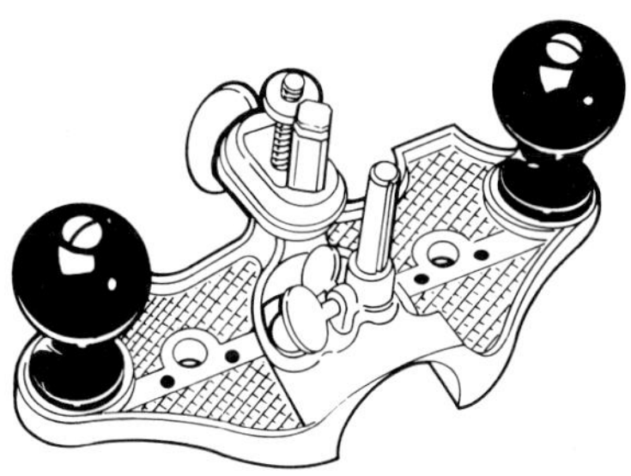

This instrument is another fine tool that, used with care, is quick and efficient. Rebates (rabbets) are step-shaped cuts along the edges of a piece of wood.

Mortice chisel
This implement is rapidly becoming a specialized tool and hard to find. However, a strong reinforced handle, thick metal blade and leather padding, mean that it can stand continuous heavy mallet blows, which makes this tool vital if you need deep mortices in hard wood.

Firmer chisel
A firmer chisel is fitted with sturdy square-edged blades to cope with light mortice work. Three chisels, sized 6, 9 and 12mm (¼, ⅜ and ½in) are enough for most projects.

Bevel-edge chisel
This is a very useful tool as the thinner, tapered ground blade can get into awkward spots. A set of these is handy. Do take very good care of them as they are easily chipped on the edge.

Lip-and-spur drill
A lip-and-spur drill, used together with a hand drill or power drill, makes a neater, cleaner hole than metalwork bits.

Carpenter's brace

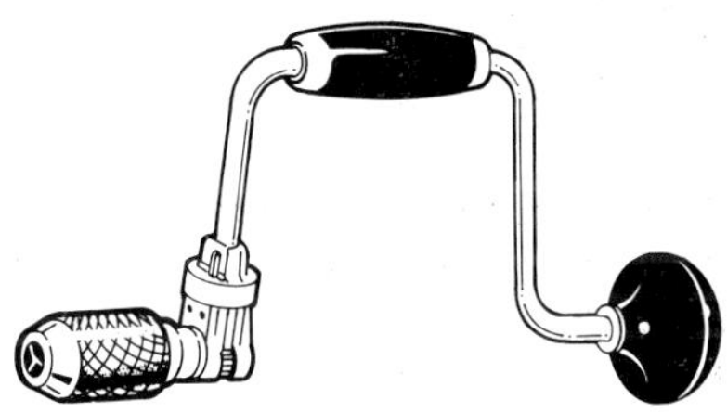

This is a powerful hand-tool for heavy work. It takes special corkscrew-like bits called *augers*. A useful accessory is a screwdriving bit.

Augers are expensive and, unless you have a special project in mind, high-speed flat bits for power drill use will serve.

Assembly tools

Careful assembly of the parts of a completed project is essential. Many potentially excellent jobs are spoilt by working carelessly and too fast. Only when all the parts have been tried for fit can assembly begin.

Joints must be tested carefully to ensure they are not too tight.

Shoulder (bench rabbeting) plane

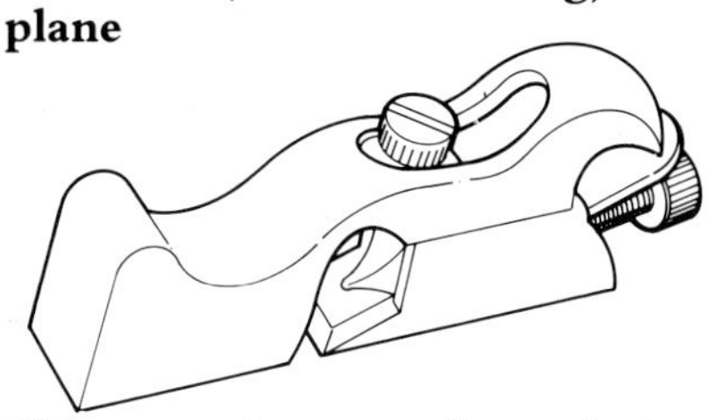

This comprises a small metal plane with a blade covering the width of the sole. It is ideal for cleaning up tenons and rebates (rabbets).

Paring chisel

This is a long, thin tool, designed to help clean inside grooves and the housing slots used for shelves.

Cleaning-up tools

'Cleaning-up' is the trade term used to describe all the tasks necessary before polishing or painting begins.

Good cleaning-up demands very sharp tools. Long pieces of wood must be made very straight and smooth; small steps in joints levelled; and dents removed.

Jointing plane

This is a heavy iron plane, up to 600mm (24in) long. Used with care it can level the front of a chest-of-drawers, or flatten the top of a table.

Jack plane

This implement will true-up surfaces if you fit a straight blade. A more usual task for the jack is cleaning up rough-sawn or dirty milled lumber. When worked this way a slightly curved blade is used. This takes off a thick shaving without digging in at the corners. Spare plane blades or 'irons' are available.

Smoothing plane

A tool which removes steps and bumps from small areas such as door panels and drawer fronts. The basic design is similar to the jointing and jack planes, but on a smaller scale. The smoothing plane is excellent for fitting small doors and other odd jobs.

Low angle block plane

This tool is vital for cleaning end grain, which is easy to split when trimming rails to fit. Its special blade is able to smooth even difficult woods such as elm.

Warrington hammer

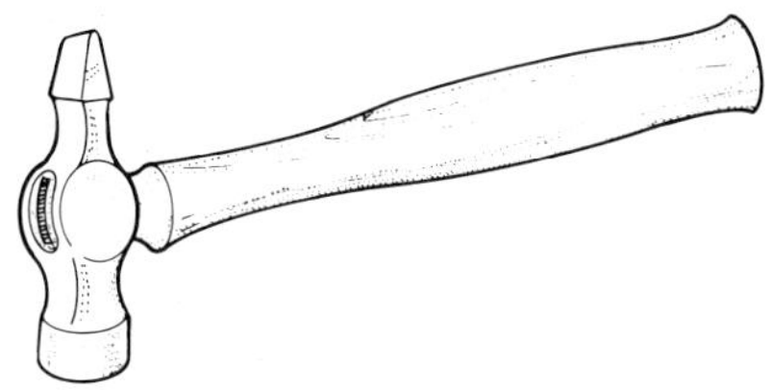

The Warrington hammer is a tool used by the cabinet maker for driving small pins and nails. The cross-pein type is best. One weighing about 170g (6oz) suits most needs.

Ratchet screwdriver

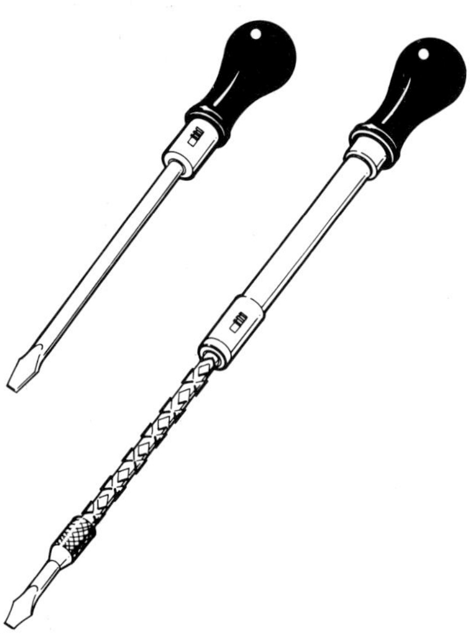

This tool comes in several sizes and types. A simple ratchet will save an aching wrist. If you have many long screws to drive in it might be wise to invest in a spiral ratchet ('Yankee' screwdriver). Note, however, that this tool takes some time to learn how to use.

Bradawl

A bradawl is used for making start holes for small screws and pins. The square shafted type, called a cage awl, is the restorer's favourite.

Smoothing tools

When the joints have been levelled and the article is complete, it is time to smooth off.

Cabinet maker's scraper

A cabinet maker's scraper is a simple square of steel, about 100 × 50 × 1mm (4 × 2 × 1/32in). Although not hard to master there is a knack to sharpening it. (See page 32.)

Sanding block

A sanding block can be bought, or made from a piece of scrap softwood about 100 × 50 × 25mm (4 × 2 × 1in). Papers of 80, 120 and 240 grit will suffice for most tasks. On flat surfaces, use a cork or rubber sanding block. Holding the paper in your fingers will make hollows in the work.

The sharpening tool

Care and sharpening of hand tools are vital if they are to work well. Since edged tools need to be razor-sharp, no tool-kit is complete without an oilstone (whetstone).

The India combination oilstone (whetstone)

This is the best oilstone (whetstone) for general use. Use the fine side for regular sharpening and turn over to the coarse side for re-shaping damaged or worn tools.

To use the oilstone (whetstone), sprinkle with thin oil and, with the flat side of the blade uppermost and the tool at an angle of 30 degrees to the stone, rub on the surface.

Take care to move around the stone since constant rubbing in one spot will dent the surface, rendering it useless.

When a minute burr can be felt on the extreme edge, turn the tool over and, with the tool *flat* on the stone, rub once or twice more only. Wipe off the oil. The tool can now be used.

Wood

Despite the excellent plastics introduced in this century, wood is still the first choice for many applications. Of the thousands of different tree types, only a very few are used commercially at present. Many more, however, are available as thin decorative veneers. The range of wood-based material has been increased by the processing of wood into manufactured boards.

Wood is divided into two groups: hardwoods, which are mainly obtained from leaf-shedding (deciduous) trees and softwoods, which are mainly evergreen (coniferous). This simple grouping is confused by the fact that some hardwoods – balsa for example – are very soft, and some softwoods – pitch pine – are very hard.

Newly-felled wood contains large amounts of moisture; wet wood shrinks considerably on drying and is prone to decay. These factors make unseasoned wood unsuitable for most purposes. To reduce the moisture level, logs are sawn into thick boards and stacked under cover. Over a period of time, which varies with the climate and thickness and type of the wood, the moisture level drops to a constant figure.

Raw wood is available in a number of different forms and finishes. Whole logs are sawn up into sizes which suit the market. The sizes used to describe the width and thickness of sawn wood are called 'nominal' sizes.

The nominal size is fairly accurate for rough-sawn wood: for example, sawn wood sold at 50 × 25mm (2 × 1in) would normally be very close to that size. When the wood is planed smooth, however, the actual size will be reduced to around 45 × 22mm (1¾ × ⅞in). Despite this loss, the wood is still sold at the larger nominal size. If an exact size of planed wood is required, be sure to order it 'finished size'.

The price will vary according to its quality. There are several ways of grading wood. The way the log is sawn affects its value. The best type of hardwood is called 'quarter-sawn'; the cheapest, 'slash-sawn'.

Trees grow in many awkward sizes and shapes and the raw material produced may be sound or shoddy. This unpredictability does not suit production-line manufacturing and that, together with rising costs, combine to foster interest in processed wood.

Plywood is made from thin sheets or 'veneers' of wood. These are usually peeled from whole logs rotating in a giant lathe. The peelings are trimmed to size, coated with glue and pressed together to form boards up to 2m (6ft) wide and 5m (16ft) long. Thickness varies from 1mm (1/24in) to 25mm (1in). Many types are available but the main grades in order of rising cost and durability are: interior, moisture resistant (MR) and marine grade. These boards can be printed to imitate handsome woods. The finished material can be sawn and jointed like solid wood.

Chipboard (particleboard) is the most popular and cheapest wood substitute. Formerly restricted to light duty in dry conditions, improvements in manufacture have made it suitable for hard use. About half the cost of plywood, its quality depends on its density, that is, how closely the woodchips used to make it are glued together. Tough on tools, chipboard is not suitable for complex jointing because of its 'crumbly' nature. It is, however, stable in conditions of varying humidity.

Medium density fibreboard (MDF) is a material new to the DIY field and is growing in popularity. Like a superfine grade chipboard (particleboard), it can be jointed and moulded with great success. MDF is recommended for complex interior work that has to be painted, for example, wardrobes and panelling.

Shown here are a few of the most useful and widely available wood species. Small samples such as this can only give a very general impression of their appearance which in fact can vary widely.

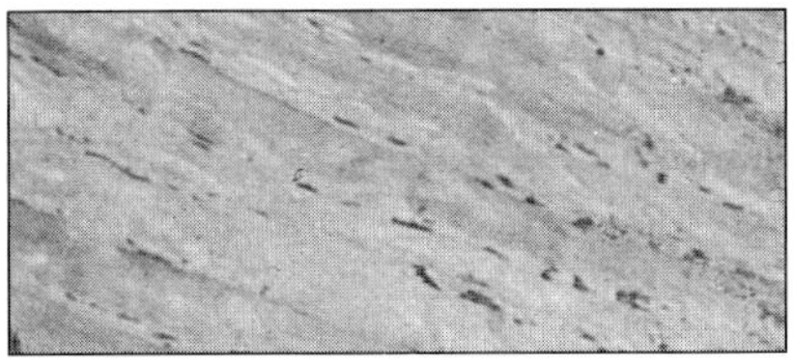

Oak: the 'queen of woods'.

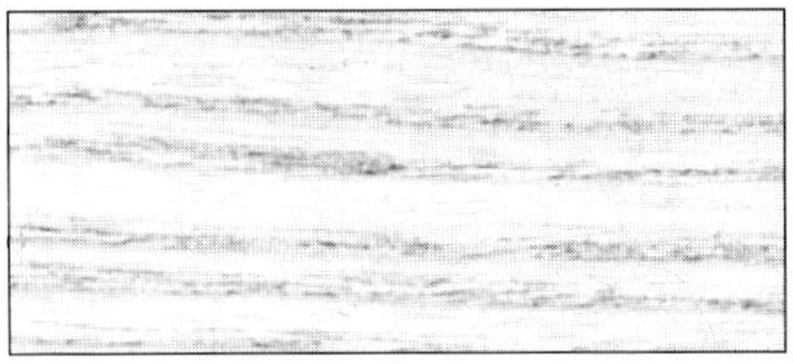

Ash: tough and springy hardwood.

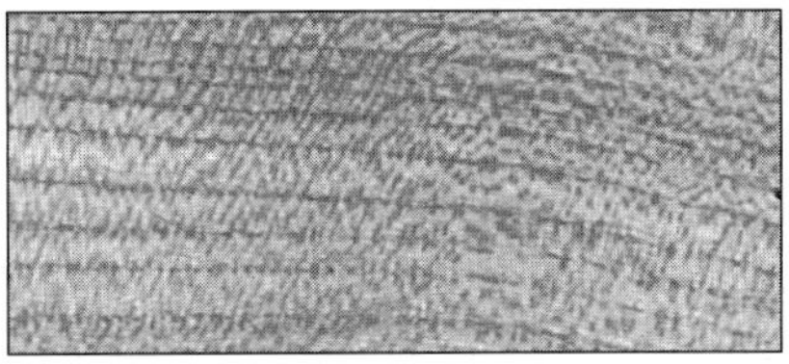

Elm: favoured by chair-makers.

Lime: often used for woodcarving.

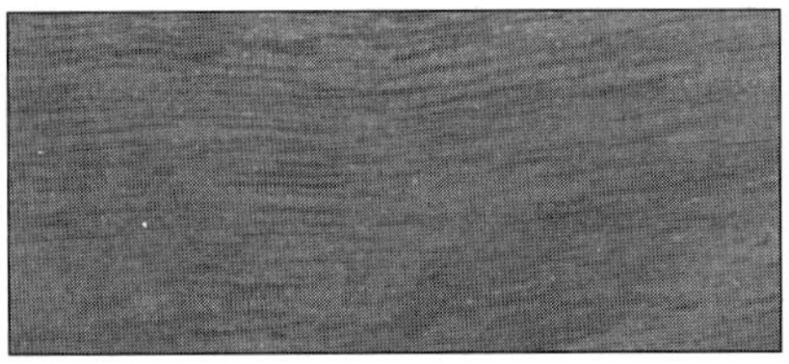

Mahogany: a very popular wood.

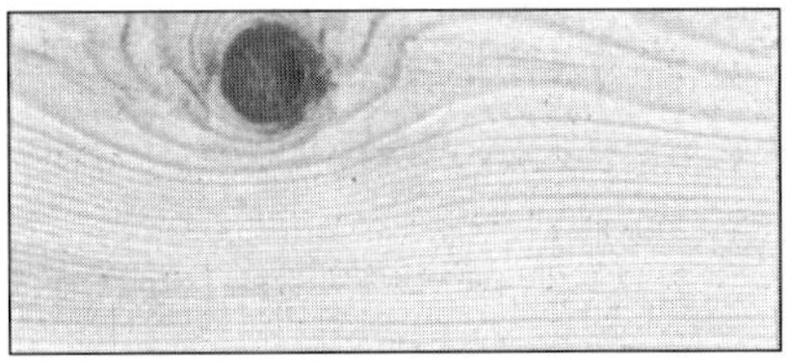

Scots redwood: best for joinery.

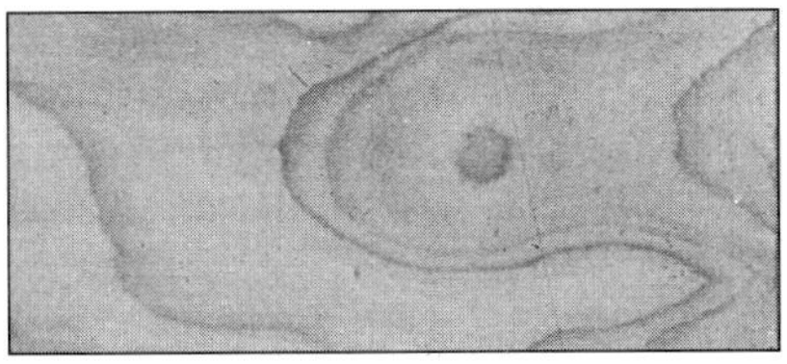

Yew: produces lovely figuring.

Types of Wood

Species	Appearance	Characteristics	Uses
■ **Afrormosia** *Pericopsis elata*	Yellow to mid-brown; grain sometimes erratic; striped.	Attractive and easily polished. Glues well, but nailing not recommended.	As veneers and solid wood for furniture; exterior joinery and boat-building. Also used as lower-cost teak (qv) substitute.
■ **Apple** *Malus sylvestris*	White to pale pink; grain often twisted; pleasing markings on some samples.	Attractive, hard and quite heavy. Fine grain means it carves well. Not for outside use.	Marquetry veneers and inlay work; wooden jewelry; model building; fine carving.
■ **European ash** *Fraxinus excelsior*	Creamy-grey; often finely figured. May have black heartwood and pink streaks.	Attractive and easily polished. Glues well. Nailing not recommended. Prone to decay and discoloration when used outside.	As veneers and solid wood for furniture; bent chair frames and boat parts. Also for hammer handles and sports goods.
■ **Beech** *Fagus sylvatica*	Pale pink to light brown. Grain not pronounced except in quarter-sawn wood.	Plain in appearance, it can be stained and polished to imitate almost any other wood. Machines well with sharp tools. Tough, but prone to fungal attack in damp situations.	Furniture; flooring; wood-turning; sports goods; food storage use.
■ **Boxwood** *Buxus sempervirens*	Golden-yellow; fine grained; usually sold in small pieces.	Hard and prone to splitting. Takes shellac polish, and glues well, but nailing not recommended.	Its small size limits its use to ornamental turning, carving, inlay on furniture and mathematical instruments.
■ **Ebony** *Diospyros*	Brown to jet-black; grain sometimes erratic; zebra-striping and dramatic figuring common in some varieties.	Attractive and easily polished. Glues well, but nailing not recommended. Extremely hard and heavy. Blunts tools rapidly.	As veneers and inlay for furniture; musical instrument parts; small turnery artefacts.
■ **Elm** *Ulmus spp*	Many varieties. Mainly mid-brown and well figured wood. Interlocked grain common in some species.	Attractive and easily polished. Glues and nails well; can be steam-bent.	As veneers and solid wood for furniture; fencing; joinery; boat-building; coffin making.
○ **Douglas fir** *pseudotsuga menziesii*	Cream to pale red-brown; grain straight and well marked.	Strong, clean working and lasting. Glues and nails well, but must be treated for exterior use.	Construction and joinery timber; also used for bridge building in the USA and as a source of paper-pulp.
○ **True firs** *Abies spp*	Many varieties; all creamy-white; straight grained; sometimes knotty.	Light, weak wood, with a tendency to woolliness.	Used as a low-cost substitute for spruce; much used for packing cases and paper-making.
■ **European lime** *Tilia vulgaris*	Yellow to pale-brown; grain always even; little figuring.	Plain, but easily polished. Glues and nails well, but lacks strength.	Carving and turning; brush handles; picture frames.
■ **African mahogany** *Khaya ivorensis*	Reddish brown; grain often erratic; striped figuring common.	Stable, attractive and easily polished. Glues and nails well, but hard to plane and saw cleanly.	Furniture; boat-building and plywood manufacture.
■ **American mahogany** *Swietania spp*	Red to mid-brown; grain straight, but sometimes erratic in highly figured wood.	Strong, reliable, handsome and easily polished. Nails and glues well; needs sharp tools on figured wood.	As veneers and solid wood for furniture; exterior joinery; boat-fitting. Also used for pattern-making.

■ *Hardwood* ○ *Softwood*

Types of Wood

Species	Appearance	Characteristics	Uses
■ **American maple** *Acer spp*	Creamy white. Hard types, like rock maple may have a pink tinge. Finely figured.	Rock maple is heavy and hard. Soft maple is easier to work, but may be hard to glue.	Furniture and joinery work; veneers; dance floors; other heavy duty surfaces. Not recommended for outside use.
■ **European oak** *Quercus spp 1*	Golden-brown. Grain usually straight and open.	Can usually be sawn, cut, carved or turned. Avoid using iron nails which will corrode. Glues well.	As veneers and solid wood for furniture; exterior joinery; floors and panelling.
■ **American oak** *Quercus spp*	Yellow to mid-brown; may show pink or ochre tint. Straight grain; attractive figuring.	Hard and heavy. Good to work, easily polished and glues well, but nailing not recommended.	As veneers and solid wood for furniture; exterior joinery; flooring; barrel-making; wagon and lorry building.
○ **Parana pine** *Araucaria augustifolia*	Yellow to mid-brown, often streaked with red. Grain straight and unobtrusive.	Attractive and easily polished. Glues well, but nailing must be done carefully. Easy to work by hand.	Furniture parts; mouldings; staircases; window sills.
○ **Pitch pine** *Pinus spp*	Yellow to mid-brown; grain clearly marked and straight. Resinous.	Heavy and hard on tools; great strength. Can be hard to glue but nails and screws well.	Heavy construction; wagon-building; some church joinery. Used as a source for rosin and turpentine.
○ **Scots redwood (Red pine)** *Pinus sylvestris*	Yellow to mid-brown; grain sometimes erratic around knots; striped figuring.	Easily worked. Glues well and nails and screws securely.	Furniture and construction work. Exterior joinery must be well maintained to avoid rot.
■ **Rosewood** *Dalbergia spp*	Rich purple-brown; creamy sapwood sometimes present. Dark brown or black figuring.	Hard and heavy, but a tendency to brittleness. Attractive and easily polished. Glues fairly well, but nailing not recommended.	As veneers and solid wood for furniture; cost rules it out for most other applications.
■ **Sapele** *Entandrophragma cylindricum*	Mahogany-like; golden or ruddy-brown; grain sometimes erratic; striped or banded figuring.	Hard to stain evenly, but easily polished. Glues and nails well, but cannot be steam-bent.	As veneers and solid wood for furniture; joinery work of all kinds; boat-building. Also used to manufacture plywood.
○ **Spruce** *Picea spp*	White to cream; grain straight and mild; sometimes knotty.	Unexciting but useful. Glues well; nails easily. A tendency to woolliness demands sharp tools.	Low-cost construction work; musical instrument parts; newspaper pulp.
■ **Teak** *Tectonia grandis*	Yellow to golden-brown; grain clearly marked; usually straight.	Oily nature and abrasive mineral content makes it hard to glue and machine. Stable and highly water-resistant.	As veneers and solid wood for furniture; exterior joinery; boat-building and outfitting. Anywhere where durability and pest resistance are important.
■ **Walnut** *Junglans spp*	Mid to dark brown; grain sometimes erratic; beautiful figuring common. Also curl and burr forms as veneers.	Showy, elegant wood, easily polished. Glues well, and can be fastened; avoid iron nails though.	Available from Europe, US, and Africa. As veneers and solid wood for furniture; gunstocks; turned items; writing boxes.
○ **Yew** *Taxus baccata*	Yellow sapwood and purple-brown heart. Small size of many trees means much is knotty and erratic. Lovely figuring.	Attractive and easily polished. Glues well, but nailing not recommended. Straight grain is easy to work but natural hardness and twisted grain is difficult.	As veneers and solid wood for furniture; fencing; high-class reproduction chairs; picture frames.

Preparation work

Carefully examine the wood before buying it and reject any that is wet or has obvious splitting. When buying long lengths, look along them for any serious twisting. Bowing – bends along the length – and curving – 'cupping' – across the width are also faults to be avoided. Wood is expensive and should never be bought unseen.

Try to obtain wood that can be easily reduced to your required size. Sawing by hand is hard work, so plan ahead.

Power-milled commercial wood is planed all round ready for use. This cuts out much hard preparation work, but the surface should be cleaned up with a jack plane.

Select a suitable length and find the worst end. This is often the original 'mill end', bearing marks of the lumberjack's saw, which usually contains deeply embedded grit and paint, and sometimes short cracks. At least 25mm (1in) should be trimmed off to give a clean start. Hold the square up to the edge of the wood and mark with a knife. Holding the piece to be worked on firmly in a vice or on a saw-horse, cut off the scrap piece with a panel (hand) saw. Be sure to keep on the waste side of the line. Measure off the length needed, and repeat the squaring and cutting processes. Saw the workpiece to slightly more than the finished length and width.

After sawing to size the edge will need re-planing smooth. Fix the wood securely in a vice and, using a long plane set to take a fine shaving and held square to the face, clean off the saw marks.

Thicknessing and trueing

After the wood has been roughly cut to size it will need reducing to the exact size required. This may involve its thickness, width and length. This part of the work must be carried out with care and precision since, if the parts are not flat and straight, it will be impossible to joint them together. Reducing the wood to the correct thickness is called thicknessing. Ensuring that the faces are flat, with both edges at 90 degrees to the face, is known as trueing. To thickness a part, fix the wood in the vice and plane off any saw-marks on the edges. Once they are smooth and square, with a marking gauge set to the thickness required, scribe a line along both edges of the piece.

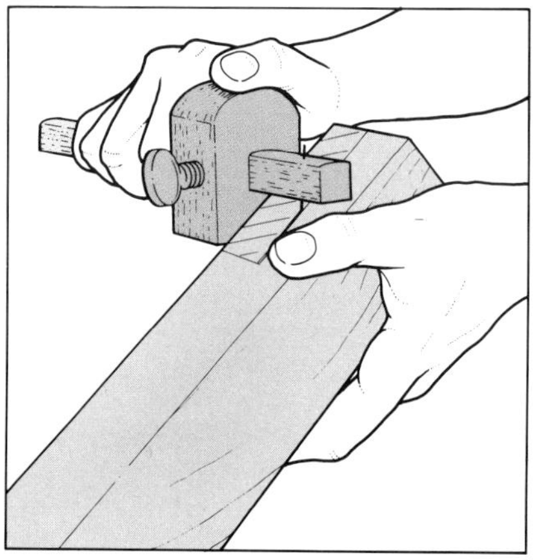

Using a marking gauge.

Mark the wood so that the worst side will be planed off. With the piece held flat on the bench, plane from corner to corner across the face. Check often to ensure that you are keeping the surface flat. Use a steel straight edge, or the blade of a square. Stay parallel to the gauge lines. When about 1.5mm (1/16in) above the gauge lines, plane along the length until the thickness required is achieved.

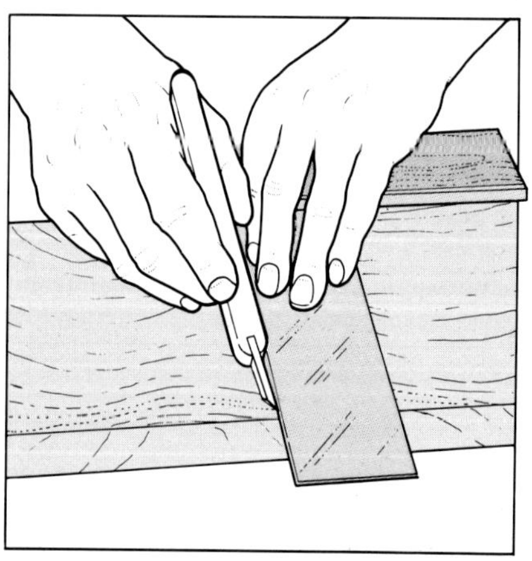

Using a square and marking knife.

Wood can also be reduced in width by gauging and edge planing. Check the surface is flat and square. This can be done with a steel straight edge and a small square.

Trimming end grain

End grain is tricky to work on as the wood tends to splinter out. To prevent this happening, joiners and cabinet makers use a gadget called a shooting board. To use the board, press the workpiece against the stop and slide a sharp plane along the board and over the end grain. The stop will prevent the back edge from splintering, and will hold the wood square. The shooting board can be used to trim parts in length and, if carefully used, will leave them smooth and square. A long plane is generally favoured for this work. Do not try to take off a thick shaving when working cross-grain as this will cause the plane to snatch and splinter the wood.

Sizing

Many woodworkers find the accurate sizing of parts difficult to achieve. It is easy to make measuring mistakes that will ruin a costly piece of wood. To avoid this problem, many craftsmen try to use a rule as seldom as possible. Measurements are made by marking off of the job in hand, or by comparison with other parts. For example, drawer fronts are marked for length by fitting them into the cabinet, not by measurement.

A useful way of avoiding problems with dimensions is to prepare a rod. A rod is a full size drawing of a job, drawn on a piece of board. Since the drawing can be laid on the bench, workpieces can be laid on top of it, for comparison. However, as a full size drawing of a whole door or window frame would be inconvenient, the usual practice is to reduce the width, showing only the

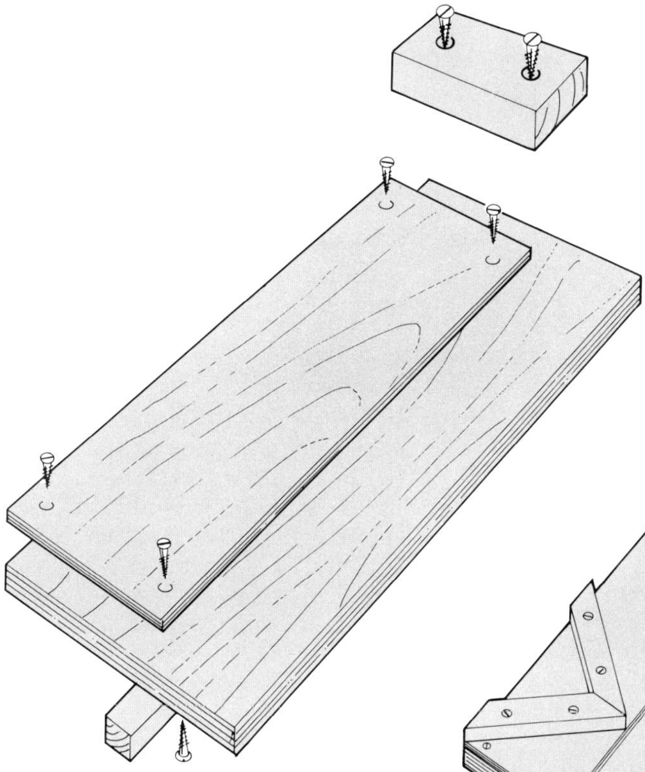

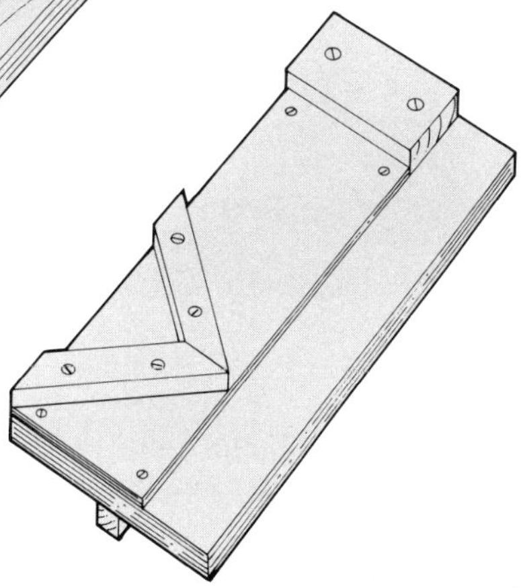

A simple shooting board

This important aid to good workmanship is simple to make, but take care to get all the angles exactly right or it will become a means of spoiling rather than improving your work.

Use a piece of flat plywood, about 450mm (18in) long by 175mm (7in) wide and 12mm (1/2in) thick. Another piece 400mm (16in) long, 125mm (5in) wide and 6mm (1/4in) thick is screwed and glued to it as shown.

A strip of strong hardwood, such as beech, is fixed across the end. Glue and clamp it at an angle of 90 degrees. When the glue has set, strengthen it with two long screws as shown.

Two further pieces of wood can be fixed as shown to trim mitre joints. Wax the bed so that the plane slides easily. A piece of hardwood 25mm × 25mm (1in × 1in) screwed to the base will enable you to hold the board in the vice during use.

To use the shooting board, employ a sharp plane, set to take off thin shavings. Press the workpiece up against the chosen stop with the left hand, with about 1.5mm (1/16in) projecting over the bed. Lie the plane flat, firmly pressed against the bed and base, and slide it along so that it trims the overhang smooth.

principle joints of the upright members, as these are usually the most prone to errors.

When making identical parts, always compare them with each other. If they are handed left and right, like the front legs of a chair, make sure you 'pair them off' and that you do not make two for the same side! Lay the two parts side-by-side and mark out the joints and so on by squaring across from one to another.

Fine sawing

Professional woodworkers cut most of their joints with a tenon (back) or dovetail saw. This is quicker than paring the wood away with a chisel, and practice enables near perfect joints to be cut in one operation. Tapping a wedge of wood into the start of the cut will keep the saw free until the cut is completed. The most important rule is to keep the handsaw sharp and clean. If it is rusty or blunt, it will not cut straight and will always tend to wander along the grain of the wood.

Never ever use a jointing saw to cut chipboard (particleboard) or fibreboard. These contain a large amount of resin glue which will blunt the saw teeth rapidly. For these jobs use a panel (hand) saw or a metal-cutting hacksaw.

Finally, remember that, once buried in the wood, a handsaw cannot be forced to change direction. Twisting the blade in the cut will only strain it. Always ensure that the saw is correctly lined up before you go too deep.

Fitting joints

Even the very best of craftsmen occasionally have trouble in getting joints to fit.

Before you start to glue up any job, you should ensure that everything will mesh together by dry fitting the parts. If a joint requires more than a firm tap with a mallet to get it to close, then some of the excess wood must be removed. The trouble-spots in a joint can usually be detected by close study of the parts after attempting to put them together. Places where wood has to be removed will be shiny, or the surface fibres will show signs of crushing. Excess can be pared away from these spots with a sharp bevel-edge chisel, held almost parallel to the surface of the piece. Use the widest chisel possible as this will help to plane the joint surface flat. Remember always to chisel away from your body, and keep your free hand out of line with the cutting edge. Blunt tools are dangerous whereas sharp ones will stay under your control.

Planes, chisels and drills

Coordination and concentration produce good woodcarving. Hand and eye working together produce beauty from the wood.

For a plane to work well it must be really sharp. Amateurs often neglect this important consideration.

Using planes is fairly easy. Bear in mind that they are designed to remove only a thin shaving without trouble, and will work best when they are smoothing down the woodfibres rather than tearing them up. Working with the grain is best.

Grooving planes

Grooving planes are simple and efficient tools which will work well on mild-grained wood.

Some of the more elaborate types of grooving plane, known as 'combination' planes, are able to make simple mouldings. These are very useful for restoration work since, used properly, they can achieve traditional patterns of moulding which have been used for the last 150 years.

Sometimes examples of old wooden moulding planes turn up in junk shops, but more often in antique shops, where they are beginning to command high prices. They are worth buying if you intend to do a lot of restoration work. Only buy a complete plane with the correct blade fitted. The blade shape should exactly match the moulded sole. Don't worry if it is grimy or rusty. A good rub with steel wool and linseed oil will work wonders. The cutters can be sharpened with small curved slipstones like those used for carving tools.

Rebate (rabbet) planes

The rebate (rabbet) is another useful type of special plane. Like the grooving plane, this tool needs to be sharp and finely set. It is capable of making large rebates, working with or across the grain. There is a small disc of metal fixed to one side of the soleplate on the rebate plane. This disc, called the spur, is only used for cross-grain working. The spur severs the wood fibres before the plane reaches them.

Bevelling

Bevelling is an operation whereby the edge or face of the wood is planed away at an angle. On flat surfaces it is a fairly simple matter to pare away wood with a small block plane. It is more difficult to achieve curved bevelling, the ideal tool for which is a spokeshave. It is sometimes difficult to get the right angle and maintain it. A special adjustable bevel gauge can be used for setting out and checking the bevel angle.

Using chisels and drills

Chisels may be driven into the wood either by hand pressure or by blows with a mallet. The secret of using chisels successfully, to chop mortices, pare joints, or make grooves, is to make sure they are extremely sharp all the time.

A main failing of novice woodworkers is that they only look at the cutting edge when they are working. What they do not realize is that if the chisel is not held straight, with the whole shaft and handle pointing in the desired direction, the cut is bound to go wrong. When chopping out a mortice or housing joint (dado), for example, always ensure that the chisel is square to the face of the wood on the final cuts. When cutting grooves with a chisel it is important to use the tool to cut away the waste; never lever wood out of the groove. The latter can cause deep splitting.

The correct alignment of the tool is also important when using a hand or power drill. Parts held together with dowels, which are small wooden pegs, will need careful boring to ensure that the parts align correctly. Sometimes it helps to stand a large square up on the work so that you can compare the alignment of your drill with it. (Dowel joints are described in more detail on page 22.)

Remember that the hand tools used today are the products of an evolutionary process that has spanned hundreds of years. Most do their job superbly – if maintained and handled with respect.

Woodturning

Woodturning is an absorbing and relaxing pastime and a vital technique for restorers to master.

Choose the type of wood to be used very carefully. Make sure the wood is well seasoned and free from knots. For intricate work, choose fine textured woods such as beech or mahogany; coarser textured types such as oak and Scots redwood, however, are suitable for straight sections and slow curves.

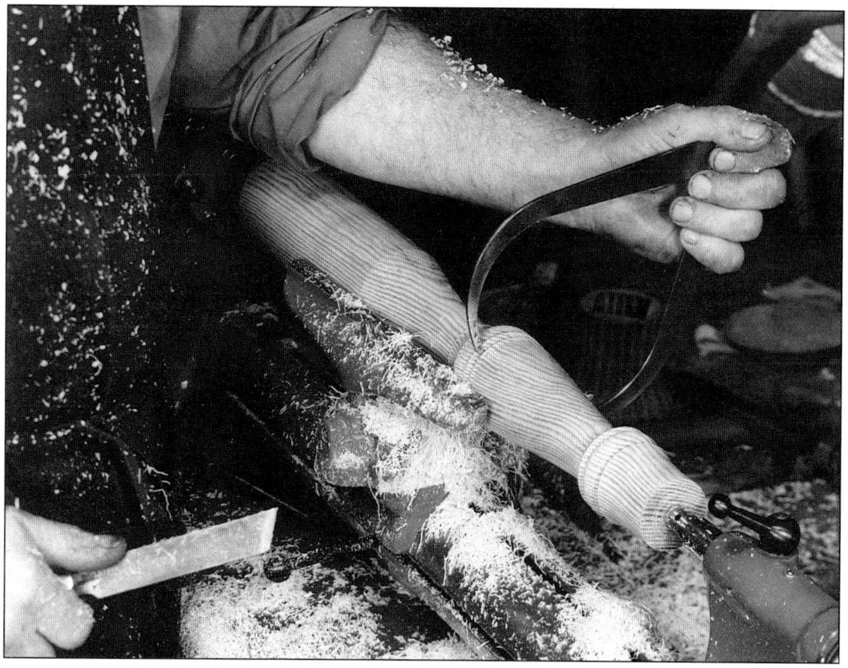

When turning on a lathe, calipers are used for measuring the diameter required. The skew chisel shown is used when the lathe is working.

Working with a lathe

All lathes have the same basic parts.

The bed

This is the base of the machine; the other parts are made to slide along it. This enables various sizes and types of work to be done.

The headstock

A sturdy bearing in a metal casing, this has the electric driving motor attached. In the case of a drill attachment, the drill replaces the headstock completely.

The driving centre

A small metal part, with spikes or vanes on one end, and a thread or taper on the other. This transfers motion to the workpiece.

The tailstock

Used for spindle-turning work, this supports the free end of the work. The actual fixing point is called the dead centre.

The toolrest

This is used as a steadying support for the hand-held chisels used in turning work.

Small items can be turned on the lathe using one of the many types of chuck available. The two most useful are the cup chuck, which holds small pieces of wood suitable for turning egg-cups and ornaments, and the screw chuck.

If you plan to make such items as table lamps, you will need a hole boring attachment. This consists of a special spoon-bit drill which can be fed through a hollow dead centre into the work. Using this device, holes up to 900mm (36in) long can be made in the hardest wood.

A pair of large dividers are useful for measuring and marking out details on the work. The divider point is used to scribe lines directly onto the turning workpiece.

Tools for turning

Spindle gouge

Available in several sizes and types, the gouge does all the rough shaping of bowls and spindles.

Skew chisel

The skew is used for planing smooth the ridged surface left by the gouge. This chisel is factory-ground on both faces to a sharpness angle of 30 degrees. Sharpen by rubbing on the oilstone (whetstone), ensuring the cutting angles are maintained.

Parting tool

This is a thin-bladed tool used for separating the workpiece from the waste wood.

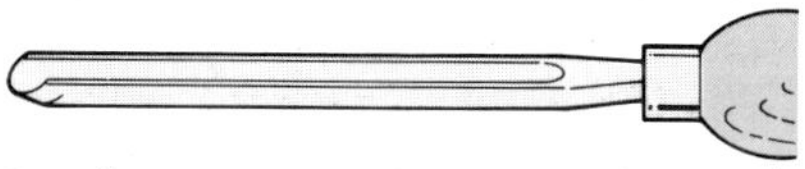

Spindle gouge

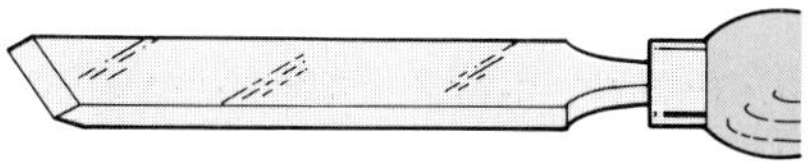

Skew chisel

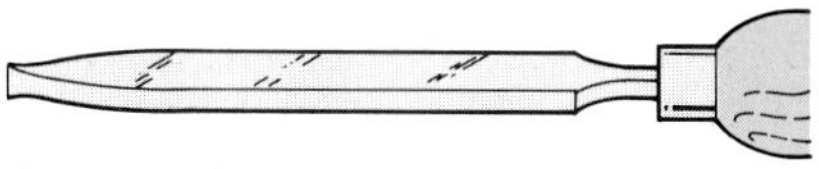

Parting tool

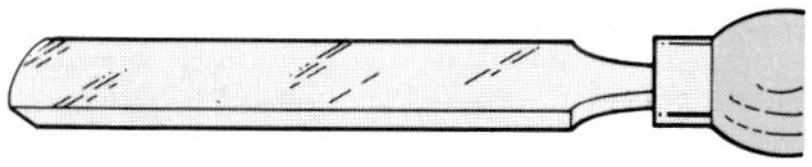

Round-nosed scraper

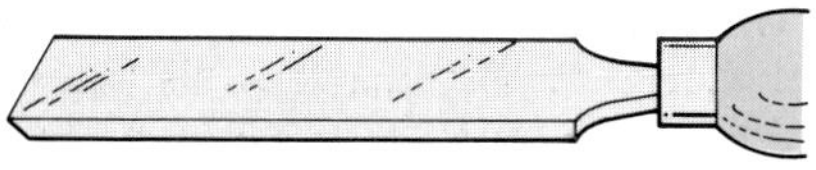

Square-nosed scraper

Scrapers

Many types of scraping tool are sold for lathe work. Amateurs are often encouraged to use scrapers for all kinds of work, since they are easy to handle. Resist this temptation since, on the lathe, these tools leave a ragged surface that needs hard sanding to give a good finish.

Scrapers are sharpened by grinding the edge to an angle of 60 degrees and 'turning it over' to achieve a burred edge.

Spindle turning

Using spindle turning you can make chair legs, stair spindles, and ornamental items like candlesticks.

To make a turned item such as a chair leg, first select a square of wood big enough to make the replacement. Allow 50mm (2in) extra on the length, and make the thickness at least 6mm (¼in) bigger than the maximum diameter of the old piece. Find the centre of each end and mark it clearly. Plane the corners off so it is octagonal in section. This makes the first cuts easier, and reduces the chance of splinters.

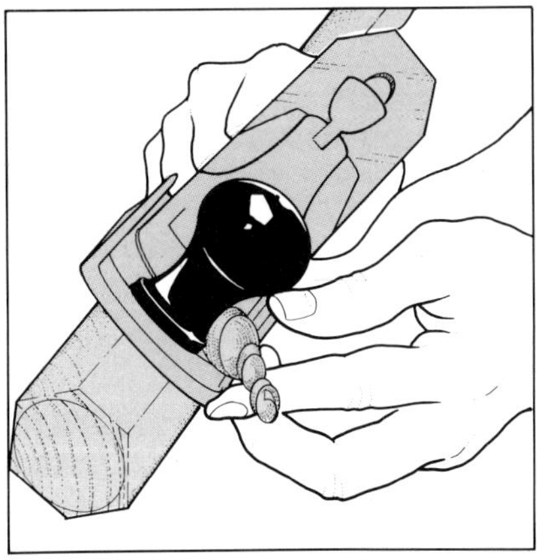

Plane the wood to an octagonal shape.

Wearing safety glasses, mount the wood between the driving and dead centres of the lathe. Ensure that the centres are exactly positioned on the marks made in the ends of the wood. The workpiece must be firmly fixed by the spiked centres to avoid it flying out.

Position the tool rest level with the wood. Rotate the work by hand before starting the lathe to ensure the workpiece is not striking the tool rest. Select a speed of 1,000-1,500 rpm. See that all the parts of the lathe are locked tight and start up.

Take a sharp spindle gouge and, with the handle firmly held in both hands and pointing downwards, press the tool down onto the rest. Advance the cutting edge toward the work. As the gouge touches the wood, steady it and, keeping the same distance from the work, slide the tool along the rest.

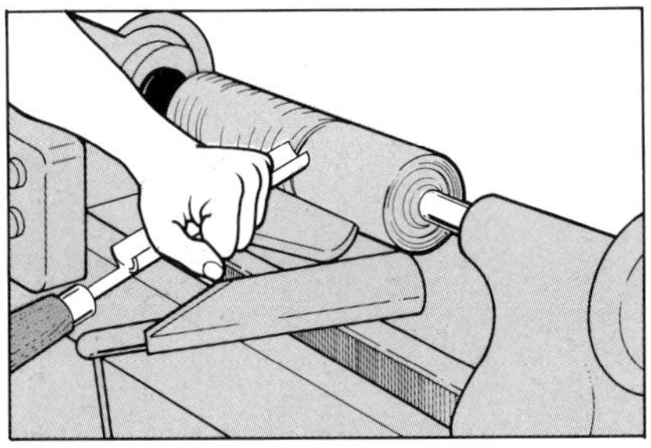

Present the spindle gouge to the wood.

A stream of shavings should now be coming off of the piece which is turned into an even cylinder of wood. Stop the lathe. The details of the part can now be marked firmly in with pencil. Re-start the lathe. Cut the hollows with the gouge; other details can be put in with the skew chisel corner, or parting tool. Always work from the larger to the smaller diameter, to avoid cutting against the grain. When all the mouldings have been cut, use the parting tool to cut down both ends of the piece until thin wooden strips connect it to the waste at each end. Stop the lathe. Separate workpiece and waste with a saw. Finish the work with sandpaper.

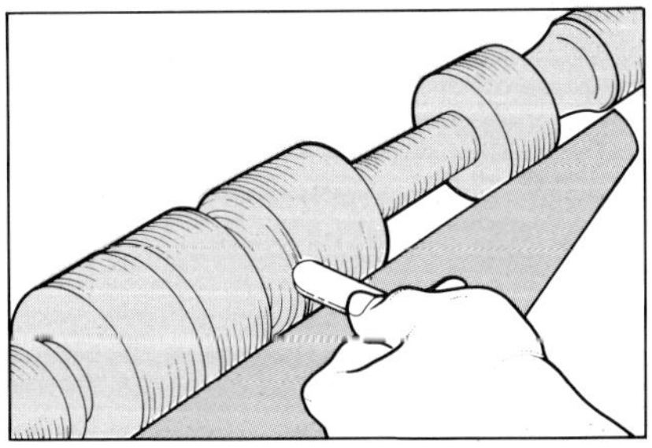

Detailed cuts can be made with the gouge.

Faceplate turning

Wooden bowls and plates require a different method of turning to chair legs. To make all parts of the surface accessible to the tool, the work is fixed to a metal disc, or faceplate, with strong screws. The faceplate is, in turn, attached to the headstock of the lathe. The work is then rotated and the outer shape of the bowl cut.

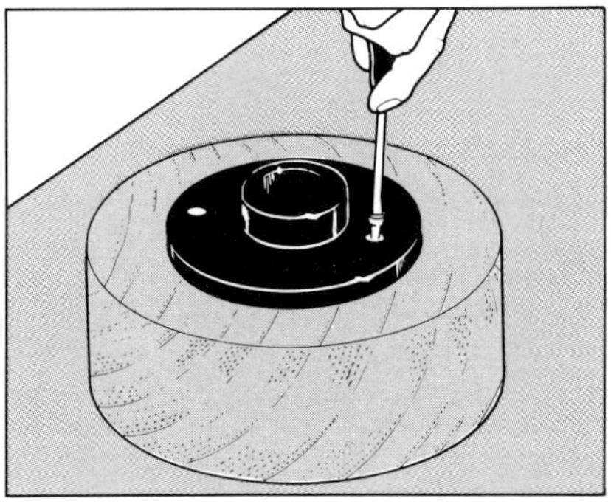

Mounting the wood onto the faceplate.

When the outside is finished, take the parting tool and scribe a line on the flat part of the work facing you. This line marks the inside edge of the rim of the bowl. Working steadily, using a 9mm (⅜in) gouge, hollow out the inside of the workpiece. When the inside is clean, tidy up the rim with a sharp parting tool and sandpaper smooth. The final finish can be applied on the lathe. Use olive oil for salad bowls, or wax polish for ornamental work.

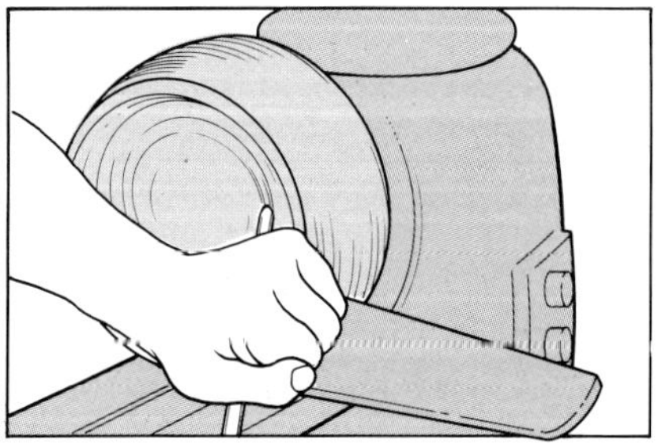

Hollowing out the inside of the work.

Joints

Like bridges and skyscrapers, simple joinery and furniture are structures under stress. Chair frame parts, for example, may carry loads of several tons if the person sitting on the chair leans backwards. To withstand the strain of use, the parts of all structures must be firmly fastened together. This is the function of joints in woodwork.

Types of joint

A butt joint is the simplest of all joints. The parts are put together with glue, without any tongues or other strengthening devices. The best type of butt joint is where parts are glued together edge to edge, as in the boards of a table top. When making edge joints, take particular trouble over the fit of the parts. Plane the edges straight and square before gluing and clamping together. End grain, which is the wood exposed when it is cut across the direction of growth, is fibrous and weak and will not glue well, as the fibres tend to pull out of the wood under stress. Reinforce the joint with tongues where the ends meet.

Tongue and groove joints are of two kinds. One of the simplest for the small workshop is the loose tongued type which is best for fastening boards edge to edge. Make a groove in the edge of each board, taking care to keep it in the centre. For 25mm (1in) boards, a groove about 6mm (¼in) wide, and 10mm (⅜in) deep will suffice. Cut a strip about 18mm (¾in) wide from a piece of plywood, thick enough to fit the groove snugly. This is the loose tongue. Glue inside the grooves and along the board edges, pushing the tongue into one edge. The two boards should now be clamped together and left to dry. This makes a very strong joint.

The other version of this joint has a groove worked into one board and a step-shaped reduction in the other to make a solid tongue.

A mitred joint is where two meeting pieces of wood, each cut to an angle of 45 degrees, join to make a right angle. They make good, neat corners on picture-frames, small boxes, and other light-weight items. The simple mitre is not very strong. Its chief advantage is that it makes it easy to join together complicated mouldings.

There are many variations on the mitre, including the mitred half lap or mitre with feather and mitred bridle. The mitred half lap has overlapping surfaces on one face, usually at the back, and a mitre on the side seen. The mitred bridle is made exactly as the plain bridle (see below), except that the seen side of both parts is cut at 45 degrees rather than at right angles. Both these joints are used when making picture frames which have to be veneered or gilded afterwards, since they are much stronger than plain mitres.

Screwed or pinned joints are usually made for lightly loaded structures, or for unseen parts of furniture, or shelf supports, etc. The parts to be joined are generally flat and square and not generally tongued or morticed.

These simple joints can often be made with or without the help of glue, but the glued joint will be far stronger because screws or nails will not hold well in end grain wood. Parts can be dovetail-nailed together for added strength. This is done by driving the pins in at angles so that they resist direct pulling from the wood. Screwing or nailing into hardwood will require the drilling of pilot holes. These will improve the strength of screw joints and reduce the chances of splitting.

A halving joint is often used in carpentry work. Where two pieces of wood cross they are each reduced in to exactly one half thickness, and then glued or pinned together. The depth of the halving can be marked out with a marking gauge and the width with a pencil or knife. Make a series of saw cuts across the waste to the full depth of the joint and then pare away the waste wood with a sharp bevel-edge chisel.

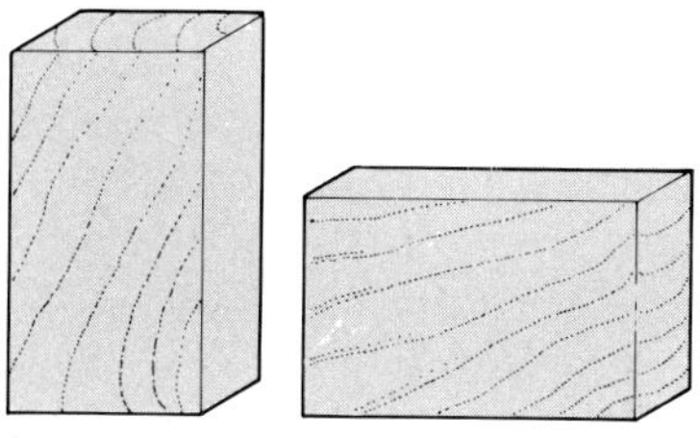
Butt joint

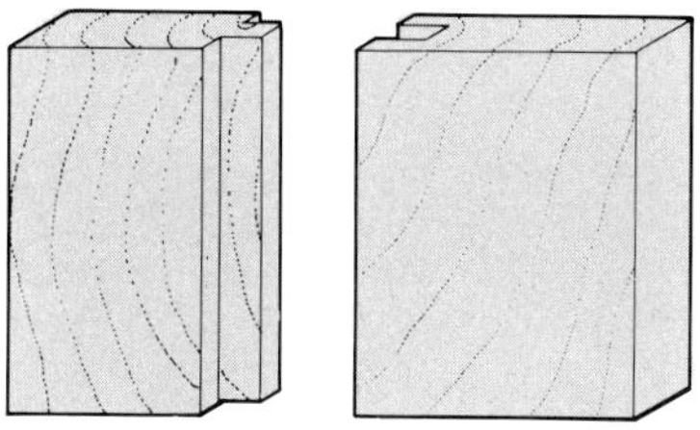
Tongue and groove joint – solid tongue

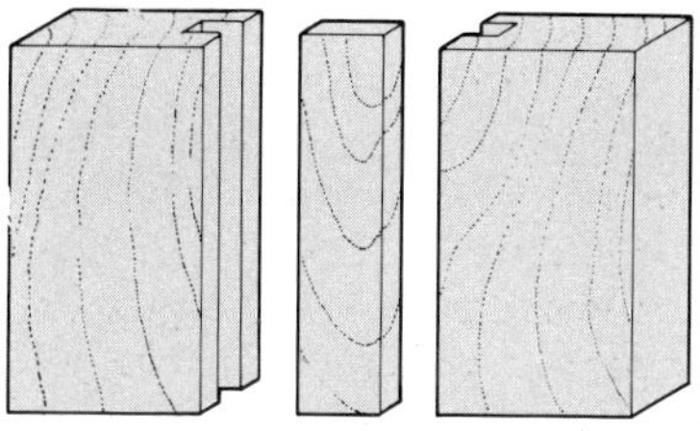
Tongue and groove joint – loose tongue

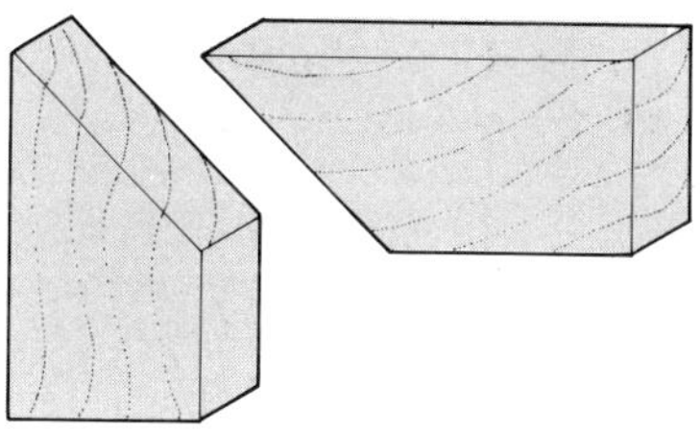
Mitred joint

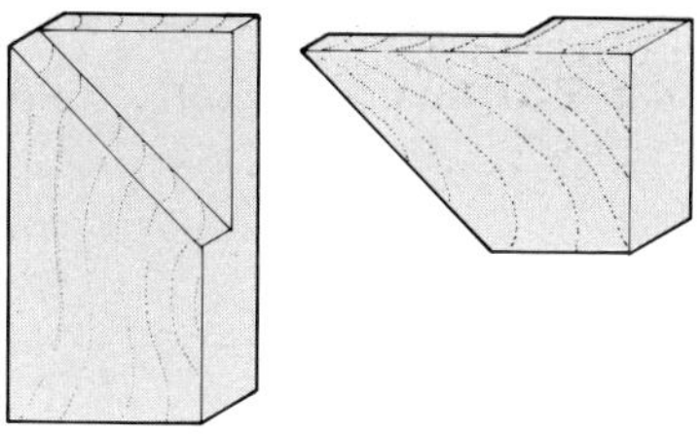
Mitred half lap joint

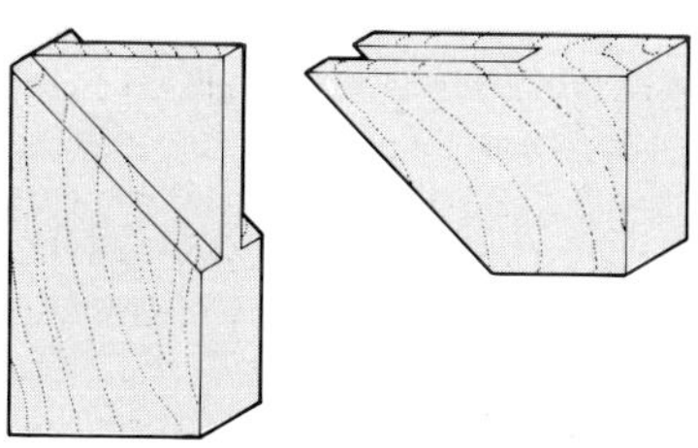
Mitred bridle joint

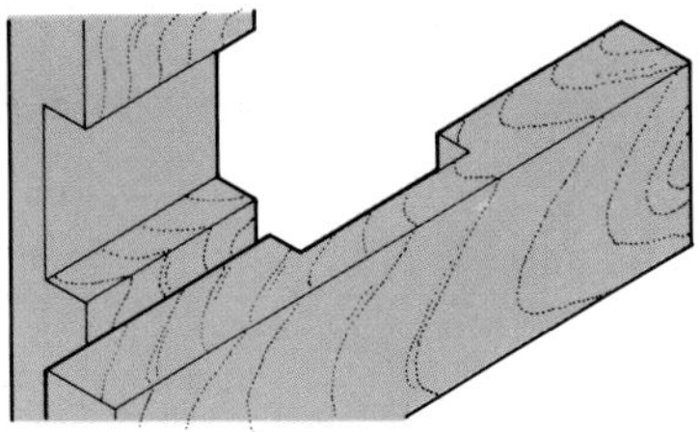

Halving joint – cross halving

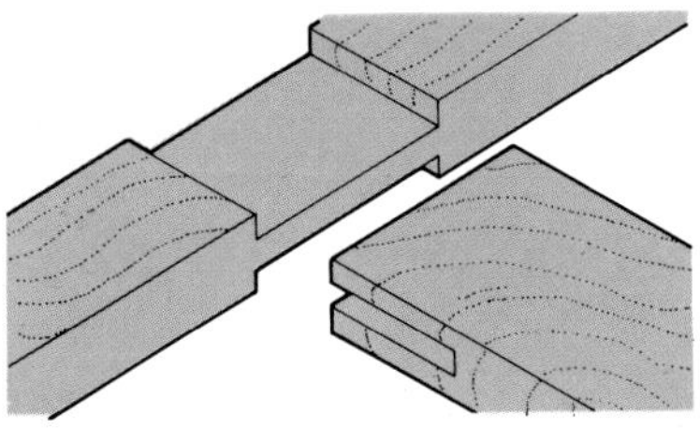

Bridle joint

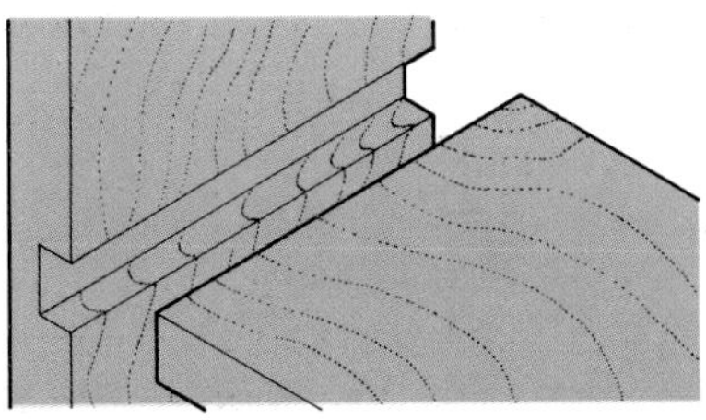

Housing joint (dado)

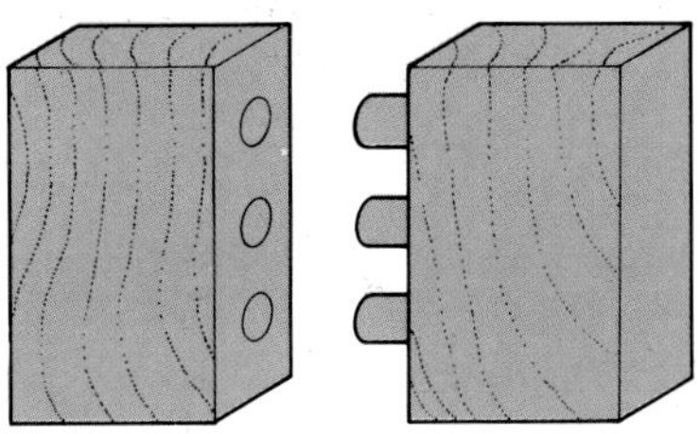

Dowel joint

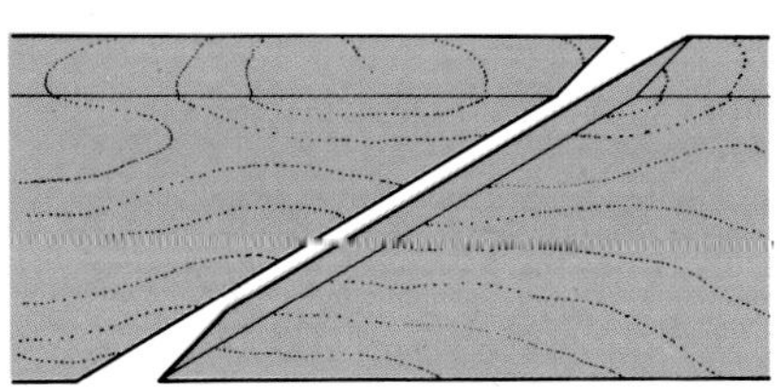

Scarf (scarph) joint

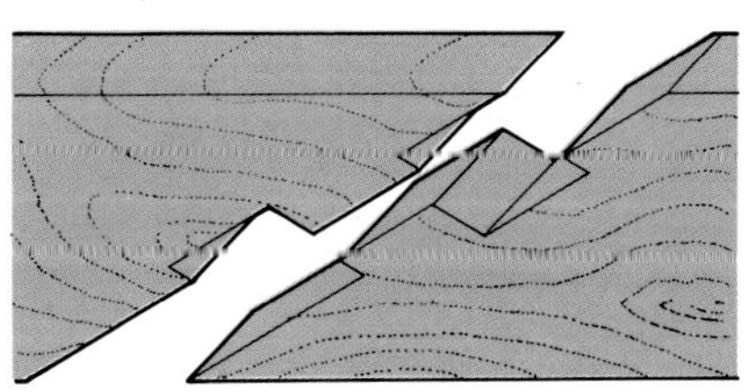

Hooked scarf (scarph) joint

Halving joints are used in simple frames for kitchen cabinets, and in roof and floor beam joints.

A bridle joint is a refinement of the halving joint, used where pieces of wood meet in a 'T' or 'L' shape, for smaller door and window frames. To make the bridle, divide the thickness of the wood into three parts in the area to be joined. Set the gauge to this thickness and mark along each workpiece. The central core is then cut out from one piece, with a tenon (back) saw and mortice chisel. The outer waste is cut from the other piece of wood, so that the two areas to be joined lock neatly into each other.

A housing joint (dado) is a simple method of creating a strong load-bearing joint suitable for shelving. The housing (dado) is a groove in the cabinet side, usually around half the thickness of the shelf wood. The housing may extend right to the front of the carcase – a through housing – or end before the edge, when it is known as a stopped housing (or stopped dado). The outline of the housing groove must be carefully marked in with a square and marking knife. The tongue on the shelf is best set out with a marking gauge.

To cut through housings (dados), carefully saw inside the lines with a tenon (back) or dovetail saw, and pare away the waste. The usual depth for a housing groove is about one-third of the total thickness of the cabinet side. The tongue on the end of the shelf can be worked with a saw or rebate (rabbet) plane.

Stopped housings (dados) are more difficult to cut, as they need to be chopped out with a sharp chisel. Take care to get the sides of the groove and the shelf tongue perfectly square. This will avoid problems with gaps along the line of the joint.

A dowel joint, which uses wooden pegs glued into holes to hold parts together, requires careful setting out as the dowel holes in the two parts must line up exactly. This type of joint is the best way to join together chipboard (particleboard) panels. Dowel joints are also common in chairs made since the nineteenth century. A number of special jigs to help with dowel jointing are available. A simple method of marking out the occasional dowel joint is to make a card template of the part to be jointed and prick the dowel centres through onto both components. Take care to keep the drill holes in line to ensure easy entry of the dowels.

If you make your dowels from a wooden rod, put a saw slit along the length to avoid trapping glue in the dowel hole. As well as making a strong edge-to-edge or corner joint, dowels can be used to join parts end-to-end.

A scarf (scarph) joint is the best means of jointing short lengths of wood together to make ridge beams and rafters. Scarfs are also used to graft new pieces onto broken or wormy parts.

The simplest scarf (scarph) is the lap type. Here, the two parts are bevelled away on the glued faces. The bevel should be a shallow one, so the width of the overlap is around six times the thickness of the wood.

Hooked scarf (scarph) joints are stronger, but tricky to make. Instead of the flat, wedge-shaped, meeting faces used in the lap scarf, the hooked scarf has two small steps on the faces. An advantage is that it can be glued and clamped together without sliding apart.

The mortice and tenon joint is the building block of all solid wood joinery. This joint consists of a tongue, or tenon, in one piece of wood which fits snugly into a hole, or mortice, in another piece. The joint is extremely strong and is used in structural work of all kinds such as door frames and window frames.

There are simple rules for the size of parts in a mortice joint: tenon thickness should be one-third the thickness of the framing wood and the depth of the mortice should be half to three-quarters the width of the frames.

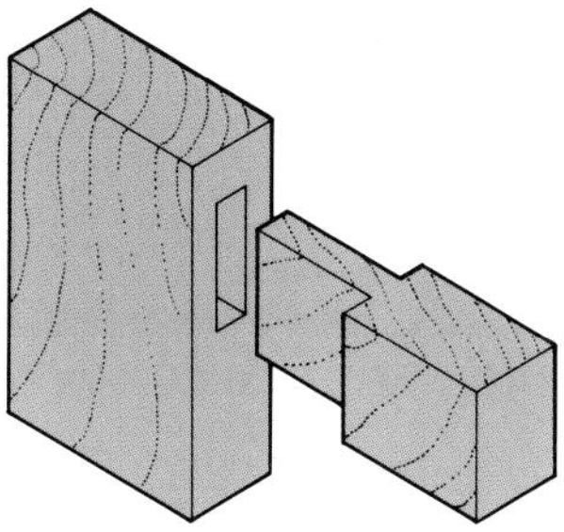
Mortice and tenon joint

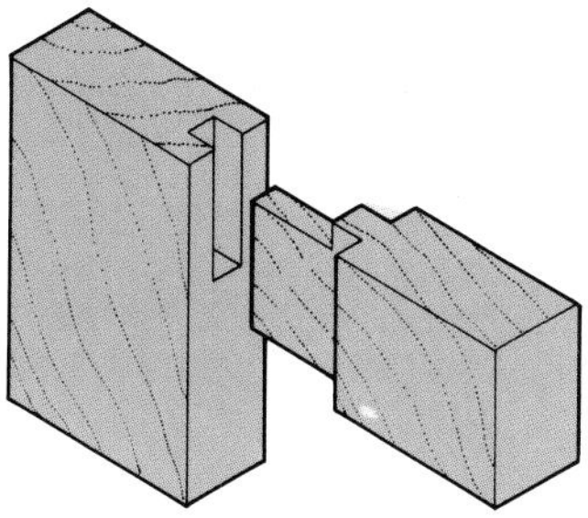
Haunched mortice and tenon

How to make a mortice and tenon joint

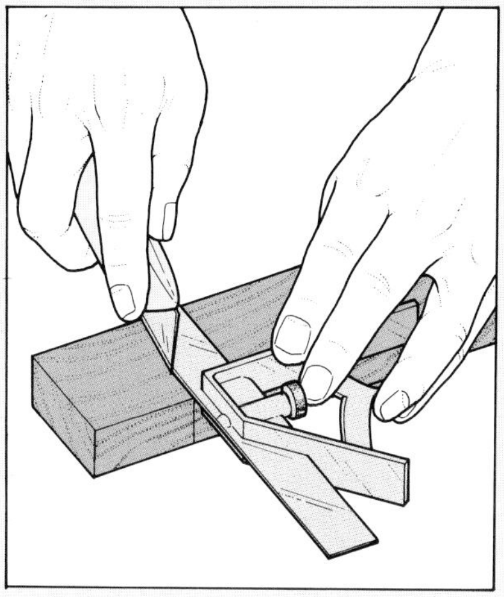

1. *Set the parts out with a square, gauge and marking knife. Follow the simple one-third thickness, one-half depth rule.*

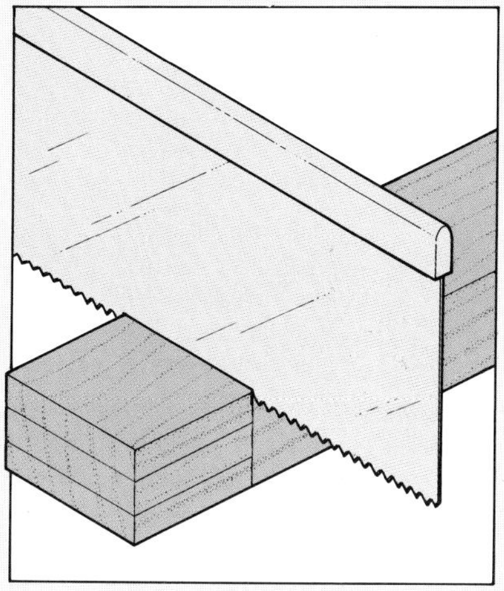

2. *Saw the tenon out with either a dovetail or tenon (back) saw. Cut the shoulders first, taking care not to go too far into the wood.*

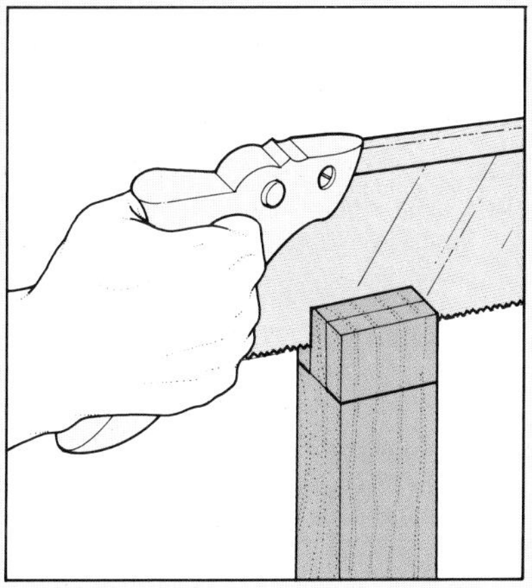

3. *Fix the wood upright in the vice and saw down the waste side of the gauge line. Clean up the joint with a bevel-edge chisel. Make sure that the shoulders are perfectly square to the wood surface.*

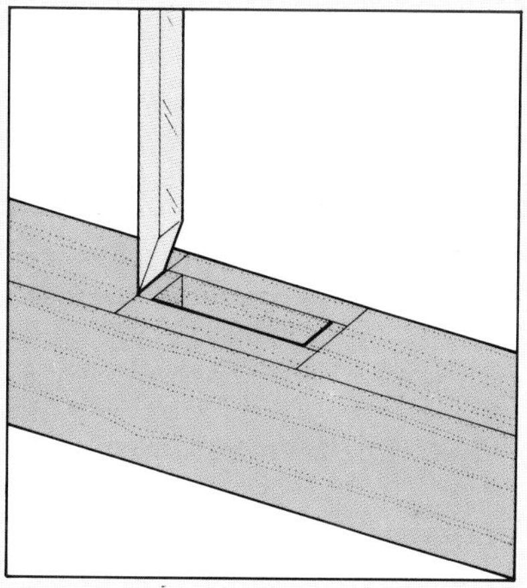

4. *The mortice should be chopped in with a firmer chisel. Remove the waste in the centre of the mortice. Make sure that you cut diagonally downwards from both ends towards the middle. Finish off with vertical slicing cuts.*

Sometimes the tenon is allowed to protrude right through the frame member and then wedged in position. This is called 'fox-wedging'. Foxed tenons sometimes crop up in old chair frames (see page 33). When a loose tenon joint has to be tightened up, the tenon can be made wider again by tapping a small wedge into it. This can be done by slitting down the mortice with a tenon (back) saw and wedging the saw cut open. The joint may be designed so the wedge is pushed into the tenon by the bottom of the mortice as the joint is assembled. Restorers call this a secret wedged tenon.

Where the full thickness of the wood is put into a larger mortice, the tenon is said to be 'barefaced'.

In another variant of this joint the tenon is reduced in width. This has the advantage that the mortice hole is completely covered by the tenoned member when the joint is assembled. This reduction in width is known as shouldering. A variation on the reduced width tenon is the 'haunched' or rabbeted tenon.

To make a simple mortice joint, follow the captions on the left.

A dovetail joint depends on a series of interlocking wedge-shaped fingers of wood, the smaller ones being called pins and the larger ones tails. (The name 'dovetail' derives from a dove's tail feathers.)

Dovetail joints are used to hold together drawers and solid wooden furniture. The joint is quite strong, and, if well cut, will remain intact even if the glue perishes.

A simple variant, the through, or sliding, dovetail is often used for furniture work as described in captions to illustrations on page 24.

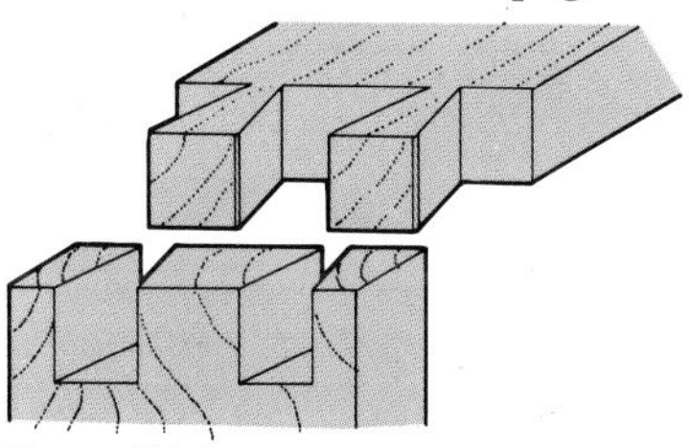
Dovetail joint

Making a through dovetail joint

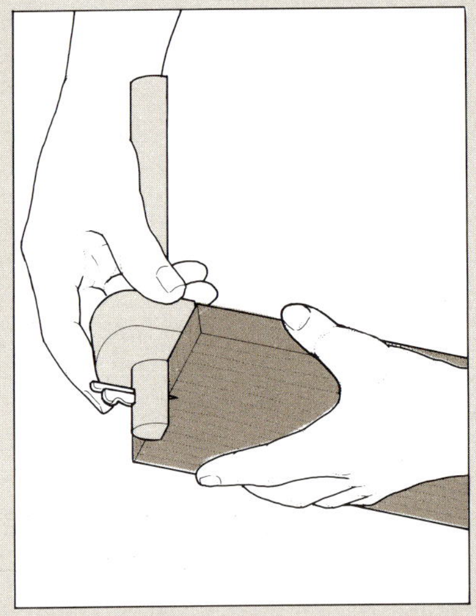

1. *Set a gauge to the thickness of the wood and gauge along both sides of the ends of the wood.*

2. *Mark the pins out on one piece. A small template can be made to give the right slope to the pins – about 1:7 is usual. Spacing of the pins generally varies between 25mm and 50mm (1in to 2in).*

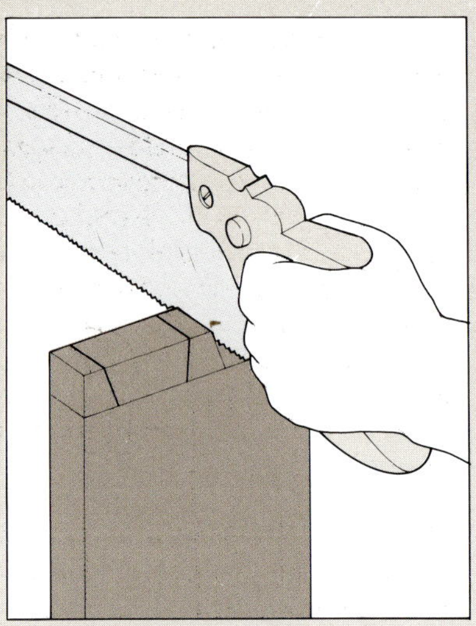

3. *Placing the work upright in the vice, cut down the pin slopes to the gauge line with a dovetail saw.*

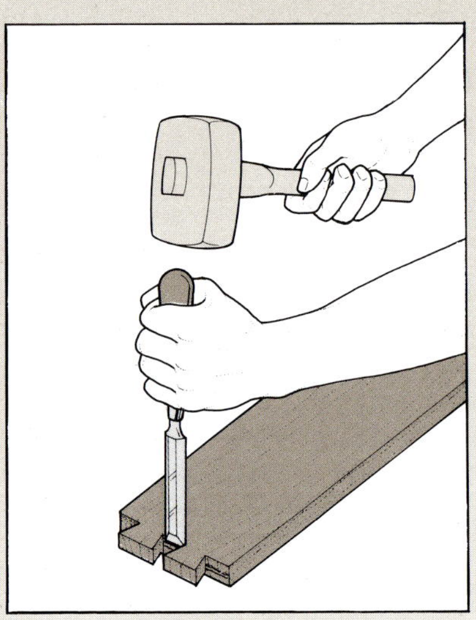

4. *Saw slots can be used to mark the position of the tails on the other workpiece. Remove the waste from the parts with a sharp chisel and saw.*

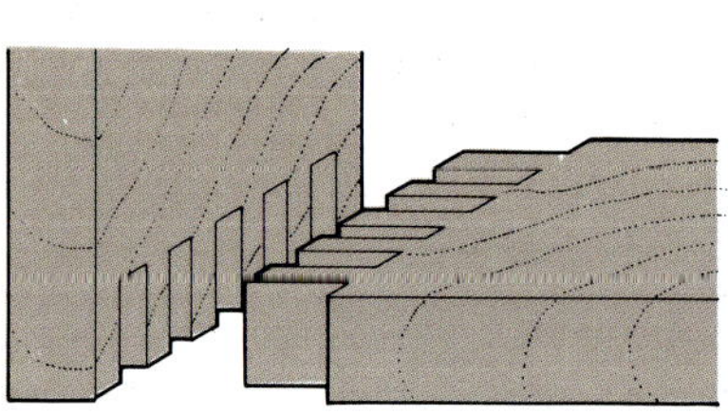

Finger or comb joint

A finger or comb joint is similar to the dovetail joint in appearance, but is simpler to make. The two parts to be joined are cut with a saw and chisel to a series of equal fingers and spaces which interlock.

This is a modern joint, little used in restoration work.

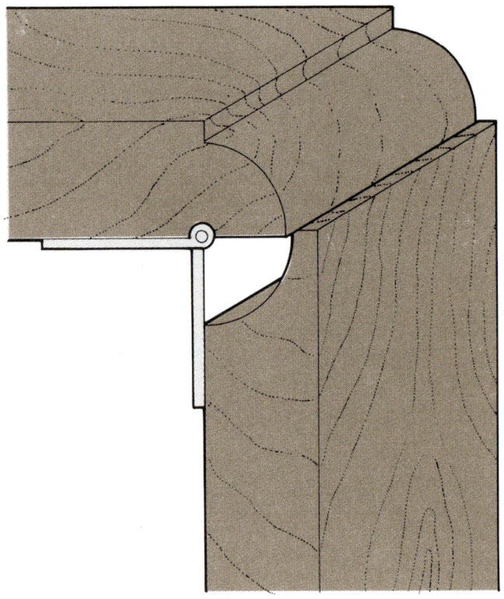

Rule joint

A rule joint is used on table leaves and some bureau flaps. This cunning contrivance is a sign of quality in old furniture, but is prone to damage. The basic purpose of the joint is to improve the appearance of the article and to conceal the gap between the top and the leaf of the table when lowered. The two parts of the rule joint are not glued together but are connected by a hinge. One of the parts to be joined is moulded to a convex curve; the other is hollowed out to a concave shape. This enables the two parts to fit close together and slide – without actually touching. The rule joint is not simple to make and requires careful profiling so that the convex and concave curves of the two parts fit together without binding. Carefully draw a cross-section of the joint and make card model templates of the shapes required. The templates can be used to check that the joint is being correctly shaped.

A curved scraper and moulding plane can be used to make the concave part of the joint. The convex part is more easily made with rebate (rabbet) and block planes. It is a good idea to make two shaped sanding blocks, one for each side, to give a good final finish.

The rule joint is also known as a drop-leaf or table joint.

Gluing and clamping

There are two main points about glues to bear in mind. It is most important that the glue does not bridge gaps in joints. The strength of a glued joint depends entirely on there being only a thin film of glue between two close-fitting surfaces. (The only exceptions to this rule are the two-tube epoxy adhesives and resin glues which fill small gaps.) The surfaces to be joined must be really clean. Dust, grease, old polish and wax will all weaken the bond strength.

Scotch (animal) glue is made from old bone and scrap hides. Its great virtue lies in its ease of application and reliability. To prepare the glue, take about 250g (8oz) and put into a small saucepan. Barely cover with cold water and leave to soak overnight. After soaking, the pan with the glue is heated in a pot underneath which contains near-boiling water. When melted to an even syrup, it is ready for use.

The glue must be used hot, since it has no real sticking power when cool. It acts very quickly. Clamps can be removed from unstressed parts within 10 minutes. Remove excess glue with a hot, wet cloth.

Animal glue has low water-resistance and cannot be used outside.

PVA glue comes ready for use in liquid form. It is therefore woodworkers' first choice for many applications. The glue has good strength and will bond together almost any porous surface. Allow three to four hours for setting before unclamping glued joints. Full strength will be attained after 24 hours. Excess glue can be removed with a hot, wet cloth.

Some PVA glues claim to be moisture-resistant, but as a general rule they should only be used for interior work.

Resin glues are sold under many brand names. They are strong, waterproof and will fill small gaps. They will join many materials but will work well only in warm surroundings, and when the joints are clamped together.

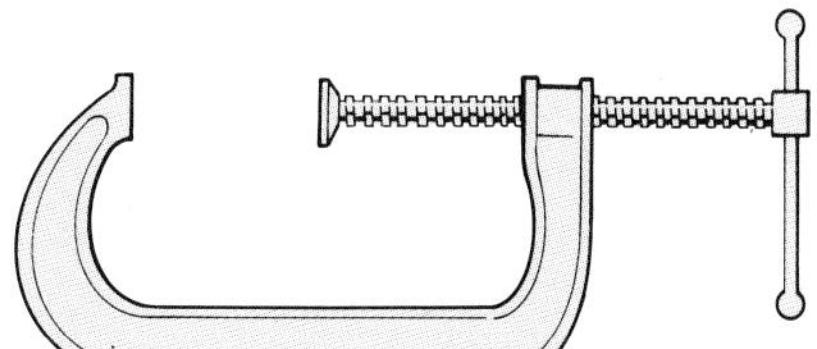

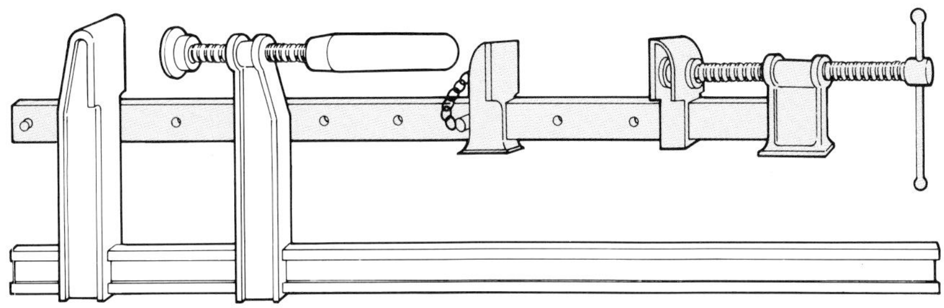

There are a large number of clamps readily available. The most commonly used is the G-clamp (C-clamp).

The sash (bar) clamp is very often used for cabinet-making (middle).

The rack clamp (below) is a very versatile modern clamp. It can be fitted with protective pads to avoid damaging the wood.

Once prepared for use, resin glues have only limited life, so only mix enough for your immediate needs. Clean surplus glue off woodwork with hot water and always keep the joint under pressure for the time stated in the instructions.

Contact glues are mainly made from rubber and plastic resins, dissolved in spirits. Adhesives such as these are unsuitable for small, heavily loaded joints. Compounds of contact glues are best for fixing plastic laminate worktops or jointing foam rubber or fabric.

The solvents used to make most contact glues are toxic. Always work with the maximum possible ventilation and turn off electric heaters and gas pilot lights.

Epoxy glues are the strongest and most versatile of all adhesives available for DIY use. The resin and hardener must be mixed as recommended. The curing time may vary between five minutes and many hours, depending on type. Generally, a slow-setting type of glue will give a stronger bond than the more instant brand.

Since epoxy resins can be irritating to the skin and eyes, wear gloves and wash your hands carefully after you have finished working.

Cyanoacrylate glues, also known as superglues, often perform badly and are not recommended for the amateur enthusiast.

Clamps

Clamps hold together parts while the glue is setting and squeeze out any excess glue. This allows the glued parts to move closer together and improves the appearance while increasing the bond strength. Put scraps of waste wood between the metal parts of the clamp and the workpiece. Remember that clamps can exert tons of pressure and never use excessive force to push parts together. Several types of clamp are available.

G-clamps (C-clamps)

G-clamps (C-clamps) are powerful tools, best used for small parts since they have limited reach. The 100mm (4in) size is most useful.

Sash (bar) clamps

Sash clamps, which are available in wood or metal, are used for assembling large structures like window frames and furniture carcases.

Rack clamps

Rack clamps are a promising recent innovation. They have a longer reach than G-clamps (C-clamps), and may prove to be less costly.

Inlay and veneering

Marquetry from the Chippendale workshop in Yorkshire, showing ivory inlaid on an ebony background, together with engraving.

Inlay, a decorative treatment, has been used on fine furniture in ancient Egypt and the West since the bronze age. This work involves cutting geometric or other ornamental designs from wood about 3mm (1/8in) thick. The cut pieces are laid on the surface to be inlaid and marked round. The marked areas are then cut out and the inlay pieces glued into the cavities. The craftsmen who used to do this type of work developed great skill and inlaying of precious stones, ivory, bone and metal, as well as coloured woods, was perfected.

Attractive as inlay work was, the taste for furniture made from scarce imported woods such as ebony, and the later demand for extravagant ornament, exceeded its scope.

Veneering, which is covering furniture and joinery work with thin saw-cut sheets of decorative wood, flourished in Britain during the early seventeenth century. The most highly figured and rarest woods were saw-cut into sheets, at first around 4mm (5/32in) thick and, as the skill was developed, reducing to 2.5-3mm (3/32-1/8in). These sheets were then glued down on the surface of furniture made from oak or pine in such a way as to give the impression that the furniture was made from the more exotic veneer.

Wood that was too wild-grained or weak to use in solid form was used to great effect, and ways were developed whereby veneers could be cut and laid in patterns.

By about 1670, elaborately cut and joined veneer sheets, made from many contrasting veneers glued onto paper, were introduced. These were laid onto the furniture surface paper side up. After gluing down, the paper could be scraped away to expose the veneers beneath. This craft had two schools of design. The oldest, parquetry, was based on geometric shapes, circles, cubes and lines. Marquetry, a development of the seventeenth century, involved the same techniques, but used them to produce natural forms such as flowers and foliage. This work was done by fixing sheets of contrasting veneer together at the edges and tracing a design on top of the pack. Using a simple saw frame called a donkey, the craftsmen cut the pattern, producing a complex design made up from parts, all of which fitted exactly.

Much old furniture features lines of veneer mosaics. These are called inlay bandings, and were made up in block form. The blocks were sawn into slices which were then laid in the usual way. This technique of slicing up blocks of layered veneers reached its highest level of complexity in 'Tunbridge ware'.

This involved creating elaborate scenes or patterns in large blocks, assembled like glued bundles of matchsticks. The blocks were then cut into sheets and were used to completely cover boxes and small furniture.

By the beginning of the nineteenth century, methods of veneer cutting had improved and thin knife-cut veneers were produced.

Only thin veneers are available today; if you are looking for modern fake antiques, first look at the thickness of the veneer.

Traditional methods of dyeing and scorching in hot sand are still used to colour the inlay bands and marquetry panels available from cabinet making specialists. Old patterns are still available, which means it may be possible to match exactly a piece over 100 years old.

Veneering today

Much of the furniture around us today has been veneered. The shrinkage of the ground or underlying wood, caused by central heating, may mean that the veneer has been damaged. Most damaged surfaces can be repaired using relatively easy techniques as outlined on page 61. Note, however, that the repair of costly eighteenth century veneered furniture should not be undertaken by novices.

If in doubt seek expert guidance.

Re-veneering panels

There are two methods suitable for re-veneering. The first, a modern technique, is to select suitable veneers and trim to a size 12mm (½in) larger than the part to be veneered. If matching parts made up from several pieces of veneer, cut the veneers and join with gummed paper tape before gluing down. Spread a thin, even coat of white PVA glue on both veneer and groundwork. To prevent the veneer from curling up, damp the unglued side with water. Leave for about 20 minutes and, when the white glue is almost dry, iron down the veneer with an electric iron set for cotton. (The bottom of the iron can be protected by covering the work with clean, brown paper.) Press down hard with the iron, and cover the work with a heavy board until cool. Leave for at least a day before trimming the surplus veneer off.

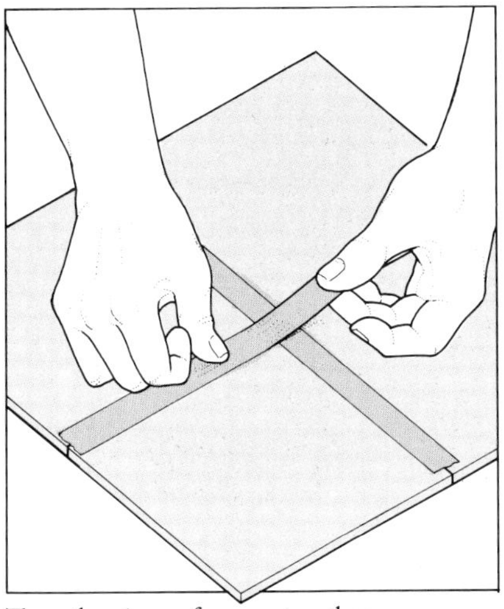

Tape the pieces of veneer together.

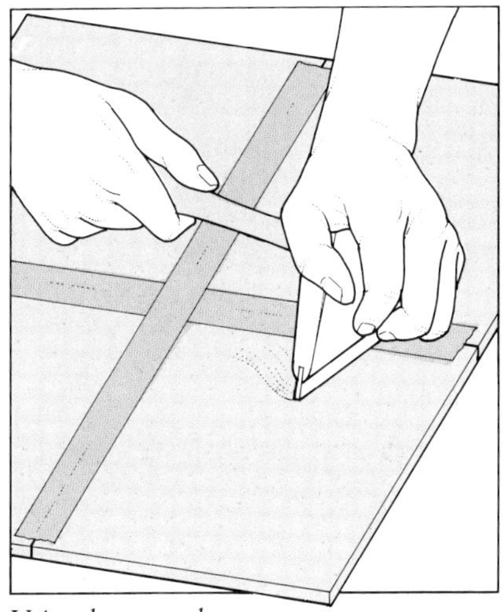

Using the veneer hammer.

Veneers can also be re-laid using traditional techniques. The simplest method is to prepare a pot of fresh, thin, animal glue. Prepare the veneers before they are laid.

Joints must be carefully cut with a scalpel and straight edge and firmly fixed together with gummed paper tape. Brush the animal glue evenly onto the groundwork and put aside. Then brush the glue thinly onto the back of the veneer. The un-glued face of the veneer may need damping to stop any tendency to curl up. (To do this, some workers dip the glue brush into hot water.) Lay the veneer, glued side down, onto the groundwork and position it carefully. The cool glue will not have much power to stick, so this should be a simple job. With an electric iron, set to medium heat, press down on the veneer. Work from the centre toward the edge, taking care to squeeze out as much of the glue as possible. Removing the surplus glue is most important. On small parts this can be achieved with a paperhanger's seam roller – a small wooden roller about 30mm (1¼in) in diameter and 25mm (1in) wide – or the pein of a cross-pein hammer. The traditional tool for larger panels is the veneer hammer.

The wooden veneer hammer is pressed down onto the surface, and pushed along with a wriggling motion. The combination of heat and pressure will force the glue out, producing a thin, strong glue film. The technique is simpler than it sounds, but there are nevertheless a few pitfalls to avoid. *Never* let the iron overheat the glue. Any signs that the glue is boiling beneath the iron should be watched for, and the iron turned down before continuing. If this is not done the job will fail, as overheating spoils the glue. Another danger to look out for is letting the panel get too cool. This will stop the glue from flowing. Aim to have plenty of steam coming off the surface, without boiling. Set the panel aside for at least two days before trimming off excess veneer.

Any small blisters can be repaired by cutting them out and inserting a little fresh glue. Re-heat locally and press down. Quickly clamp a block over the spot and leave to dry.

Successful veneering needs practice and patience; it is one of the great skills of cabinet making.

Woodcarving

Geometric panels and free-flowing relief carving, used to good architectural effect.

Few other crafts ask so much in terms of aesthetic appreciation and exacting workmanship as woodcarving. A skilful use of tools has to be balanced with an expert eye for design. One of the major obstacles to good woodcarving is the inability to draw. It is true to say that if it cannot be drawn, it cannot be carved. The would-be carver must practise drawing as much as tool-handling, striving to develop an eye for beauty of line and form.

Tools of the trade

Few crafts employ so wide a range of tools as woodcarving; over 300 types of chisel are readily available. Most professional carvers have a hundred or so tools, of which perhaps 20 may be regularly used. The reason for the need for so many tools is that woodcarvers strive to achieve results with clean cuts, rather than whittling waste wood away. This means that tools which cut a detail in a single stroke are preferred.

Another type of woodcarving – known as 'whittling' – is becoming increasingly popular, based on the methods of American craftsmen. Using these techniques, simple tools – two or three different knives – can produce amazing results, but the lack of any method used to drive the knife with a mallet limits the range of work possible.

The carving mallet

The carving mallet has a conical top and is made from hard, dense wood. It is used to drive the tool when hand pressure is not enough.

Gouges

Gouges are the orthodox carver's main tools. These are semi-circular in cross-section and various widths and diameters are available. Straight gouges are fine for most work, but for deep cuts and hollowing out details a curved gouge is vital.

Flat tools

These are like the carpenter's chisel, except for the way the blade is sharpened. They are used for paring flat and convex surfaces, and 'chopping-in' straight lines.

Veiners

Veiners are used for grooving and detail work. The blade is 'U' shape in section.

'V'-tools (parting tools)

These have 'V'-section blades. These are very useful for fine line-carving and lettering work.

Buying carving tools calls for restraint. It is very easy to spend too much money on tools which you cannot master easily. The best course is to buy only one or two examples of each type of tool until your skill and enthusiasm for the craft grow.

Types of carving

Most woodcarving falls into one of four main categories.

Chip-carving, also known as incised carving, is the oldest and easiest method to use. The carving, which can be elaborate, is done with a knife or chisel. Chips of wood are cut away from the surface, or 'ground', building up a pattern of geometric shapes. Lettering and representational carvings can also be done in this way.

Relief carving is technically more demanding than chip-carving. The design is carved from a panel by cutting back the ground and detailing the raised parts. This was the style of carving exemplified by the old masters of the art such as Grinling Gibbons, a prominent British craftsman working in the seventeenth century.

Pierced carving is a refinement of relief carving, where the ground is cut right through. The finished work may be mounted on a contrasting panel. Piercing is usually done with a saw or drill, and the modelling work effected with ordinary carving tools.

Wood sculpture, like conventional sculpture, is done in the round. This means that, unlike carved panels, it can be seen from all sides. Some of today's wood sculptors work on specially made blocks, built up from small, dry pieces of wood glued together. This is to overcome the difficulties of drying large pieces of solid tree. Sculptures may also be assembled from small parts, each shaped before assembly. The great degrees of artistic skill involved in this work means that it has produced some of the best – and some of the worst – examples of the carver's art.

Gilding

Gilding – the art of covering mundane materials with a thin skin of beaten gold – has been practised for at least five thousand years. As far as can be ascertained, the tools and techniques have remained virtually unchanged and products of the craft have survived in perfect condition since the time of Tutankhamun. The gold leaves are hammered on a slab, cut and beaten again. This process is continued until they reach a thickness of 1/10,000mm (1/250,000in) – so thin that a light will shine through them. (1,000,000 pieces of gold leaf make a pile 100mm – 4in – high!) The leaves, each about 75mm × 75mm (3in × 3in) square, are then slipped into a book made from tissue paper, each leaf separated from the next by the paper. Twenty-five leaves comprise one book.

Tools

Gilding tools are simple and usually inexpensive. An ordinary supplier of artist's materials will provide most of them.

Cushion

This is made from some 12mm (½in) ply or softwood which is covered with a piece of soft baize or flannel and over this a layer of fine washleather (chamois) is stretched. A paper screen about 75mm (3in) high, wrapped around one end of it, will prevent draughts blowing the gold onto the floor where it will be hard to pick up.

Gilding knife

A gilding knife is used for cutting up the leaves on the cushion.

Tip

This is a thin, flat brush, used to transfer gold from the cushion to the work.

Gilder's mop

A gilder's mop is an ordinary No. 3 camelhair brush. Used to press leaf onto the workpiece.

Burnishing tool

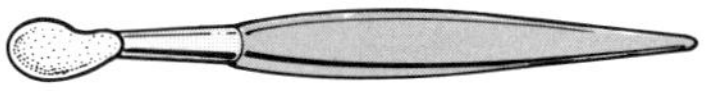

This implement is a smooth piece of synthetic agate, set in a handle.

Materials

Gold leaf

Gold leaf comes in two types: transfer gold and loose leaf. Transfer gold is stuck onto paper with wax. It is easier to handle than loose leaf.

Rabbit skin size

This is a thin glue solution, used to prepare gesso, the foundation for water gilding.

Gilder's whiting

A refined form of common whiting.

Bole

Bole is fine, red clay powder which is mixed with weak rabbit skin size to the thickness of thin paint. It makes a very smooth top coat for the gilding to be laid on.

Gesso

Gesso is made from gilder's whiting and rabbit-skin size and is mixed to the consistency of thin cream. It is used to fill and cover the wooden surface to be gilded.

Methods of gilding

Gold leaf can be fixed to the work by the use of either oil or water.

Water gilding requires the work to be covered with five or six thin coats of gesso. This should result in a perfectly smooth surface. Take care not to fill the fine details of carved work. Gesso must be applied warm, but never boiled.

The coats will take an hour or so to dry and should all be applied within a 24-hour period.

Dazzling examples of gilding.

The work is then given two to three coats of bole. The final stage of preparation is to polish the bole with a soft rag.

A leaf of gold is transferred to the cushion with the gilding knife and cut into suitable pieces. The tip of the knife is brushed on one's face to charge it with electricity, so that it will attract the leaf. The place where the leaf is to be laid is moistened with sized water and the leaf quickly floated onto it. The gold is pressed around the contours of the work, using the gilder's mop.

The burnishing tool should be used the following day. Rub the burnishing stone over the surface until the gold begins to gleam.

Oil gilding is a simple process in which the leaf is pressed onto a thin coat of tacky varnish. Special varnish called gold size is used. A flawless surface must be prepared, and the surface may be painted with ordinary undercoat and gloss. Finish the painting with a coat of red or yellow and smooth with very fine wet or dry paper. Coat the workpiece thinly with gold size, using a flat artist's brush. Ensure that the whole surface is covered evenly, without runs or thick patches. Leave the work to dry, away from dust. When the size is almost dry the leaf can be laid, using the tacky gold size to hold the leaf down.

Restoring Furniture

It is extremely likely that in any old house renovated traditional furniture will look better than anything modern. Best of all is a fine antique, of course, but it is not necessary to spend the fortune required to buy a Chippendale chair, a Hepplewhite cabinet, or a Shaker table in order to have a beautiful piece. Auctions and stores which sell bric-a-brac are sources of furniture built over the last hundred years and items are often available at low prices, albeit in a somewhat dilapidated condition. Also, many homes have old pieces of furniture that have perhaps been inherited and then abandoned in corners because the effects of age and wear have left them marked and shabby.

However, with a little bit of work, these apparently unpromising pieces can be turned into attractive objects that are an asset to any room. Moreover, you do not have to pay large sums of money to professionals as this is work you can generally do yourself. As well as having the satisfaction of producing something that will give you pleasure, there are the added bonuses that the task of restoring furniture is pleasant and rewarding, does not usually involve difficult skills and need not call for the purchase of expensive tools.

Furniture, in fact, provides one of the most enjoyable sources of restoration for anybody who enjoys creative work. When you start to restore a piece of furniture, you will not only find out how it was made but also, if you do the job properly, learn techniques which have been used by master craftsmen for centuries. These, of course, are worlds away from the practices involved in producing the machine-manufactured furniture of today. And, when you have finished, you will have a unique piece bearing your personal stamp.

As an amateur you cannot expect to acquire all the skills of a professional cabinet maker, furniture restorer or upholsterer, but you will undoubtedly learn a great deal and, with practice, your techniques will continue to improve. All that is required is a certain manual dexterity, a fair selection of tools, some space to work in and, above all, time and patience. Fine tables, chairs and cabinets were not made in a hurry – and cannot be restored in a hurry either. They demand the same degree of care and affection that went into their making. There are no short cuts and it is best to take your time; herein lies much of the satisfaction of this engrossing craft.

One important piece of advice to bear in mind is to spend time assessing a piece of furniture before starting to work on it. If you think the item may be of particular value, do not rush into working on it as such a piece needs to be handled with special care – in fact, you would probably be safer not to attempt to restore a valuable antique yourself. In such a case, seek professional valuation and advice first. For other pieces, look for the tell-tale holes that are evidence of woodworm and for any structural damage, as either of these will weaken the parts of the structure in need of repair. Always examine how a piece has been constructed before starting to strip off the finish and knock it apart, as this will be an irreversible process and you do not want to find later that you have a heap of wood which you cannot reassemble. If the structure is at all complex, make notes and sketches.

This chapter describes structural work on wooden and wood-framed upholstered furniture. For wood finishing, see Chapter 3.

The time was when every locality had a carpenter or cabinet maker who would produce most of the community's furniture. Today, nearly all furniture is mass produced and it is not easy to find craftsmen capable of restoring items using traditional techniques. Old time craftsmen, as their modern counterparts, were aware of the importance of the quality and care of their tools and respect for materials. The amateur furniture restorer should develop the same concern.

Tools and equipment

Fine and detailed work on furniture is hopeless if your tools are rusty, dirty or blunt. It should be a matter of habit always to oil tools before putting them away to prevent them rusting and to sharpen and clean them before use.

Bradawl

Small, pointed tool for making holes, usually for starting off screws.

Cabinet maker's (paint) scraper

A thin rectangle of steel with sharpened edges, used for taking off finishes or removing very small amounts of wood. Curved scrapers are used for shaped work such as turned legs or mouldings.

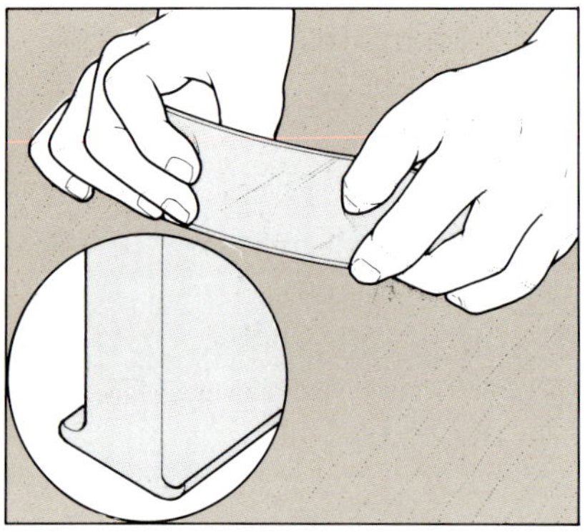

A cabinet maker's scraper is useful for removing thin shavings of wood and for taking off old finishes.

Chisels and gouges

Bevel-edge chisels can undercut an angle such as a dovetail joint. Start with 6mm (¼in), 12mm (½in) and 25mm (1in) sizes. For cutting a deep slot, a mortice chisel will be useful and a paring chisel (with a long bevelled-edge blade) will help to remove the wood. Gouges aid cutting inside and outside curves.

Trimming knives

The normal utility trimming knife, with replaceable blades, is essential.

Drills

Some means of drilling both large and small holes is necessary: a hand drill and brace will suffice, given a suitable selection of drills and bits, but an electric drill is easier and quicker to work with.

Hammers

A fine pin (light weight) hammer is an essential tool and can double as an upholsterer's hammer.

Mallet

Needed for use with chisels and for dismantling and assembling joints.

Measuring rules and marking and profile gauges

The traditional rule is of the folded boxwood type, but retractable steel tapes are probably easier to use and a rigid steel ruler will also serve as a straight edge for cutting. A marking gauge, cutting gauge or mortice gauge (with two marking pins) will take some of the guesswork out of marking woodworking joints, and a profile gauge, with adjusting needles, will faithfully reproduce any shape and act as a template.

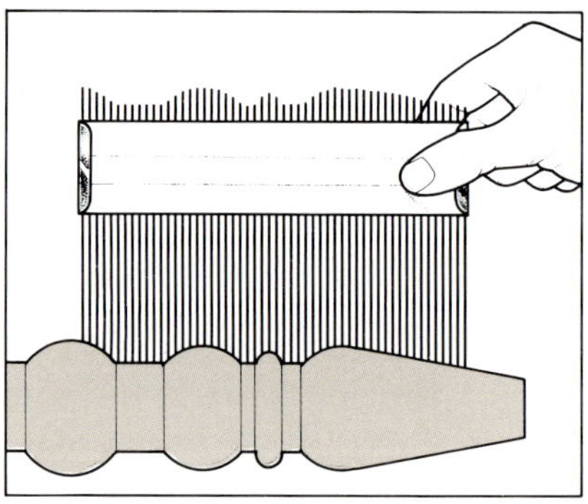

A profile gauge can act as a template.

Nail removers

Pincers can be used for removing nails, providing some of the nail is protruding and the surface is protected. Otherwise use an upholsterer's ripping chisel (tool).

Planes

The most useful size of bench plane is the jack, with a soleplate about 360mm (14in) long; a block plane is also useful for end-grain and final smoothing. Useful additions are a spokeshave, a two-handed plane (drawknife) with a convex soleplate for smoothing curved surfaces, a rebate (rabbet) plane with a blade the width of the soleplate, a router for cutting recesses and slots and a combination plane which is used to shape mouldings.

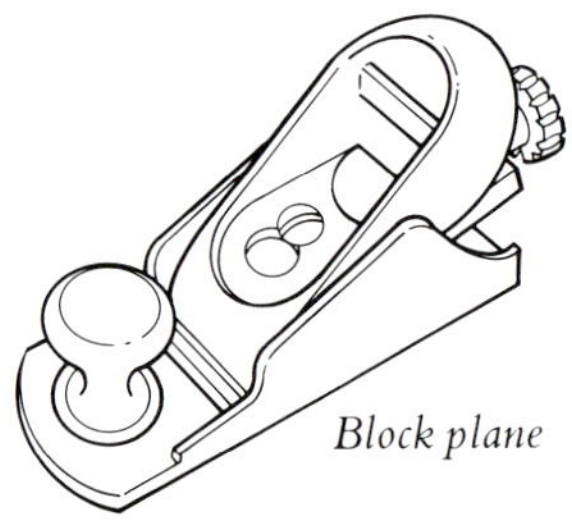

Block plane

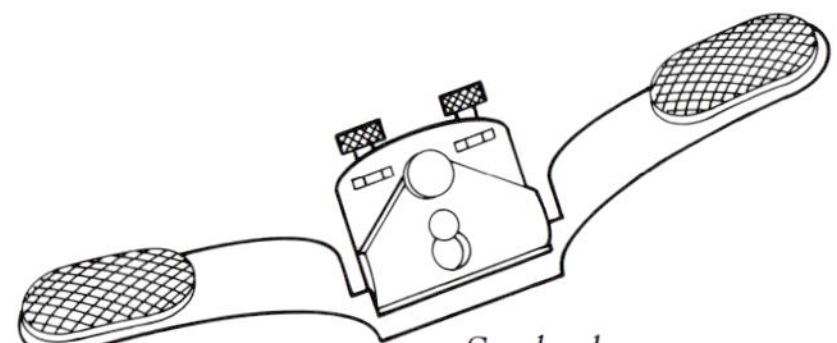

Spokeshave

Screwdrivers

A good selection of screwdrivers is always useful: cabinet makers' screwdrivers, for example, do not have the tapered end of an engineer's screwdriver.

Saws

Tenon (back) and panel (hand) saws are useful for cutting up wood; a dovetail or gentleman's saw is needed for detailed work. A coping saw is useful for cutting curves, and a powered jigsaw (sabre saw) takes much of the hard work out of the job. A padsaw (keyhole saw) is necessary for cutting shaped holes, for example, in door panels.

Vices and clamps

Ideally, you will have a proper workbench with a woodworking vice for holding wood. A selection of clamps for holding wood while it is being glued is also necessary: the most useful are large sash (bar) clamps, different sizes of G-clamp (C-clamp) and – possibly – an edge-clamp for securing lipping and other edge finishes.

Repairs to chairs

Some repairs to chairs, such as regluing a loose joint, can be carried out fairly simply; others, such as mending broken legs or repairing damaged joints, will involve dismantling the chair first.

The most vulnerable part of a chair is the joint between the seat and the back legs. This is put under a lot of stress when people lean back on the back legs of a chair. So, when assessing an old chair, this is the first fault to look for: tilt the chair onto its back legs and press down on the top and the seat to see whether the joints are loose. Also, have a look to see whether the corner blocks under the seat are in place and secure, and whether any of the joints have previously been strengthened with screws and nails.

With just one loose joint, it ought to be possible to squeeze some glue into the joint and clamp it up; if several joints are loose, or some are damaged, it will probably mean dismantling the chair.

Dismantling chairs

Before starting to take a chair apart, it is necessary to find out exactly how it has been made, in particular, what type of joints have been used – mortice and tenon or dowel joints. (For more detailed information about the joints described in this section, see Chapter 1 pages 21-24.) The different joints require different methods, discussed below, to take them apart. Some mortice and tenon joints may have been strengthened with wooden pegs put in at right angles to the tenon.

No two joints, legs or rails of a chair are ever identical and it is important to mark the joints in some way – craftsmen use a system of notches – so that they can be put back together the same way round. Using a notebook will help – especially if you are dismantling an upholstered chair. Or you could identify each part with masking tape on which you can write 1-1, A-A, B-B and so on.

The first parts to remove are the corner blocks under the seat. These will normally be glued and screwed in place and may come off when the screws are removed. If not, the glue will need to be softened.

Dowels or pegs securing mortice and tenon joints will need to be drilled out. Do this using a small drill bit first (after paring the tops off any pegs so that they are level with the surface) and then a drill slightly larger than the first but smaller than the diameter of the peg or dowel. The remaining wood can then be cleaned out, using a sharp-ended tool such as a ground-down screwdriver or bradawl. There may also be screws holding joints together (possibly hidden under wooden caps) which will also need to be removed. Nails should be pulled out with pincers, taking care not to damage the wood surface. Raise them first with a ripping chisel (tool), if necessary.

Where wedges have been used to strengthen mortice and tenon joints, the wedges will have to be removed with a narrow chisel before the joint can be separated. Concealed wedges (in a fox-wedged joint – see page 23) are more difficult to remove and necessitate the use of a thin saw blade to cut down to the position of the wedge so that the remainder of the tenon can be broken off.

Some joints can be separated by

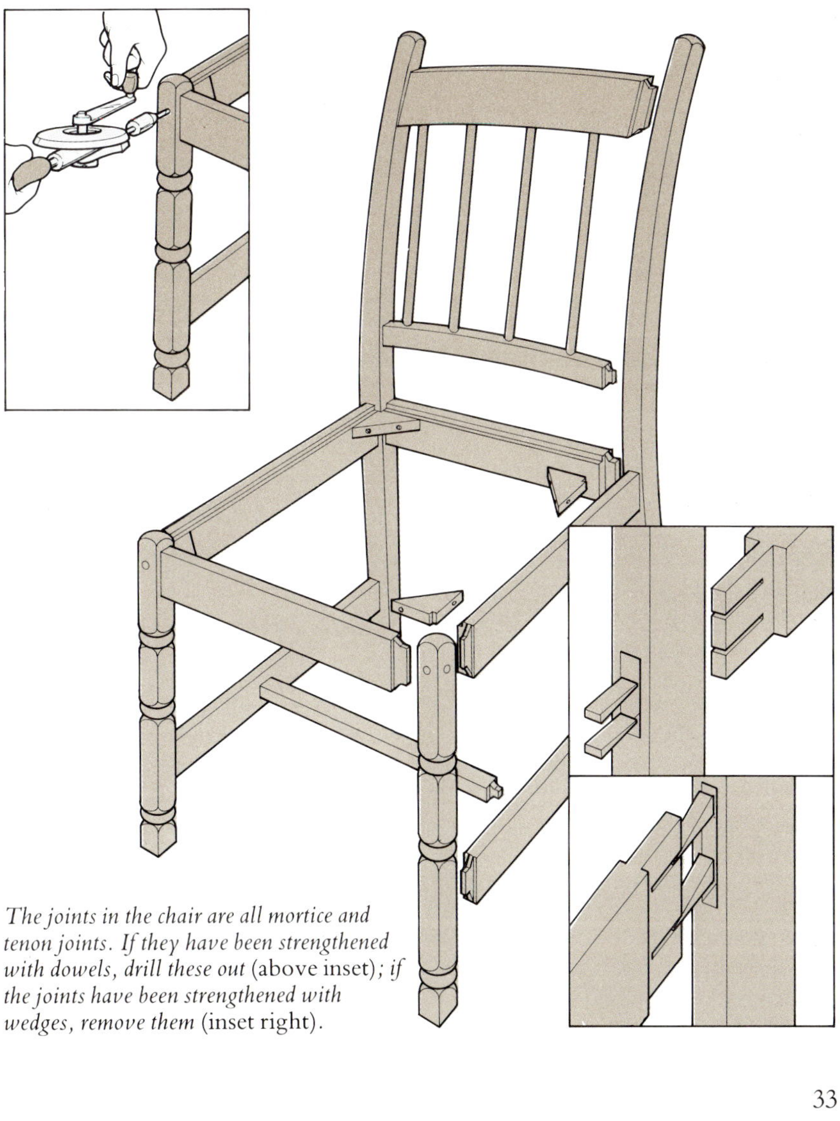

The joints in the chair are all mortice and tenon joints. If they have been strengthened with dowels, drill these out (above inset)*; if the joints have been strengthened with wedges, remove them* (inset right).

Methods of freeing joints

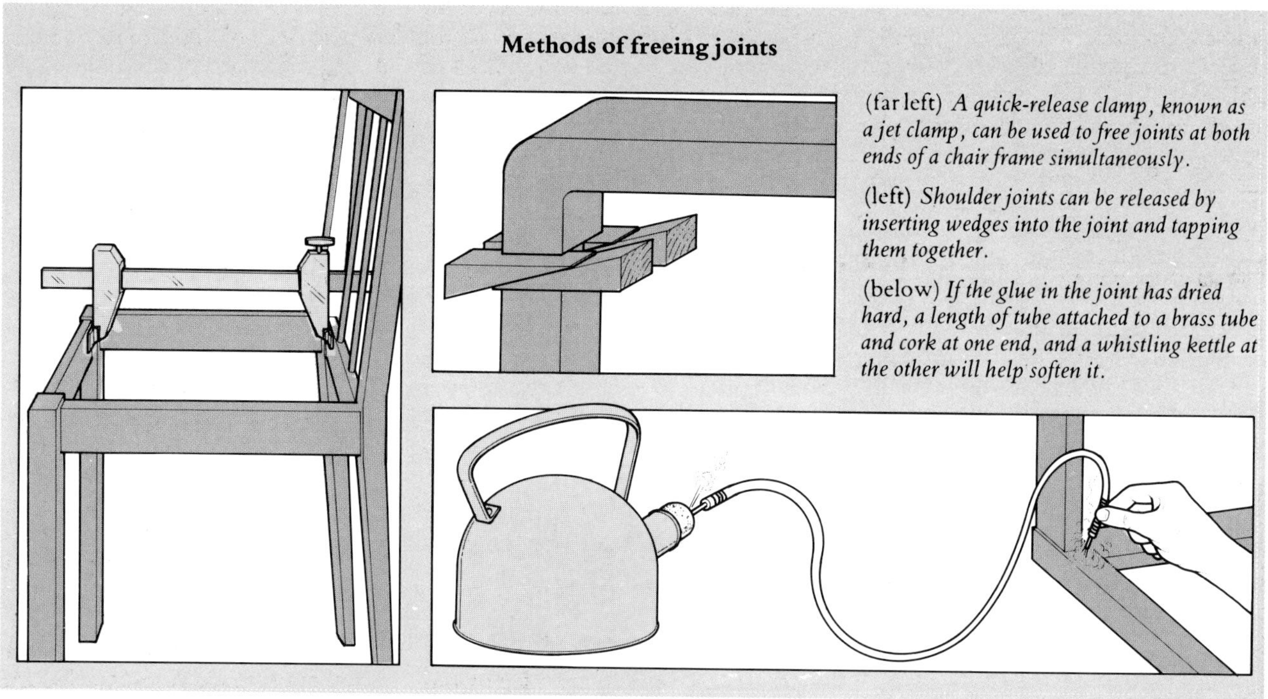

(far left) *A quick-release clamp, known as a jet clamp, can be used to free joints at both ends of a chair frame simultaneously.*

(left) *Shoulder joints can be released by inserting wedges into the joint and tapping them together.*

(below) *If the glue in the joint has dried hard, a length of tube attached to a brass tube and cork at one end, and a whistling kettle at the other will help soften it.*

using a mallet with a waste piece of softwood or packing ('softening') to protect the wood surface. Tap the joint on each side alternately so that it is not put under stress and, if there are joints at both ends of a piece of wood as in a frame, work on the two together. An alternative is to use a special type of quick-release clamp (sometimes known as a 'jet' clamp) – not available in the US – which can operate in reverse. By 'tightening', the two ends are slowly moved apart. When freeing shoulder joints – such as where the top and sides of a chair back meet – wooden wedges inserted into the joint and tapped together will separate the joint.

If the joints will not come apart, it means that the glue has dried hard and will need to be softened. Traditional woodworking glues can be loosened by using moist heat – by wrapping a hot damp cloth around the joint or by directing the steam from a kettle at it. More extreme measures include soaking the whole joint in hot water or drilling a small hole down the side of the joint and inserting a brass tube into a holed cork and plugging it into a whistling kettle. A length of tubing attached to the brass tube will direct steam into the joint.

Freeing joints made with modern working glues, such as PVA adhesive, is much more difficult and may involve soaking in hot water for a matter of days.

After dismantling, *all* the glue should be removed from the old joints with a sharp chisel, followed by hot water and a rag. Allow the wood to dry thoroughly before reassembling.

Loose and broken joints

If the only problem found with a mortice and tenon joint is that it has merely worked loose, regluing it and fitting new or larger wedges, should be sufficient to secure it. If, however, the joint has worn or has broken, some repair work will be necessary.

Mortice slots often split at the edge and, provided no wood has actually broken out, can usually be repaired by working glue into the split with a brush and clamping the mortice up together again. If wood has broken out, new wood will have to be set in.

Where the sides of a mortice and tenon joint have worn, the answer is to cut them so that the sides are square and parallel and to glue on strips of wood with the grain running in the same direction, matching where it will be exposed and trimming down to the original lines.

If part or all of the tenon is missing, a new piece will need to be

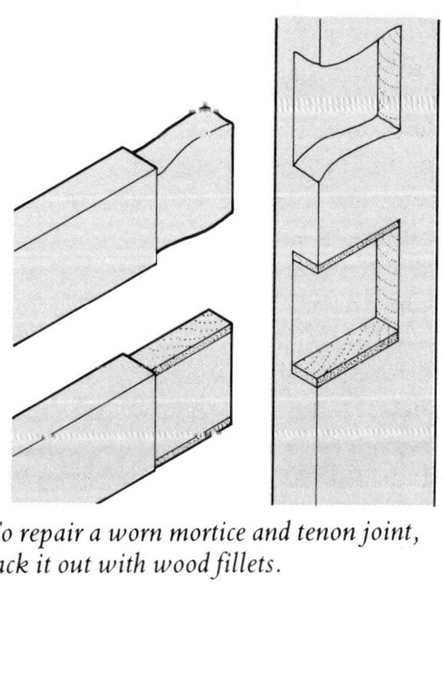

To repair a worn mortice and tenon joint, pack it out with wood fillets.

inserted using a stopped housing or angled bridle joint (see page 22). Beech is a good wood to use for this, unless the new piece will show, in which case it should be made to match the original as far as possible.

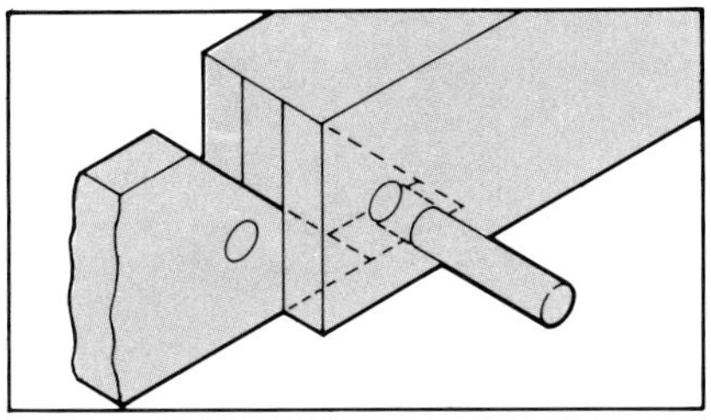

Repairing a broken tenon.

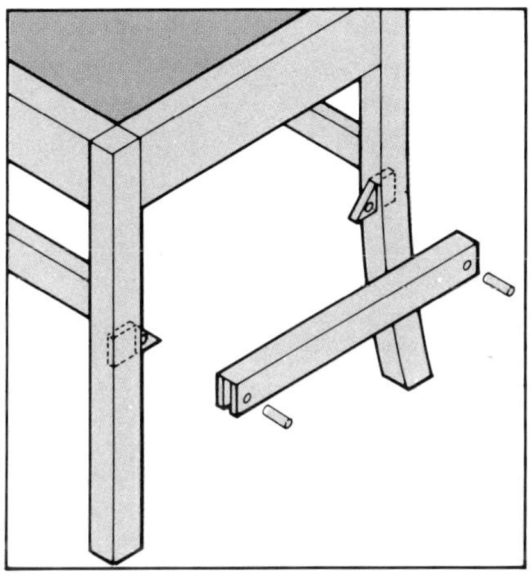

False tenons fitted with dowels.

If a dowel joint has broken, both parts will need to be drilled out and replaced with new dowelling. Where the dowels are concealed, hardwood dowelling can be used, cut to length with a slight taper on each end and a groove cut along the length to allow the glue to escape. Where wood has broken out at the side of a single dowel, such as at the top of a chair leg, a temporary dowel will need to be inserted *before* the new wood is set in so that the new hole can be drilled properly.

On some furniture, the pegs – dowels – used to strengthen mortice and tenon joints are made from the same wood as the chair and, to preserve the original appearance, you could make your own dowels – as the original craftsman would almost certainly have done. Using a woodturning lathe is the simplest method, but the alternative is to cut a piece of wood to a square the same size as the hole diameter and then to plane off the corners to give an eight-sided section. (With large dowels, it will be necessary to plane twice to give a sixteen-sided section.) The wood can then be rounded with glasspaper (abrasive paper) held in the hand. An alternative method of making dowels on site, which traditional craftsmen used, is to cut holes in a piece of 6mm (1/4in) steel of the appropriate diameter and bang through hardwood pegs, chiselled to fractionally larger than the drilled holes. The steel will act like a plane to shape the dowel or peg to the right size.

Broken legs and rails

Sometimes a broken chair leg or rail can simply be glued together if the break is clean – that is, not ragged – without the need to dismantle the chair. Screws can be used to strengthen the joint, fitted into counterbored holes which are then filled with wooden plugs to match the surrounding wood and planed and sanded flush. If, however, a new piece of wood needs to be set in, another leg or rail may well be needed as a pattern for shaping the first one.

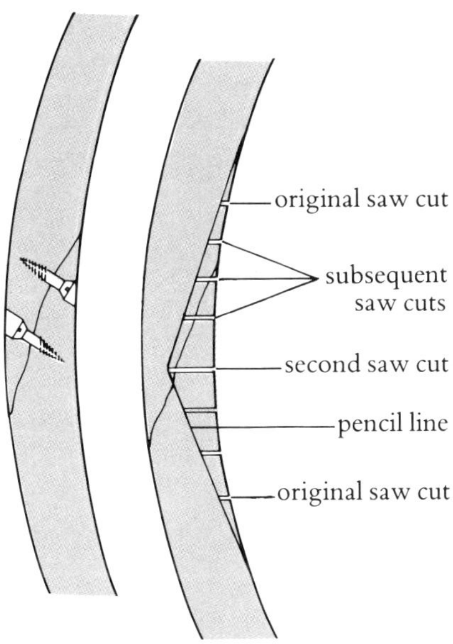

Screws (left) *or a brace* (right) *can be used to reinforce a broken leg.*

Where the break is clean and more or less straight across the leg or rail the joint can be strengthened by adding a brace, preferably at the back of the leg. Wood will have to be cut away to do this. Glue and clamp the broken ends together and, when set, make a series of saw cuts in a shallow 'V' shape, going no further than halfway through the leg. Using a sharp chisel, remove the wood between the saw cuts to give a smooth, flat surface. Then select a new piece of wood of matching grain and cut it to size and shape matching the missing section. Glue and clamp the brace and plane it flush.

With a square section leg, a diagonal cut is made across the leg and a new piece of wood cut, using another leg as a guide. The wood is cut slightly oversize, taking care to match colour and grain and is then shaped flush, having been glued and clamped. One problem is that the joint will tend to slide as it is clamped up: professionals use a 'shouldered' scarf (scarph) joint (see page 22) to prevent this happening, but this is not easy to cut successfully.

With broken turned legs, the repaired joint is supported by a wooden dowel or steel pin inserted

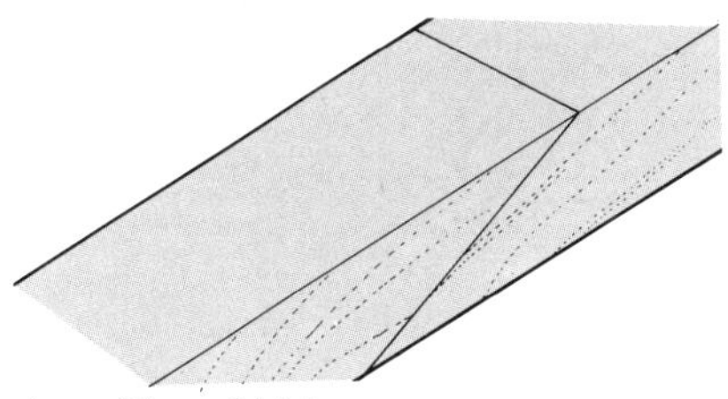

A scarf (scarph) joint.

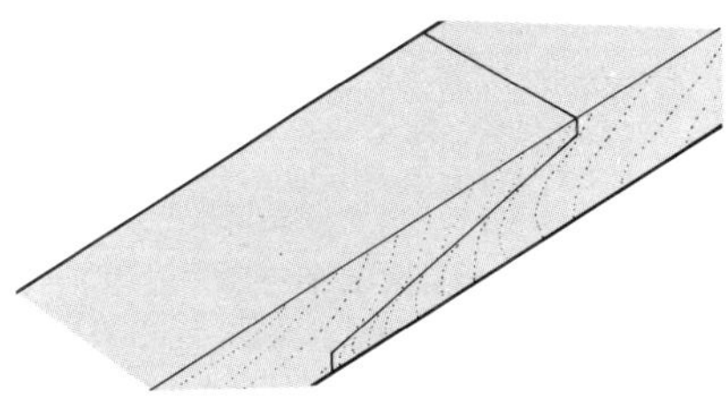

A shouldered scarf (scarph) joint.

into the middle of the leg. Turned legs are liable to break where the decorative turning is narrow. This can be repaired with a dowel to brace the pieces of the leg from the inside.

If the break is near the top of the leg that is jointed into the underside of the seat frame, it can be drilled down from the top.

Remove the broken end from the seat frame and glue and clamp it to the rest of the leg. When set, drill down with the largest drill bit that will pass through the narrowest part of the turning, without weakening it. The drilled hole should extend into the lower half of the broken leg. Make a groove along the length of the dowel (for even distribution of the glue). Glue the dowel into the drilled hole. Mending a break near the middle of the leg or on a morticed leg is a little more complex and is described in the captions to the illustrations on the left. It might be easier to have a whole new leg turned; make sure that the turner has the same pattern, such as the other leg, to work from.

Broken rails are usually more easily replaced than repaired. If it is just the mortice and tenon joints that have gone, it may be possible to fit false tenons into the old mortice slots which can then fit into angled bridle joints cut into the rails.

Setting in new wood

Use replacement wood that matches the original in colour and grain; cut the new wood *oversize* so that it can be finished flush after it has been set; make the join lines for the new wood straight and flat and fit the new wood so that the grain runs in the same direction as the old.

Finding the right replacement wood may be the greatest difficulty. The best source will undoubtedly be other old furniture, as new wood will always look new, however much it is stained and finished. This is true even if new wood is 'antiqued' by using glaze or 'distressed' by hitting it with nuts or chains, by puncturing it with nails, or even by

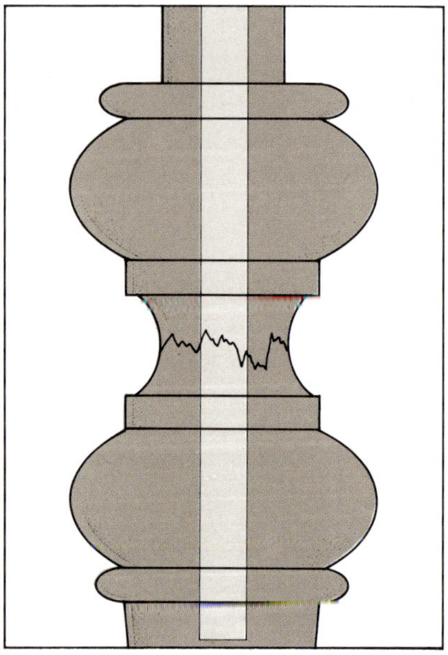

A dowel can be glued into a drilled hole to strengthen a turned leg repair.

A rocking chair may appear to need little restoration, but check the joints carefully in case they have worked loose with the rocking action.

Mending a middle break

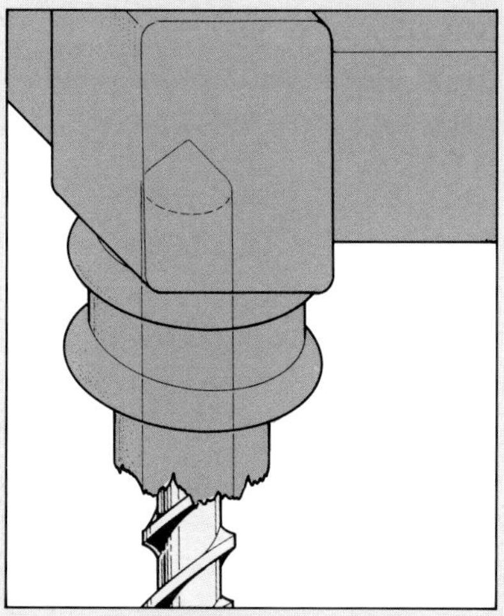

1. *With the broken bit of leg removed, drill a hole upwards through the remaining part to take the dowel.*

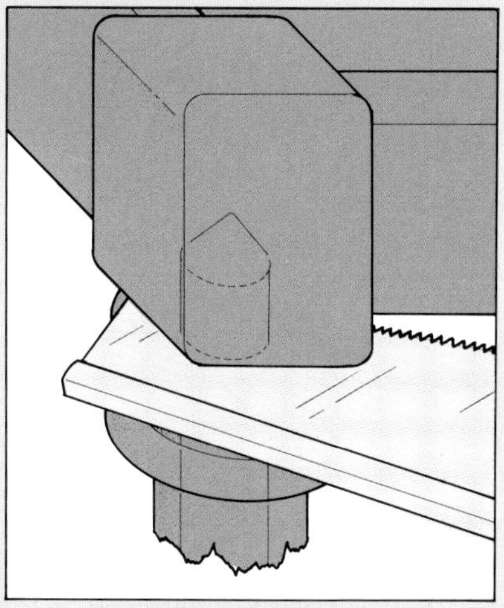

2. *Cut through another turned section further up the leg, using a fine-toothed saw. Keep the cut square to the wood.*

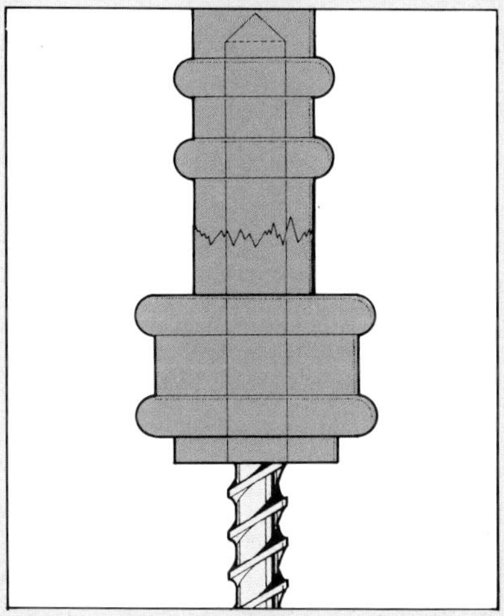

3. *Glue the cut off section to the rest of the leg to give you a register for drilling down into this part.*

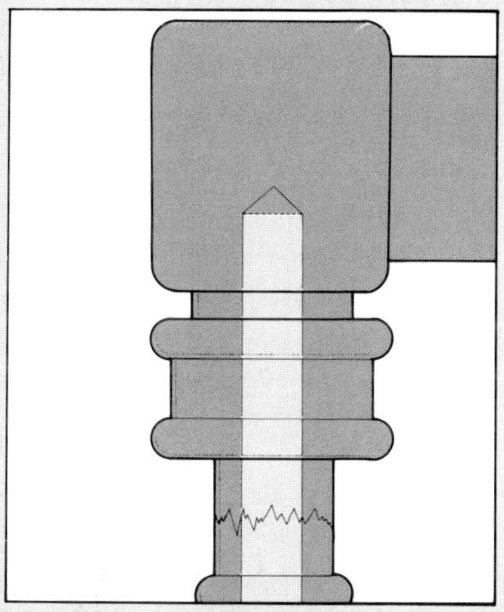

4. *Drill further down the leg and then fit the dowel and glue the leg back onto the chair.*

burning it with a lighted match. These may seem to be drastic actions to take after all the previous careful and painstaking work undergone; nevertheless, these techniques are commonly used in the reproduction furniture and antique trades to make furniture look old.

New wood is usually set in where a mortice joint has broken, taking some of the rail or frame with it. A new piece of wood is cut oversize and also angled at the ends, and the matching faces are perfectly flat. The wood can then be used as a template for marking the hole to be cut to take it. To cut the back of the recess in the wood perfectly straight, use a metal straight edge, clamped to the wood as a cutting guide. When the new wood has been cut, fit the pieces together. Have several 'dry run' attempts until you are sure it is a perfect fit. It

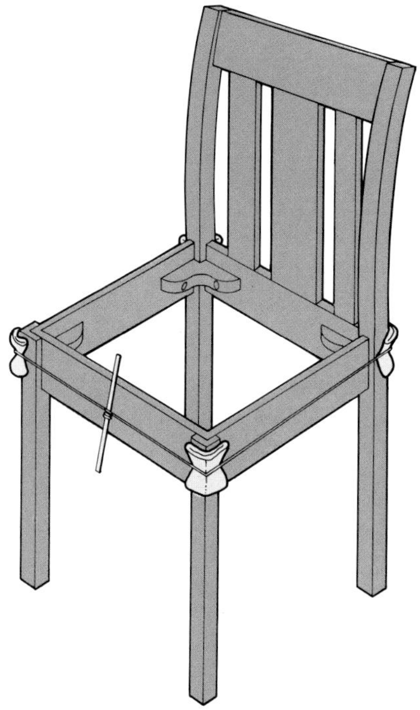

Using a Spanish windlass to clamp a chair.

can then be glued and clamped in position and, when the glue has dried, planed flush and the mortice recut.

Reassembling chairs

All the old glue must be removed from joints and the wood allowed to dry before attempting to reassemble. Have a dry run first to make sure that all the joints fit properly and that the chair is true and square before clamping it up with glue.

Some designs of chair are very difficult to clamp up properly and you may have to resort to special techniques to ensure a proper fitting. You can use a Spanish windlass which is a tourniquet of rope or twine wrapped around the parts under repair, to be held and twisted together with a stick until they are tight. As with using clamps, the wood surface must be protected from damage. Another technique, applicable to curved surfaces, is to construct a 'saddle' out of leather pinned to wooden blocks which, for example, can be used to hold the curved back on the top of a chair.

Repairs to tables

Many of the repairs to tables – loose joints, missing bits, and so forth – can be dealt with in the same way as for repairs to chairs which have been outlined above. For repairs to veneer and methods of removing stains from polished surfaces, see Chapter 3 on wood finishing.

There is, however, one group of repairs which are peculiar to tables which result from the wood shrinking in centrally-heated houses. The furniture, of course, was not originally designed to cope with warm, dry atmospheres and the shrinkage which this type of climate produces leads to tables cracking and splitting on the top.

A small split may enhance the look of an old table, but a large split will need repairing. It may be possible to close up the split by clamping it with glue, but in time it may split again. Usually, fitting a new fillet of wood into the split will be the answer. The split itself will be tapered and the first thing to do is to make a saw cut down the split so that a thin, parallel fillet can be inserted. Use a fine saw, for example a dovetail saw, and choose a strip of thick veneer for the fillet. If the split is very wide at the open end, you will have to repeat the operation twice.

(right) *Round tables are good for seating lots of people at a time.*

(below) *This old pine table has been stripped and varnished for protection.*

The fillet is glued in place with the table clamped up and then, once the glue has dried, planed down until it is flush with the table surface. Finish off with a cabinet maker's scraper to make sure that it is absolutely level. A good way of ensuring the new fillet is not noticeable is to stain the surface (see page 65). Finally it will be necessary to polish to match the table top.

Some tables, especially round, ornate ones, are made in two halves screwed together, and shrinkage of the wood may cause these two halves to move apart. Here the solution is to undo the screws holding them together and retighten them with the table halves clamped together. If glue is to be used, the two halves will have to be removed and any old glue cleaned off before clamping them up in position with new glue. Clamping may be a problem, especially if the table is large. One solution to this is to use a circular leather strap, nailed to two blocks of wood which are then clamped together; another method involves rigging up a wedging system whereby blocks are nailed to a flat horizontal surface so that wedges can be driven in between them and the table, thereby forcing the two halves together.

So that the glue does not have to take all the stress, hardwood 'butterflies' can be used to reinforce the join. These are cut to size (about 6mm – or ¼in – thick) and the table will have to be clamped up while the recesses on the table bottom are marked. Release the clamps and cut the recesses. The butterflies are left slightly above of the surface so that they can be planed flush after the glue has dried.

When reassembling a table after mending a split in the top, it is likely that the screw holes of the frame and table no longer quite line up. If this is the case, simply turn the table round through 180 degrees: the original holes will be covered and it is extremely unlikely that the opposite holes line up at all, so new ones can be made.

Some tables have hinges which may well have worked loose or have broken. There are many reasons for this – sometimes it may have been caused as result of the table shrinking. It is very important to find out why the hinge is no longer working – it may, for example, be necessary to set in a new piece of wood rather than closing up a split, which may well not prove satisfactory.

If hinges of your table need replacing, you may have to fill the existing screw holes with dowels glued in place so that new screws can be put in – the old holes may be slightly out of position.

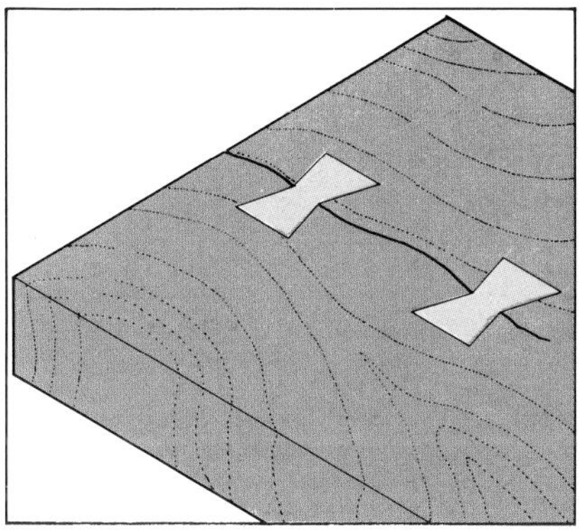

'Butterflies' used to reinforce a table join.

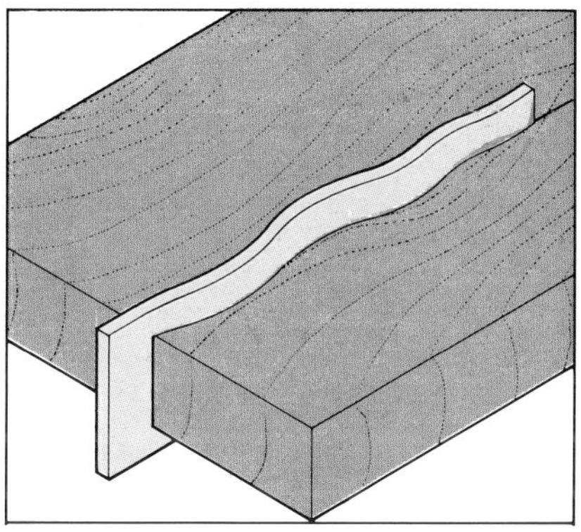

Repairing a split with a fillet of wood.

Two methods of clamping

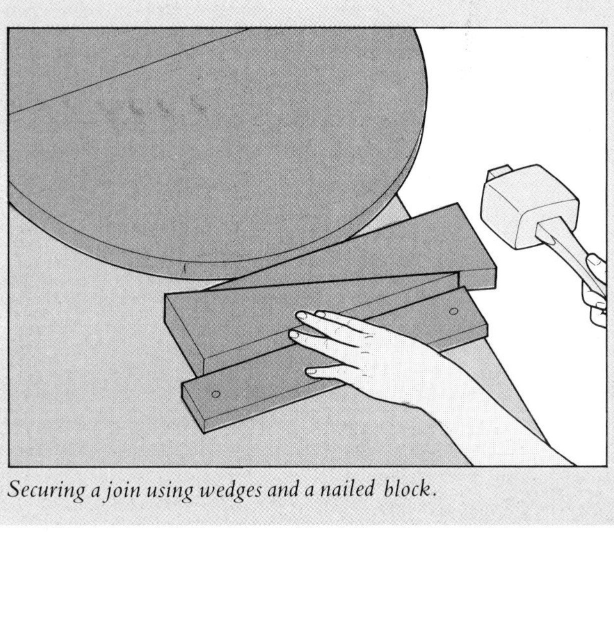

Securing a join using wedges and a nailed block.

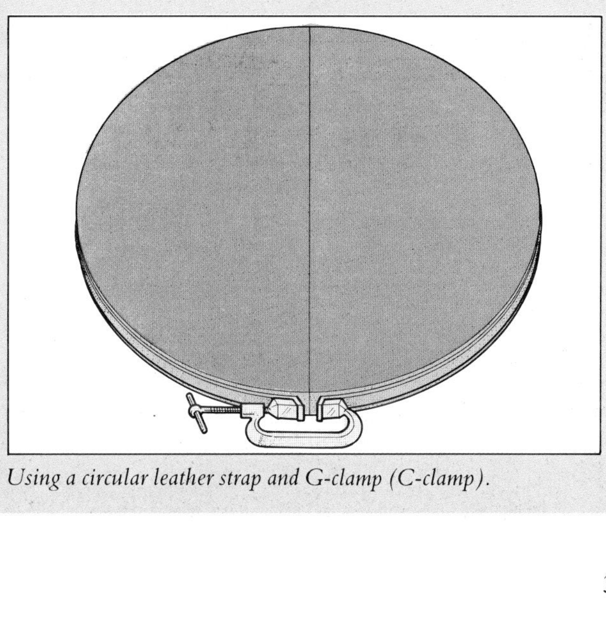

Using a circular leather strap and G-clamp (C-clamp).

Repairs to cabinets

On the left is a beautifully functional nineteenth century mahogany glass-fronted corner cabinet. The picture above shows a mid-eighteenth century secretaire chest with many small drawers and insets typical of the period.

Most cabinets will fall into one of two categories – those built with solid side panels and those built with side panels fitted to a frame.

Many cabinet frame and panel repairs involve the same techniques previously described in this chapter for chairs and tables, but there are three special areas that may need attention which are described below: drawers, doors and metal fittings.

Drawers

The main problem with drawers is likely to be wear on the runners. Usually, drawers are of two different types. The first is where the whole drawer rests on the runner; the second is where the runner, screwed to the side of the cabinet, slides into a groove in the middle of the drawer side. Either way, the runners are likely to have worn, as is the drawer itself.

If the drawer has a worn groove, cut a larger groove and fit a new, oversize, runner. The best tool for recutting the groove is a router or circular saw where both the depth and the direction can be controlled. Where the drawer sits on the runner, and both have worn, it will be necessary to set a new piece of wood into the bottom of the drawer and to replace the runner.

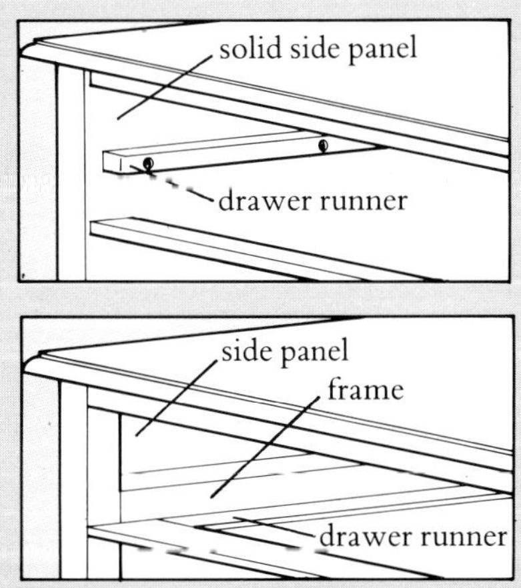

Alternative types of drawer frame construction.

Repairing worn drawers

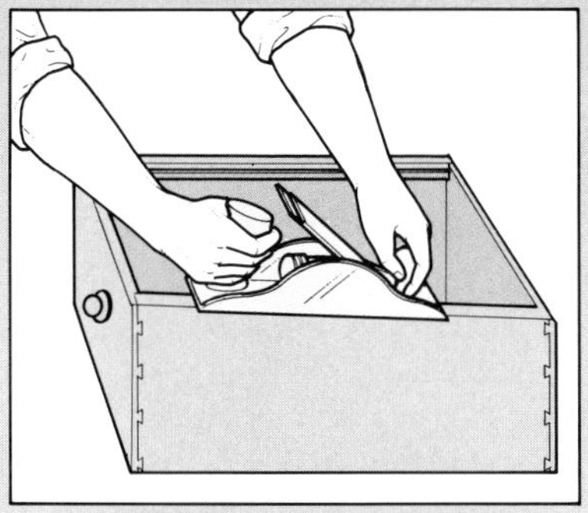

1. *Turn the drawer upside down and remove the base. Plane the worn surface flat until just below the level of the wear. Glue a strip of new wood, already planed flush to the side panel, flush with the inner face of the drawer side.*

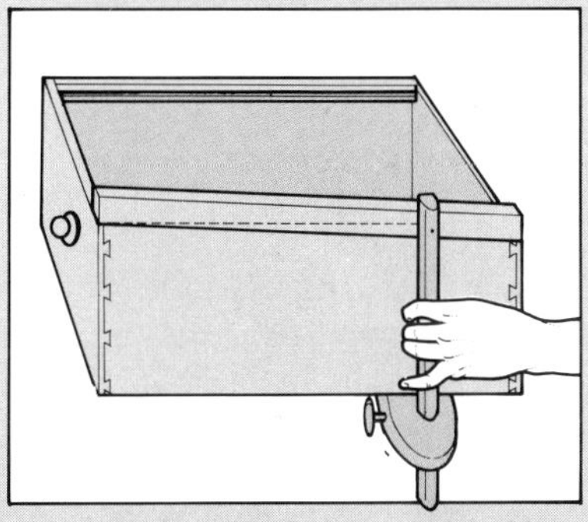

2. *Using a marking gauge, scribe a line along the new wood parallel with the top edge of the drawer side. Plane the strip level with this line.*

Another item to check for in drawers is missing or damaged front stops. Other potential problems are loose joints at the corners, missing or damaged drawer bottoms and missing or damaged dustboards – which protect the contents of a drawer from both airborne dust and sawdust generated by the wearing of the runners.

Doors

Doors are not easy to deal with and the trickiest are elegant, curved glass doors: if the glass in these breaks, it will be best to get a professional to replace it as the job is too difficult for the DIY enthusiast. The most common problem with cabinet doors, however, is that they will not close properly.

Where hinges are badly worn, the door may begin to drop or sag at an angle. It is advisable in this case to replace the hinges. However, if the hinges are only partly worn, it may be possible to swap the hinges from top to bottom. If the screw holes have become enlarged, fill them with wood filler and wait until it dries. Refit the hinges. With a badly sagging door, it may be possible to pack a hinge recess with a waste strip of narrow wood, for example, balsa or plywood or veneer. Hinge recesses may also need to be deepened with a chisel.

Metal fittings

The most common metal fittings that are likely to need attention are hinges which may rust or loosen because of constant movement. Handles and locks are also problem areas. Broken or damaged handles can usually be replaced, but it will almost certainly be extremely difficult to find an exact match and some elementary metalwork will be necessary to 'convert' a similar handle to the shape and size you want. (For more information on metalwork, see Chapter 5 on Metalwork and Metalware.) Broken handles can be mended by brazing. It is also possible to solder, but it is usually best to replace the handles, unless they are genuinely antique, in which case a professional should repair them.

The usual problem found with cabinet locks is that the key is missing. On a simple lock, however, you may be able to make a new key yourself from a suitable blank, but with more complicated locks probably the only way you will be able to deal with the situation is to replace the lock or get a locksmith to cut a new key for you.

Glossary

Bridle joint: used to join a thick leg in the centre of a thinner rail.

Butterflies: hardwood wedges used to hold two pieces of wood together.

Counterbored: a hole in wood which is larger for part of its length. When using auger-type bits, the larger part of the hole is made first.

Distressing: giving furniture an antique look by simulating wear.

Dowel: thin, circular piece of wood used to make or secure joints.

Dustboard: thin sheets of wood between drawers in a cabinet.

Fox-wedged joint: mortice and tenon joint with concealed wedges which force the tenon apart.

Lipping: thin piece of wood used to finish an edge.

Mortice and tenon: common joint. The male tenon fits into the female mortice.

Notches: used by craftsmen to mark joints for reassembly.

Packing: softwood block used to prevent damage to furniture when dismantling.

Paring: slicing action used with a chisel to remove wood across the grain.

Pegs: protruding dowel: widely used on very old furniture.

Saddle: device cut to enable awkward shapes to be held for gluing.

Scarf (scarph) joint: wood joint cut on an angle for joining wood end-to-end.

Stopped housing: a joint cut partway into the wood.

Undercutting: the chiselling method used for cutting dovetails.

Upholstery

Upholstery in a striking pattern, combined with soft furnishings in the same design, can be used to unify the decoration of a room. Here, even the table is draped in the matching cloth. Its floral design is named after the famous English Sissinghurst garden.

Upholstery is a traditional craft requiring knowledge, skill and experience. It can be rewarding for the amateur – provided that he or she is prepared to start with simple tasks such as repairs or replacements, move on to jobs such as recovering a padded seat, and work up slowly and patiently to the more complicated tasks.

You will need plenty of space, time and patience. It is hard work and tough on the fingers so you may need to wear leather gloves. Work slowly, and be prepared to undo and repeat parts of the job which don't quite work out first time.

In this section of the chapter, two types of chair are looked at in detail. These include the majority of skills needed for upholstery. The first is the 'stuffed-over' seat, which is a chair where the stuffing (filling) sits on webbing attached to the chair frame. This is an extension of the similar 'drop-in' seat, where only one layer of stuffing is used (as opposed to two in the stuffed-over seat) and no stitching of the hard-edge (or edge roll) is required.

The second type of chair is a simple sprung chair which, in the example given in this chapter, is like a stuffed-over seat with springs. More complicated sprung chairs are mentioned on page 52 but, for the amateur, it is better to start with a simple one.

There are many things to remember when upholstering. The first is that each chair or sofa is slightly different and so the instructions given will need to be modified if the item you are working on does not quite fit. The secret is to take careful note of how the chair is constructed as you take it apart.

Unlike many other jobs which involve dismantling and reassembly, a stripped-down chair looks nothing like the finished article, as it is simply a bare frame and a pile of upholstery materials. The professional upholsterer will have a clear picture of what the finished product is going to look like, but the beginner will need to make a careful note of exactly what the article looks like – if necessary, drawing detailed plans, before beginning to dismantle. Imagination is needed to see the final shape of what appear to be formless piles of stuffing. A common mistake beginners make is not to realize how much the various processes compress the various layers and so put too little stuffing in the chair. On average, reckon that stuffing will compress to one-third of its original shape. If you discover at any stage that there is simply not enough stuffing, don't panic: it is usually possible to untack one or more layers and insert some more. There is a specialist tool called a regulator which is used for moving the stuffing around under the covering materials to where it is required.

Tools and equipment

Upholstery can be done with just a few special tools, but having the correct ones helps to make each task easier. In addition to the tools listed below, specialized implements such as G-clamps (C-clamps) (to hold a chair steady) will be useful (see page 32). A sturdy workbench will provide an easier, more comfortable, working height than working on the floor – cover the bench with a blanket so that the 'show' wood of a chair is not damaged. If you have no workbench, put a blanket down over the floor and be careful where you drop old tacks and anything else that could scratch the polished wood or catch the fabric.

Needles

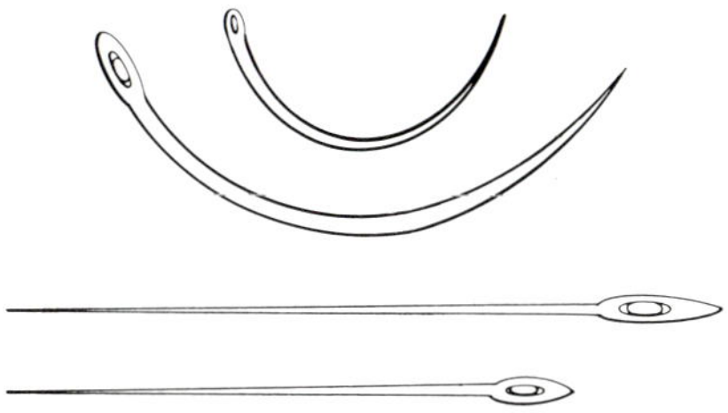

Curved needles and double-ended needles are used in upholstery to sew through the materials from one side. Double-ended needles are available in sizes ranging from 100mm to 400mm (4in to 16in): the 200mm (8in) double-ended needle is a good size to start with. Two sizes of curved needles are needed: one 50 to 75mm (2 to 3in) long for sewing hard edges and one 125mm (5in) long called a spring needle for securing springs to webbing. Remember to store needles away carefully, with a cork or something similar on the pointed ends.

Regulator

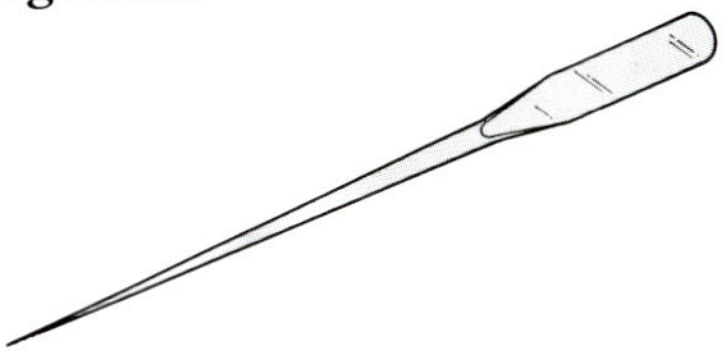

A regulator is a long metal spike (shaped like a bodkin) which can be pushed through a calico or scrim covering and waggled about to redistribute the stuffing below. It is useful when you are sewing a hard edge. The flat end is used to tuck fabric into narrow places.

Ripping chisel (tool)

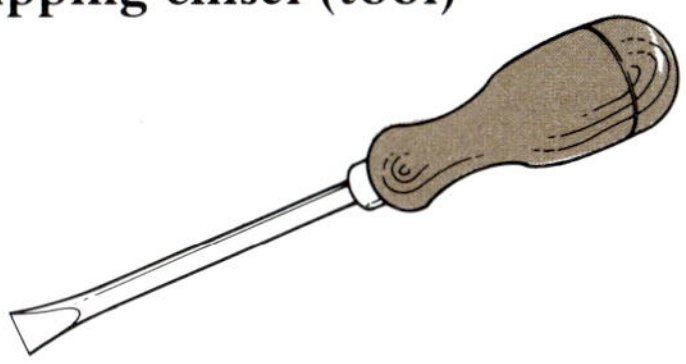

A ripping chisel (tool) is used to remove old tacks. One end of the chisel is placed under the tack head and the other end is tapped gently with a wooden mallet to ease the tack out. Make sure the tack comes out along the grain of the wood, or else the wood may split. An old chisel or screwdriver, used with care, will do instead; grinding a 'V' groove will prevent slipping.

Skewers (upholsterer's pins)

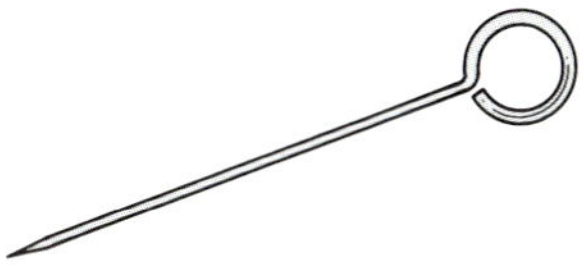

Long metal skewers (pins) are used to hold material in place as you work and to secure an edge before it is sewn.

Tack lifter

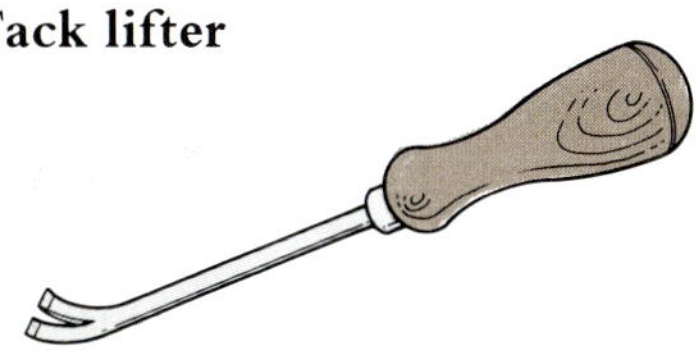

A tack lifter is used for removing old tacks. It has a curved claw head which you work under the head of the tack to lift it out of an old frame. Some hammers and pincers have a tack lifter at one end, but these are often too thick for upholstery work; a separate tack lifter is worth having.

Tailor's chalk
Tailor's chalk is useful for marking sewing lines and positions of springs without making a permanent mark.

Upholsterer's hammer
In upholstery, tacks often have to be driven in tight places without damaging the polished wood, so an upholsterer's (or *cabriole*) hammer needs to have a small head. Often, one end of the head is magnetized, so that the hammer acts as an 'extra hand' and is able to pick up tacks and position them while you hold the webbing or fabric tight. Some upholsterer's hammers have a claw end for removing incorrectly positioned tacks.

Upholsterer's pliers

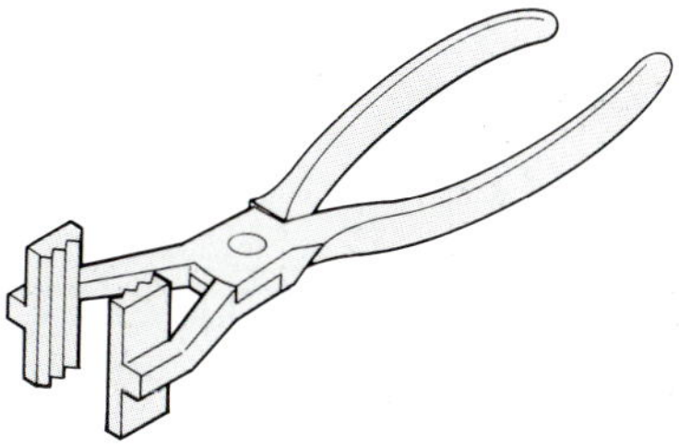

Special pliers for upholsterer's work have wide serrated jaws for gripping and tensioning fabric covers. Because they are used for leatherwork, they are sometimes called 'hide stretchers'.

Webbing stretcher

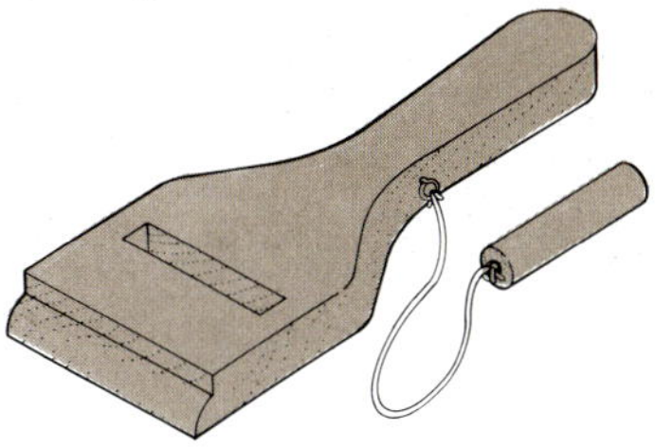

A webbing stretcher is used to tension the webbing support of most seats. It is possible to make do with an offcut of wood or home-made tool, but this is not recommended. The proper tool is preferable for this job – and it is not expensive. The usual webbing stretchers are made in one of two designs, both of which are equally effective.

Upholstery materials

The common materials used are listed below in the order you would use them to upholster a chair; as you strip a chair down, you will find them in roughly the reverse order.

Webbing
For most upholstery, you will use the woven type of webbing which is 50mm (2in) wide. English black and white twill webbing is the best type to use; if you are offered jute webbing from the Far East, check that it is perfectly dry.

Tacks

There are two types of upholstery tack, both with a very sharp end, which can be pushed by hand into the wood. *Improved* tacks have two small lugs under the head for extra grip when securing webbing and hessian (burlap). *Fine* tacks are smaller and are used for securing linings and top covers. They are also used if the wood is very hard or if the piece you are nailing into is narrow. Both types of tack are available in sizes ranging from 6mm (¼in) to 25mm (1in); if you buy a stock of 10mm (⅜in), 13mm (½in) and 15mm (⅝in) tacks, you should be equipped for most jobs. Use the longer tacks where you are fixing materials that support the upholstery – the hessian and the webbing.

Staples

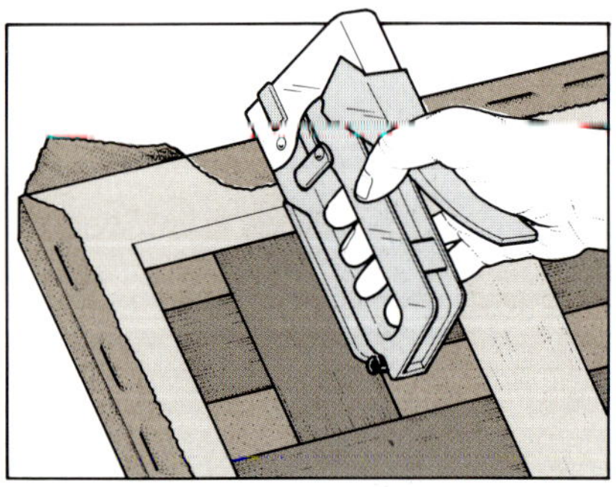

If you have a staple gun, staples can be used for tacking. The thicker types of wire staple which are hammered home are useful to anchor the laid cord (or twine) used to lash the springs. Although tacks can be used for this job, staples give a more secure fixing and are very much easier to work with.

Hessian (burlap)
Hessian (burlap) is a strong coarse cloth, made of hemp or jute. For the cover over springs, a heavy grade is needed; for the layers between stuffings an open weave hessian called *scrim* is used.

Springs

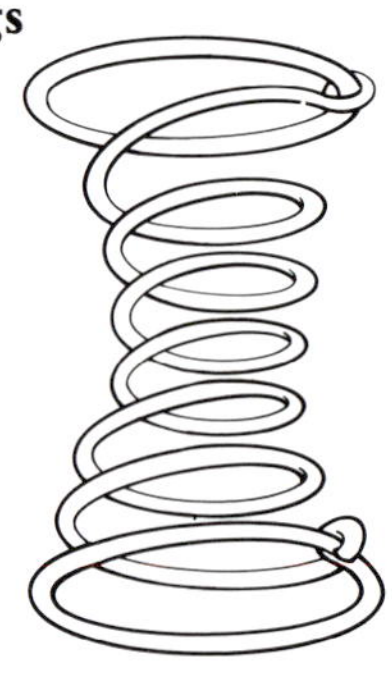

The springs used to give resilience to a chair seat (and sometimes to the back and arms as well) are made of copper-plated wire or lacquered steel. They come in different sizes from 100mm (4in) to 300mm (12in) long and are made from different diameters (gauges) of wire. If you find you have to replace one because it is bent or has lost its bounce, it is in fact best to replace them all so that the new seat will wear evenly.

Laid cord
This is a soft, strong cord which is better than twine for lashing the springs together (though twine is often used for this purpose).

Twine
Jute or hemp twine is available in three grades. Medium (No.2) twine is the most useful as it can be used for sewing down springs and is fine enough for stitching.

Stuffing
Horsehair was the traditional stuffing material used, and it is still widely believed to be the best. If you find a chair stuffed with horsehair, find someone who will wash and 'card' it for you (that is, comb it free of tangles) so that it can be reused. Of all the other stuffing materials, *hoghair* has the best resilience. Algerian grass and coir (the prepared fibre from the husk of the coconut) are the main alternatives to hair.

Wadding (batting)
Wadding (batting) is a loose, fluffy material which looks a little like sheep's wool and is used to pad below (or sometimes above) the calico cover to give a smooth finish to the stuffings and to stop hair or fibre prickling through the calico and top covering fabric. *Felted cotton waste* may be used.

Calico
Calico is a strong cotton cloth with a fine weave which goes over the stuffing to hold it in place and stop the fibres or hair prickling through.

Gimp
Gimp is a decorative braid, about 15mm (⅝in) wide, used to trim chairs. Brassed or enamelled chair nails (known as *upholstery nails)* can also be used as a trim.

Gimp pins

These fine tacks, ranging in size from 4mm (¼in) to 25mm (1in), are used to nail on the braid or gimp used to finish some upholstery.

Chair cord
Chair cord is a decorative twisted cord which is sometimes used in place of *piping* (which is a fine cord encased in a pipe-like fold). It can look very effective, but it may be difficult to get a good colour match with your fabric.

Black lining
Black lining is thin, black cambric or calico and is used to finish off the underside of a chair.

Stuffed-over seat

A stuffed-over seat has no springs. It is commonly used for dining and 'occasional' chairs. The stuffing is applied in two layers over the webbing, the first layer being stitched on all sides to make a 'hard' edge to give shape and support to the seat. The cover either comes right over the frame or is tacked to the sides, leaving decorative wood to show.

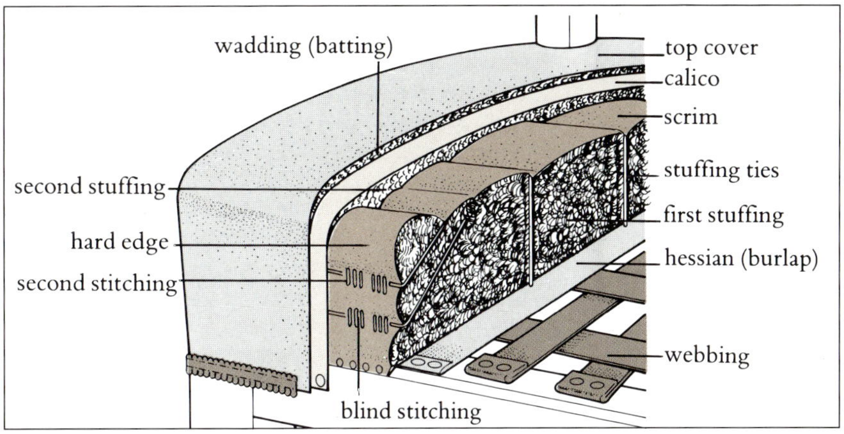

Stripping off old upholstery

Turn the chair upside down and clamp it securely. Remove the old tacks, using a ripping chisel (tool) or old screwdriver and work with the grain of the wood to avoid splitting the wood. Start to remove the tacks at the corners, working towards the centre of the rail. You will find that a downwards lever action on the chisel helps to flip the tack out. Some tacks will break; these must be pulled out with pincers or punched below the surface.

It should be possible to loosen the tacks that hold each layer of the upholstery, starting with the black cambric lining. Cut through any threads holding gimp or braid edging in place. Try to remove all the tacks before turning the chair upright. Then lift off the upholstery, layer by layer. Have a notebook handy to record the materials (including tacks) and method of construction of each layer (look particularly at the corners) and, as far as possible, keep and mark each layer for future reference. (Drawings and/or photographs will also help at this stage.)

After the first few layers – top cover, wadding (batting) and calico – have been removed, the second stuffing can be pulled out. Cut the stitches securing the edge and remove the scrim, first stuffing and hessian (burlap). Finally, remove

(top right) *Cross-section of a stuffed-over seat.*

(bottom right) *This heart-back chair contains a stuffed-over seat.*

the webbing with its tacks, noting its width and marking its positioning on the chair.

Cleaning up the frame

Once all the materials have been removed, inspect the stripped frame carefully; it may need some repair (see pages 33-37) or treatment for woodworm. Fill all of the tack holes, using sawdust and wood glue pressed into place. This will also strengthen the frame. Polish up any parts of the frame which will be exposed when the upholstery is finished, not forgetting the legs.

Fixing the webbing

The purpose of the webbing is to provide a support for the rest of the upholstery and, ultimately, for the person sitting on the chair. On a stuffed-over seat the webbing is fitted to the *top* of the frame.

Before fixing the webbing, mark where it is to go, following the notes you made when dismantling. Space the webbing evenly across the chair. The front to back webbing is fitted first, working from the centre outwards. Fix the webbing as described in the captions to the illustrations shown on the right.

Fitting the hessian (burlap)

The main purpose of the hessian (burlap) layer is to prevent the stuffing falling through the webbing so it needs to fit snugly all round – and especially at the corners. Cut a piece of hessian 50mm (2in) larger all round than the chair frame. Lay it over the frame so that the weave of the hessian lines up with the chair frame. Fold over the back edge by 25mm (1in) and tack at 25mm (1in) spacings along the back rail, fitting the tacks outside the ends of the webbing and working outwards from the centre. Pull the hessian tight to the front rail and tack along that rail at 50mm (2in) spacings. Fold back the surplus and tack again between the first tacks. Deal with the side edges in the same way, tacking one side through the folded-over edge and the other, through the single edge first, while pulling gently, and then through the folded over edge. Make neat folds at the front corners; at the back, cut into the fabric to enable a neat fold round the back uprights.

Fixing the webbing

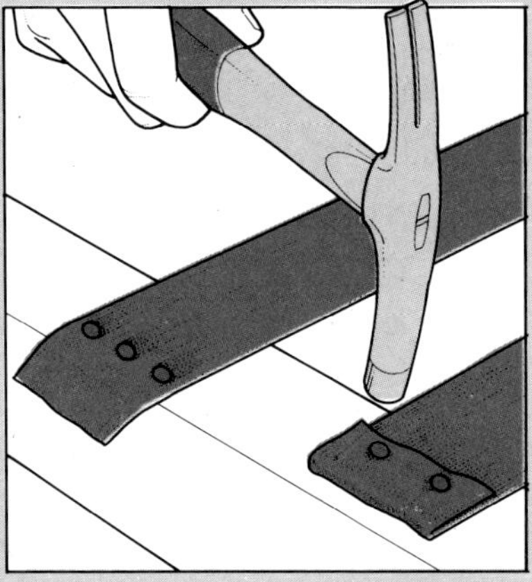

1. *To fix the first web, lay the roll of webbing across the chair so that it overlaps the back rail by 20mm (3/4in). Knock in three improved tacks in line about 13mm (1/2in) from the frame edge and fold over the end. Knock in two more tacks so that the five form a 'W' shape. This staggering avoids splitting the wood.*

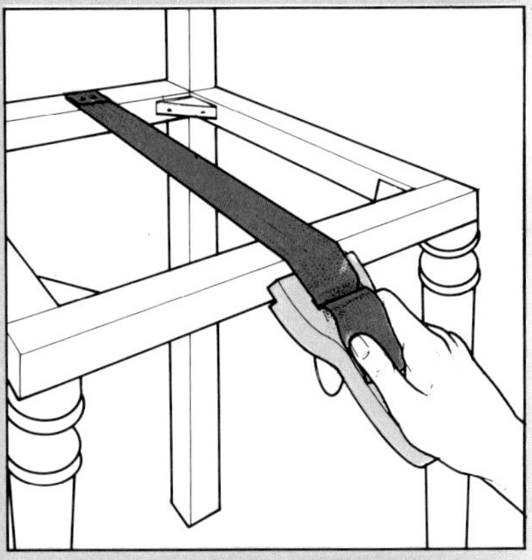

2. *Take the webbing to the front of the frame, using a webbing stretcher or home-made wood block to pull the webbing tight. Holding it tight, hammer three tacks in a line across the webbing 13mm (1/2in) in from the edge of the frame.*

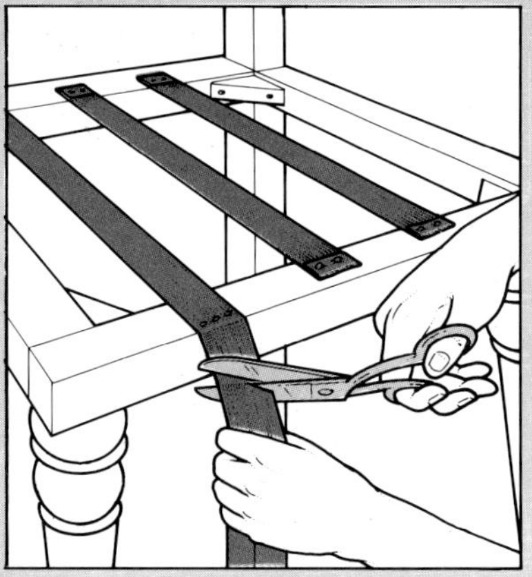

3. *Cut the webbing 20mm (3/4in) beyond the frame and put in two more tacks as before to make the 'W'. Make sure the tacks are fully hammered home – remove and replace any that are crooked. Place all the front-to-back webs in this way, leaving not more than 50mm (2in) between adjacent webs; fan out towards the front if the chair is wider there.*

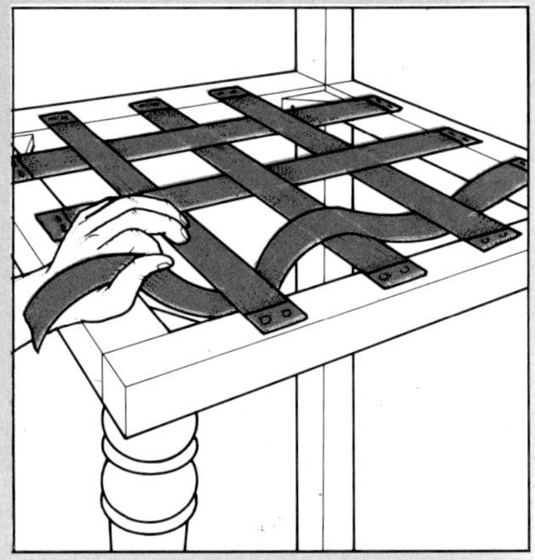

4. *Weave the cross webs between the front-to-back webs and then fix the end of each web with the five tacks in the same way. Although it is important that the webbing is taut it is nevertheless essential to beware of over-tensioning a delicate frame which might then easily snap.*

If the webbing strips have been left unfolded, the ends are folded *over* the hessian with the final two tacks securing the hessian as well. Beginners may find it easier to fit temporary tacks, put halfway in, at the centre of each rail and at the corners before finally hammering home the securing tacks once the hessian is pulled square and tight.

First stuffing

The first layer of stuffing gives the upholstery a solid base. It is held in place by loops of twine, called stuffing ties (or bridles), attached to the hessian (burlap). Thread a curved needle with medium twine and secure it with an upholsterer's slip knot – see box – in one corner of the hessian. Make a large loop stitch about 75mm (3in) long, and secure this loop with a back stitch into the hessian so that the next loop overlaps by about 35mm (1½in). Without cutting the twine, make similar loops all round the edge of the frame and then stitch a second lot in the centre, finishing with a double-hitch.

Tease out a handful of stuffing, tucking it under one of the ties. Tuck enough handfuls under each tie to take up the slack in the loop. Tuck more handfuls down between the rows of stuffing held by the ties. Next, tuck palm-sized chunks of stuffing under the edge ties to get a substantial springy lip which slightly overhangs the frame all round.

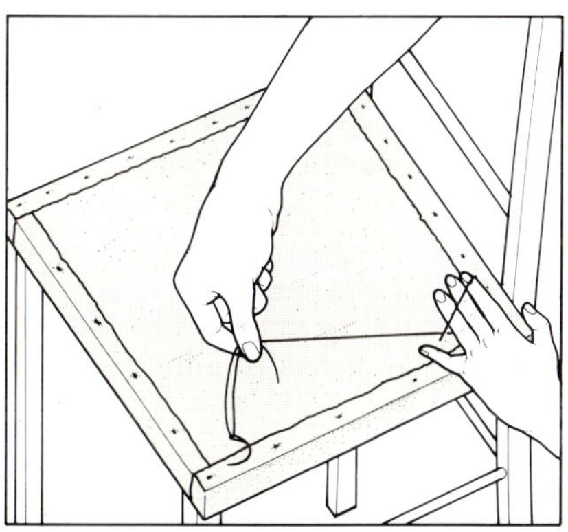

Sewing stuffing ties onto hessian (burlap).

Upholsterer's slip knot

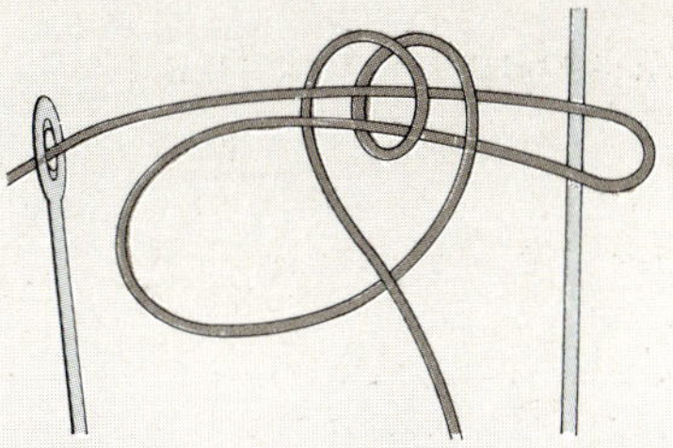

The first stitch in upholstery is usually secured with a special slip knot called an upholsterer's knot. It is made very easily as follows: thread a needle with a length of twine and pass it through the material in which the knot is to be made until about 100mm (4in) is left free. Grip the two pieces of twine together, leaving about 50mm (2in) free. Form a 'D' shaped loop with the free end on top of the two pieces; pass the free end around both pieces and back up through the 'D' shaped loop; pass it round and through the loop again. Pull the knot tight with the main length of twine.

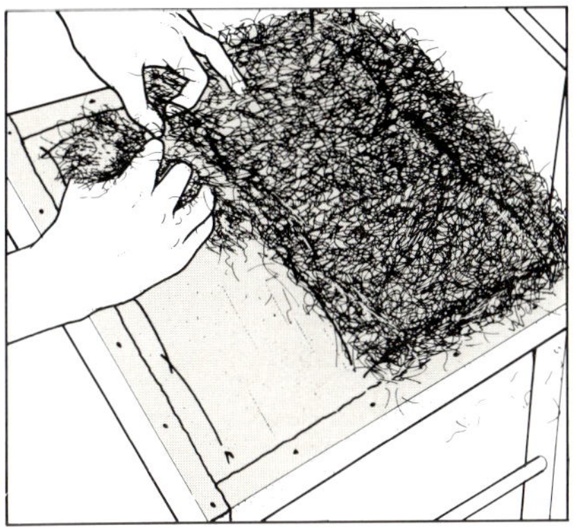

Tuck handfuls of stuffing under the ties.

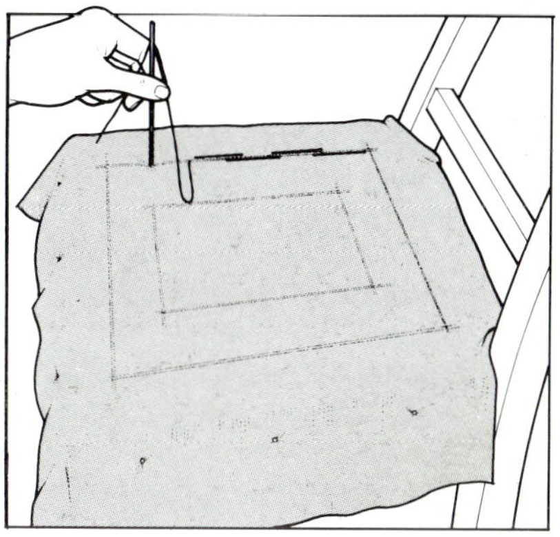

Sew along the square to secure stuffing.

Aim to keep the stuffing evenly distributed and the lip straight. The stuffing should be the correct height when compressed by hand.

Cover the stuffing with a square of hessian (burlap) scrim big enough to overlap 50mm (2in) all round. All woven material such as hessian, scrim or calico can be cut square by pulling out (drawing) a single thread to give a cutting line. Position the scrim so that the weave aligns with the chair and put three holding tacks down each side of the frame. Now the scrim needs to be tied to the hessian so that the stuffing is fully secured. Draw a square on the scrim 100mm (4in) in from the edge of the frame, using tailor's chalk or a felt-tip pen. Push a double-ended needle down through one corner, out below the hessian, and back again about 8mm (5⁄16in) away. Tie an upholsterer's knot and pull the twine tight. Push the needle in again about halfway along the line to the next corner and make a similar stitch. Do the same at the next corner and continue round the square. Finish with a stitch at the centre of the square and tie a knot. On large seats, you will need three or four stitches along each side of the square with perhaps a second square inside the first.

Making a hard edge

It is important that the edge of the chair has a firm, hard edge to keep the rest of the upholstery in place.

The first task is to ensure that there is enough stuffing. Remove the three temporary tacks from the

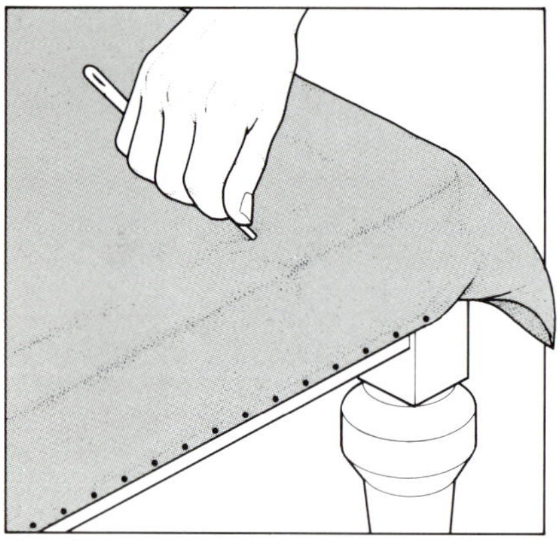

Regulate stuffing towards frame edge.

back and draw the scrim over the lip of the stuffing. Pull the scrim taut and then slacken it about 6mm (¼in). This slack will be taken up when the hard edge is sewn. Tuck the end under the lip and, following a straight thread line, tack at 25mm (1in) spacings through a double thickness into the chamfered edge at the top of the frame. Leaving the corners open, tuck and tack the scrim on the sides and front in the same way. Add extra stuffing through the corners, pushing it along with a regulator. At the back, cut the corners to enable the scrim to fold round the uprights. At the front, first ensure that there is plenty of stuffing, then take the flap of scrim and reverse fold it so that the flap is inside. Slipstitch together the meeting edges with fine twine.

Work round the chair, adjusting the position of the stuffing with the sharp point of the regulator and pulling it forward to the edge of the frame to get an even sausage-shaped lip. The sausage should overhang the edge of the chair by around 10mm (⅜in); if there appears to be too little stuffing, open up the scrim at the corners and add more.

The next job is to sew the hard edge in place. Starting at the back of the chair, follow the instructions given in the captions to the illustrations below.

When you come to the end of a piece of twine, use a reef knot as close to the scrim as possible to join on the next piece. On the last

Blind stitching

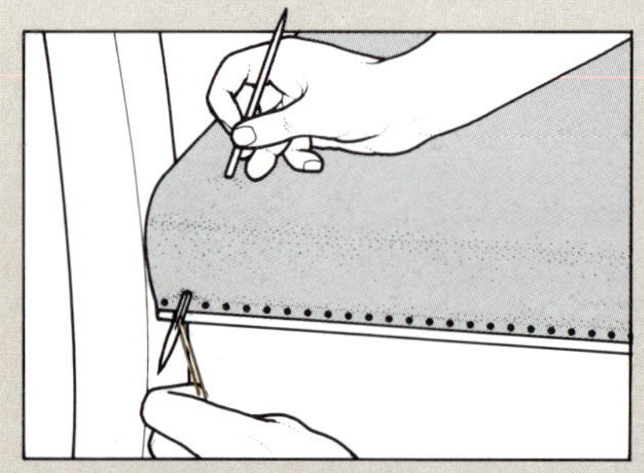

1. *Insert a double-ended needle fitted with medium twine into the bottom of the sausage-shaped lip about 13mm (½in) from the left-hand corner. Make a stitch to secure the twine. Angle the needle so that the point will emerge through the top of the stuffing about 75mm (3in) from the edge.*

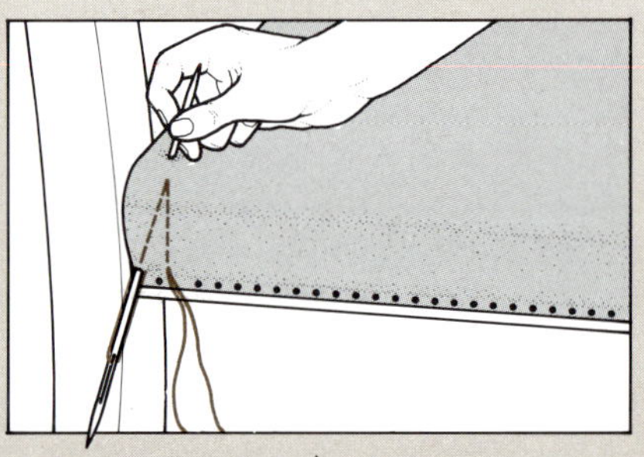

2. *Pull the needle right through the material. Then make a back stitch to bring the needle back down to the back corner and tie off with an upholsterer's knot. (How to do this is outlined in the box on page 47.)*

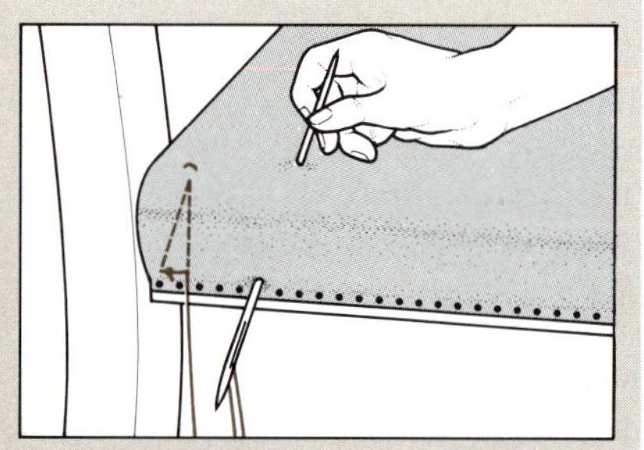

3. *About 40mm (1½in) to the right of the knot, push the needle into the sausage at the same upward angle as before. Angle the stitch to the left as well so that the point emerges on the top of the stuffing 75mm (3in) from the edge and 13mm (½in) back from where the stitch began.*

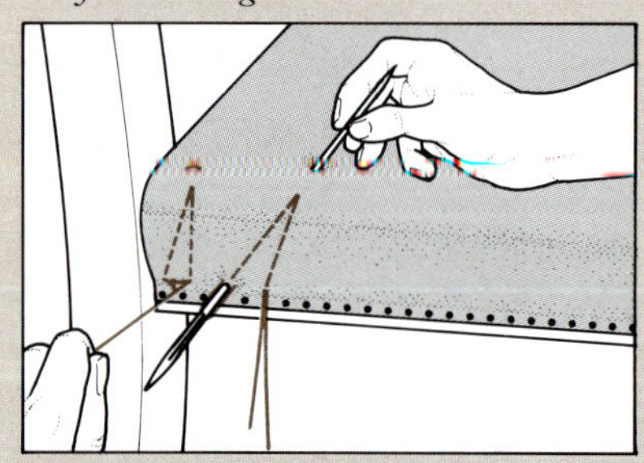

4. *Pull the needle through the scrim until the second eye begins to appear but stop before it comes right out. Turn the needle at a new angle to bring the point back out at the lower edge 25mm (1in) to the left of where the needle went in.*

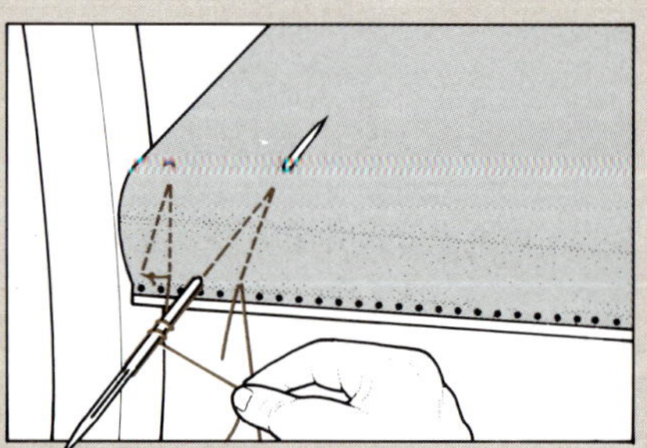

5. *As the needle is drawn out, stop and make two anti-clockwise (counter-clockwise) turns of the twine round the needle. Draw the rest of the twine through these loops and pull it tight to make a tight stitch which will not slip.*

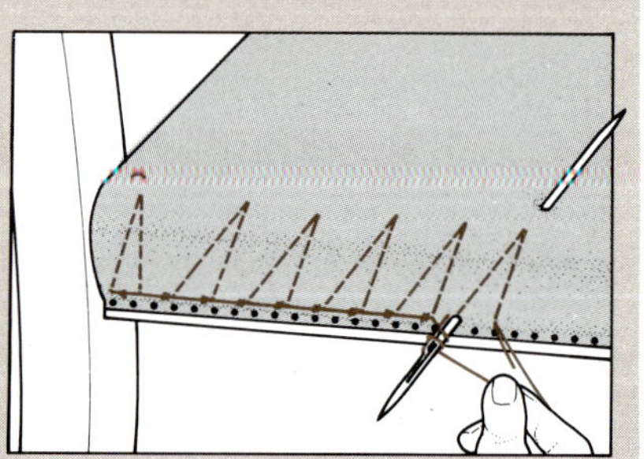

6. *Repeat this 'blind' stitch (which never comes through the scrim) around the chair, moving along 40mm (1½in) each time and adjusting the stuffing with the regulator where necessary to get an even, well filled roll.*

corner, secure the last stitch with a knot. On some chairs, a second row of 'blind' stitches will be needed, but on most stuffed-over chairs you can go straight on to the second or 'top' stitching.

Second stitching

The second stitching makes an 'edge' roll around the seat of the chair. Start this second row of stitches about 6mm (¼in) above the 'blind' stitches, following the step-by-step stages outlined in the illustrations on the right.

If the roll is uneven, adjust it with the regulator; if the roll is flopping over, make the stitches more vertical; if the roll is too soft, insert another row of stitches.

Second stuffing

The second stuffing (about half as much material as the first stuffing) fills hollows left by stitching and provides the final shape of the chair. If the ties through the scrim have enough slack, use them to secure the second stuffing. Otherwise, sew a row of stuffing ties round the edge of the well created by the hard edge in the same way as for the first stuffing.

Tuck stuffing under each tie and then between to form the final shape of the chair. Pack it firmly behind and against the hard edge, especially at the front. Tear up a piece of wadding (batting) and lay it over the stuffing so that it reaches onto the

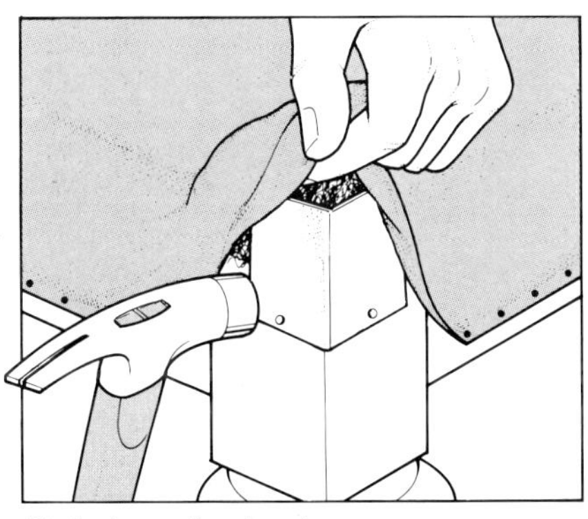

Tack pieces of card at the corners.

Second stitching

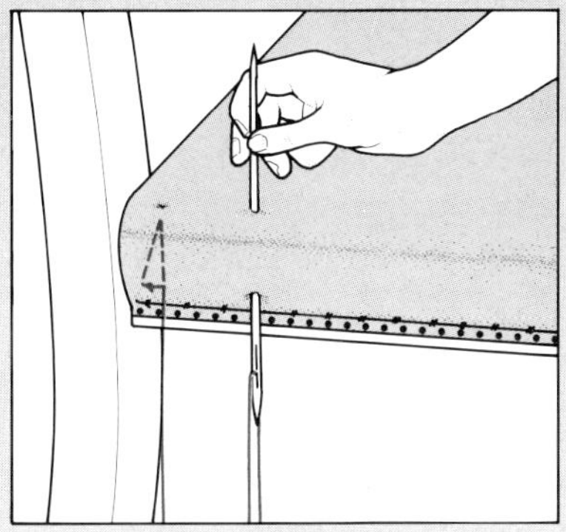

1. *Make the stitch with the upholsterer's knot to start. Then insert the needle at the same upward angle as before, this time keeping the needle straight – the point should emerge on the top in line with where it went in about 60mm (2½in) from the edge, that is 20mm (¾in) nearer than the blind stitches.*

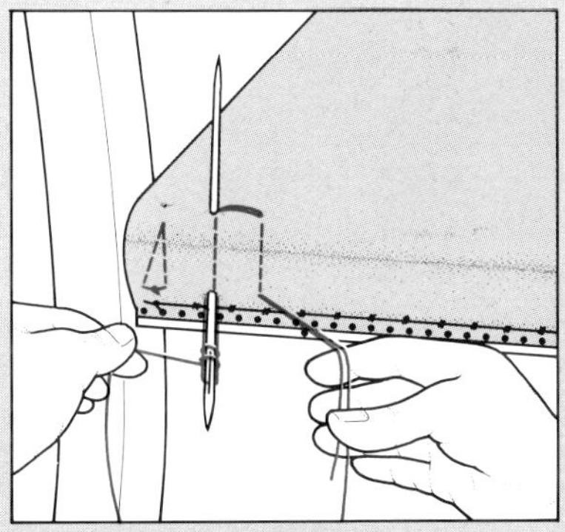

2. *Draw the needle right through the scrim and make a backstitch 13mm (½in) to the left; twist the two turns of twine as before and draw tight.*

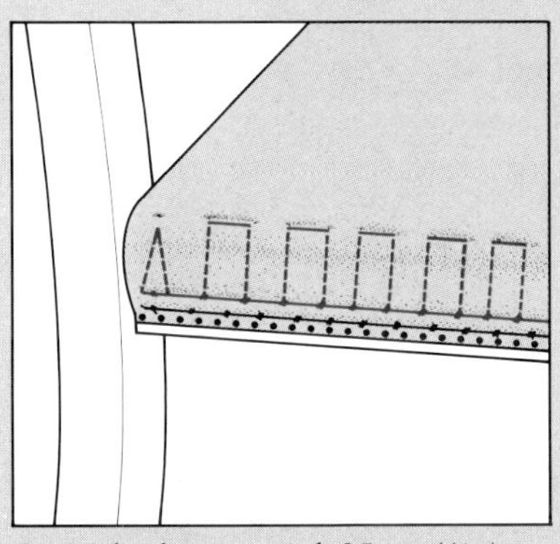

3. *Make the next stitch 25mm (1in) along, again coming through the scrim, and continue round the chair.*

hard edge: this prevents the hair of the stuffing coming through. Finally, tack small pieces of card, folded around each of the front corners.

Cut the calico larger than the chair and lay it squarely in place. Tack the calico temporarily with two or three tacks on each side. Keeping the weave straight, ease the calico firmly over the stuffing with one hand and, holding it in position with the other hand, tack it in place. At the back corners, cut the calico to fit; at the front, make a parcel-like fold, taking the excess material from the front round to the side of the frame. Establish a neat crease down the front and slipstitch the edge with fine twine. Some upholsterers prefer to put the wadding under the calico (as described here); others put it on top between the calico and top covering.

Top covering

Fix this in the same way as the calico, paying attention to the positioning of the material and the balancing of any pattern to the corners. Trim the lower edge with braid tacked with gimp pins or glued and sewn into place, or finish with close nailing. Tack the cambric lining to the underside of the chair.

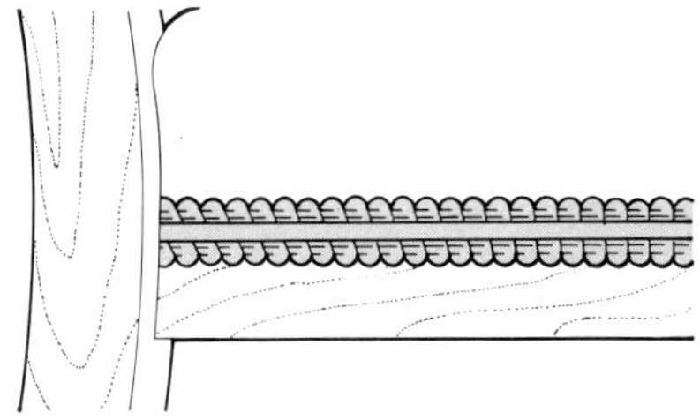

Two methods to finish off a stuffed-over seat. Close nailing (top) *and braid* (below). *Both secure the seat cover.*

Simple sprung chair

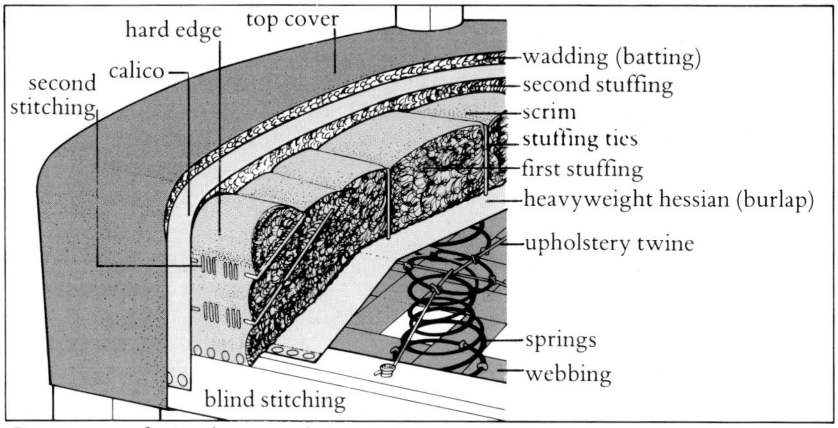

Cross-section of a simple sprung chair.

With a simple sprung chair, although the upholstering follows much the same stages as described previously, there is, of course, the extra stage of fitting the springs between the webbing and hessian (burlap).

Many sprung chairs will have padded or sprung backs and some will have fully upholstered arms. There may also be a second set of springs on the front edge.

First stages

The old upholstery should be stripped off and the bare frame prepared as described previously on page 46. When dismantling the chair, check the springs to see whether or not they can be re-used. Provided they are not distorted and bounce back readily when compressed by hand, they should be all right.

Fitting the springs

Fit the webbing to the seat, as described on page 46. With a simple sprung chair, the webbing is attached to the *underside* of the chair frame and positioned so that the springs sit on the junction between the webs. Place the springs on the new seat webbing as they were in the seat before you took it apart. A simple sprung chair will typically have five springs: one placed centrally and the remaining four near the corners of the chair with their joined ends pointing inwards. The springs are sewn to the webbing and lashed down to the chair rails.

To sew them to the webbing, thread a large, curved needle with No. 1 or No. 2 upholstery twine. Starting with the central spring, bring the twine up through the webbing and down over the bottom coil of the spring and tie a simple knot, keeping the stitches close to the spring. Without cutting the twine, make two more stitches round the base so that the spring is secured in three places. Work round the other springs in the same way, looping from spring to spring, without cutting the thread. Knot the twine and cut after the last spring.

The exact method of lashing the springs will depend on their number and position. For example, where three springs are in a line, the laid cord is lashed to the top coil of the central spring and the inside of the outer springs, and the second coil on the outside of the outer springs

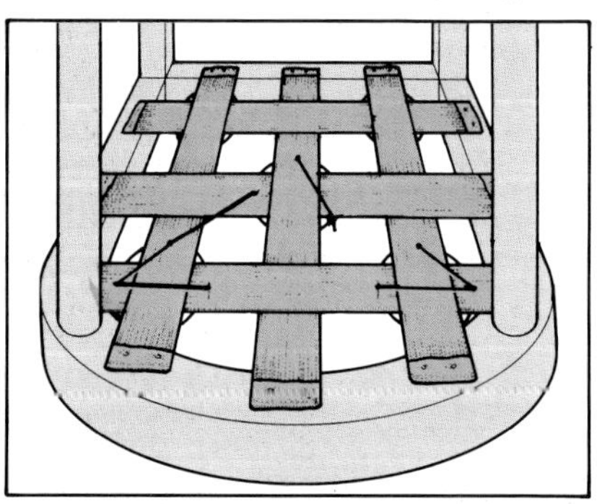

How to secure springs to webbing.

Lashing the springs

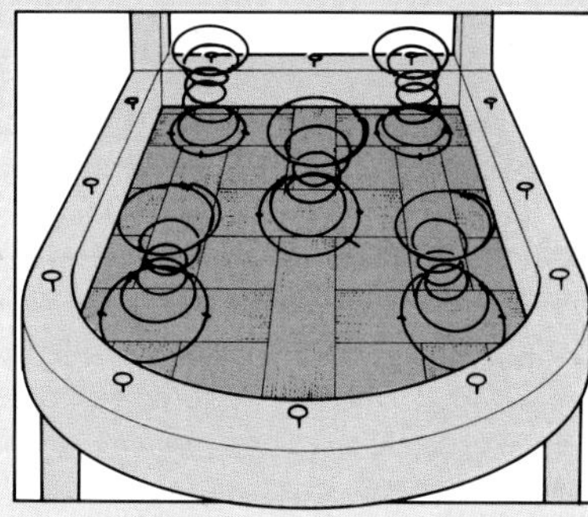

1. *Knock 20mm (3/4in) improved tacks (or wire staples) into the tops of the chair rails in line with each spring.*

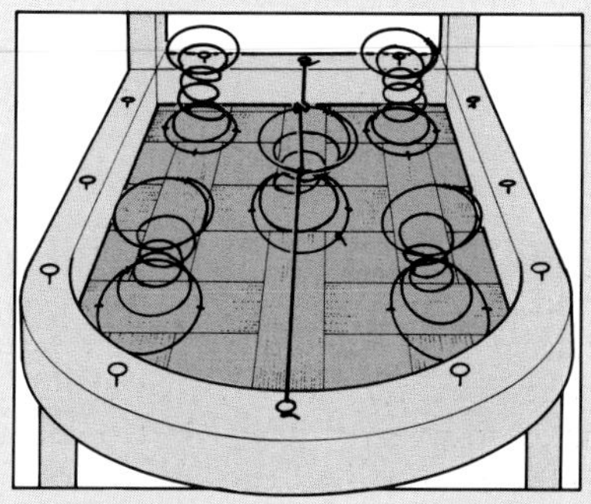

2. *Cut a piece of laid cord about twice the depth of the frame (front to back). Knot to the tack in the back rail. Hammer home. Tie the cord to the spring on the side nearest the back rail, while compressing about 25mm (1in). Cross the spring and tie a second knot on the other side. Knot the cord to the tack and knock home.*

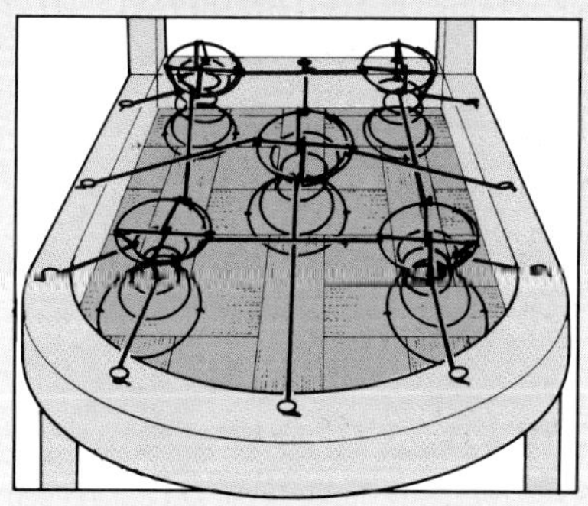

3. *The outer springs are tied down in a similar way, except that the knot on the spring nearest the edge is tied to the second coil down and the free end of the cord is brought back from the tack to attach to the top coil. The process is repeated so the springs are lashed front-to-back and side-to-side.*

Fitting the hessian (burlap)

Cut a piece of heavyweight hessian (burlap) to fit over the springs with 50mm (2in) to spare for tacking. The hessian should fit neatly with no slack, without compressing the springs. Tack the hessian in place around the frame in the same way as for a stuffed-over seat (see page 46) and then sew the springs to the hessian in the same way as they were sewn to the webbing. You will find it easier in the long run to tack the hessian temporarily in place before folding it over the edges and securing firmly.

Stuffing the seat

Sew stuffing ties around the chair as for the stuffed-over seat (see pages 47-49) and put in the first stuffing, building up the lip which will eventually form the hard edge. Fit the scrim squarely and tack it temporarily down each side. Mark a square 100mm (4in) in from the edge and sew through the stuffings as described for the stuffed-over seat.

Making the hard edges

This process is identical to making a hard edge and second stitching of the stuffed-over seat (see pages 47-49). Tuck under and tack the scrim, leaving the corners open. Adjust the stuffing in the sausage-shaped roll of stuffing; add more if necessary; and then close the corners. Starting at a back corner, sew the two rows of stitches (blind and top) that make the hard edge.

Second stuffing

Sew ties two fingers' high to take the second stuffing and feed the stuffing under and between the ties. Build up some extra in the centre to give the seat a gentle dome. Lay a piece of wadding (batting) over the stuffing and tack the calico in place, using a light card to stiffen the front corners as with a stuffed-over seat.

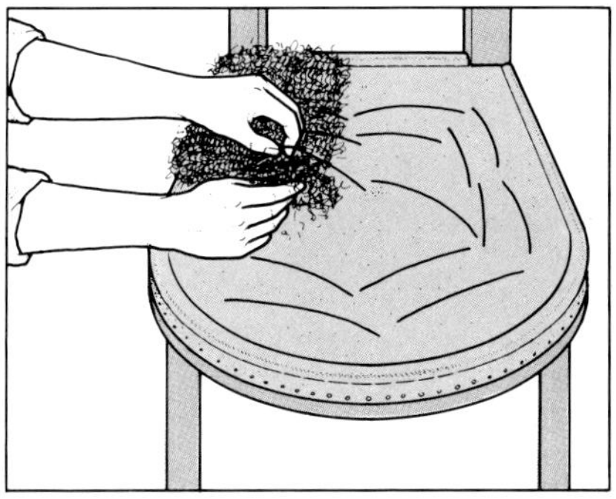

Fitting the cover

Fit the seat cover in the same way as for a stuffed-over seat. Finally, trim the bottom edge of the chair with braid and fit the cambric lining.

(left) *Putting on the second stuffing.*

(below) *This simple styled American elbow chair has no fussy decoration. When re-upholstering, treat the seat and back as two separate parts.*

Other types of chair

The techniques described earlier in this section cover the most important elements of traditional upholstery. But no two chairs are identical and you may need to adapt the techniques. When you have some experience, more complicated types of chair can be tackled.

Drop-in seat

A drop-in seat – as found on many dining chairs – is probably the simplest type of chair to re-upholster as the seat pad can be worked on away from the chair. There are usually no springs and only a single stuffing held in place by bridle ties. The chair frame gives a firm edge to the seat. The webbing is fitted to the top of the seat pad, followed by hessian (burlap), stuffing ties, stuffing, wadding (batting), calico, and finally the cover as for a stuffed-over seat, described on page 49. The calico and top cover are taken right under the seat panel (so extra material needs to be allowed for this) and care needs to be taken to get a neat, pleated finish at the corners – this will involve cutting away some of the material.

The button back and cabriole legs are the main features of this armchair. Although rather large, such chairs are often very comfortable to sit in.

Padded seat

A padded seat (also called 'pincushion' seat) often fits in a rebate (rabbet) on the top of the chair frame. Consequently, all the layers are applied from the top of the frame, starting with the black lining which is held in place with the webbing tacks. Take care to graduate the edges to avoid lumps. The cover can be left with a raw edge, hidden by a braid trim glued round the rebate and sewn to the top fabric. The work may sound easy, but these frames are usually very delicate so treat them gently. The steps are: black lining; hessian (burlap); stuffing; wadding (batting) and calico; top fabric and braid. A padded back is made in much the same way, but in addition needs a top cover on the outside back.

Chairs with backs

Re-upholstering a simple padded back is very similar to a stuffed-over chair seat (see page 45).

Where the back is curved, the vertical webs are fitted first and the side-to-side webs keep the shape of the back (unless it is 'tub'-shaped, in which case it has to be the other way round).

In some instances, only side-to-side webs are used, and this is especially likely if the chair has a central tacking rail. Remember that chair backs need covering on both sides. This may seem an elementary point but it is often forgotten.

A sprung chair back is similar to a simple sprung seat, except that the springs used are smaller and generally softer. The vertical webbing is often tacked to the outside of the top rail and the inside of the bottom rail to bring the lower springs forward.

Chairs with arms

Where chairs with wooden arms have stuffed pads, the webbing and hessian (burlap) stages are omitted. The stuffing ties have to be tacked in place onto the arms and the scrim which covers the first stuffing will need to be cut large enough to allow for the sewing of the hard edge around the arm pad. Sewing the hard edge will be easier with a curved needle – as the wood may get in the way. The calico and top cover are put on after a second layer of stuffing and tacked to the wooden arm. Gimp or braiding is used to finish off.

Where chairs have sprung arms, with the springs supported on wooden boards, the springs are secured with staples directly into the board, or with a piece of webbing laid across the bottom coils and tacked to the board. A second strip of webbing is laid across, and sewn to the springs to secure them. In this type of chair (a balloon-type armchair, for example) hessian (burlap) is put over the webbing, followed by stuffing, wadding (batting) and calico before the top cover is fitted.

More complicated sprung chairs

Arm chairs, wing chairs and (on a larger scale) sofas and *chaises longues* come into this category. Often the arms, and/or back, are sprung as well as the seat and there may be additional springs along the front of the seat. Deep buttoning can be an added complication – see page 53. The way to upholster such a chair is to consider the back, the arms and the seat as four separate pieces and to get the back and arms to the first stuffing stage before starting on the seat springs. The back and arms also get their second stuffing before the seat, but the seat is the first part to be covered with the top fabric.

Buttoning

Buttons, covered in the same fabric as the upholstery, are a popular way of finishing off a chair or sofa.

The buttons can be attached so that they sit flush (or *float*) on the top cover or they can be *deep buttoned*, that is, set into the stuffing. (An example of deep buttoning can be seen on the back of the chair in the photograph on the opposite page.) Although flush buttoning is the easier method for a novice, deep buttoning is very much more effective.

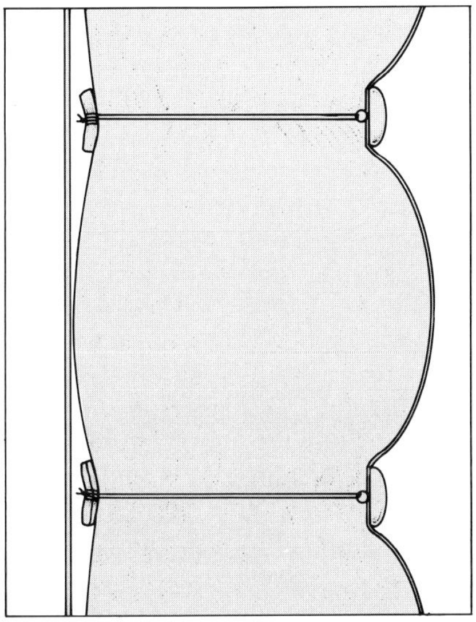

Twine and toggles used to secure buttons.

Deep buttoning pulls the top fabric down into a hollow in the stuffing. The fabric is folded into pleats which radiate from one button to the next. Usually, the pleats are made to run at angles to create a diamond-shaped mound between the buttons, but on arms, or narrow pieces of upholstery, there is often a single row of buttons with the pleats running vertically.

The old top cover makes an excellent pattern piece if you are recovering a piece that was previously buttoned; otherwise you have to plan your button positions on a piece of paper cut to the size of the area to be buttoned. This then has to be transferred to a second paper pattern piece for the calico and top fabric on which you must include an allowance for the bumps and hollows of the stuffing. Although it is quite possible to make a guess at the size of the bumps and hollows it is really best to measure when you have reached the second stuffing stage, marked the button positions and have regulated the stuffing into shape. You will have to make a hole in the wadding (batting) at each button position and move the stuffing so that there is a properly shaped hollow to take the button.

Most of the hard work comes next as you install the calico and make adjustments to the stuffing to get the buttoning even. Position the calico and tuck it loosely into the hollows. Stitch it in place at the buttoning points of the two lowest rows, with twine going through to the base hessian (burlap). Put in the pleats, using the flat end of your regulator under the calico and something like the back of an old spoon on the top side to make a crisp pleat. Have the pleats facing down so that they don't catch dirt. Move on row by row, adding or removing stuffing if necessary to even out the diamond shaped areas between the buttons. When the centre is finished, pleat the calico from the edge buttons to the frame and tack.

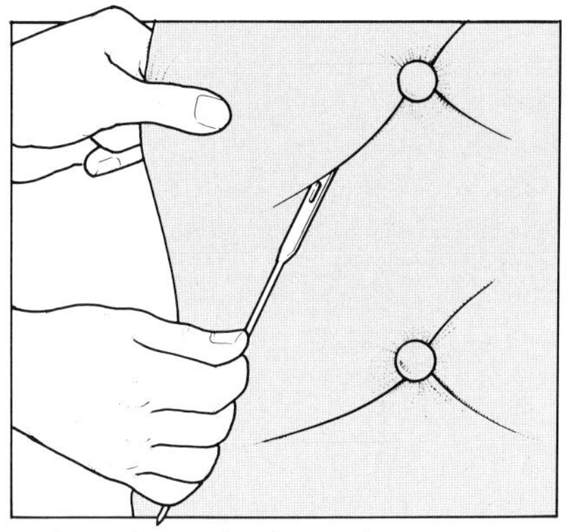

Making pleats using the regulator.

The cover is fixed like the calico but this time you use the buttons to secure the fabric. Recheck the button positions on your second paper pattern, using a flexible steel rule to measure from button to button and use the pattern to make small holes in the top fabric with a regulator. The buttons are attached two rows at a time, using a metre of medium twine for each button and securing the button from the back of the chair with an upholsterer's knot tied round a toggle made from a rolled up square of hessian (burlap). Start with the button in the middle of the bottom row and sew a loop through the button from the back. Draw each knot just tight enough to hold the toggle in place. Make the pleats while the knots are loose and then, when the whole chair is buttoned with the pleats all set, draw the knots tight and tie each off with two half hitches.

Glossary

Blind stitch: method of stitching to make a hard edge, making a loop around the stuffing.

Bridles: loops of twine to hold stuffing in place.

Chamfer: a bevel filed or planed on the corner of a piece of wood (the top of a chair rail, for example).

Grain: the direction of wood fibres.

Hard edge: the outside of a chair seat or back, sewn to make it firm.

Slip knot: special knot used to secure twine.

Staple: sometimes used instead of tacks.

Stuffing: filling used in upholstery.

Tack: specially shaped nail.

Toggle: piece of hessian (burlap) sewn into the back of the chair to secure the button at the front.

Top stitch: second stitch used for making hard edge.

Caning

A nineteenth century Brentwood rocking chair with a cane seat and back.

Cane has been used for cabinet doors, bedheads, stools and, of course, the seats of chairs. The cane itself comes from the bark of the creeper *rattan*, which is shaved to take off the knots where the leaves join the vine. The hard part of the vine is removed to make chair cane and the remainder is cut into the softer cane used in basket making. Cane has a 'direction' – if you pull a piece through your fingers, pulled one way it will catch slightly. It should always be woven in the smoother direction and should be fitted so that the shinier of its two sides is on top.

Before cane can be worked, it needs to be softened in lukewarm water for a couple of minutes – if the water is too hot or the cane is left in too long it can discolour and become too brittle. When working with cane, keep it clean and avoid even the slightest split in the material as this will weaken the final result. While you work, squeeze the cane to smooth it out and also to remove any excess water.

There are many methods of caning, but by far the most popular is the 'six-way' pattern of weaving, described below, which involves seven separate stages – including a finishing or beading stage.

Tools, equipment and materials

You will probably already have the majority of tools needed for cane work. These include the following:

Electrician's sidecutters: for cutting cane.

Light hammer: for driving in the holding pegs.

Pliers: for pulling cane through holes.

Pointed tool: such as an awl.

Punch: for removing old pegs from the holes and driving in new ones.

Sharp knife: such as a utility cutting knife.

You will need some temporary pegs to hold the cane in position as you work. A craftsman would make his own tapered pegs, but for an amateur an ideal temporary measure is to use golf tees. You will also need some wooden pegs cut from hard wood dowelling or some pegs cut from basket cane for final fixing.

The cane is sold in six numbered sizes, with No. 1 the thinnest and No. 6 the thickest. For replacing a chair seat, No. 3 could be used throughout, or a mixture of No. 2 and No. 4. Cane is sold by weight – typically in 60, 250 and 500g bundles (2, 9 and 18oz). For an average chair 60g (2oz) should be enough, but this depends on the size of the chair. If in any doubt about the size of cane to use, take a piece of the old material to the supplier and measure the spacing and diameter of the peg securing holes. The correct size can then be recommended.

The six-way pattern

Before starting re-caning, all the old cane should be stripped from the chair by using a sharp knife around the inside of the chair seat. Take a photograph of the caning pattern first if it is at all unusual. The beading running along the edges should be cut through carefully, and all loose cane removed. Use your punch (or blunt nail) to remove any old pegs and clean out the holes; if glue has been used, the holes will need to be drilled out.

Caning is the *last* operation on a chair, so any repair work to the frame and all finishing, such as staining and polishing, should be done first, before you start to cane.

Prepare the cane by soaking a few lengths at a time in warm water for a few minutes. Do not leave the cane in water for too long: if you are not ready to use it, take it out and put in a plastic bag.

The six-way pattern of weaving consists of six different strands of cane: two 'vertical' (from front to back); two 'horizontal' (from side to side); and two across the diagonals.

The method of working is to position the chair so that you are facing the front. Each layer is put on separately and the end result is an attractive criss-cross pattern with octagonal holes. The first working is vertical, the second horizontal and the third diagonal. These are repeated a second time so that altogether there are six workings. Finally there is the finishing off. The workings are illustrated in the diagrams on page 57.

You can use the same size of cane throughout (No. 3, for example) or use smaller (No. 2) for the square weaves and larger (No. 4) for the diagonals. No. 6 and No. 2 are usually used for beading.

First vertical weave

The first layer of caning is produced by simply lacing the cane from the holes in the back of the frame to the holes in the front. Start from the hole in the middle of the back (or one of the two holes if an even number) and position a length of cane so that about 100mm (4in) is poking down through the hole from the top. Wedge the cane with a tapered peg (or golf tee) and take the length to the hole in the front, making sure that it is the right way up (shiny side on top), that it goes in the 'smooth' direction and that there are no wrinkles. Pull the cane down through the equivalent hole in the front rail and insert another tapered peg to hold it. Make a sharp turn to the left, folding the cane to form a right angle. Getting this 'twist' done properly is important – it ensures that the cane lies flat on the underside of the chair. Make another 90 degree twist and bring the cane up through the next hole on the front rail and then take it to the next hole on the back. The cane needs to be kept tight, but not too tight – it will shrink as it dries and this will tension it.

At the back rail, go down through the next hole and transfer the peg from the front rail to secure the cane. Work from front to back like this, continuing to transfer to the temporary peg as you progress, until you come to the end of a length of cane. Simply push the end bit down through the holes (making sure that there is at least 75mm – 3in – free underneath) and fix a peg. Do not transfer this peg yet. Then go to the next available hole over on the *opposite* rail, thread a new piece of cane through, peg it and lace back to the first rail. Note that a new piece of cane is never tied on to the end of the last piece; you simply start again from scratch.

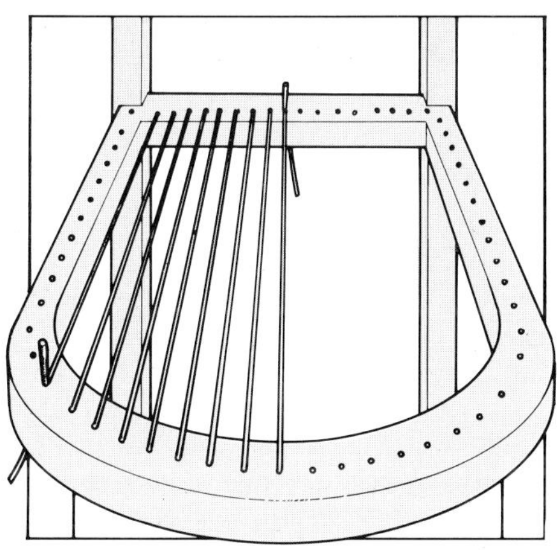

Start caning by working from the middle out towards one of the sides of the chair.

Work across the chair until you get to the edge, but do not use the corner holes. Weave the other half of the chair in the same way. On a chair which tapers from front to back, you may need two or three extra pieces at the sides. Experiment to find the best holes to put these in so that the lengths lie parallel with the lengths on the main seat. Peg these lengths in place.

First horizontal weave

The first horizontal layer is laced in very much the same way, starting at the back (but leaving the corner holes free) and working forwards. It is simply laid *over* the first layer and not woven in and out. Once you have completed your first horizontal weave, you should now have a square lattice pattern with four empty corner holes.

First diagonal

This layer is the first to be woven. Starting at the empty hole in the front right-hand corner (on the left as you look at it), weave the cane *under* the vertical canes and *over* the horizontal ones. If the sides of the chair are curved, or the number of holes on the front and back differs from the number on the sides, it will be necessary to put more than one cane through some of the holes to maintain the correct pattern. This will certainly be true at the corners.

Second vertical weave

The second vertical pattern is laced in the same way as the first vertical layer, using the same holes. It is laid over the three layers you have done already and the canes are positioned slightly to the left of the first vertical layer.

The six-way pattern

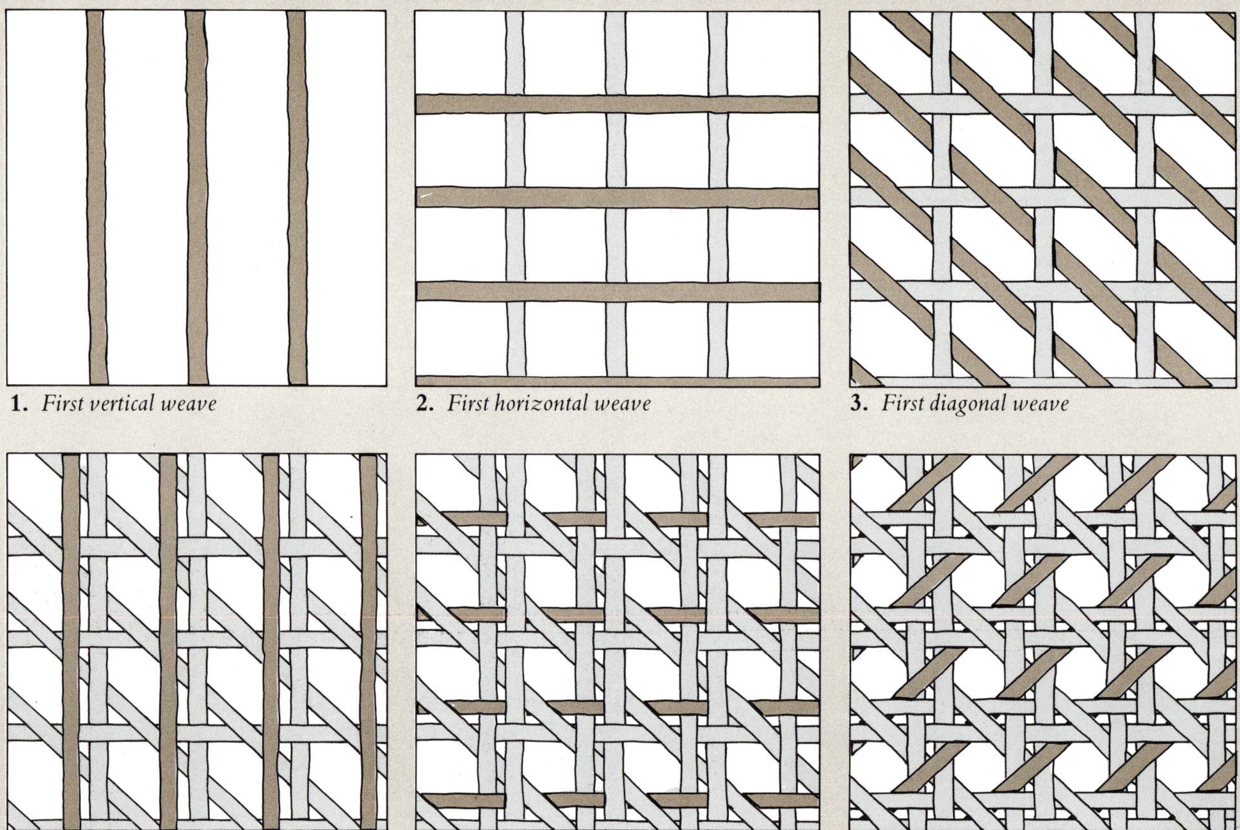

1. *First vertical weave* 2. *First horizontal weave* 3. *First diagonal weave* 4. *Second vertical weave* 5. *Second horizontal weave* 6. *Second diagonal weave*

The work becomes a little complicated at this point and it is important to keep your head and refer to a drawing of the pattern so that you can remember which strand is which.

Second horizontal layer

The second horizontal layer is woven using the same holes as the first horizontal layer. Make sure that the caning is positioned slightly to the rear of the first horizontal layer.

Each strand is woven:
☐ under the first diagonal course
☐ under the first vertical course
☐ over the second vertical course

As you proceed with the work, you will see the pattern slowly emerging. It is important that you check for mistakes all the time. If you do make a mistake, simply unpick the cane (carefully) and do the job again.

At this stage, very careful work is needed to avoid splitting the cane. It helps to pull the cane tight after each four or five 'stitches'.

Second diagonal

This is woven in the opposite direction to the first diagonal course, but this time the diagonal canes go under both horizontal canes and over both vertical ones.

You may have some difficulty in the final stages getting the cane under the layers that have already been laid. Use a sharp pointed tool, such as an awl, to lift the cane carefully so that the new piece can go underneath. Keeping the canes already installed moist (but not wet) as you go will help to keep them pliable while you work.

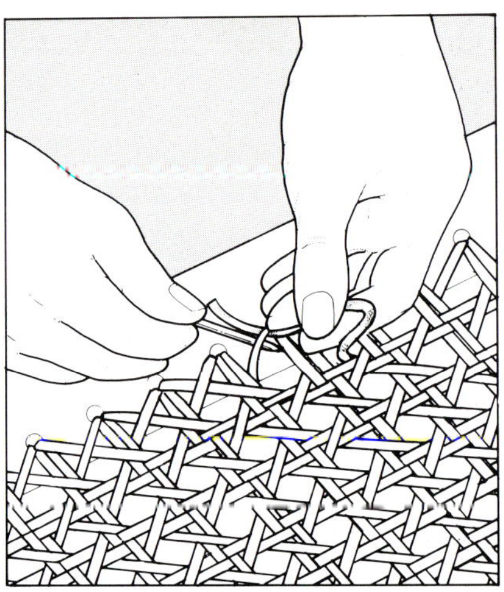

Using a nail to lift the cane.

Finishing off

One way to finish off the caning of a chair is to fit wooden pegs, or pegs made from basket cane, into each hole. The pegs, which are slightly shorter than the depth of the chair rail, are driven in with a hammer and punched just below the surface with a punch of the correct size. All temporary pegs should be removed as you go and loose ends of cane held under slight tension as the holding pegs are driven in. Finally, cut off any loose strands below the surface.

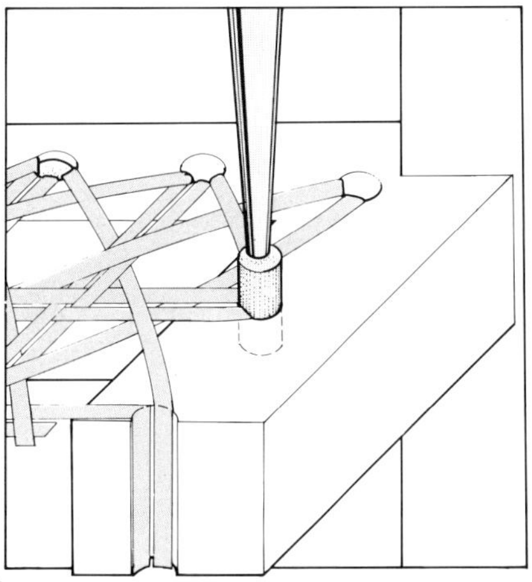

Driving in the holding peg.

Caning is often used for the seats of delicate bedroom chairs, as shown above.

Beading

Another, more attractive, method of finishing is a process known as beading. Here, half the holes are pegged and half are left free. Work round the chair, pegging every other hole as described previously, but leave the four corner holes free: if the hole you want to peg has a loose end of cane going through it, take the loose end up through the next hole and hold it while this hole is pegged before removing the temporary peg holding the loose end in place. Don't worry if you are left with two unpegged holes in the middle of a rail.

For beading, two sizes of cane are needed: No. 6 to form the bead itself and No. 2 to hold it in place. Cut lengths of No. 6 cane about 50mm (2in) longer than the sides of the chair and taper the ends.

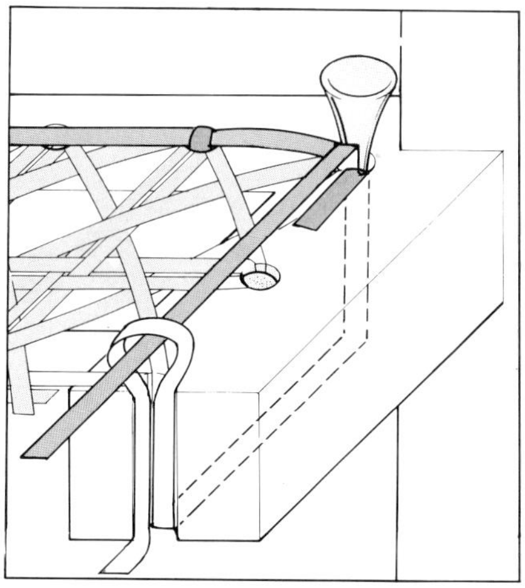

Pull the cane through to tighten the bead.

Take a long length of No. 2 cane and pass about 50mm (2in) of it up through one of the rear corner holes. Put the end of the No. 6 cane into the same hole, from the top. You must then secure both canes with a peg.

Go to the first free hole and pass the No. 2 cane up through the hole, over the No. 6 cane and back down again. Pull the cane tight and pass on to the next hole. When you get to the corner, push the prepared end of the No. 6 cane in, together with the end of the next piece, and drive in a peg to secure them. The free end of the No. 2 cane is passed diagonally across the corner so that it can start to secure the next piece of beading through the first free hole.

Work round the chair like this until you come to the hole where you started. Here, the free end of the No. 2 cane is passed back up through the hole and secured by a peg, together with the two ends of the beading which, of course, meet at this corner.

Wood Finishing

The ready availability and familiarity of wood make it easy to forget that it is a material of great beauty. Each piece has been created by a natural living process, and as a result has its own quality and characteristics. These have to be respected for that beauty to be realized, especially in the treatment of the grained texture of the wood's surface. Care and attention are always rewarded.

If it is exposed, wood stains and marks easily, so practically any wooden object needs sealing and finishing to protect its surface. Wood on the outside of a house is subject to the ravages of the elements, while that on the inside is subject to the marking effects of spillages, scuffing and burning. While the exterior calls mainly for protective treatment, interior articles need both protection and a carefully applied, attractive finish as they are seen more regularly at close quarters. Good quality materials and equipment are therefore absolutely essential to produce pleasing and worthwhile results.

The basic steps in treating wood finishes are surface preparation, grainfilling, stopping, staining and application of the final finish. Not all of these may be necessary; much depends upon the condition of the wood being worked on. The type of wood and the finish required will determine whether it is necessary to fill the grain or to use a stain. Bleaching may be required if the wood is to be lightened or if stains are to be removed from old wood.

It should always be remembered that there are limits to what wood finishing techniques can achieve. For example, white woods cannot be made to look as though they are expensive hard woods. It is quite impossible to stain pine or ramin and expect it to have the grain configuration of walnut or mahogany, even though the colour may be a very close match.

This bannister was stripped of paint and varnished to show its intricate mouldings.

Wood finishing is a vital part of the process of restoring furniture and the history of the various techniques involved in the craft is fascinating. Until the early nineteenth century, furniture, if not painted or gilded, was finished mainly by waxing, oiling or varnishing. The oils and varnishes available in earlier times did not have the hardness, clarity and durability of the modern varnishes, which are based on synthetic and natural resins, blended with oils, solvents and other ingredients. The wax was usually beeswax and the oil linseed. The varnishes would have been made from a variety of natural resins, such as sandarac, mastic, Venice turpentine, elemi and rosin, all of which were obtained from various trees. The resins were melted by heating them in a pot over a fire and subsequently they were thinned with turpentine, which was obtained by distilling the gum obtained from pine trees. The solid left after the distillation was rosin.

Cabinet makers would have made their own finishes and the recipes for these would have been closely kept secrets. However, in 1803, *The Cabinet Dictionary* by Thomas Sheraton was published in London. It contained an 'explanation of all the terms used in cabinet, chair and upholstery branches, with directions for varnishing, polishing and gilding'. Sheraton claimed that polish was to 'give brightness to any substance' and varnish was defined as 'a clear limpid fluid, capable of hardening without losing its transparency'.

Well-known cabinet makers of that time, such as Hepplewhite and Chippendale, usually finished their furniture with beeswax. A cork was rubbed onto a block of wax and then rubbed hard over the wood to spread the wax over the surface. This process was repeated many times. Fine brick dust, sifted to remove coarse particles, was rubbed over the surface with a cloth to grind the wax into the wood and to remove the clamminess. This procedure was slow and laborious. It was found to be easier to apply a soft wax made by melting beeswax and adding turpentine. If the wax was to be used on mahogany, red oil was added, made by heating linseed oil for 12 hours with a quantity of alkanet root. Dragon's blood, a coloured resin obtained from Asian trees, was also added when a stronger mahogany colour was required.

Quite often, furniture was finished with oil and brick dust only, the work being left for from two to seven days between applications for the oil to harden. Brown and black varnishes were made using asphaltum, a solid, brown-black bitumen which, when dissolved in varnish, gave a black solution. Lamp black was also added, which was made by burning resins from pine and fir trees and collecting the smoke on glass. Varnishes were usually applied one coat per day and then left to harden before being rubbed down with powdered pummice and water to make level. This process would remove the top layers of the varnish, exposing the underneath layers which would not have hardened completely. The work was left for one or two days to re-harden and then rubbed with tripoli powder and water, washed and left as before, rubbed again with rottenstone and water and finally polished with flour and oil. This left the surface with a bright gloss finish. Over the years, the furniture would have acquired a beautiful patina, mainly due to the change in colour that occurs as wood ages and partly owing to the effect of various finishes that had been applied.

Around 1820, the methods outlined above began to give way to French polishing, a craft that is still widely practised today. Although relatively slow in comparison to other wood finishing techniques, it produces a superb finish and, while it is susceptible to marks and stains, the craftsmanship involved can be very satisfying to achieve.

Modern technology has given rise to many wood finishing products, based on synthetic and natural resins, blended with oils and solvents, which are as hard and clear as, and more durable than, traditional finishes. However, without knowing their different properties, the amateur might well have difficulty in selecting the right finish for a particular job.

So, despite the wide choice of techniques available, many craftsmen hold firmly to the belief that the timeless beauty of fine furniture is best enhanced by traditional finishing methods.

(left) *Stripping off the paint has revealed the beauty of the wooden chest-of-drawers.*

(right) *A deep mahogany wood has been exposed and a sheen provided with a varnish.*

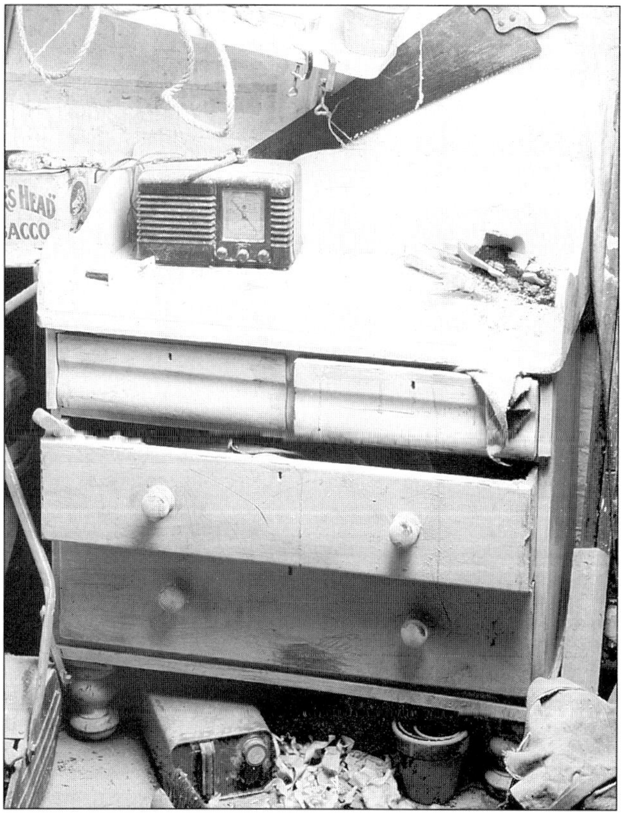

Cleaning and surface defects

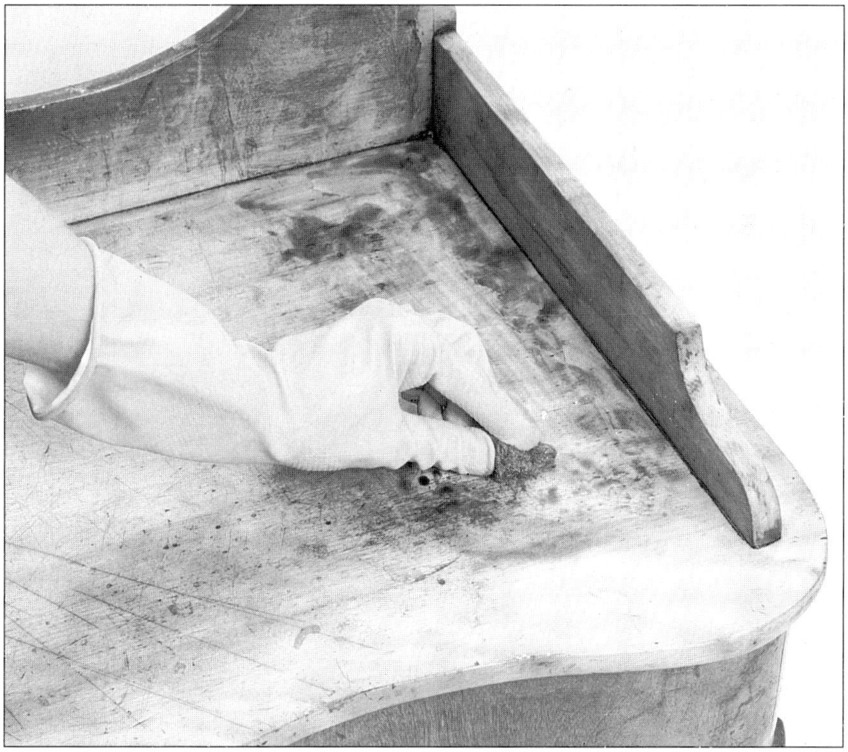

Old wax and dirt are being removed from the wood surface with a pad of fine steel wool. No scratches will occur if only gentle pressure is applied.

Shabby antique furniture quite often only requires cleaning to restore the surface to good condition. It is very important to make sure you don't damage the surface of the wood. This is very easy to do as the patina is very thin and, if it is disturbed, the wood will show through a much lighter colour.

The first step is to clean with paint thinner on a coarse rag. The paint thinner will dissolve any wax polish. It is possible that this treatment may not be sufficient to remove very old wax, in which case the paint thinner can be applied with small pads of steel wool, rubbing with the grain. The resulting solution should then be wiped off with a clean rag. Do not use water or soap to clean old furniture because, if there are any cracks in the finish or veneer, the water will cause the wood to swell.

Surface defects

The most common surface defects are heat and water marks on tables and sideboards.

If the mark has not penetrated the finish through to the wood, it can often be removed with a mild abrasive. Metal polish on a soft cloth should be rubbed over the damaged area, finishing off with a clean soft cloth. If the mark is in the top layers of the finish, the abrasive will remove the finish and the mark.

If this treatment does not work, the only satisfactory remedy is to strip the finish.

Scratches, if they are superficial, can be rubbed with fine wet and dry paper until removed. The gloss can be restored with metal polish, or with burnishing cream. If, however, they are too deep to remove by sanding, and you do not want to strip the whole surface, they can be filled with a clear finish or a varnish stain of the appropriate shade, thinned with paint thinner or solvent. Apply very carefully with a small artist's brush or toothpick to the scratched area. Administer several times until the area is slightly higher than the surface. The damaged area should then be rubbed smooth with fine wet and dry paper and brought back to a shine by burnishing.

An alternative and much simpler method of making a scratch less noticeable is to rub shoe polish of the nearest shade over the damaged area. But the only really satisfactory way of treating scratches that have penetrated through the finish is to strip and refinish.

Burn marks can only be removed by stripping the old finish completely and scraping the damaged area with a knife until the charring or discoloration has been removed, afterwards sanding with fine paper. If this treatment leaves a shallow indentation in the wood, dampen the area to make the grain of the wood swell. This may remove the indentation; if not, fill the area with wood filler or extra coats of finish until the level has been brought up to the surrounding area.

Small cracks may be filled with paste-wood filler or plastic wood. Large cracks should be filled by inserting a sliver of wood, using a suitable adhesive.

For a blistered veneered surface, try standing a hot iron on a damp cloth over the affected area. This may re-soften the glue so that the blister can be pressed down. If this happens, stand a weight over it and leave overnight. Otherwise, cut the blister with the grain using a razor blade and insert an adhesive in the hole. Then stand a weight on top until the adhesive has set. The same treatment applies to inlays that are lifting. If pieces of veneer have broken away from the surface and have been lost, buy some more, matched to the nearest grain type and cut to fit the damaged area. Before sticking the new veneer into place, make sure that all traces of the old adhesive have been removed. The new piece of veneer should be stained to match the old veneer.

Stripping

It is very likely that, having cleaned the surface of the wood, you will find that it is so badly scratched or marked that it will need to be stripped and the bare woodwork treated as new. Even if the woodwork has not been damaged, you may wish to remove the old paint to expose the natural beauty of the wood, which can then be varnished or stained and varnished.

If you are going to strip and repaint the woodwork, the old finish can be removed with a blowtorch or hot air stripper. If, however, the woodwork is to be re-finished with a clear sealer or varnish, or stain and varnish, a chemical solvent paint remover should be used. Even a clear finish should be removed if the wood is to be made lighter or darker in colour. Remember that bleaches and dyes only work on bare wood.

Alkaline paste and powder removers are also available, but are not recommended for use on wood which is to be stained and varnished as they can discolour the surface.

If you are stripping antique furniture, it is best to use a chemical solvent paint remover as it will have no effect on the patina of the wood. Never use water-based paste type paint removers, blow lamps or hot air paint strippers.

Old finishes should not be removed by sanding as thin veneers can easily be damaged. Orbital and disc sanders score the wood. These will show in the finished film when a clear finish is applied. Many woods, for example, mahogany, acquire a beautiful deep colour with ageing and this would be removed by sanding.

Chemical solvent removers

If possible, remove furniture and small articles into a well ventilated room and stand on a large polyethylene sheet.

Undo the container cap to release vapour which may have accumulated inside the container. Re-seal and shake it vigorously. Pour the contents into a container wide enough to accommodate the brush to be used for stripping. A thin coat of remover brushed over the surface will cause the top layers to soften, and sometimes a bubbling effect will be noticed.

Now make a second application, applying liberally with a dabbing action. This will press down the layers of paint which may have lifted and ensure further penetration of the paint remover.

Leave for a short while and, if the finish can be removed easily, scrape it off. If, however, the paint is very thick, a further application of remover will have to be made, using a short, sharp dabbing action.

Remove the old finish with a flat scraper. If there are small traces of the old finish left, these can be removed with steel wool. Carvings and mouldings can be cleaned with a small piece of pointed wood or a wire brush.

After the old finish has been completely stripped, the surface should be wiped with a clean rag and paint thinner. As solvent paint remover will not raise the grain of the wood, sanding is not normally necessary. Many solvent paint removers can be rinsed off after use with water or paint thinner. As water raises the grain of the wood, it should not be used for rinsing off unless the wood is to be bleached after stripping. When the wood is dry treat as new bare wood.

(left) *An art nouveau tobacco box is being stripped to reveal its fine points. It will later be sealed with a varnish.*

(below) *Pointed wood removes finishes from mouldings after chemical solvent remover has been applied.*

Wood preparation

Before any finishing operations are carried out, it is essential that the surface of the wood is perfectly clean and smooth. Even the slightest imperfection in the surface of the wood will be very apparent as soon as a finish is applied. Plane marks must be removed by sanding, starting with the coarse grit and working down to the finer grades. Alternatively, they can be removed with a cabinet maker's scraper, which is a thin piece of steel, approximately 100mm × 50mm (4in × 2in) with a burr on the edges. The wood should be subsequently sanded with flour abrasive paper used with a cork block, or fine garnet paper, to produce a silky smooth surface. Particular care should be taken when sanding near the edges. If the block is tilted as it moves over the edge, a rounded edge will be produced which will spoil the appearance.

If an orbital sanding machine has been used, it is nevertheless essential that the surface is finished by sanding with the grain by hand afterwards. If this is not done, small circular scratches, resembling fish scales, will be seen in the final finish.

Particular care should be taken to make sure that all traces of glue or adhesive have been removed.

Wood fillers

Any cracks, nail holes or countersunk screw holes should be filled with wood filler. Traditionally, cabinet makers finishing their work with French polish would often fill holes with beeswax which was melted into the hole with a hot knife or lighted match. Beeswax, however, is too soft to make a satisfactory filling agent and cannot be used with many modern finishes where the solvents would soften the wax. Paste-type wood fillers are available in a range of natural wood shades. Many of them can be thinned with water and are satisfactory for filling damaged areas or holes; if, however, the damaged area is on the edge of the work, plastic wood, or two component fillers which require mixing immediately prior to use, should be used.

Wood fillers usually shrink slightly and should, therefore, be applied so that the filling is slightly above the surface. When dry and thoroughly hard, these areas can be sanded so that they are level with the surrounding wood.

Unfortunately, wood fillers always appear as lighter or darker than the surrounding wood and are noticeable because they break the natural configuration of the grain. This only matters if the work is to be coated with a clear finish or stain and a clear finish. However, the areas filled up can be made less noticeable by painting them with artists' colours to match the surrounding wood. With practice, the grain configuration can be faked. However, this operation is skilled and requires a good eye for colour.

As a general rule, if the wood requires a lot of filling, it would be better to paint rather than employ a clear finish.

Grainfilling

A major problem when applying clear finishes is that, owing to the nature of the wood, the finish will sink into the pores. This occurs even when many coats of French polish or varnish have been applied. Sinking may be noticeable as soon as the finish has been applied, or may occur many months or even a year after the surface has been finished. The problem can be overcome by applying several coats of the finish and rubbing down, when dry, with fine garnet paper or, preferably, with wet and dry paper until the pores of the wood have been sealed. The alternative is to use a grainfiller before applying the finish.

In the past, plaster of Paris and plaster-based fillers were used extensively for filling the open grain of wood. The plaster was sprinkled onto the wood and a cloth, dampened with water or methylated spirits, was then used to rub the plaster into the grain. Plaster of Paris dries white, so it was necessary to wipe the surface with linseed oil to make the substance transparent. However, over a period of time, the oil

Chart showing types of cutting paper

Abrasive paper:
Made from ground bottle glass. Suitable for rubbing down all types of wood and paint.

Garnet paper:
Made from crushed garnet. Available in a wider range of grit sizes than abrasive paper and has a much softer cutting action, which results in a finer finish. Used for rubbing down wood and paint.

Emery paper:
Used mainly for metalwork.

Aluminium oxide paper:
Mainly used on metal and hard wood. As it wears, the points of the grits round off so that the cutting action decreases. Has a faster cutting action than either abrasive paper or garnet paper.

Wet and dry paper (silicon carbide):
The hardest grit available, being only one degree softer than a diamond. Used for metals and painted surfaces. When in use, the particles break, providing new cutting edges.

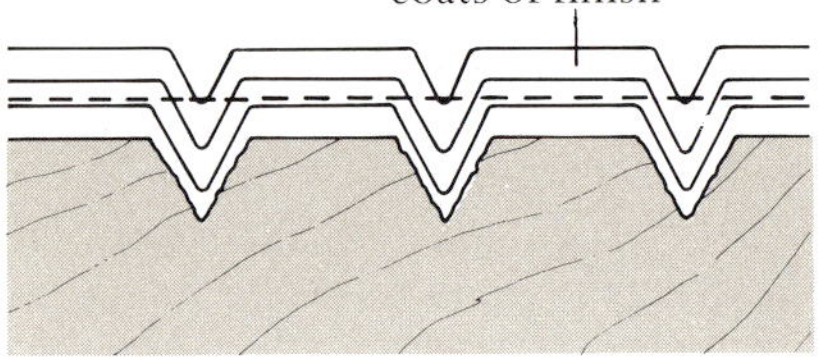

Cross section of wood

If the wood has not been filled before applying a finish, the surface will appear to have an open grain. After applying the finish, rub down the surface to the bottom of the hollows. Apply a final coat of finish.

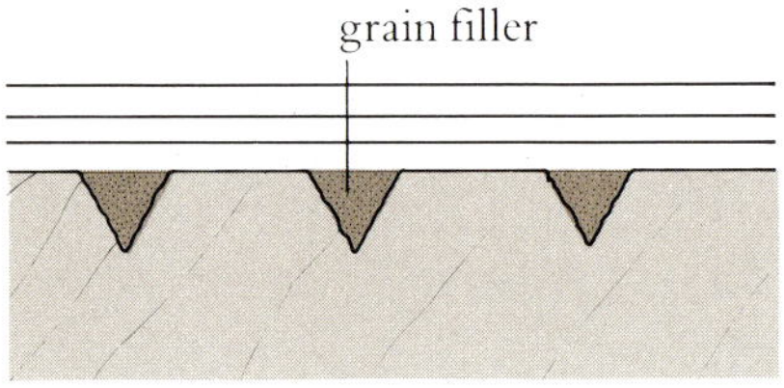

Wood filled with grainfiller will not need rubbing down as the grainfiller prevents the finish from sinking.

oxidized and the plaster showed white under the finish. This could be prevented, to a certain extent, by mixing pigments with the plaster to colour it to match the colour of the wood to which it was being applied.

Plaster-based fillers have another disadvantage in that they may react with some modern finishes. Bearing this in mind, it is better to use ready-made paste fillers which are available in a range of natural wood shades. Usually, they can be thinned with paint thinner to a consistency of a thin cream. The thinned grainfiller should be wiped firmly across the wood, using a piece of hessian (burlap) or coarse rag. In areas where grainfiller has not been applied the finish will sink into the grain, so the wood should be carefully checked to make sure that no area has been missed out. As the surplus grainfiller will set extremely hard and be difficult to remove, the surplus is removed by wiping across the grain with a clean rag before the grainfiller has hardened.

It is unwise to use grainfiller on wood that is being waxed or oiled as open grained wood looks best.

Bleaching

Bleaching may be used to lighten the colour of wood or remove stains such as those made by ink or water.

The traditional method of bleaching woodwork was to use a saturated solution of oxalic acid, made by dissolving crystals of oxalic acid in hot water. Oxalic acid is a poison and the container should be carefully labelled accordingly and stored well out of the reach of children. If you are going to use this method, the solution should be applied to bare wood with a brush. After use, dispose of both acid and brush, and wash your hands thoroughly.

Oxalic acid is not a powerful bleach and stains are more easily removed, and the colour lightened, by using a two-part wood bleach. This consists of two solutions, usually labelled 'A' and 'B' or '1' and '2'. The first is applied to the bare wood and, after about 10 minutes, the second solution is applied. Don't be alarmed if the first solution causes the wood to go darker rather than lighter. The first solution acts as a catalyst which causes the second solution to liberate oxygen. This acts as the bleaching agent.

After the second solution has been applied, the wood should be left for several hours or overnight. If the wood is very dark, or very badly stained, the bleaching action can be repeated after two hours. The scum which forms on the surface of the wood should be removed by scrubbing in water. The wood should then be rinsed with a solution of acetic acid (white vinegar) and water to neutralize the alkaline bleach.

When the wood is dry it can be stained to the desired shade or, if you wish to keep the wood as light as possible, it should be treated with white or transparent French polish.

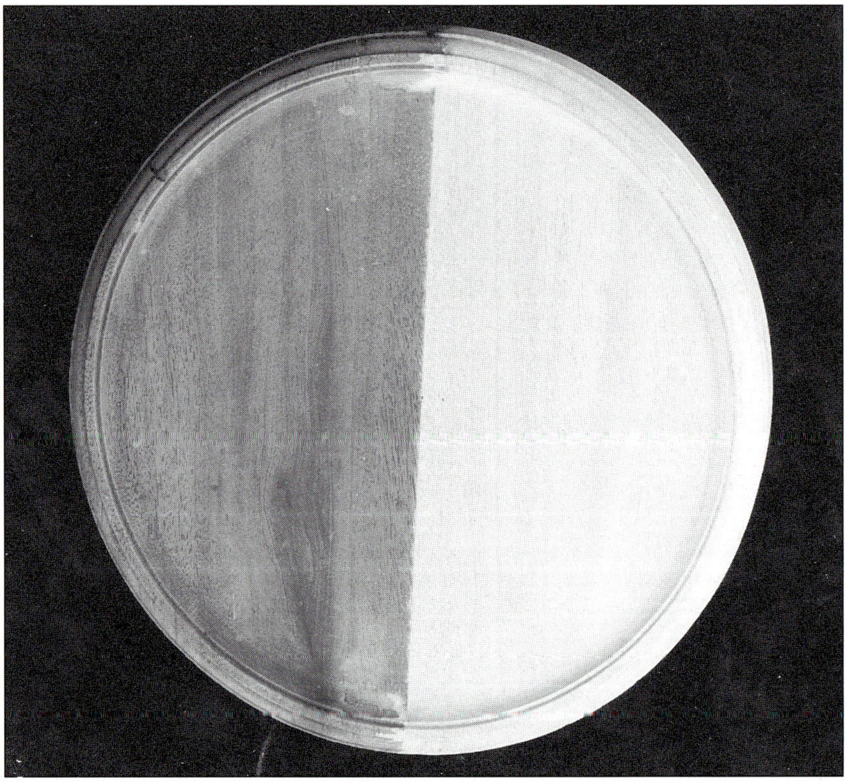

The wooden table top above shows the stark contrast between before and after bleaching.

Staining or dyeing

Before applying a finish to wood it is often necessary to stain the wood to a different shade. The recipes below given by the English furniture-maker Thomas Sheraton illustrate how staining was accomplished in the nineteenth century:

For black stain
1 pint strong vinegar
2 oz fine iron filings
½ lb pounded galls

Diffuse for three hours on hot cinders. Increase heat and add four ounces of copperas; then add water in which has been dissolved one ounce of borax and indigo and boil to a froth. Apply to wood after washing with *aqua fortis* and water.

For making new mahogany match old
Apply soft soap and leave on the surface until the wood has darkened.

Or to make redder
Slake quick lime with urine and apply to wood hot.

The latter method most certainly would be very unpopular today!

However, one does not have to go to this trouble as with modern, ready-mixed stains, which are readily available, staining is a quick and fairly simple process.

Most natural hard woods do not need staining as they have an attractive colour which is enhanced when a finish is applied. However, it may be necessary to change the hue, either to match other pieces of furniture, or because a different shade would be more attractive. Here it should be noted that, while a soft wood can be stained to imitate, say, oak or mahogany in colour, it is impossible to imitate the grain configuration of hard wood.

It is important that all traces of glue around joints or elsewhere on the wood surface are removed as the stain will not penetrate it.

Wood stains are manufactured from transparent synthetic dyes, or natural dyestuffs dissolved in water, methylated spirits (denatured alcohol) or hydrocarbon solvents, usually paint thinner or paint thinner and naphtha. They do not contain any pigment and will, therefore, not obscure the grain of the wood. Most wood surfaces darken after treatment, even when a clear finish has been applied, but stains dry to a lighter shade than when first applied. Mahogany or walnut stains seen on a showcard in a store may look entirely different when used on different types of wood. A dye is transparent and, because of this, the basic colour of the wood will affect the final colour. Wood can never be stained to a lighter colour than it is initially and if, therefore, you wish to stain a dark piece of wood lighter, it must be bleached first. You should also note that certain woods, such as pine, cannot be stained to an even shade as the soft sap wood will absorb far more stain than the hard wood and will give a striped effect.

Before applying stain to furniture, test either on a spare piece of similar wood or on a piece of the furniture that would not normally be seen, such as the underneath of a chair rail or table. If you are just applying a clear finish, and do not have a spare piece of wood, damp a small area of the furniture with water. The change of colour will approximate to the effect of the finish.

The cheapest wood stains are those based on water. They are sold as powder or crystals, the most popular being Vandyke or mahogany. Vandyke crystals will produce a rich brown shade, although the final colour will vary according to the type of wood to which it has been applied. For mahogany, a small amount of ammonia can be added to produce a warm colour. The crystals or powder should be dissolved in boiling water. The amount of stain to water varies according to the strength required, but a good starting point would be 25g to 1 litre (4oz per gal) of water. Strain the solution through muslin before use, to remove undissolved crystals. The stain can be used hot, in which case it will 'take' more quickly than if it is left to cool.

Water stains cause the grain of the wood to swell and the wood requires re-sanding after they have been applied and allowed to dry. This can cause patchiness as, when the surface is being sanded, stain may be removed more in some areas than others. If a water stain is to be used on wood, the wood can be dampened with water beforehand and allowed to dry. The surface can then be lightly sanded smooth before applying the stain. The application of the stain will cause the grain to swell somewhat, but not to the same degree as when applied to dry wood.

Water stains are also not as penetrating as alcohol and oil stains and usually have to be applied twice for a dark shade.

Spirit stains are manufactured from aniline dyes dissolved in methylated spirits. They are available in colours ranging from natural wood shades to more exotic colours, such as reds, greens and blues. They are more powerful than water stains and are both penetrating and very quick drying. However, they are not widely used for staining bare wood, but more for tinting or colouring French polish. To make your own, dissolve 60g (2oz) in 4.5 litre (1 gal) of mineralized methylated spirits (denatured alcohol). When the stain has been dissolved, approximately 120ml (4fl oz) of transparent French polish should be added to fix the stain to the wood.

The most widely used stains are the oil stains, manufactured from oil soluble dyestuffs dissolved in paint thinner and naphtha. Some also contain bitumen, which is a dark brown mineral and in solution gives warm brown shades.

Stains should be applied with a cloth because if a brush is used the

Two identical whitewood chairs have been finished with different coloured stains, illustrating the exciting transformations that can be achieved with the use of wood stains. One chair has been stained with an oak coloured dye, the other stained to give a Burmese teak effect. Although the grain configuration remains the same, there is no doubt that the effects are stunning and radically alter the appearance of the chairs. Stains of a similar type can be mixed with each other to produce an infinite range of shades. Before staining the wood, remember to test the colour of the dye on part of the object that will not be seen – in the case of the chairs, for example, the underside of the chair seat – or a spare piece of the same wood used for staining. Both chairs have been finished with a coating of hard wearing varnish.

(below) *A chair is in the process of being varnished. Note the dramatic contrast between the varnished and unvarnished parts.*

wood will often be darker where the full brush first touches the surface, particularly when the stain is being applied to soft, absorbent wood when it would appear uneven. When applying stain to carved or moulded surfaces, make sure that pools of stain are not left as they then dry much darker than the surrounding areas.

The end grain of wood is more absorbent than the surface. It is important that the stain is diluted considerably with the correct solvent before applying to the end grain, otherwise the wood will appear much darker – in some cases almost black.

Instead of diluting the stain, the end grain can be given a coat of thin glue size or transparent shellac. This will reduce the absorbency of the end grain, but it is important to make sure that not too much sealer is applied, otherwise the stain will not penetrate at all.

You may experience difficulty in obtaining water and spirit soluble powders or crystals, as they are not now widely stocked. Bichromate of potash can be obtained from pharmacists, but you will probably find it easier to use a ready-mixed oil stain. If you want unusual colours for wood, such as green and blue, coloured writing inks can be used.

Traditional finishes

Many people, especially dealers and collectors, prefer traditional finishes on wood as they are more authentic. However, a lot of time has to be spent applying them as you cannot cut corners with traditional wood finishing techniques.

French polishing

French polish is both a proper and a collective noun. As a collective noun it covers all polishes made with shellac and alcohol. As a proper noun it refers to one specific type of material made from flaked shellac dissolved in industrial alcohol.

There has always been a mystique about the art of French polishing, but in fact it is a process that can be carried out by any competent amateur with a little practice.

French polish is suitable for use on all light and dark woods, when a light to medium-brown tone is required. Button polish is used to obtain an orange or golden tone and white French polish, which has a milky appearance, or transparent polish, is used on light-coloured or bleached woods, where the natural colour is to be retained.

It is essential that French polishing is done in a warm, dry, dust-free room. If polishing is carried out in damp conditions, 'blushing' will occur. This is the term used to describe the way French polish appears as it dries white, not to be confused with 'blooming' which is a deposit like the bloom on a grape, which can occur on the surface of the polish at any time after it has been applied, and which can usually be removed by wiping with a damp cloth.

Making the polishing pad

The processes of polishing consist of bodying in, building up and spiriting out. The polish in all three processes is applied with a polishing pad, the dimensions of which depend upon the size of the hand and the size of the work being polished. It is made by wrapping cotton wool (batten) in a soft rag as shown on the next page. When the pad has been made it is unwrapped and the polish poured into the cotton wool. *On no account should the polish ever be poured directly on to the rag*. The rag acts as a strainer and ensures that no scratches occur on the surface as a result of any foreign body that may have

This large kitchen dresser has received a full wax treatment, which has accentuated its magnificence and enhanced the beauty of the wood. Careful maintenance will ensure its continued usefulness.

inadvertently entered the polish. Polish should be poured into the cotton wool until it is saturated. The rag is then wrapped round the cotton wool again to make a pear shaped pad and pressed on to a spare piece of wood or cardboard to squeeze out the excess polish. If it is too wet, ridges of polish will be left on the work, which can only be removed by rubbing down with abrasive paper.

The first applications of polish should be made by rubbing up and down over the surface quickly with the polishing pad without exerting too much pressure. On no account should the polishing pad be passed over polish that is not dry.

If the wood has not been filled, the first coat of polish may make short fibres in the wood stand above the surface, in which case, after the polish has been allowed to harden, the surface should be rubbed in the direction of the grain with fine paper so that only a mild cutting action is obtained. The paper should not be used with a block, as too much pressure may be exerted.

The paper should be held by the thumb and little finger with the other three fingers over the paper, so that a very fine control of pressure is obtained. Any irregularities on the surface can be felt by the fingertips.

Further applications of polish are made by rubbing in a circular or figure of eight motion, passing quickly and lightly over the surface. It is important that at all times the polishing pad is slid onto the surface from the side with a gliding action and lifted off in the same way. At no time should it ever be lifted from the work in the middle or applied to the middle, as a mark will be left which will be very difficult to remove.

After the first few applications of polish, the pad will not slide so easily over the surface. When that happens, apply a very small amount of linseed oil to the base of the pad. If too much is applied, the surface will either have a smeary effect, as the linseed oil does not dry quickly, or it will sweat on the surface.

After four to five applications the work should be left for several hours to harden. Between applications, store the polishing pad in a screw-top container to prevent it drying and becoming hard. A little methylated spirits (denatured alcohol) can be added to the pad whilst it is stored in the jar, to keep it soft and moist. If it dries and hardens, it should be discarded and a new one made.

Spiriting out

When a sufficient layer of shellac has been applied to give the consistency of colour required, the final operation of 'spiriting out' is done. This is the stage at which the high gloss finish is obtained. Start the process at least 24 hours after the previous application of French polish. The pad should be charged with French polish that has been thinned with methylated spirits (denatured alcohol) and squeezed so that it is almost dry. When dabbed onto white paper it should leave just a damp impression. It is then moved over the surface, in circular movements, using considerable pressure, and finishing off in straight, even sweeps, backwards and forwards with the grain, sweeping on and off the ends. This action dissolves any high spots on the surface and, as the pad dries, it has a burnishing effect.

When French polishing work that has carved areas, it is not always possible to use a polishing pad, in which case these areas can be coated by applying the French polish with a flowing action, using a bearhair or camelhair brush.

Quite often, when wood has been stained, a coat of French polish will make one part of the wood look darker or lighter than another. If this happens, you can make lighter areas darker by dissolving analine spirit soluble powders in methylated spirits and adding the coloured methylated spirits (denatured alcohol) to the French polish. When

Making a polishing pad

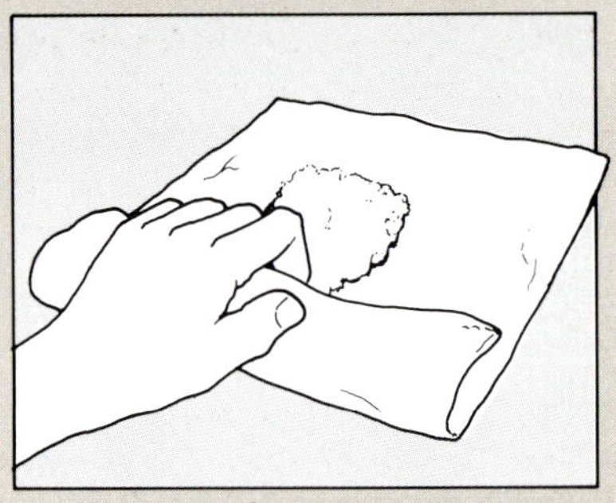

1. *Place piece of cotton wool (batten) in soft rag, ensuring that bottom of pad is perfectly flat with no external stitching or creasing. Fold front of rag over cotton wool.*

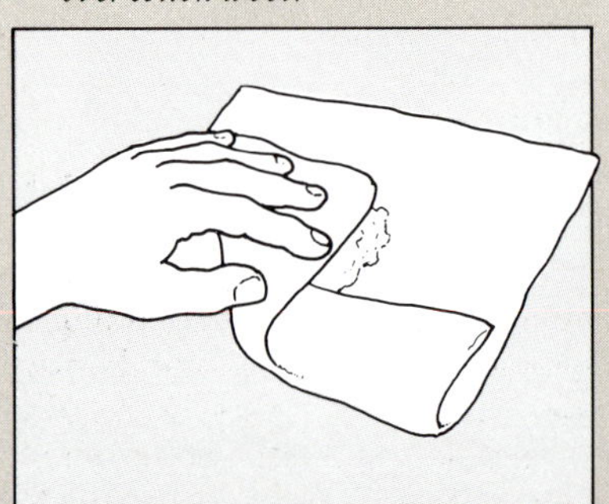

2. *Fold front corners of pad.*

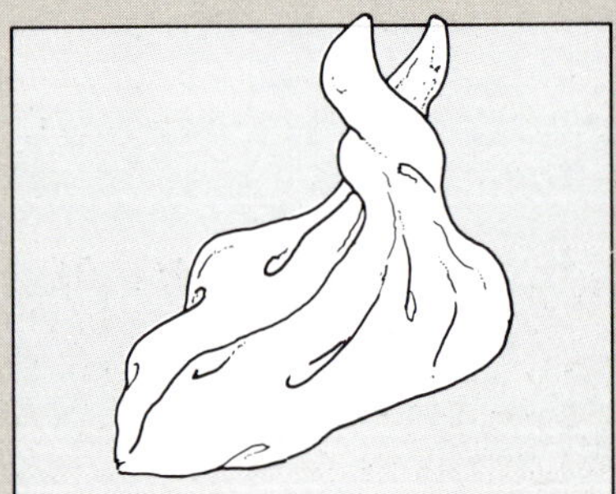

3. *Twist end to make shoe shape with flat base.*

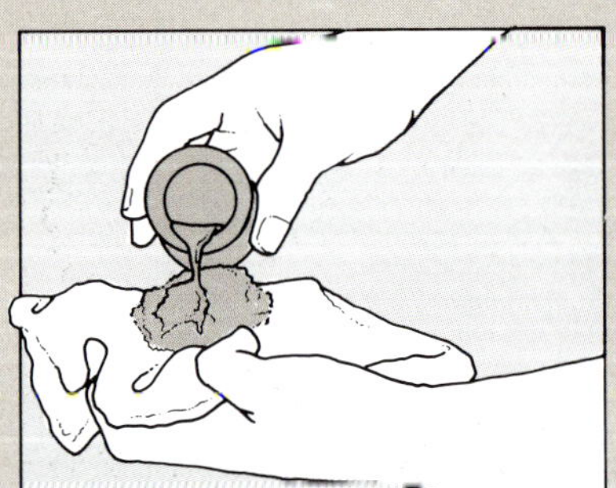

4. *Hold polishing pad and unwrap. Saturate cotton wool with polish.*

colouring wood with tinted French polish, it should be thinned so that very light layers of coloured polish are applied to the surface, otherwise it will leave ridges.

A high gloss finish is not always required. Many people prefer – and many articles of furniture look better with – a satin or matt finish. If so, the surface can be dulled down by sprinkling it with fine pumice powder which is brushed with the grain with a soft shoe brush. It is also possible to make the surface matt by firmly rubbing in the direction of the grain with steel wool and wax polish.

French polish can be applied over practically any finish without lifting problems. This is because the only solvent used in it is alcohol which does not dissolve the resins and oils in oil finishes and varnishes.

Before attempting to French polish any article of furniture, it is advisable to practise first on a spare piece of wood.

Oiling and waxing

Antique furniture is not normally finished to a very high gloss. If you wish to keep as close as possible to the original appearance, the furniture can be oiled or waxed. Although linseed or boiled linseed oil were used traditionally, modern oils such as teak and Danish oils will dry more quickly and have better durability and resistance to heat and solvents.

The oil is applied liberally with a soft cloth. Rub it hard into the wood, and wipe off the surplus after a short while with a clean rag. Further applications should not be made until the previous one is completely dry. Teak and Danish oils normally take four to six hours to dry, boiled linseed oil 24 hours, and ordinary linseed oil three days. A rag or cloth used for applying oils should be kept in an airtight tin between applications, or opened out to dry. It must not be left crumpled up as it may catch fire by spontaneous combustion. Depending on the absorption of the wood, many applications of oil may be required to produce an attractive finish. When the oil is dry and hardened, it may be buffed by rubbing it with the grain with a soft cloth to produce an attractive soft, lustrous surface. An oiled surface can be re-oiled or waxed at any time.

The circular table, having been oiled, is being buffed, revealing the rich mahogany.

If you wish to wax furniture, it is advisable to seal the surface first with one or two applications of French polish, or even with a coat of oil. This will prevent the wax sinking into the wood, which will eventually cause it to become a greyish colour, because dirt gets sucked down with the wax. Sealing the wood before waxing also makes it easier to remove the wax at a later date with paint thinner, as it will not disturb the sealer.

Proprietary ready-made hard wax polishes are satisfactory for use on furniture, but you may make your own pure beeswax polish according to the following recipe.

Place the beeswax in a container within a pan of boiling water and melt. When it has melted, pour paint thinner or pure turpentine slowly into the molten wax, stirring vigorously to prevent lumps of wax forming as it is cooled by the solvent.

The source of heat must be extinguished before the solvent is added to the hot wax, as a vapour is given off which is highly flammable. The proportion of wax to solvent depends upon whether a very hard or soft wax polish is required. A good starting point is 250gm (about ½lb) of beeswax to 1 litre (2 pints) of paint thinner or pure turpentine.

A wax polish should be worked over the surface of the wood, using a soft cloth, and the excess removed with a soft shoe brush or yellow duster. It should always be applied sparingly and left for the solvent to dry out before the final buffing. It is far better to make many light coats of wax than one or two thick ones, as these will be difficult to buff to an attractive sheen because of the retention of solvent. If the furniture is carved or has a moulding that makes it difficult to wax with a cloth, apply the wax with a small shoe brush or toothbrush.

Special effects

Special wood finishing effects can transform an inexpensive and rather drab piece of furniture into a stunning showpiece. The effects can be exciting but represent a challenge to the home restorer as the results are often unpredictable.

Ebonizing

There are two main methods of ebonizing. With the first, the wood is black but the grain can still be seen. The wood is first coloured with a black penetrating stain, and, when dry, finished with black French polish. This can be bought as a ready-made solution; otherwise French polish can be turned into black polish by adding 60g (2oz) of black analine spirit dye to 4.5 litres (1 gal) of French polish. It is also possible to colour a clear polyurethane black by adding a black oil stain to it, but this will thin the polyurethane so that more coats than normal will be required to obtain a satisfactory finish.

If you want to obliterate the grain completely, so that the surface is a high gloss jet black, like Chinese lacquer, the wood should be painted with black undercoat or a blackboard black paint and, when dry, rubbed to a smooth finish with fine paper. It may then be finished with a black French polish or black polyurethane. A jet-black finish can also be obtained by using a cold-cured lacquer made black with a pigment, not a dyestuff. The coating is, therefore, opaque and no undercoat is required.

Liming

Liming effects make the grain a lighter colour than the rest of the wood. They are obtained either by fuming with ammonia and subsequently rubbing in lime to produce an attractive contrast, or by staining the wood to any desired shade and filling the grain with a contrasting colour. Only woods which have a pronounced open grain are suitable for liming, oak probably being the best. The grain should be opened up as much as possible by brushing with a stiff wire brush. The wood is then stained if required and sealed with the chosen finish before the liming paste is applied. This will enable the surplus paste to be wiped off without staining the wood, leaving it only in the grain. When the sealer has dried, rub the liming paste hard across the grain with a piece of coarse rag. After a short time, wipe the surplus paste off with a clean rag, dampened with paint thinner.

If you cannot find liming paste a suitable substitute is the pigment that settles on the bottom of undercoat paints. It should be carefully lifted from the bottom of the can with a spatula or knife, left to stiffen and then rubbed across the grain, as described above.

The work should be left overnight and a final coat of finish applied to seal the liming paste in the grain.

Fuming

The traditional process of fuming (which makes the wood darker) by using liquid ammonia is not recommended because of the fumes it gives off. It is preferable to darken oak chemically by brushing a solution of caustic soda over the wood. Extreme caution must still be taken, as a caustic soda solution is highly corrosive. The work should be carried out in the open or in a garage. Remember to wear protective rubber gloves and a rubber or polyethylene overall.

'Antiquing'

'Antiquing' furniture – giving a look of old paint – can be carried out by painting with a base colour or glaze, made by thinning ordinary paint with paint thinner and, when dry, painting on a contrasting colour, wiping the surface across the grain almost immediately with a cloth dampened with paint thinner, so that the second colour fills the grain in the same way as a liming paste. The base colour is usually white or an off-white shade.

The picture below shows the stark elegance of ebonized wood used for these slim-line cane chairs.

Varnish stains

How to coat a surface evenly

1. *Brush the varnish in one direction, making sure that you work it well into the surface being worked on.*

2. *Brush at right angles to the first brushing, using slightly less pressure than before. Make sure that the brush strokes blend with each other.*

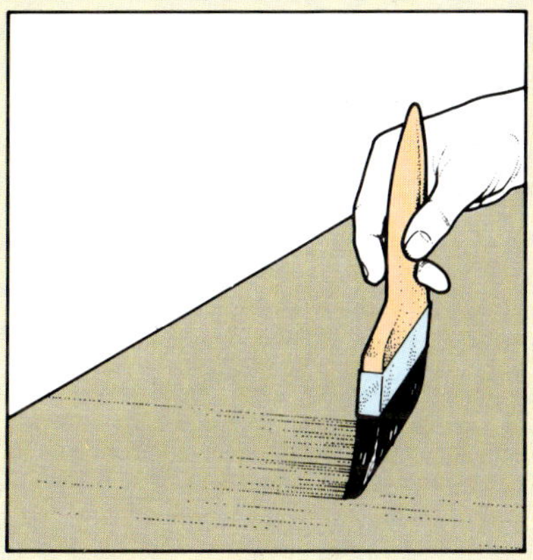

3. *Brush again with less pressure across diagonals of the piece. This constant cross-brushing will ensure good coverage.*

4. *Brush as first brushing, but only scanning the surface, so that the object is evenly covered. When the object is dry no brush marks should be visible.*

Varnish stains may be polyurethane- or oil varnish-based. They are similar to an ordinary varnish, but contain dyestuff or transparent pigments so that a finish and colour can be obtained in one operation. It is very important that varnish stains are brushed on evenly, as any unevenness in application will result in a variation of shade. Each successive coat of varnish stain will darken the surface. Therefore, if the required shade is achieved with one or two coats of varnish stain but, at the same time the finish is still not satisfactory, further coats should be applied using unstained material, either gloss, matt or satin, according to the effect needed.

When applying a varnish, it is essential that a good quality brush of the appropriate size is used. It is no good trying to varnish a door, for instance, with a 25mm (1in) brush. A 62.5mm (2½in) or 75mm (3in) brush will cover the surface much faster and with fewer brush marks. Also, it is important to remember that, because varnishes are relatively slow drying, application should always be carried out in a dust-free, warm atmosphere.

If the wood has been stained with an oil stain, the first coat of varnish should be applied with a minimum amount of brushing, as the solvents in the varnish may make the stain run slightly, creating an unevenness in colour. This irregularity may, however, be prevented entirely by applying one coat of transparent French polish to the stained wood with a piece of rag and allowing it to dry before varnishing.

A varnish should be cross-brushed over the surface to obtain good coverage and then finished off with light, sweeping strokes along the length of the work. Try to keep a wet edge on the varnish, so that, as you proceed along the work, the varnish blends on the surface and the brush strokes are not visible when the varnish dries.

It is impossible to finish wood with one coat of varnish. If the first coat is in any way uneven, it should be allowed to dry thoroughly and lightly rubbed down in the direction of the grain with fine paper before further coats are applied. Because varnishes take some time to dry, it is very difficult to obtain a surface that is completely free from imperfections, probably due to dust settling on it as the varnish is drying. This does not matter with items such as shelves, doors or wall cladding. On furniture, however – for example a table – the feel of the surface would be spoiled by the presence of any irregularities. If a polyurethane finish is left for several weeks to become thoroughly hard, it may be rubbed down with fine wet and dry paper. It can then be burnished with a burnishing cream or the type of rubbing compound used to restore the shine on vehicle body work. The gloss will not be as high as that obtained with acid-cured lacquers or French polish, but it will be a great improvement on a brush finish. If a satin or matt finish is required, instead of using a burnishing cream the surface can be rubbed in the direction of the grain with steel wool and a wax polish.

Clear varnishes and oils

Clear varnishes and oils include a very wide range of wood finishes. Some of these are for specialized use only, and some are to a greater or lesser extent, toxic and flammable. Make quite sure that empty containers are well wrapped before being disposed of, and always follow the manufacturer's instructions when using them.

Cellulose lacquers

Cellulose lacquers are mainly used by furniture manufacturers. They are quick drying and can be applied by spray gun. They also have a very low flashpoint and are consequently more hazardous to use than many other finishes. If you do decide to use them, take all precautions necessary to prevent the risk of a fire, and make quite sure that the room used is ventilated properly as the fumes are very powerful. Never use cellulose lacquers inside the house; always use them in a garage or other separate building.

Polyesters

Polyesters provide a very hard, clear film which may be burnished to a mirror-like gloss. Their pot life is short and they are usually applied with special spray equipment or by curtain coating – a process whereby the finish is applied to flat pieces of wood which are passed on a conveyor belt under a curtain of falling polyester.

Polyurethanes

Polyurethanes are probably the most widely used finishes for interior woodwork. There are three main types available: two-pack, moisture-cured and air-drying. The two-pack give the toughest and most durable finish, but they are toxic to a certain degree and are mainly used in industry. Moisture-cured polyurethanes, which dry by reacting with the moisture in the air, produce hard, durable finishes, but they are slow drying and usually take about 12 hours, depending on the humidity in the atmosphere, before they can be handled safely. Air-drying polyurethanes dry much faster than the two-pack variety, usually in one to one-and-a-half hours, but they do not dry to such a hard finish. There are some air-drying polyurethanes available which dry to a high gloss, matt or satin finish. The matt and satin finishes are obtained by incorporating powders into the formula which cause the polyurethane to dry with a slightly rough finish. Whether the finish dries with a matt or satin appearance depends upon the powders used. Products which contain these powders do not feel as smooth to the touch as a gloss polyurethane which has been matted by rubbing down with fine steel wool and wax polish.

There is considerable variation in quality between the brands of polyurethanes. The quality depends very much upon the type of oil used to modify the polyurethane and also the amount of polyurethane contained within the formulation itself.

Oil varnishes

Oil varnishes are slow drying and usually take eight hours or longer to dry. They are not normally used for interior woodwork, but do, however, give very good protection out of doors.

Cold-cured lacquers

Cold-cured lacquers are usually based on urea formaldehydes and melamine – or combinations of the two. They give clear, hard films which are durable and resistant to most solvents and may be burnished to a mirror-like gloss, or rubbed down to a satin or matt finish. The lacquers do not dry until they are mixed with an acidic hardener, which acts as a catalyst, making the components in the coating cross link and polymerize. They are used extensively in industry, but the curing is initiated with infra-red heat instead of an acid hardener.

These lacquers are probably the best finishes for furniture, but they are not always easy to buy. They cannot be used over existing finishes and are for use on new work or furniture that has been stripped. The lacquer is usually almost colourless and has to be mixed with an acidic hardener before use. You must use a glass or polyethylene container. Metal must not be used as it will react with the hardener. The proportions used are usually one part hardener to four parts lacquer. Once mixed with the hardener, the lacquer will start to cure and will form a gel and then a solid, even in a closed container. The mixed coating must, therefore, be used within the period stated by the manufacturer, which is usually within three days, although some cold-cured lacquers may have a pot life of 24 hours or less. Therefore, it is necessary that you read and follow the instructions very carefully.

Cold-cured lacquers may be applied with a brush, roller or spray gun. When applying with a full brush, use a flowing action and a minimum amount of brushing, as the lacquers dry so quickly – depending on temperature, usually in one to one-and-a-half hours.

For a high gloss finish, at least three coats are recommended. For a mirror-like gloss, the last coat is rubbed down with fine wet and dry paper and the surface then brought to a high gloss with a burnishing cream. Alternatively, the surface may be rubbed to a satin or matt finish with steel wool or wax polish.

Cold-cured lacquers produce a surface that does not darken with ageing and has extremely good resistance to heat, solvents and abrasions. They are not recommended for exterior woodwork, however, as their resistance to continued moisture is not as durable as a marine or yacht varnish.

External woodwork

External woodwork is usually painted. However, if an attractive hardwood has been used it may be varnished, oiled or stained.

Clean the existing paint or varnish surface with detergent or sugar-soap. Rinse and wash thoroughly with clean water. Make sure the surface is dry before proceeding further and, if it has been varnished, make sure that no gloss remains. Very often, external wood will have become badly weather-stained if the surface coating has failed. If this has happened, the old finish should be removed by stripping and the bare wood bleached. Always use a paint stripper; never burn off the old surface if you are re-coating with a clear finish.

Before varnishing or oiling, exterior woodwork should be treated with a clear wood preservative. There are several types of organic solvents. These are preservative chemicals dissolved in paint thinner or petroleum oil. Organic solvents are very usefully applied to wood already attacked by fungi or insects, but if it is at all affected by wood rot the rotten pieces must be cut out and replaced. If the surface is no longer smooth it will be impossible to apply any coating that will stay intact for more than a short time. The wood must be brought back to a smooth condition by planing or by deep sanding. In extreme cases, it must be replaced with new wood.

The most common finish for external wood is varnish. For maximum durability, apply a minimum of four coats. Multiple coats are particularly recommended for wood which has to survive the harsh weather conditions of parts of Northern Europe, the US and Canada.

If the wood is bare, the first coat should be thinned to enable it to penetrate the wood better. Also, it is essential that at least one coat of varnish is applied to the top, bottom and side edges of doors to prevent moisture being absorbed, as, if it is allowed to penetrate sealed woodwork, the expansion and concentration of the wood will make the varnish crack and eventually flake and peel from the surface. For this reason varnishes usually first fail at the joints.

Ideally, wood should not have a moisture content of more than 18 per cent when it is varnished. Wait for a warm, dry spell before varnishing wood that has been left exposed during a wet period.

If a high gloss finish is not required, external woodwork can be treated with a good quality teak or Danish oil. Because an oil finish soaks into the wood and does not leave a thick protective film on the surface, it will have to be re-oiled at least once a year. Before this is done, the surface of the wood should be cleaned, preferably by rubbing it with a rag and paint thinner. If necessary, use steel wool to remove surface grime.

Some exterior wood stains contain special compounds which resist rot and mildew and repel termite and other wood-destructive insects. Brush or spray the stain on in generous proportions and let the residue soak in. Apply regularly.

This distinctive building shows how external woodwork can enhance a home.

Painting and Wallcovering

The traditional crafts of painting and wallcovering have seen a great many changes over the last three hundred years. Before ready-mixed paints became available, it was necessary for painters to mix the colour and medium at the place where they were to be used. This meant that only the houses of the wealthy were painted. Elsewhere, whitewash was used to cover both interior and exterior surfaces, made by mixing burnt lime with size and water.

Ready-mixed paint became available during the late eighteenth century and painted interiors became more common as the less wealthy could afford to undertake the work.

Wallpapers in their current form also became available in the late eighteenth century. In 1839, a printing machine which produced decorative wallpaper in roll form was invented and gradually this form of wallcovering gained currency. Prior to this, wallpaper was printed as panels on heavy card and nailed to the walls directly or onto a wooden frame. (Alternatives to printed panels were stretched or hung fabrics or wooden panelling.)

(above) *A beautifully restored bedroom, carefully redecorated with wallpaper specially printed to match the original.*

(left) *The living room of a carefully decorated nineteenth century cottage, using traditional materials in the period style.*

Professional decorators resented the arrival of the new materials. Nevertheless, because interior decoration on a grand scale required skills which approached an art form, the best practitioners of this new craft survived. They were called on to produce graining, marbling and similar effects, as well as stencil friezes.

Changes in fashion have meant demands made on painters and decorators have varied. On the whole, the work has become easier for the less experienced to tackle.

It is well worth making the effort to ensure that any decorating job is done well as the benefits are there to see for a long time. Professionals always pay a lot of attention to preparing the area to be decorated. Always follow the recommendations made in this book and bear in mind manufacturers' instructions. If you are stripping old paintwork, first test an out-of-the-way area to determine its strength. And take care when attempting to remove wallpaper from old walls.

It is not only important to prepare properly. You must use the correct materials. Good quality materials give better results which outweigh their extra cost.

Although modern finishes may look out of place in an old setting, nevertheless, there are some contemporary materials which provide splendid effects and look just as good as their traditional counterparts.

The effort involved in acquiring good painting and wallcovering skills is amply rewarded by knowing you have mastered new techniques and will achieve a high level of craftsmanship when decorating your walls.

Painting

Painting today is a highly developed craft. If you learn to apply painting techniques, you will not only save yourself time and effort but also end up with a decor to be proud of.

Most modern paints contain four basic ingredients: pigments or colour, resin to act as a binder, plasticizer to keep the paint elastic after drying and a solvent which renders the paint thin enough to be applied by brush or roller and which evaporates as the paint dries. Emulsion (latex) paints use water as a solvent.

Alkyd-based paints will wrinkle and peel if applied to fresh plaster because the alkali and water the plaster releases will deform the paint film. Indeed, some types of paint will actually damage particular surfaces. Emulsion (water-thinned latex) paint will engender rust if applied to an unprotected ferrous metal surface.

Primers or sealers are essential protection for raw surfaces or old, friable plasters such as those frequently found in very old houses. Undercoats are also necessary as they contain coarser pigment particles than top coats and provide a greater depth of colour; they are especially effective under alkyd finishes. To avoid costly errors it is worthwhile seeking the advice of paint manufacturers, suppliers or professional decorators before purchasing your paint.

Tools

Using the right tools is as important as choosing the right paint. Like most jobs, painting requires both general-purpose and specialized tools. Have on hand a rule, hammer, screwdriver, sanding block, abrasive paper and a quantity of clean rags. The more specific tools, listed below, will help you to carry out your interior painting neatly and efficiently.

Brushes

At least three sizes of brush are needed: a 75mm (3in) brush, for

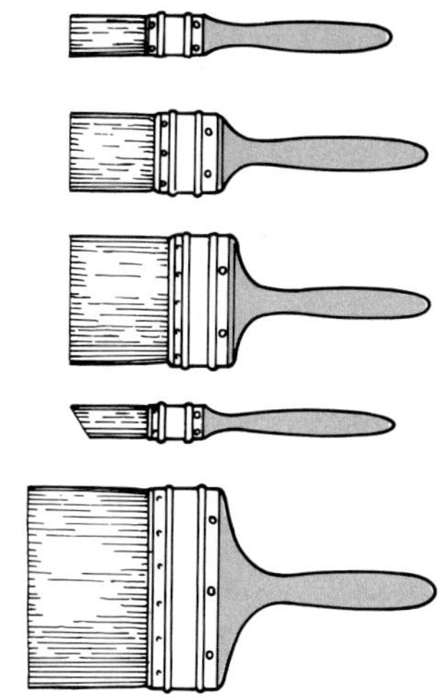

wide, flat areas such as flush doors, a 50mm (2in) brush for skirting boards (baseboards) or door panels and a 25mm (1in) angled brush for narrow areas such as window frames and mouldings.

Dust sheets

Dust sheets protect furniture and floors from drips or splattering. They can be either plastic for furniture only or twill sheeting.

Knives

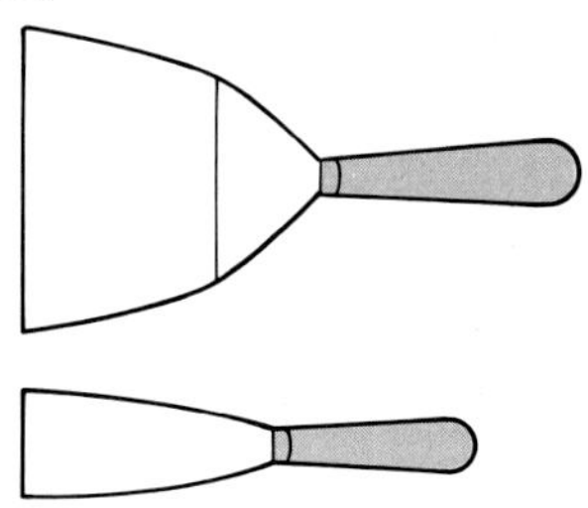

For removing wallpaper and patching wallboard or plaster before painting, you will require both wide and narrow rigid stripping knives and flexible bladed filling knives.

Masking tape

Masking tape is extremely useful in precision painting. Also, you may need a roll of jointing tape to cover wallboard seams.

Protective clothing

For protection during both preparation and painting, you will need the following: a pair of rubber gloves, a suit of overalls and some form of head covering.

Rollers

You will need a variety of rollers for different painting situations; a roller tray, for rolling on paint; a spring roller frame and sleeve (ideally, lamb's wool) and an extension pole to reach high areas.

Shave hook

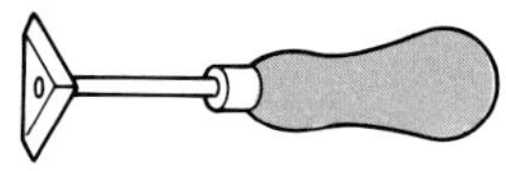

A shave hook is a small, triangular or heart-shaped blade, mounted onto a shaft. It is used for stripping paint from mouldings.

Tack rags

Tack rags are sticky cloths, made by impregnating open-weave cloth (such as mutton – cheese – cloth) with non-drying, resinous varnish. If wiped very lightly over a prepared background they will pick up any residue of dirt or dust.

Window scraper

It is important to make sure you have a window scraper available for removing dried paint from glass.

Planning the work

Whether you are painting a single room or redecorating the entire house, you will achieve the best results with the least fuss if you take time to plan your work. First you need to know how much paint to buy and how long the entire job – preparation, painting and cleaning up – is liable to take you.

Don't estimate how much paint you will need in a paint shop – it will be impossible. It is best to calculate the area you will have to cover before you leave home.

Given a normal rectangular room, first measure the length and width to the nearest 0.5m (1ft). Add the dimensions together and multiply the sum by the room's height.

Double the result and you have the area of your walls in square metres (yards). From this figure you can deduct 1.5sq m (5sq ft) for each normal sized window and 2sq m (6½sq ft) for each door. The ceiling area is the length multiplied by the width of the room.

If the room is unusually shaped, each wall area must be calculated separately and added together for the total area. A stair well often forms a triangular shape. For the area of this triangle, multiply the lengths of the horizontal and vertical sides and divide by two. The skirting board (baseboard) and picture rail areas are the product of the height plus width, multiplied by the perimeter of the room.

A lot depends on the covering capacity of the paint and the type of surface to be painted. For example, if the walls are smooth, you can reckon on covering approximately 15sq m with one litre (160sq ft with 2 pints) of matt or semi-gloss paint. By dividing the total wall area by the most pessimistic coverage figure (in this case, 15) you will find the maximum amount you need for the first coat. (If you are applying finishing paint directly to porous, rough or unpainted walls, the coverage will be considerably less.) Estimating time involves another set of variables. You will probably cover about 7sq m (24sq ft) of ordinary surface in one hour. An average-sized room could be given one coat of paint in a day. If you are applying two coats, you must allow time for the first coat to dry – a matter of hours for emulsion (latex) paint, or overnight for semi-gloss. Generally speaking, you can reckon on two days to paint a room and clean up afterwards. However, painting is often the quickest part of the job. Unless you are working on new surfaces, the repairs and preparation will be a major portion of the work. This is especially the case in old buildings where walls and woodwork may require stripping and patching. Another important variable is your own physical condition. Painting requires more lifting, stretching and bending than the average daily task, so take care not to overdo things. If you schedule the work to include tea breaks and lunch you will finish the day in better condition than you would if you had no food or drink.

Painting can be a messy job. Before you start, clear the room of as many portable objects, such as chairs, lamps and tables, as possible. Then cluster the bulky furniture, rugs and suchlike in the centre of the room and cover them with dust sheets. Remove curtains, rails, pictures, nails, hooks and, where feasible, electrical fittings, remembering to switch off at the mains. Protect the floor by spreading newspapers along the skirting boards (baseboards) and the rest of the floor with dust sheets. Assemble all the equipment, tools and materials for the job on a worktop (such as a trestle table) so that they are ready to hand.

The success of interior painting depends largely on the care with which the surfaces have been prepared. Thorough cleaning and removal of flaky paint, distemper, cracks or holes are essential.

Preparation

When preparing a surface for painting or wallcovering, you may need to carry out some, or even all, of the following procedures, which (in the UK) are known as 'making good'.

When painting over existing wallpaper, make sure it is in good condition. The odd peeling corner can be stuck back with wallpaper paste, but paper in bad condition should be completely stripped off using a chemical paint stripper. Remember, too, that if the paper has a bold pattern, at least two coats of paint will be needed to disguise it – and unless a paper has been specially formulated to be overpainted, it may bubble in places.

Filling is the technique of filling up holes in plaster or woodwork to achieve a smooth surface. Fillers can be either oil- or water-based. Oil-based fillers are used principally to repair holes in woodwork. The first step is to remove any loose or rotting wood with a chisel. Always coat the inside of the hole with a good primer before you use the filler; otherwise the oil may be absorbed by the wood, leaving the dry filler to drop out.

For small holes or cracks in plasterwork, it is best to use a water-based filler. First, use a stripping knife to chip back all the crumbling edges of the hole until you come across firm plaster. Next, undercut the edges by removing some of the plaster with a shave hook. Having provided a 'key' with the undercut, blow or vacuum out all the dirt. Now, moisten the back of the hole and apply a layer of filler to within about 6mm (¼in) of the plaster surface. Score the filler lightly and allow to dry. Then fill in the remainder of the hole with more filler until it stands a little above the surface. When completely dry, this can then be sanded flush.

Filling is a method of dealing with small cracks in plaster. Using a shave hook, open out the crack into a 'V' to take the filler. Having moistened the enlarged crack and surrounding area, work in the filler with a narrow filling knife, leaving it above the surface. When dry, sand it down with a fine abrasive paper.

If, having scraped off small areas of old flaking paint and sanded the surface, there is still a noticeable step between the painted and scraped areas, this can be evened out by painting the area with a thinned down water-based filler.

Where plasterwork is shabby, but not so bad as to warrant major repairs, applying a lining paper will present a smooth, taut surface for painting or wallcovering. The paper should be butt joined, that is, joined edge to edge to avoid a visible overlap seam. Seal the paper with a thin coat of size (see pages 94 to 95) before painting.

Colour

The complex and subtle nuances involved in the perception of colours are very much in the eyes of individual beholders. No two people ever mean exactly the same things when describing colours – a factor psychologists have been aware of for over a century.

Used imaginatively, but with care, colours can enhance the appearance and proportions of a room. People tend to stick to safe colour schemes, such as plain white or cream walls. A room containing these colours may well lack character and appear to be rather cold, although it may have a chaste charm. With the multitude of colour paints available, it would be easy to try out a more adventurous colour scheme. By all means leave the reds, blues or yellows to the really brave and daring. Try out a subtle mauve, lilac or apricot and you may find you have transformed the area painted into a real living space.

Colours which have been 'distressed' or broken up by, for example, ragging or stippling (see pages 79 to 83), are often much more flattering than flat, opaque, colours which tend to shrink a room and highlight defects. For example, brushing on a simple tinted glaze one shade darker than the ground colour will make the walls appear to recede and will also at once improve the appearance of the room.

A great deal of thought and a basic knowledge of the qualities of colours are required. Do not assume that because you like a colour it will therefore be suitable for your wall or ceiling. Much has to be considered to avoid a garish result, such as the amount of natural and artificial light entering the room, where the light falls, and what the room is being used for.

Primary colours are those from which all other colours are derived. They are red, blue and yellow. Secondary colours are two primary colours mixed together: for instance, red and yellow give orange. When two secondary colours are mixed, they give rise to tertiary colours; orange and purple, for example, making russet. There are an enormous number of permutations, so you can spend many hours working out colour schemes.

The warm shades of the walls and ceiling offset the furniture and fittings.

A useful division is into warm colours (those tending towards red or yellow) and cool colours (those inclining towards blue). White tends to have a blue or yellow shade and can affect any colour you mix it with. For example, a brilliant white almost always contains a high proportion of blue to bring out its whiteness; it is not, therefore, recommended as a base for mixing.

Warm colours, such as red, yellow, magenta or emerald, cheer up a bleak north-facing room. These are sometimes called 'advancing' colours as they appear to bring the walls closer together. Cold colours, such as dark green, grey or purple, are known as 'retreating' colours as they tend to give a wall depth.

Colour can create optical illusions as, for example, with trompe l'oeil panel painting (see page 84). It can also be used to change the perceived dimensions of a room. If, for instance, you want your ceiling to be lowered it can be coloured either with a dark shade or with contrasting dark colours. A frieze or picture rail in contrasting colour will stop the eye from travelling upwards. Conversely, carrying the wall colouring up to the ceiling, or painting it a lighter shade, will tend to give the illusion of a higher ceiling.

Nowadays, white and its more fashionable variant cream is extensively used. However, it rarely seems to be handled properly. It is essential to note that white or cream walls must be pure and without shadow. This means that at least three coats of paint must be applied if the proper effect is to be achieved. If less coats are laid on, the result will appear to be skimped and look dirty, especially if, as is often the case, paint is being applied over a darker surface.

It is quite wrong to think that white is the only choice for rooms with exposed wood. In fact, old cottages with lots of beams are rarely so well proportioned that they look and feel right with the stark contrast of white walls and very dark beams. Never apply brilliant white. Cream is much safer.

Stippling

For centuries, decorators have known that flat, uniform colour is inert and unyielding. Borrowing freely from artists, they have used tinted glazes, water colours and very many conjuring tricks with paint to transform its appearance to suggest marble, fabric porphyry and other precious materials. Among the most successful of their techniques has been the stippling process which has been used by generations of decorators, either to soften colours or to disguise brush marks. By using a fine stippling brush the painter is able to distribute the paint evenly over the surface of the wall to get an imperceptibly grainy texture, known as 'orange peel'.

Most modern stippling is carried out either with a stippling brush or a crimpled cloth pad which is dabbed firmly against a thinly applied wet glaze, lifting off specks of the glaze to reveal the base colour.

Brush stippling gives a good, delicate-looking finish, rather similar to the bloom on a peach. However, it is slow and tiring work, and the brushes, too, are expensive. If you are decorating large areas, it is usually easier, and less tiring, to use a cloth pad. This gives an effect similar to rag-rolling, but is tighter and more uniform in appearance. Stippling with a cloth pad also offers a wider range of textured effects. Half the fascination of stippling is the scope which it offers for experimentation. Even crimpled newspaper has been used to remarkably good effect for this purpose, producing very bold results, but it cannot match a delicate brush finish.

Stippling is usually carried out using transparent colours over a white or light coloured base. This allows just enough of the base coat to show through and soften the glaze. Thus, a bright red over white will appear as soft pink, or a brown on cream as *café au lait*.

Wall surfaces to be stippled should be reasonably sound and smooth – athough the odd bump or crack does not present a problem. It is important that the base coat should be non-porous so that the stipple can register evenly. The transparant glaze can be coloured or tinted to suit your own taste by means of stainers (tints) or artists' oil colours.

Stippling is less tiring – and much easier – if two people work together.

Having mixed the glaze, the first painter applies a thin film over a strip of wall. At the same time, the second painter is following behind, stippling the surface while it is still wet and malleable.

It is very important to keep the pressure on the brush or pad firm and decisive.

The glowing colours used for stippling the walls of the room shown above create a cosy atmosphere.

Sponging

This attractive decorative effect can be achieved by applying one or more harmonizing or contrasting colours over a pre-painted surface. Standard emulsion (latex) paints are used for this technique which is suitable for many wall surfaces. Muslin, cheesecloth and crimpled paper are some of the materials that can be used to apply the colour. Perhaps the most satisfactory is a coarse honeycomb marine sponge, cut in half to provide a flat side. When decorating a large area, choose a fairly open textured type. Before using, soak the sponge in clean, cold water so that it expands fully and squeeze dry.

Suitable paints for sponging are either matt or silk (water-based) emulsion (latex), or eggshell or satin finish (oil-based) paint. You will need a clean paint tray for sponging colour, a honeycomb marine sponge, a bucket of clean water, a sheet of paper or board, painted with the wall base colour. A 75mm (3in) or 100mm (4in) brush is suitable.

The surface to be decorated should be prepared in the normal way. Wall areas should be painted with a good quality matt or silk (water-based) emulsion (latex), but an oil-based eggshell paint is best for woodwork. Allow to dry completely. It is advisable to use a lighter shade for the base coat and a darker shade for the sponged pattern. Before attempting any broken colour work, try out the effect on a spare piece of pre-painted paper or board to get a feel for the amount of pressure needed when using the sponge, and to determine the correct density.

Pour a little of the paint onto a paint tray and brush it out in a thin layer. Remember that the sponging colour should be of a slightly thinner consistency than that used for the base coat. Dip the dampened flat side of the sponge into the paint. Test the effect by dabbing it a few times on the pre-painted paper or board. The colour should then be dabbed on the wall, using an even, light pressure whilst maintaining a loose wrist action. Hold the sponge at varying angles and wave it randomly across the surface to avoid lines in the finished work. Occasionally, it may be necessary to rinse out the sponge. Allow the paint to dry and, if required, add a second colour to produce a multi-colour effect, filling in any blank areas to leave a mottled but even pattern.

You can also use masking tape to mark out the wall. When sponging, fill in alternate areas of the design to create a lined pattern on the surface. Remove the tape as soon as the decoration is complete.

Sponging achieves an effective mottled finish.

Ragging and rag-rolling

Ragging and rag-rolling are among the oldest traditional methods of producing 'distressed' or broken colour effects and have been developed from stippling. The techniques do not require a very great deal of expertise but they can, if properly carried out, create very decorative and striking finishes. The process involves pressing bunched up rags or chamois leather into wet glaze which has been applied over a pre-painted surface, creating a bold open pattern with considerable variety and depth.

Ragging and rag-rolling are, in fact, both facets of the same process, the only difference being in the way they are applied. A coloured glaze is either 'ragged off' or 'rolled on'.

When ragging, you simply bunch up the rag or leather and dab it about the glazed area, using a loose wrist movement.

Rag-rolling, on the other hand, involves wrapping the rag into a loose sausage-shape and rolling it over the wet glaze in various directions like a rolling pin.

In both cases, the result should be an irregular pattern but, paradoxically, one that gives the impression of uniformity. However, unlike other methods of 'distressing', a ragged surface should not be uniform or else the pattern becomes insistent and annoying.

Varying pressure on the rag, rolling it 'this way and that way', and even rearranging the rag itself, will create a subtle, varying flow of colour, softening angles and making small areas seem more spacious.

Ragging and rag-rolling are ideal for decorating large areas of wall such as stairwells or corridors and woodwork. The process is easy, once you have acquired the knack, but it is time-consuming and tiring, which is why it is best carried out by two people.

The bold effect of a ragged finish makes it unsuitable for bright, hard colours, the most pleasing result being achieved by using soft pastels over an off-white base, that is, white, tinted with a little raw umber for a grey cast or raw sienna for a warmer cream.

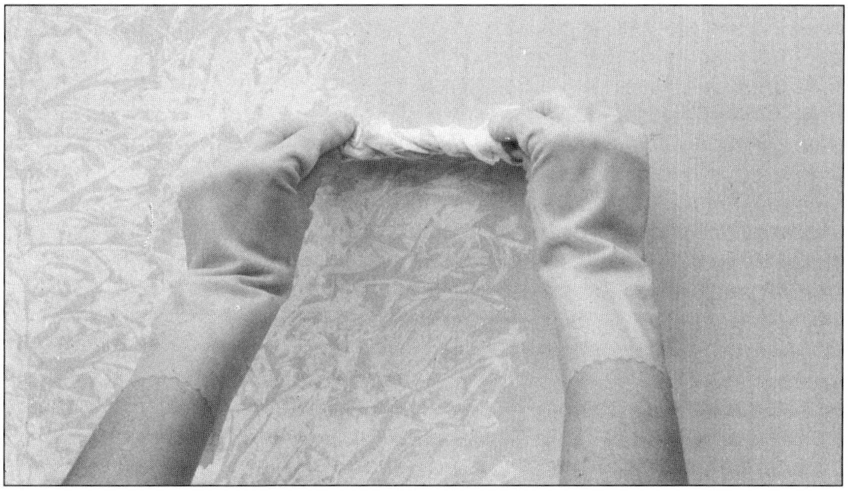

Rag-rolling a sausage-shaped rag over the surface produces 'distressed' effects.

Colours ideal for the glaze are blue-green, greenish-grey or pink with a touch of brown. Colour on colour can also be very effective, particularly if the two colours have similar tone and intensity, while off-white on brilliant white can give the appearance of delicate marble.

Before starting the techniques, however, try out the effect on a fairly large piece of card or hardboard. This will allow you to judge the result of your colour choice and get used to the amount of pressure needed to achieve your objective.

Tools and materials

Colouring agents

Colouring agents consist of universal stainers (tints), artists' oil colours, or oil-based paints.

Glazes or washes

Ragging with an oil glaze gives a crisp pattern; thinned oil paint, or a wash or thinned emulsion (latex) produces a softer effect. Usually, a litre (2 pints) of glaze or paint is sufficient for a small room.

Rags and brushes

You will need a 75mm (3in) paint brush to apply the glaze/wash and a 'flogger' or long bristled brush to create a texture. You will also need a good supply of rags or a piece of leather to 'distress' the glaze. Rags can be of any texture – old sheets, net curtain, mutton (cheese) cloth or even hessian (burlap), but they must be of a reasonable size (380mm – 15in – square) and they must be well washed and lint free. Use the same type of rag throughout. Rags can be used dry or with a glaze – wrung out in paint thinner – for a soft effect.

Paint thinner

Paint thinner is needed to thin glaze or oil paint.

Preparation

The surface to be decorated should be prepared for painting in the normal way. In common with most special wall-finishes, ragging with a transparent oil glaze (glazing liquid) is best done over a mid-sheen, oil-based paint. Tint the glaze to the required depth of tone, using oil stainers, tubes of artists' colours or any oil-based paint. Thin with paint thinner for easy application. If you are using a leather cloth, however, both the base coat and the glaze should be water-based emulsions (latex paint). This produces a softer effect. Again, the base coat should be a mid-sheen, silk emulsion; matt

The cold colours used to create depth have been softened by the grey rag-rolled walls.

emulsion is more absorbent. It is best if one person applies the glaze and another carries out the actual ragging. Make sure the base coat is clean and dry before you start.

Method

Starting at the top of the wall, apply the coloured glaze over an area of about 2sq m (6sq ft). Oil glaze needs to be worked over thoroughly to eliminate brush strokes. Do this by stippling the surface with the flat part of a clean, long-bristle brush. Using the 'flogging' brush, start from the bottom of the glazed strip and draw it upwards over the surface glaze to create an even textured appearance. Pay attention to corners as dark or light areas of colour can give an uneven finish. Rag pads will soon become hardened with a build-up of paint and glaze, and will have to be replaced often. Make sure you have plenty to spare. Remember, rags soaked in paint thinner present a very real fire hazard, so dispose of them safely.

When using an emulsion (latex) wash, apply a small strip at a time and fade it out towards the edge so that the adjacent overlapping strip does not form a ridge. Dry edges can be softened with a wet sponge to make the paint workable.

When finished, allow the glaze to dry thoroughly. If desired, a second harmonizing or contrasting colour can be ragged on to give an exciting multi-coloured effect.

Finally, when the work is complete and dry, it should be protected with a finishing coat of matt polyurethane varnish.

Dragging and colour washing

Dragging is another way to distress or break up colours. Essentially, the pre-painted surface is covered with a wash or glaze of nearly transparent colour and then brushed down from top to bottom with a dry brush, dragging off fine strips of colour so that the ground colour shows through. This technique can animate the plainest of rooms with colour, highlights and shadows. Dragging is well within the capabilities of the amateur enthusiast and, in fact, the most interesting techniques have often been achieved through blind ignorance! What is required is both the right materials and an adventurous nature.

The tools needed are very basic: a paint brush and a longer bristled dragging brush. Buy the largest dragging brush you can – it will speed up the work. Having applied the base coat, the material for dragging can be oil-based glaze or wash, a mid-gloss oil paint which has been thinned or an emulsion (latex) which has undergone a similar process. Dragging glaze or wash should be applied very sparingly.

Method

Dragging is best carried out by two people: the first applying the glaze and the second following immediately afterwards dragging in the glaze. The process can be achieved by one decorator only, but in this case note that it will involve very quick work to make sure that the glaze is not dry before dragging. For evenly dragged walls the surface should be smooth, regular and painted with a ground colour. The best results are achieved on a base of oil-based paint.

The first painter applies a narrow band of glaze or thinned out paint (about 450mm -18in-) from ceiling or cornice to the bottom. Keep the film thin or it will run. Having done this, the second painter drags the surface by setting a dry dragging brush at a slight angle to the wall and running it very lightly from top to bottom, keeping as steady a pressure as possible on the brush. While the second painter is dragging, the first painter is painting the next section. It is very important that each drag runs into an adjacent wet patch or the effect will be patchy. Build-ups of glaze at the top or bottom of the wall should be 'feathered' out with a dry brush.

Unless you are extremely careful, there is no way that the drag lines can be absolutely plumb. However, wavy lines will not be noticeable.

Two-directional dragging gives a woven effect similar to Thai silk.

Keep a steady pressure on the brush to provide an even effect.

Colour washing

Colour washing is a much blander form of dragging, which gives a soft, delicate dapply watery colour effect. The base coat is normally a warm white which can be brought to life by a colour wash in pink, russet or even pale blue.

The favourite medium for colour washing used to be distemper, but modern equivalents such as thinned down oil paint or watered emulsion (latex) can give an equally pretty effect. Whatever you use, colour wash should be thinned by about one part solvent to nine parts paint.

Application is simple. Slap the colour on loosely in all directions, making an effort to avoid brush marks or hard edges. Leave a good bit of the base colour uncovered, and, when the first coat is quite dry, repeat the treatment. This will cover the bare patches and also intensify the colour already applied. You will then see the effect come alive on the colour-washed surfaces.

The soft lines produced by dragging and colour washing provide a subtle background.

Trompe l'oeil

Trompe l'oeil, which literally means 'to deceive the eye' is an architectural extension of artistic illusion. Fine examples of trompe l'oeil were found on exposed walls in Pompeii, and Pliny recorded that the artist Zeuxis painted a bunch of grapes so lifelike that 'the fowls of the air descended to peck at them'.

The technique is chiefly used to create an illusion of relief and depth on a flat plane. There are many Italian churches where the apse behind the altar exists only in the eyes of the congregation!

Trompe l'oeil is not easy. Unless you are a skilled artist, it is best to stick to fairly simple tasks such as door panelling.

Method

Paint one coat of flat or mid-sheen, oil-based white paint on the door and architrave. This will be the base coat. Allow to dry and then mark out the panelling with a pencil and straight edge. The lines forming each panel should be about 12mm (½in) apart – a box within a box. Each panel should be about 80mm (3½in) inside the door edges. The space between upper and lower panels may be a little wider.

Make up a small amount of thin medium-grey paint by mixing one part white oil-based paint to two parts paint thinner and tinting with raw umber. Paint the mixture between the panel lines you have drawn, using masking tape to ensure accurate straight lines.

Add more raw umber to your mixture to darken it and paint in the two panel lines (top and side) which are nearest to the light source. This will imitate the shadows cast by real panelling.

Now mix up some more thinned white paint and umber to produce one or two shades lighter than the painted panel lines. Using a wider brush, drag this over the whole door surface.

When the door is quite dry, apply two coats of varnish for protection.

(above) *The clever use of stock borders and wallpapers has helped to simplify the work necessary to produce the effect of an old panelled staircase. The careful use of shadow creates the false impression of a three dimensional scene.*

(right) *A small, paved garden is extended by the imaginative use of trompe l'oeil. An arch and trellis work have been painted onto a wall. Through the arch there is a magnificent view of an imaginary garden, leading up to another arch.*

Marbling

All surfaces should be perfectly smooth and prepared as for re-painting. Any surface defects should be filled, using a fine surface filler. An ideal surface is obtained by applying an oil-based eggshell or satin-finish paint as a preliminary coat. Allow the ground colour to dry completely before marbling. Prepare and paint a test panel to see what the colour and effect will be before starting to marble the surface.

The method of marbling

To reproduce the marble effect it is advisable to use oil-based colours. This will allow time to create various marble patterns before the paint dries. The colouring of natural marble is nearly always translucent. To reproduce this, it may be necessary to repeatedly glaze the work, using a transparent oil glaze. Tint the glaze with the appropriate colour of oil stainers, or oil-based paint, to the required colour.

It is not always essential to reproduce the colours exactly; the style or pattern is more important. It may be appropriate to change the colours of the marble to relate to the colour scheme of the room. With many marble patterns, background effects can be achieved by applying a thin coloured glaze, using the rag-rolling technique, and by carefully cross-brushing the work, using a soft bristle brush. Allow the glaze to dry and, when applying the deeper colour, follow the pattern made by the rag-rolling effect, using a small artist's brush. Hold the brush lightly and zig zag downwards and across the work to create the irregular shaped veins. Soften the colour with cross-brushing strokes, using a soft bristle brush.

For white vein marble, first paint the surface with a thin mixture of transparent oil glaze and white paint. With this colour still wet, pencil in the light grey veins and soften carefully. The dark grey veins should then be introduced and blended with the work. All these veins should follow in a definite direction, occasionally branching out across the panel. Allow to dry hard to achieve a transparent effect. Glaze the work with a thin mixture of glaze and white. Patches of colour can be introduced, using a fitch or small brush. If necessary, small areas of colour can be removed using a crimpled piece of paper, allowing the darker coloured veins to show more clearly. When dry, the work should be coated with an extra pale eggshell, or matt, varnish.

A very simple technique is used to create a black marble. The surface is prepared and painted, using a black eggshell oil paint which is then allowed to dry. Groups of light and dark grey veins are then introduced. These should follow in one direction: down the panel. If necessary, the large areas should be lightly softened. Finally, white veins should be added at various angles running across the work.

An example of marbling is illustrated above showing veining and translucent colour effects.

White vein marbling

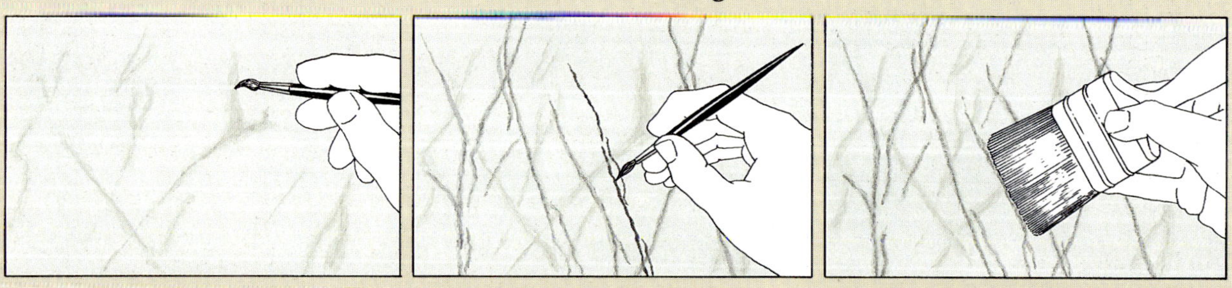

1. With base colour still wet, pencil in light grey veins and soften.

2. Introduce dark grey veins, carefully blending with the area previously worked on.

3. Ensure veins follow in definite directions, occasionally branching out across the panel.

Graining

Graining is the art of imitating wood with paint. It is a skill that needs a little patience and a knowledge of various types of wood to produce good results.

Tools

Brushes

Dragging brushes or *'floggers'* are used to 'flog' the surface and to create a straight grain effect.

A *dusting* brush can be used as a flogger and also to stipple the work.

Made from hoghair or camelhair, a stubby, short-bristle *mottler* brush has no handle. It is available in varying widths from 50mm (2in) to 100mm (4in).

Rubbing in brushes are used for applying and spreading the graining colour, and for varnishing the work when complete.

A *softener* brush blends or softens the graining colour.

Combs

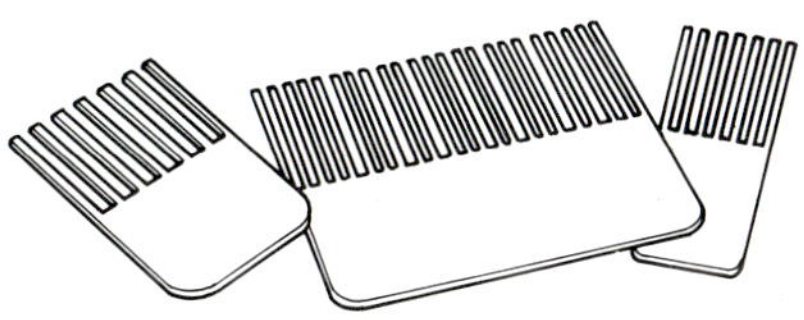

Combs are available in varying widths. The most common are made of steel and come in coarse, medium and fine grades. Rubber combs are also available.

Graining rollers

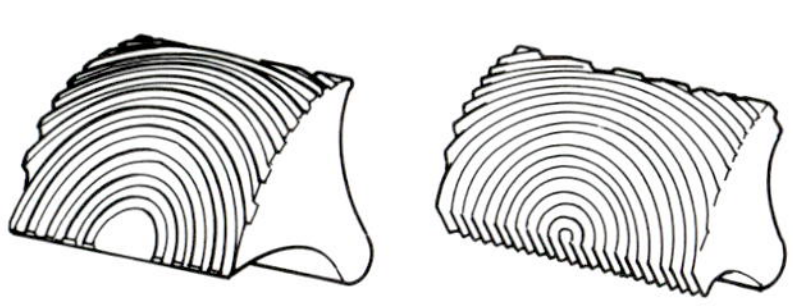

Made from rubber, these rollers are used when simulating the heartwood. They are available in a fine and coarse grain.

Pencil overgrainer

This metal plate carries a number of regularly-spaced, small brushes known as pencils, made from sable or hoghair.

Veining horn

Made from wood or bone and shaped like a window-wedge, the veining horn is covered with a piece of cotton rag and used for wiping out the dapples in oak graining.

Materials

Oil scumble is available in a wide variety of wood shades which are all intermixable. Generally, the scumble needs thinning with paint thinner.

When working on a large area, a small amount of raw linseed oil can be added to delay the drying process, allowing time for figuring the work. Use a mixture of two parts paint thinner to one part linseed oil.

Try out the colour and test for the consistency of the scumble on a piece of pre-painted cardboard before starting the graining work.

Preparation

All surfaces must be clean, dry and free from grease and dirt. The grounding colour should be perfectly smooth and hard. When mixing and matching colour for any wood reproduction, choose the lightest shade of the wood.

A close look at any wood will show that normally one of the characteristics of the pattern of the grain is a soft effect. Therefore, there should never be too much contrast between the base paint and the scumble – a tinted translucent oil glaze should be used to produce the graining effect.

Most manufacturers of scumble provide a wide range of coloured undercoats carefully matched to the various shades of scumble. When using a standard scumble colour, apply the recommended shade of undercoat. As an alternative, particularly when a special coloured effect is required, an eggshell or satin finish oil paint should be used for the ground colour.

Make sure that the base colour is completely dry and hard before attempting any graining effects.

Oak graining

To oak grain, first apply the scumble when the appropriate ground

An example of wood graining. This craft requires a good knowledge of wood types.

colour is hard and dry. Panelling should be completed by working on each section separately. The next step is to produce the straight grain and then to outline the figure work. The process of outlining figure work is illustrated below.

One of two methods is used to produce an oak sap effect. The sap is either wiped with the graining horn from the wet, scumbled surface as in dappling, or, when the scumble has dried, the figuring of the sap is painted on the surface, using the graining colour and a small artist's brush.

The first method is probably the most popular. The surface is stained and flogged as for brush-graining oak. Choose the position of the sap, usually down the centre of the work, and comb each side of this area with a coarse comb covered with rag.

For the overgraining process, apply the thin water colour glaze, completing each of the panels individually as the water scumble dries very quickly.

Use a mottler or clean folded rag to create the highlights and shades which should cross the original straight brush grain. Soften the effect by working in a horizontal direction and finish with a few vertical strokes.

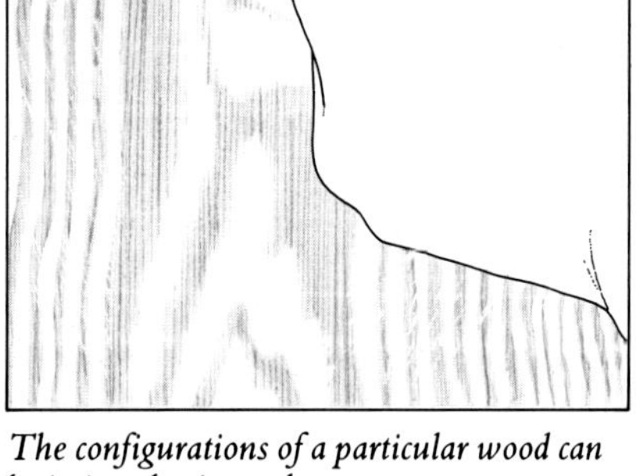

The configurations of a particular wood can be imitated using a clean rag.

Straight graining and dappling

1. *For the straight grain, cover a graining comb with a clean, lint-free cloth and apply a touch of the graining colour to the edge of the rag. Starting at the top of the work, drag the comb downwards. The strokes should not be too straight; slight swirls and gentle curves will improve its appearance.*

2. *To create the broken character of the oak grain, overcomb the work, using a fine narrow comb in a series of short, slanting strokes. For a shorter brush-grain effect, use a flogger or dragger brush instead.*

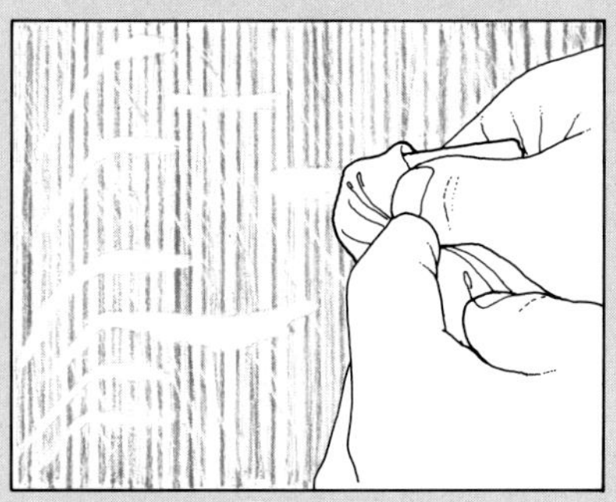

3. *For figure work, known as dappling, hold the veining horn between thumb and index finger and wipe the dapples cleanly in a suitable pattern, gently twisting the horn to create varying stroke widths. Change the position of the lint-free cloth frequently so that it wipes cleanly.*

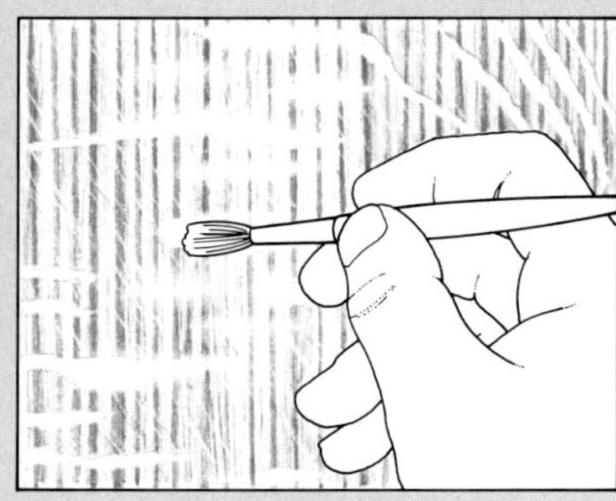

4. *Any bolder dapples are completed by softening with a small artist's brush, or by using a clean rag folded into a small pad to blend the inner edges of the dapples with the grain.*

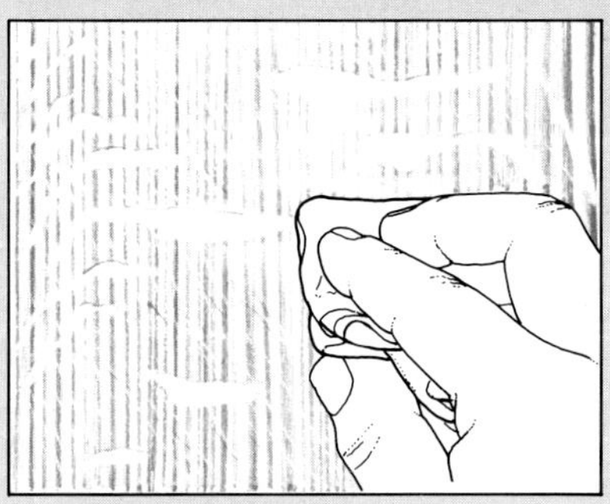

5. *The open areas in the centre of the figure work are then mottled to give the highlights and shading that are found in natural wood.*

6. *When wiping and figuring has been completed, draw a fine comb lightly upwards through the work to produce the flow of indentations.*

Stencilling

The patterns on the curtain and bedcovering have been continued on the walls, using stencils to produce an harmonious effect which emphasizes the splendour of the cabinet.

As an art form, stencilling is versatile, cheap and easy to do. You can be as creative as you please and, in a world of packaged stereotypes, a stencilled room has a rare and refreshing hand-made beauty.

Gifted and adventurous pattern-makers will want to invent their own designs, while others will find what they seek in tried and tested traditional themes. Ready-cut stencil kits can be bought, but cutting your own stencils is not difficult and can be very satisfying to do.

To make sure the colour effect works, make up proofs of your stencils on sheets of paper and hold them on the wall with masking tape. This will enable you to check colour combinations (which can play odd tricks) *in situ*, taking into account factors such as lighting and proportion.

A stencil needs to be waterproof and tough. In the past, a variety of materials has been used, including leather, lead foil, copper and oiled paper. Today, these have been largely superseded by clear, acetate sheets (available from artists' suppliers). Acetate is expensive but it is easily cleaned and lasts much longer – which is useful if you wish to build up a stencil library. In addition to the stencil material, you will need a hard cutting board and a sharp knife or, better still, a scalpel.

The first job is to transfer the design to the stencil material. If you are using a stencil card or board, all you need to do is to sandwich carbon paper between the design and the board and trace over the design with the tip of a knitting needle. Clear acetate should be placed over the design and the outline traced directly onto it with a chinagraph pen. Fix the design firmly to prevent slipping. Designs can be enlarged (or reduced) by placing them on a squared grid and scaling them up (or down) section by section. An alternative is to use a photographic enlargement.

Multi-coloured designs need a separate stencil for each colour. This poses a problem relating to registration, that is, lining up successive stencils when painting. When using acetate, this problem can be easily overcome as you simply draw the key parts of the rest of the design on the acetate making sure to align these as you go along.

If you are using an opaque stencil board, trace the different colour areas on separate stencil sheets and trim each sheet to exactly the same size. Put the sheets together in a stack and cut a small 'V' in each side of all the boards simultaneously. Mark the 'V' marks on the wall with pencil. You can now accurately align each stencil in turn.

To cut the stencil, fix the acetate or board firmly to the cutting block with masking tape. Allowing for a margin of at least 25mm (1in) around the edge of the design for strength, cut gently but firmly around the inked outline with a smooth, fluent movement. Cut towards yourself and, when you come to a curve, move the board round rather than the knife. The idea is to keep up a smooth cutting action without any hesitation. Rough edges should be carefully smoothed.

The surface to be stencilled should be sound, smooth and already painted in the chosen base colour. A 'distressed' wall finish (see pages 79 to 83) will give the stencils a richer look; dragged or colour-washed walls create a gentle contrast of texture.

A traditional stencil brush, with a clump of stiff bristles cut square at the end, gives by far the best result: a soft but definite stippled effect which can be subtly variegated to give a charming hand-made look. The stippling action lessens the risk of paint seeping under the stencil.

The main requirement for stencil paint is that it should be quick drying, especially on a multi-colour design where you may want to stencil over a colour which was put on only half-an-hour previously. Poster colours, sign writer's 'bulletin' paint, or acrylic colours are all suitable, but do not make them too thin or they will seep under the stencil and leave smudges. The paint's consistency should be creamy. Very little paint is taken up on the brush, so the colours must be intense enough to register well when only a thin coat is applied.

Regularly spaced stencils should be positioned in a grid drawn up on the wall with chalk. Make sure the lines are truly vertical and horizontal by using a plumb line and set square (try square). Remember, few rooms are symmetrical and it may be necessary to bend a stencil to fit into a corner. Hold the stencil to the wall with small strips of masking tape.

Dip just the bristle tips of the brush into the paint and, holding the brush firmly, dab or 'pounce' the brush with a slight rocking motion through the cuts in the stencil, as if using a rubber stamp. Using very little paint at a time gives delicacy to the colour, and prevents seepage. Work from the sides of the design toward the middle. Leave the colour to harden for a few seconds, then peel off the tape and move to the next spot. Continue round the room, applying one colour at a time.

When using multi-coloured stencils, make sure that each colour is quite dry before applying the next. It is important to wipe the stencil clean frequently, using a rag or tissue to prevent paint building up and clogging the details.

A covering of clear varnish will greatly prolong the life of a 'distressed' finish, especially stencilled patterns made with quick drying colours which can rub off easily. One (or two) coats of clear matt varnish can be applied easily and will allow walls to be washed down without harm to the design.

Floor stencils

Technically, floors are stencilled in exactly the same way as walls. However, squaring off a floor to

Floor stencils are original. Ensure floors are in good condition before stencilling.

take a stencil pattern is far more critical. You will need a stencil, rule, squared paper, chalk, string or a long straight edge and a set square (try square) for measuring angles. The procedure is set out below.

If you wish to stencil directly onto the floor, the surface should be sound and, if painted, finished in an opaque, flat or semi-gloss oil-based paint. If the floor is badly pitted, or there are gaps between the floor-boards, it will be better to cover it first with pre-stencilled smooth hardboard tiles.

You may have to adjust the size of the designs to suit the space available, as a number of complete designs should make up each run. A plain border around the edges of the floor could help solve this problem.

The best paints to use are the fast-drying types such as poster paints or, if obtainable, Japan colours thinned with paint thinner. These paints present little risk of smudging or smearing.

'Pouncing' with a regular stencil brush will give the crispest definition, but, when painting an entire floor with a repetitive design, it can become very tiring indeed. On the whole a 25mm or 50mm (1in or 2in) decorator's brush is much easier. Use it to brush the colour in rather than pounce it. This gives a less definite outline, but is less noticeable on a floor.

Floor stencilling is very tiring on the back muscles, so do not try to do too much at once. Also, because of the heavier pressure which tends to be exerted in this position, smears are more likely to occur. Keep a good supply of clean rags on hand to wipe them away as you go along. Be careful when lifting off the stencil not to slide it over the wet paint. Clean frequently.

The finished pattern should be left to dry for at least 24 hours before applying at least three coats of matt, semi-gloss or polyurethane varnish for protection.

Laying out a floor for stencilling

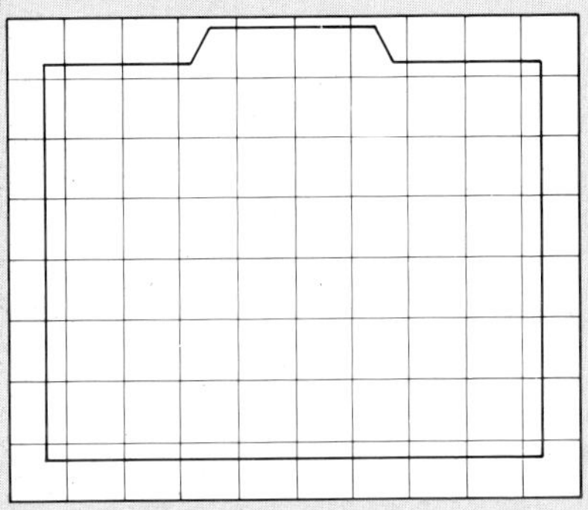

1. *Measure the floor and draw it to scale on the squared paper. To plan the layout, mark the stencil designs off along the sides of the floor plan, working from the centre of each wall.*

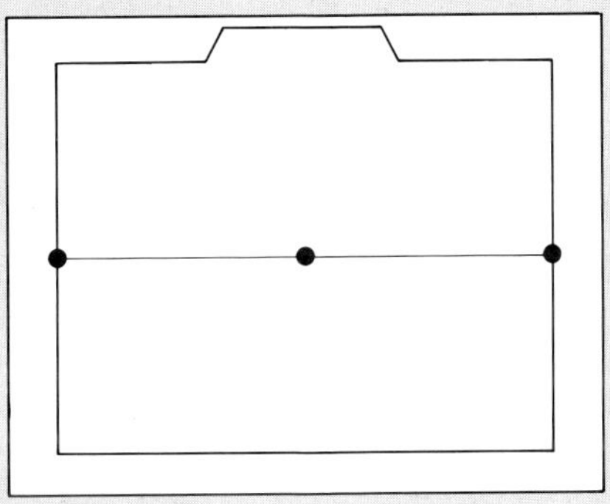

2. *Mark the centres of two opposite walls at skirting board (baseboard) level. Make a straight line across the floor between these points. The centre of this line should be the centre of the room.*

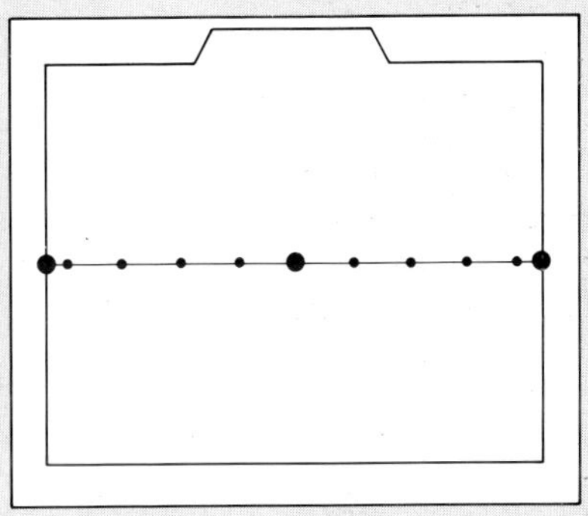

3. *Mark off the stencil widths along the centre line in both directions, working from the middle point of the floor out to the edges.*

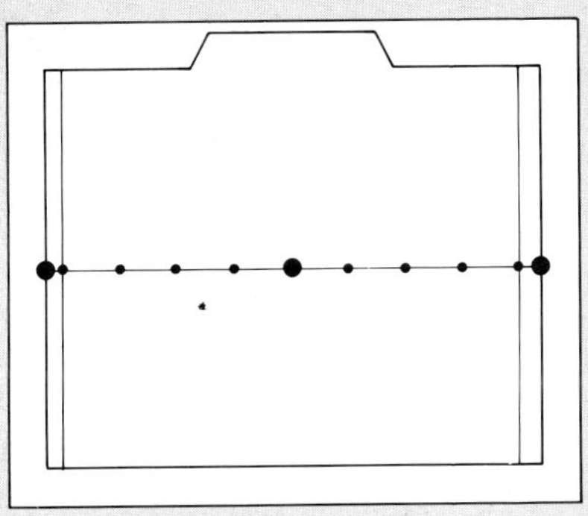

4. *At the last complete stencil position at each end, draw a line at right angles to the centre line. This will form the demarcation lines between the borders and stencilled area.*

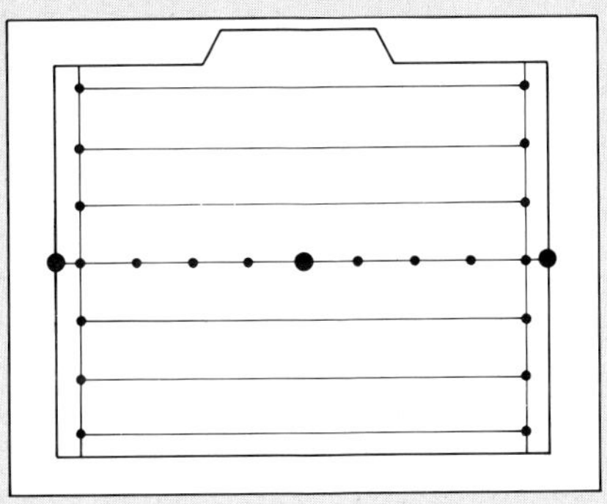

5. *Mark off the stencil widths along the two lines and join the marks. You should now have a series of parallel lines running across the room.*

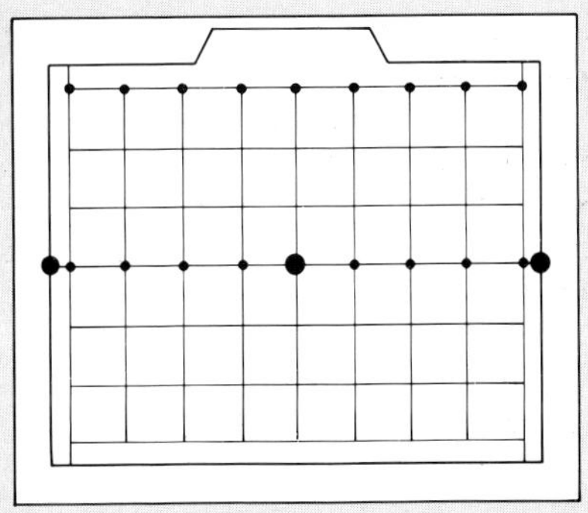

6. *Choose one of the outer lines and mark off the stencil widths from the centre outwards, joining the marks with those made on the original centre line. Extend these lines to complete the grid.*

Wallcovering

Techniques of wallcovering have not only improved over the years – the choice is far greater today than ever before. The relatively recent introduction of new materials such as vinyl, fabrics and paper/plastic combinations, together with such labour-saving innovations as pre-applied adhesives, has transformed the once arcane craft of paperhanging into a routine job for the DIY decorator.

Although these new materials would appear rather unusual to nineteenth century craftsmen, their modern descendents appreciate their excellent qualities and appearances which are compatible with traditional finishes.

Wallcovering is an attractive alternative to paint and (with the exception of such exotic coverings as silk, fabric and flock) is as easy to apply. By following a few simple rules you can achieve professional looking results, even if you have never attempted the task before.

Washable papers (those coated with a clear glaze) and the vinyls can be either flat or textured. Although not traditional, they are invaluable in areas which are subject to heavy wear and tear or have a moist atmosphere, such as children's playrooms, nurseries, kitchens and bathrooms.

More delicate coverings, like untreated paper, flocks and textured grass cloths, should be reserved for areas where appearance, rather than wear resistance, is the criterion. Some other, more unusual, coverings such as cork, woodchip, or hessian (burlap), are particularly

This richly coloured wallpaper, based on a Chinese design, could be overpowering unless it suits you and your belongings.

useful for covering uneven or badly patched surfaces. Some of these coverings will require lining – that is, an inexpensive plain paper will have to be applied to the wall before it is covered by the wallcovering.

The easiest type of wallcovering to use is known as ready-pasted (pre-pasted). This simply needs to be dipped into a trough of water in order to make the back sticky. It can then be hung straight onto the wall, thus avoiding the tedious process of mixing and applying paste.

The pattern you choose will be very important and involves more than mere aesthetic considerations. It can, for example, affect the position in the room where you start your first roll. If the pattern is small and neat, you can start from a corner or doorway without any problems but it is best to start a bold pattern over a focal point (such as a fireplace) or in the centre of a wall.

The size and type of the pattern will also dictate the number of rolls needed to complete a room. There will always be a certain amount of wastage but this will not be significant if the pattern is small and runs horizontally. Large patterns mean more waste, but off-cuts may be used both above and below windows. Where the pattern is dropped, that is, runs diagonally, pattern matching can be very difficult to achieve. However, depending on the height of the wall and length of pattern, waste can be reduced by cutting lengths from alternate rolls.

Machine-printed wallcovering rolls are cut from a single run or batch. Successive production runs can vary slightly in colour, so make sure that all your rolls have the same batch number.

With hand-printed papers, colours nearly always vary from roll to roll. Try to hang these in such a way that any slight variations are least noticeable. Remember, too, that hand-printed colours are comparatively costly and fragile. It is advisable to reserve them for areas that receive the least wear.

A reproduction floral wallpaper with predominant colours in the brown range helps to create a warm and inviting atmosphere and a cosy nineteenth century scene.

Calculating the amount of wallcovering required is simpler than calculating the amount of paint required as you do not have to allow for the porosity or smoothness of the surface. The simplest method is to measure (with either a tape measure or a roll of wallcovering) the number of roll widths around the walls and divide this number by the number of floor-to-ceiling lengths or 'drops' on a roll. Remember to allow for odd shaped areas, trimming and pattern matching.

Be generous with your estimate of rolls needed; they may be difficult to match if you want to buy more. Most suppliers will take back unused rolls.

If you are covering a surface which is in a reasonable condition, allow a full day to size (see page 94) and cover a 4m by 5m (12ft by 16ft) room. Obviously, more time will be needed if the surface needs extensive repair or if you have to remove existing paper.

Tools and equipment

Brush

A *hanging* or *smoothing* brush is used for smoothing paper on the wall.

Pure bristle brushes are best as they will not scratch the paper. A brush about 75mm (3in) long is the ideal size.

A 150mm (6in) *distemper* brush is best for applying the paste or adhesive to the paper.

Paper hangers' scissors

The ideal scissors to use are 255mm (10in) long. Professionals use much longer, special scissors known as paper hangers' scissors – about 300mm (12in) long – but these are unwieldy unless used by someone who knows how to handle them.

Pasting table

Although it is possible to use the kitchen table, it is best to use a folding table which will be used only for pasting. You will be able to move it around and it will not matter if it becomes sticky.

Plumb line

As the wallcovering must be hung truly vertical, a plumb line is an essential tool.

Seam roller

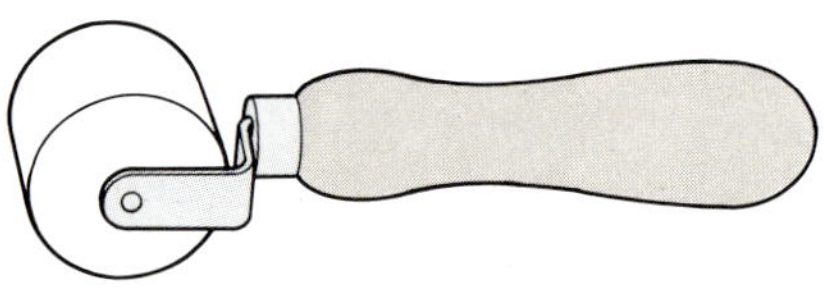

This is a small roller which flattens the join between two lengths of paper to give a smooth finish. Note that a seam roller should not be used on embossed wallcoverings.

Other items that will be needed are buckets for paste and water, steps, a cellular sponge, stripping knife, filling knife, trimming knife, clean cotton rags, abrasive paper and, of course, a pencil for marking. You may also need a casing wheel for trimming delicate paper.

If using a ready-pasted (pre-pasted) covering, the pasting equipment can be omitted. Instead, you will need a water trough, which will usually be available from wallcovering suppliers.

Preparation

Preparing a surface for wallcovering is much the same as preparing for painting, except that existing wallpaper, in almost all cases, should be removed. Papering over paper can be very risky; the moisture in the new paste can seep through the old paper and loosen its paste. If this happens, the combined weight of papers and paste will pull everything off the wall.

The paper to be removed should be soaked with a mixture of warm water and liquid wallpaper stripper for at least half-an-hour. Scoring or slitting the old covering with a paint-stripping tool or knife will help the soaking process. Use a wide stripping knife held at a shallow angle to the surface to firmly push the wet paper up from the bottom, or from one of the slits you have made. Grasp the end of the loosened paper, pull upward with a firm pressure, and it should come off easily in sizeable sections. (Do not pull it outwards, or it will rip off in your hand.) One section of the paper should be stripped while the next is being soaked.

Before hanging the covering it is best to size the surface. This comprises a water-based mixture of glue or cellulose paste which, when painted on and allowed to dry, seals the surface and provides a bonding key for the wallcovering paste.

With old, unpainted plaster surfaces, remove old wallpaper and wash the surface thoroughly to remove all traces of paste and size. Make good any defects and allow the filler to dry. Rub down to a smooth finish and apply a weak solution of size or thinned down paste. When painted on and allowed to dry, it seals the surface and prevents the wall absorbing too much moisture from the wallcovering paste before it has a chance to dry properly. It also makes sliding the new wallcovering easier.

With new plaster, provided it is sound and completely dry, there should be no problem when hanging a wallcovering. Prepare as for old plaster. If, however, there is any moisture present, hanging a wallcovering is not recommended. Sufficient time should be allowed for the plaster to dry out and any efflorescence (see page 182) formed should be removed periodically by a thorough dry brushing down. No attempt should be made to wash off the salts as they will be dissolved and re-absorbed by the plaster. Before hanging a wallcovering of this type of surface it is advisable to coat it with an alkali-resisting primer, thinned with 10 per cent paint thinner, making sure it is brushed in well. When dry, the surface should be cross lined, that is, covered with lining paper which is hung in horizontal strips.

Water paint, distemper and limewash surfaces must be thoroughly washed and scraped to remove as much of the old coatings as possible. Rinse with clean water and fill any irregularities and cracks in the surface with a plaster filler. When dry, rub this down to provide a smooth finish and prime with an oil-based stabilizing solution, thinned with 10 per cent paint thinner solution. Apply liberally and evenly, making sure no areas are missed. Allow to dry completely and cross line.

Emulsion (latex) paint surfaces may look sound, but when a pasted length of paper is hung on them a break down quite often occurs. A reliable test is to press a small strip of adhesive tape onto the emulsion paint. This should be removed immediately; if any of the paint film sticks to the tape, the surface should be primed with an oil-based stabilizing solution. If the tape is clean when removed the only preparation necessary is to apply a weak solution of size before the surface is cross lined (see below).

With oil-painted surfaces, wash down with a sugar soap (detergent) solution to remove all dirt and grease. Rinse with clean water and allow to dry. When hanging wallcoverings on this type of smooth finish, it is essential to 'key' or roughen the surface so that the paste will grip well. Usually, it is sufficient to score or scratch the surface with the use of a coarse, abrasive paper. It is also advisable to cross line this type of surface (see below).

Lining paper

Lining paper absorbs moisture from the paste, ensuring better adhesion and countering the possibility of the wallcovering shrinking. It also prevents the opening of butt joints during and after drying, particularly on non-absorbent surfaces, and provides the ideal foundation on rougher surfaces. It is not commonly found in the USA.

The material should always be hung at 90 degrees to the direction of the final wallcovering – hence the term 'cross lining'. This means that the lengths have to be hung horizontally, therefore, the long lengths required have to be gathered in short, concertina folds, similar to the method used when hanging a ceiling paper. Hang the first length along the top of the wall. The folds are then opened one by one and brushed firmly into position.

When you are hanging succeeding lengths, the edges should be either

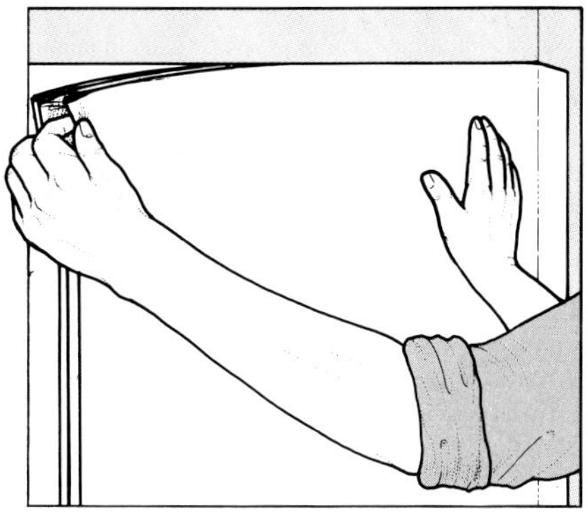

Hanging the lining paper.

placed together edge to edge or left slightly apart. Do not overlap them.

A strong paste should always be used when hanging lining paper and all joints and edges should be well pasted and brushed down firmly. Allow the paper to dry completely before covering. It is not necessary to size the lining paper before hanging a wallcovering.

Condensation quite often occurs when an oil painted surface has been decorated with a wallcovering. Thin, polystyrene wall linings can be used to combat this problem. The polystyrene veneer should be hung in accordance with the manufacturer's instructions, allowing a minimum drying time of 72 hours. The surface should then be cross lined, using a thick paste, and allowed to dry before the patterned wallcovering is hung.

Pastes and adhesives

Selecting the correct type of paste or adhesive for hanging wallcovering is very important, as an incorrect mixture can cause hanging difficulties and result in the finished job looking shoddy. There is a wide range of paste powders and ready-mixed adhesives available, all of which are formulated specially for the many types of wallcoverings.

The traditional material for paperhanger's paste used to be the best household plain flour. A similar mix is still available today. Follow the directives set out below.

The powder should first be mixed into a smooth batter, using 500ml (1 pint) of warm water. A further 4.5 litres (8 pints) of vigorously boiling water is then added to scald the paste, stirring all the time. This should have the effect of thickening up the mixture. Put the paste aside to cool and, when nearly set, pour 250ml (half pint) of cold water on the surface to prevent a surface film forming. The paste should only be used when cold.

Testing the consistency of the paste.

Normally, these quantities make a thick paste, which may require thinning with cold water to the consistency required for brushing-out. Great care is needed not to over-thin the paste. One very reliable test is to paste one corner section of the length. Take the paste brush and lay it flat on the corner of the pasted paper. If the brush lifts the length from the table the paste should be the correct strength for that particular wallcovering.

Powder adhesives are, perhaps, more convenient as they are usually mixed with cold water and can be used 15 minutes after mixing. When hanging special wallcoverings, a ready-mixed adhesive is more suitable. It has the advantage of having high adhesive properties. It is worth remembering that the more water it contains the more stretch will be experienced when the wallcovering is hung.

Hanging techniques

With certain types of wallcoverings, individual lengths may appear slightly different. Therefore, it is advisable, after hanging two or three lengths, to check that you are getting the effect you require, as most manufacturers do not allow claims for any material hung in excess of this. Also, some types are very delicate, so it is important to take great care and pay attention to detail when preparing the surface.

If you also intend to paint the woodwork or ceiling of a room, do so *before* you start hanging paper. You must also plan the starting and finishing place as, unless the perimeter of the room is an exact multiple of the pattern width, there will be an unavoidable mismatch along the edge of the last length to be hung. This will not be evident in a room that has one wall interrupted by, say, a built-in cupboard or bookcase. But in all rooms with four continuous walls you should plan ahead so that the inevitable mismatch is located in the least conspicuous place – an unobtrusive corner or over a door.

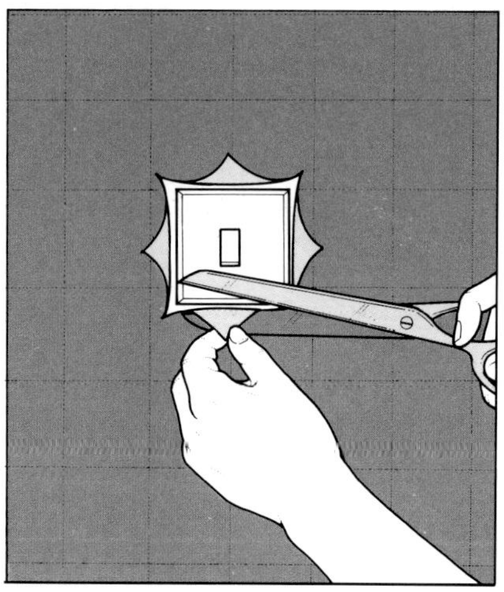

Make several cuts in a star shape.

No house has truly vertical walls, so you should establish a vertical guideline with the first length with a plumb line. Hold the line high up on the wall, near its centre, and mark the wall with a pencil at several points behind the string. Join these points with a pencil and straight edge. Re-check the alignment after hanging every few rolls, particularly after turning a corner.

When hanging patterned wallcoverings, bear in mind that the designs must be matched at the joins. It is therefore advisable to centre each wall to be decorated to give an even, balanced effect. Plan the position of the joins and mark the wall at a suitable starting point, using a plumb line and pencil. Hang the first length nearest the centre line on each wall. When decorating a wall with any external angles, avoid joining the wallcovering near the corner. All joins should be at least 50mm (2in) away from the angle.

When cutting lengths from a roll, allow at least 100mm (4in) to permit trimming at the ceiling and skirting board (baseboard).

Lay a cut length pattern-side down on the pasting table, allowing the bottom section to hang over the left side of the table. Align the edge of the paper with the back edge of the table. Paste the top section and fold it gently back over itself, so that the pattern side is uppermost. Now slide the length toward you so that the unpasted lower section is on the table and the pasted upper section is hanging over the edge. Paste the lower section and fold it onto itself so that the upper edge of the length almost touches the lower edge.

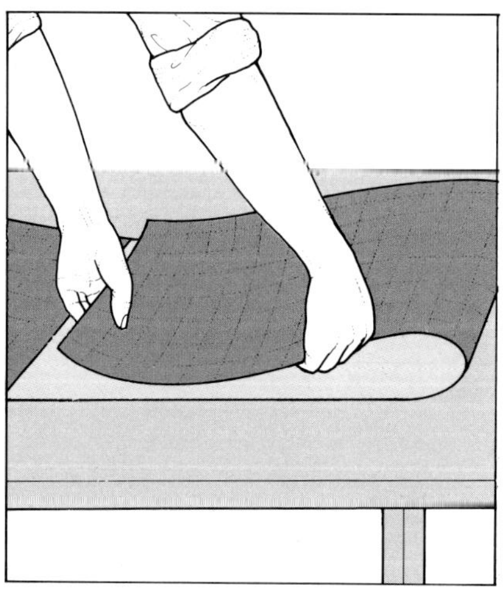

Fold the pasted section back onto itself.

For a wall length, fold with a large fold at the top and a smaller fold at the lower end.

When pasting, brush off the table to ensure an even coating of paste on the edge of the paper. To avoid marking the face of the wallcovering, move the length to the other edges of the table, pasting each section before folding the paper over.

When hanging a wallcovering with a delicate surface, it is essential at all times to keep the paste from the face of the material and it is advisable, therefore, to have only one length on the table at a time.

Set the pasted length aside to soak (see the manufacturer's instructions for the length of time required for this) and start pasting the next length. While that is soaking, you can be hanging the first length.

Roll ready-pasted (pre-pasted) paper loosely from bottom to top with the pattern inside and place in a trough of water. Place your stepladder in front of the trough, which should be below the section of the wall to be covered. With the pattern facing you, draw up the wallcovering as you climb the ladder and hang it immediately.

Inner corners are often out of true; if you try to bend more than a narrow slip around a corner, the paper will wrinkle. Professionals split a length so that one strip extends about 8mm (5⁄16in) around the corner, while the other strip is hung on the adjacent wall, just overlapping the first. This also allows for correct alignment on the adjacent wall. As the overlap is in the corner it is not noticeable.

At a chimney breast, start by hanging a length of wallcovering in the centre of the breast and then work back to the outer corners, allowing a 25mm (1in) turnround at the corners. This is particularly critical with patterned paper as this is the focal point of the room. Trim along the mantelpiece and remove as much waste as possible before smoothing into place. Cut to fit the mouldings beneath the mantelpiece.

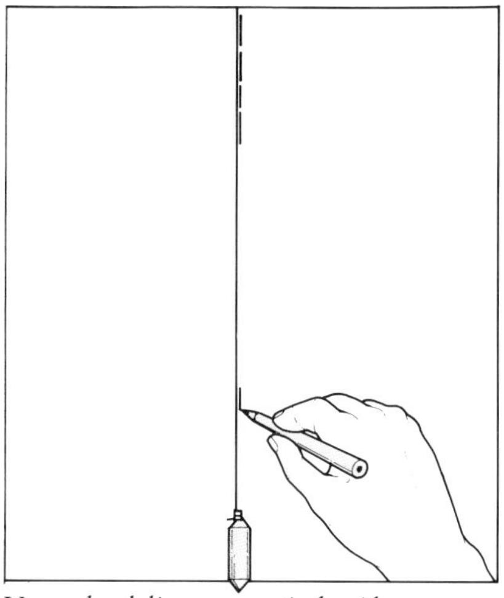

Use a plumb line as a vertical guide.

Before papering round an electrical fitting, turn off the power at the mains. Make a number of cuts in the covering in a star shape, starting at the centre of the fitting and radiating outwards to approximately 20mm (¾in) beyond the edges of the fitting. Trim off the waste and smooth the paper back into place.

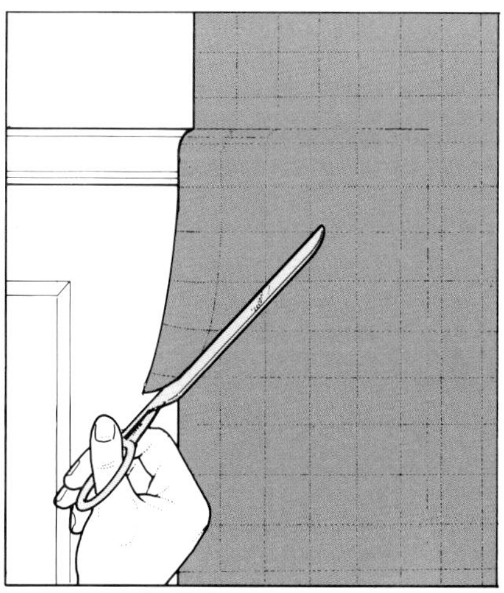

Cut the paper out towards the corner.

Where you find door frames, make a rough trimming line by running the back of the scissors which are kept slightly open along the paper at the edge of the frame. Cut along this line and make sure to press it into the angle before trimming. Then smooth into position with a hanging brush.

How to hang wallcoverings

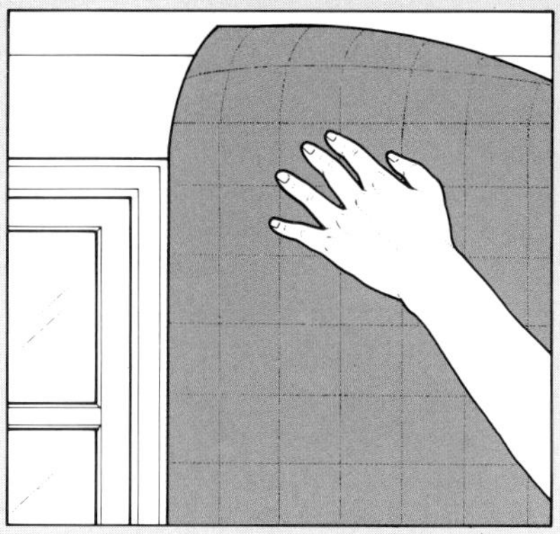

1. *Unfold the top section of the length, starting at the ceiling line and allowing a 50mm (2in) overlap for trimming. To avoid stretching, place the matching edge into position.*

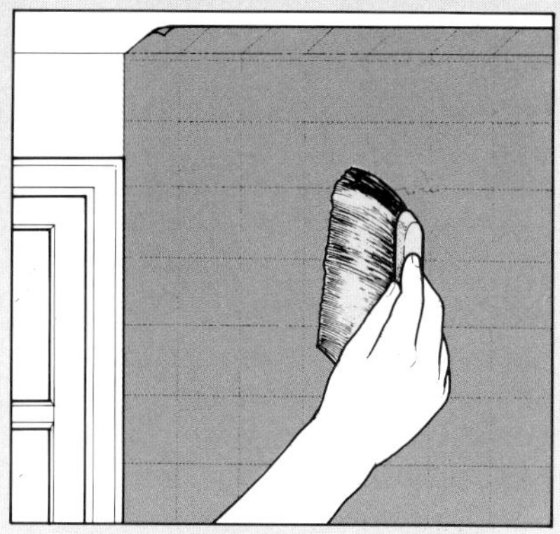

2. *Run the smoothing brush down the top half, working from the matching edge to eliminate air bubbles.*

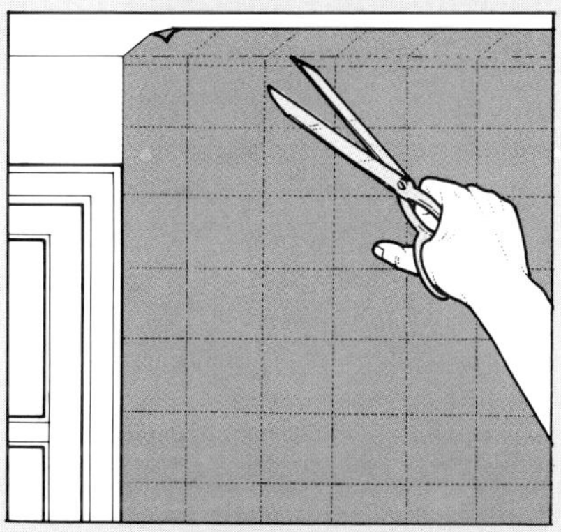

3. *Run the scissors' blade back, with the scissors slightly open, along the angles between wall and ceiling.*

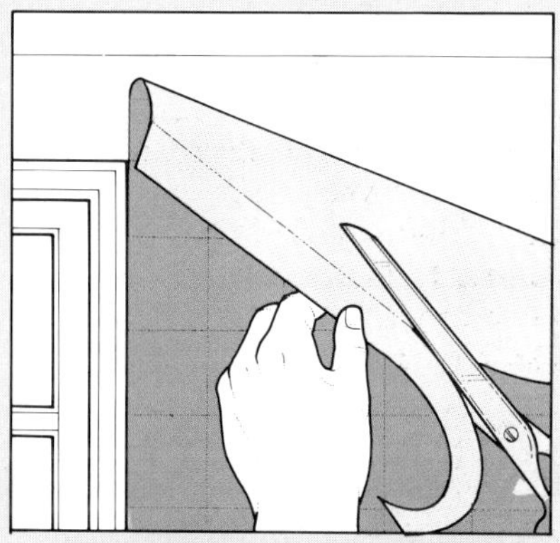

4. *Pull the paper back and trim it neatly with scissors. Wipe any excess paste from the ceiling and skirting boards and then brush the paper back into position.*

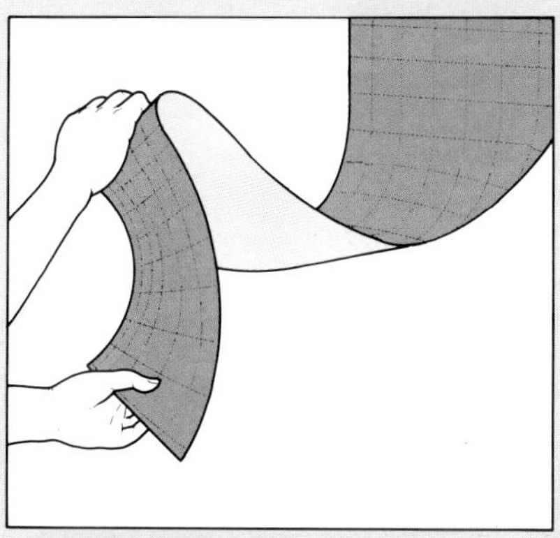

5. *When you have finished the top section, unfurl the bottom half and repeat the smoothing action with the brush.*

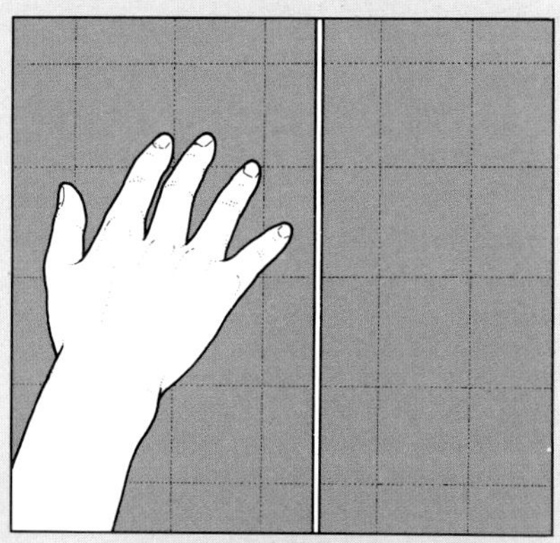

6. *Place the next length of paper on the wall and slide it into position so that the pattern matches and forms an exact butt joint with the first length.*

Lincrusta

Since it was first manufactured in the late nineteenth century, lincrusta has proved to be one of the most distinctive and durable wallcoverings ever produced. (It is not, however, available in the USA.)

Lincrusta is perfect for areas of heavy wear and tear. Its great advantage is that it disguises wall surface imperfections, and its elegant designs can be redecorated indefinitely. Unlike other wallcoverings, it can be produced in a deep relief, providing a range of interesting texture designs and accurate reproductions of wood patterns. After preparing the material, a special lincrusta glue should be applied. Before hanging, it is essential to make sure that the wall surface is firm and dry. A cross lining is recommended when using this material (see page 95) and an adhesive containing a fungicide.

The natural colour of the material is off-white and the textured designs should be painted with an oil-based matt or semi-matt finish. Emulsion (latex) or rubber-based paints are not recommended. As an alternative to painting lincrusta, many patterns, particularly the wood effects, may be decorated with a scumble and wipe (see page 87) technique. When creating a natural wood effect, the desired colour of oil scumble can be applied direct to the unpainted lincrusta surface. If a special shade is required, the lincrusta should be coated with a suitable colour of matt oil paint first.

The coloured scumble is diluted with paint thinner until the desired shade is produced. It is advisable to test the shade on a spare piece of material first. Apply the scumble evenly over an area of approximately 2sq m (2sq yd) at a time, brushing the colour well into the texture of the design. Immediately following this, take a pad of dry cotton cloth and wipe the scumble from the surface, leaving the colour in the recessed grain and detail. The harder you wipe, the more colour you will remove.

Always wipe in the same direction, or with the grain, when producing a wood effect. Allow the scumble to dry completely and, for extra protection, apply a polyurethane eggshell or matt varnish.

Preparation

Always handle lincrusta carefully to avoid damaging or cracking its surface. Cut individual lengths to size, allowing extra for trimming at the top and bottom. Match the pattern and mark each length at the top. Following the marked guideline on each edge, trim off the waste with a sharp knife and steel straight edge. Hold the knife at an angle to undercut the material to provide a more accurate butt join between lengths. When trimming, protect the table with a clean strip of hardboard.

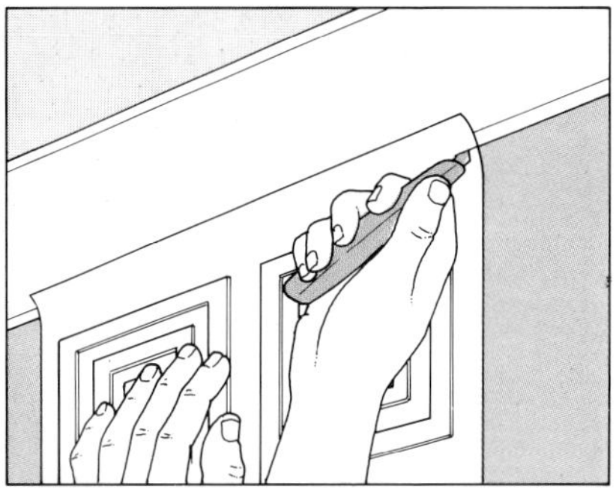

Mark the dry length of material at the top.

Sponge the reverse side of each length with hot water and leave to soak for 20 to 30 minutes. For best results, place the lengths back to back while soaking. This will expand the material to its fullest extent and will prevent blisters when hanging. After soaking, wipe the back of each piece dry.

Hanging

For hanging, hold the dried length of lincrusta in place on the wall and mark each side of the material at the top. Trim through the two marks to ensure a perfect fit at the ceiling, leaving the surplus at the bottom for trimming off when hanging. Any special cutting, around light switches or doors, for example, should be completed before pasting.

Apply the adhesive with a clean 75mm (3in) paint brush, making sure all the edges are well pasted. For extra long lengths, a mohair paint roller should be used to speed up the application. If the lincrusta glue is too thick to spread, stir it well to make it into a usable consistency. Immediately after pasting, hang the length on the wall. Smooth down, using a 100mm (4in) rubber roller or a warm, wet cloth, working away from the matching edge.

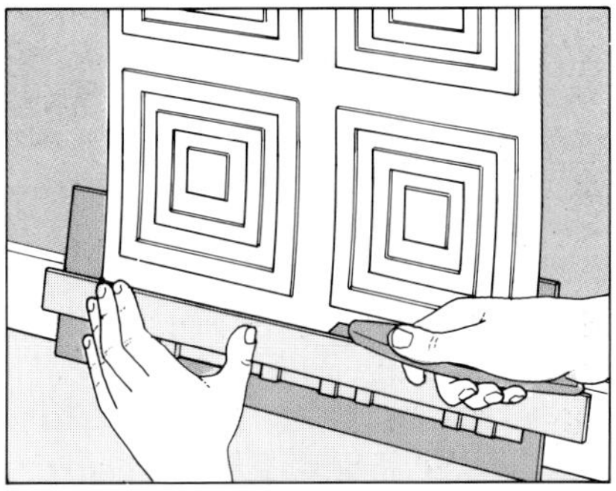

Cut the paper at the bottom.

Mark the length on each side at the skirting (baseboard) level. Place a strip of hardboard (deeper than the skirting board) behind the paper and cut through the two marks, using a straight edge and sharp knife. Brush down. Wipe any surplus adhesive from paintwork or from the surface of the lincrusta with a sponge. Make sure you hang subsequent lengths in the same manner, butt joining the edges. Check often to ensure not to overlap the lengths.

Taking lincrusta round internal and external corners is only practicable with some of the designs, and then only if the corners are rounded. When the angles are sharp, the material should be cut at the corner with a bevel edge so they will form a mitre joint (see page 21).

Allow the lincrusta to dry for at least 24 hours. Before applying any decoration, the surface should be wiped clean with paint thinner to remove any dirt and grease.

Flock wallpaper

Flocked wallpapers are a traditional decoration, closely resembling velvet and brocade hangings which they are designed to imitate. They are made by gluing silk, nylon or wool cuttings to the surface of the paper so that the design stands out in relief and has a noticeable pile similar to cut velvet.

Flocks originally consisted of shearings of wool which were dyed and then scattered on cloth or canvas which had been previously coated with adhesive or varnish. The result – if the dye was red – was a fairly good imitation of red velvet. The latter used to be both desirable and expensive, so the cheap substitute was much sought after.

By the end of the seventeenth century, the process was applied to paper and today flock papers are produced in a variety of designs and colourings. There is an increasing demand for the traditional patterns which are required to replace damaged or destroyed originals.

The paper needs very careful placing, trimming and cutting as mistakes cannot be easily rectified – and sometimes cannot be retified at all. Modern flocks may have a vinyl finish; these do not need soaking and, once pasted, can be hung immediately. Edges should be butt joined, that is, edge to edge, as it is impossible to stick the overlap with thick paste. When cutting, make sure to use a straight edge and a very sharp knife. Peel back the edge, apply more paste and roll the edge back in. Wipe off surplus paste with a sponge. Roll firmly into position with a roller covered with cloth or chamois leather. The surface of flock is very delicate, so when rolling into position hold a clean piece of thin paper on the surface to protect the pattern, which can otherwise become very easily crushed.

(above) *Traditionally designed flock wallpapers are very suitable for hallways.*

(right) *The autumn colours of this elaborate flock wallpaper bring out the rich tones of the wood, creating a pleasant atmosphere.*

Hessian (burlap)

Hessian (burlap) and natural weaves are popular wallcoverings in the fabric range. These materials are accessible and relatively cheap and, although the natural colour is buff, the materials can be dyed to suit your own taste. The material is provided either unbacked or with a paper backing. There is an attractive range of coloured weave effects. The rolls are usually trimmed. Any loose strands of material on the edges should be very carefully cut off – removing by any other method could damage the fabric.

A ready-mixed adhesive is recommended. Do not let any of the paste smear the face of the material.

When hanging an unbacked material, a 'paste-the-wall' technique should be used. If the unbacked hessian (burlap) has an open weave so that you can see through the colour, the surface or lining paper should match the colour of the wallcovering as closely as possible. Unfortunately, lining papers are often only available in an off-white finish, so paint with emulsion (latex) paint first. Allow this colour to dry before hanging the wallcovering.

Manufacturers sometimes recommend reversing alternate lengths when hanging fabrics.

Method

For paper-backed material, cut the material into the required lengths, allowing 50mm (2in) top and bottom for final trimming. Mark the top on the reverse side with a pencil and roll up each individual length with the top as the loose end.

Apply the paste liberally, but evenly, (as described on page 96) to the paper backing, paying particular attention to the edges. After pasting, fold the length carefully, back to back, and leave for approximately 10 minutes. (Always check the product label for the manufacturer's recommended soaking time.)

Carefully place the length into position at the top. Smooth down, working outwards from the matching edge, using a clean felt-covered, or a mohair, paint roller. Check for any air bubbles or blisters. Press the fabric well into the angle at the ceiling and skirting (baseboard) level, using a metal or plastic strip.

Trim off the surplus material using paper hangers' scissors.

Hang the other lengths, pushing the edges together. If necessary, carefully roll the edges flat with a seam roller, protecting the surface with a clean strip of tissue paper.

At internal angles, push the material into the corner with a thin metal or plastic strip. When hanging the fabric around an external corner, all edges should be at least 50mm (2in) away from the corner.

For hanging unbacked material, cut to the required lengths and roll each length from bottom to top. Using a mohair paint roller, apply the adhesive to the wall surface, covering an area slightly wider than the material. Keeping the hessian (burlap) rolled up, place the top section into position, leaving the required overlap at the ceiling. Smooth the material using a felt or mohair paint roller. Follow the guide line on the wall, keeping the face of the fabric from the pasted wall. Leave for approximately 10 minutes before trimming.

If the edges of the hessian are damaged, overlap approximately 25mm (1in) of material at the edges of adjacent lengths. Leave for a few minutes and cut vertically through both layers of the material with a sharp knife. Remove the two waste strips of fabric, re-pasting the wall if necessary, and carefully smooth back the edges to make a neat join.

An ebonized screen contrasts with the rough texture of hessian wallpaper.

Grasscloth

These very attractive papers are manufactured by laminating natural grass and synthetic yarns to a paper backing. The material normally requires trimming before hanging. Because the materials used are natural, there may be colour variation, particularly at the edges. To overcome any problems this might cause, it is advisable to reverse alternate lengths.

Grasscloth papers can be pasted in the normal way and a ready-mixed paste is recommended. Make sure the pasting table is perfectly clean; if necessary, cover with a strip of lining paper.

Method

Cut the material to the required lengths, allowing 50mm (2in) top and bottom for final trimming. Mark the top and bottom with a pencil on the reverse side of the material. Carefully roll up each length with the loose end as the starting edge.

Trim approximately 13mm (½in) from each edge, using an extra sharp knife and steel straight edge. Protect the table with a clean strip of hardboard. When trimming, follow a suitable part of the design.

Apply the paste liberally, but evenly, (as described on page 96) to the top section of the paper, using a clean short-bristle paste brush and paying particular attention to the edges. After pasting very carefully, fold over the length and leave to soak for a short time. Do not allow the paper to soak too long as this could cause delamination. When hanging a heavyweight grasscloth it is advisable to apply a thin coating of paste to the wall as well.

Place the top of the length into position. Smooth down, using a clean, dry felt or mohair paint roller and taking care not to allow any adhesive to contact the surface of the material. Press the fabric well into the angle at ceiling and skirting (baseboard) levels, using a thin metal or plastic trimming blade.

Gentle, textured wallpaper, such as the oriental grasscloth shown in the picture above, provides an excellent background for exotic furnishings.

Trim off the surplus material, using the thin metal or plastic strip and an extra sharp knife to prevent fraying. Another method sometimes used is to allow the adhesive to dry completely before trimming in the normal way. This avoids problems of shrinkage.

Hang other lengths, pushing the edges together. When using a seam roller, protect the wallcovering with a clean strip of tissue paper.

At internal angles push the wallcovering into the corner, using a plastic or metal strip. When hanging the wallcovering around an external corner, it is essential to make sure that any edges are at least 50mm (2in) away from the corner.

Metalwork and Metalware

Metal has been used to make domestic appliances for thousands of years but it was not until the eighteenth century that metal, principally iron, was used in significant amounts for constructional purposes. Then it was used to bolt and bracket wooden frames and to construct the structural members.

Although grander houses had employed various metals, largely for decorative purposes, for many years metal only became a significant part of ordinary domestic houses when cast iron became cheap and plentiful. Traditionally, wrought iron, worked by blacksmiths and locksmiths, had been used for fireplace equipment, decorative fittings, gates, railing and door furniture, but it was expensive so these items were not in general use.

The industrial revolution made cast iron available for uses for which it had hitherto been denied. Soon, balconies, railings, fire surrounds and many other pieces of architectural metalware were able to be made to much higher standards of decorative finish at low cost in cast iron.

One of the biggest jobs any home owner is likely to have to face with an old house is the replacement of cast iron balustrades balcony support. Usually it will be easier to have professionals undertake the work because it is is certain they will understand how the work was done originally and how repairs must be carried out. For instance, nineteenth century railings were usually anchored to the masonry by lead-filled cavities which prevented the ironwork rusting away too quickly and decorative finials were often made, not of iron, but of lead or brass.

If your home is 50 to 100 years old, and has escaped the ravages of previous owners, you are likely to have to deal with cast iron fittings such as fire surrounds and stoves and, perhaps, copper alloy door and window furniture.

Care of domestic articles, such as cooking utensils and fireplace equipment, will often demand more care and skill. However, the pleasure of seeing a renovated coal scuttle or copper kettle will make it worthwhile. Before you tackle any job, consider the risks – whether to life and limb or financial. Objects made in precious metals are best repaired by craftsman, and roof supports by qualified construction engineers. If you do decide to tackle a job, use the appropriate materials.

(left) *Polished copper kitchen utensils and an oven range.*

(above) *An ornate wrought iron stair bannister.*

Tools and equipment

Hammers and mallets

An engineer's ball pein hammer is the most versatile tool for general hammering and is essential for riveting. If the faces are polished to a mirror finish, a small ball pein hammer can also be used for planishing or sinking.

A hide mallet is useful as it does not leave hammer marks on soft metal – provided that the head is kept free from metal particles.

Bossing mallets, planishing and raising hammers are all special purpose tools necessary for serious beaten metalwork.

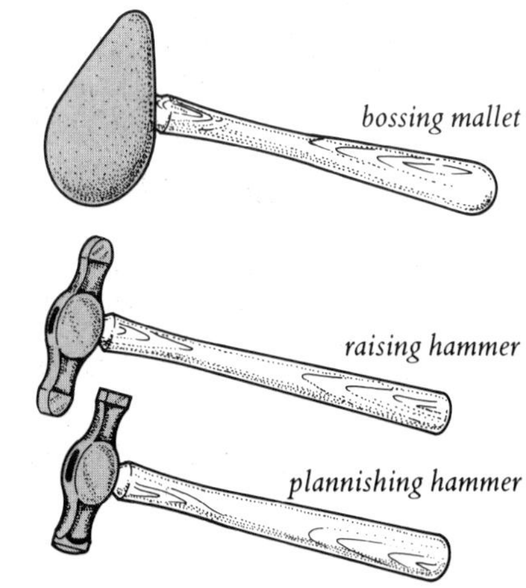

Heating equipment

A propane blowtorch is a most versatile tool, which can be used for annealing, soft and hard soldering and brazing. Oxy-acetylene equipment gives much more concentrated heat, but needs considerable skill to operate. It is also expensive to purchase and maintain. However, it is necessary if you intend to gas weld steel.

Hole cutting equipment

A two-speed or, better still, a variable speed drill are the best options. Single speed drills run too fast for most bits and will 'burn' or blunt them. A set of high speed bits ranging from 2mm (3/32in) to 10mm (3/8in) will cover most requirements and, unless you replace them as they become blunt, you will need a grindstone to sharpen them. This must be power operated as two hands are necessary to hold the drill while it is being sharpened. A drill mounted grindstone is quite suitable.

Other tools and equipment necessary have been mentioned where appropriate in the following text.

Saws and files

A hacksaw is a general purpose tool for cutting all metals. Different blades are available to suit varying thicknesses and types of metal. High speed steel blades are the hardest and will last longest, provided that they are not bent or twisted, in which case they will shatter. Low tungsten blades are cheaper and will stand more abuse. A junior (mini) hacksaw is cheap and useful for small sections. If you wish to make curved cuts, however, you will need a tension file and frame.

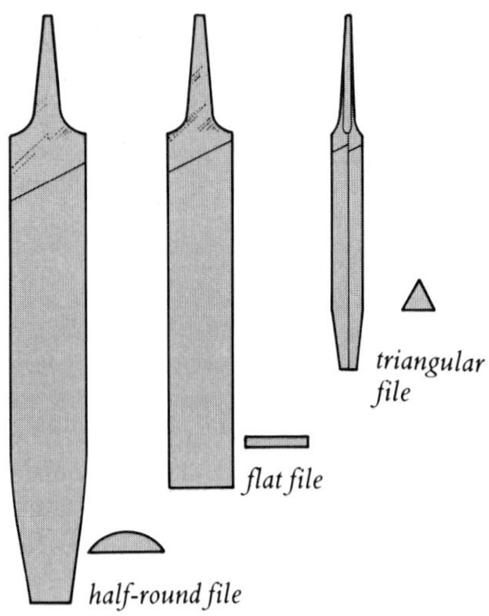

Files are available in many shapes and sizes. As a suggestion, the following three files will cope with most home metalwork: a 250mm (10in) bastard half round, a 200mm (8in) second cut hand and a 150 mm (6in) smooth three square. They should all be fitted with handles.

Rehardening a tool

Edge tools can be rehardened, but the result will not be as effective as the manufactured hardness, nor will it run the entire length of the tool.

The first step is to heat the end of the blade with a blow-torch. When it is cherry red, quench it in cold water and clean it with a fine emery cloth until it is bright and shiny.

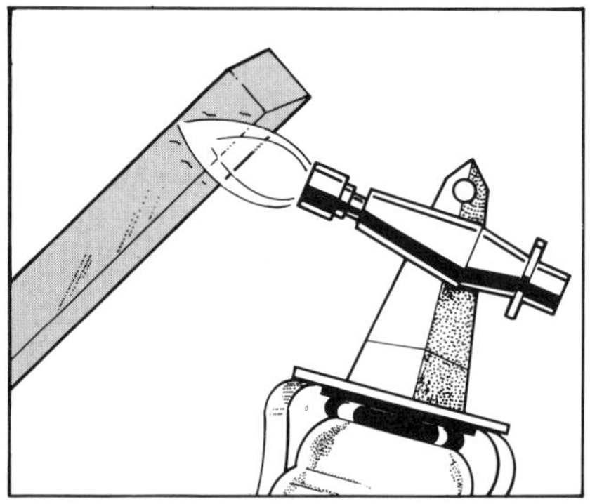

Heating the blade with a blowtorch.

The blade will now be very hard but also brittle. To temper the blade, turn down the flame on the blowtorch and apply it to the blade, about 25mm (1in) behind the cutting edge. As the blade slowly heats up, two bands of colour will appear on each side of the flame. The colour of the bands will change from straw colour to brown, then purple, dark blue, light blue and finally to grey. As more heat is absorbed, these different coloured bands will move away from the flame, up and down the blade, with the straw colour leading. Watch the band moving toward the cutting edge carefully and be ready for it to move faster as it travels down the bevel to the edge.

Immediately the edge turns from brown to light purple, quench the blade in cold water. The tip is now re-tempered and may be honed to a keen edge on an oilstone (whetstone). If you wait too long before quenching and overheat, the entire operation will have to be repeated.

Once re-tempered in this way the blade will be able to be used until about 3mm (1/8in) has been ground away. The edge will then be soft again and you will have to repeat the hardening and tempering process.

Ferrous metals

(left) *The blacksmith's forge is one of the traditional places for working ferrous metals. In this picture work is being carried out on a scroll. Some of the specialist tools used can be seen hanging on the walls.*

(above) *The footscrapers are made from cast iron which is poured molten into a sand mould.*

Ferrous metals include wrought iron, cast iron and steel. In the eighteenth century, iron became the new wonder material. The industrial revolution, which started in Europe and spread to America, was based on it, and its use in domestic architecture and household metalware increased markedly. Wrought iron had already been in use for a long time, being worked by blacksmiths for structural and decorative ironwork. Alas, it is now virtually unobtainable, despite several points in its favour; for example, it has a good resistance to corrosion and is very easy to work.

At the beginning of the eighteenth century, a new method of casting iron, using coke instead of charcoal, was devised. Gradually, wrought iron became replaced by cast iron. This form of the metal proved to be much more versatile than its predecessor and allowed for intricate designs which made it far more attractive for domestic purposes.

Cast iron is poured in its molten state into a suitably shaped mould, normally made from sand. When the iron cools it is in the required shape. Once cooled, the iron is very hard and brittle and cannot be worked or misshapen, but will break if struck very hard or dropped. If you are using cast iron, it is wise to paint it – preferably with bitumen as it will rust if exposed to air. Any damage to cast iron can only effectively be repaired by welding, using special techniques which are best left to professionals.

Today, steel is the most commonly used of all metals. It is an alloy of iron and carbon, with other metals added to give it its special properties. In its most common form it is known as mild steel and contains less than 0.5 per cent carbon. Mild steel is a relatively easy metal to work. It can be bent cold or formed into complicated shapes when heated to red heat and is readily available in many forms.

Two forms of mild steel are obtainable: black, which is shaped when hot and covered in scale with slightly rounded corners, and bright, which is more accurately rolled when cold and has sharper corners. Black is easily formed or bent, whereas bright has some stresses left in the surfaces which make it more difficult to bend. Most decorative ironwork is now produced using mild steel.

If the carbon content is slightly increased, it can then be hardened and tempered by heat treatment. This steel is known as high carbon steel and is used for most handtools.

How to form mild steel

Black mild steel is the modern equivalent to wrought iron. It can be used to make such items as shelf brackets, garden furniture, wrought iron gates and plant hangers.

It is quite possible to bend black mild steel cold, provided light sections are used. However, if heavier sections or very complicated shapes are required, heat is necessary to form the metal.

The traditional method of heating steel for forming purposes is to use a forge. However, provided the sections are not too large and a reflective (fireproof) backing of firebricks is set up, a blowtorch can be used equally effectively.

A blacksmith uses an anvil to shape his work on – this is undoubtedly the best piece of equipment to use for forming metal, but usually it is possible to substitute a large steel block. If you are thinking of making scrolls you will also need a substitute for the beak of the anvil; a steel bar tapering down from about 75mm (3in) to 12mm (½in) may be held rigidly in a vice to carry out most operations.

When forging steel, the bar is heated to orange heat. The scale is quickly brushed off, using a wire brush, and the steel is then beaten into shape on the anvil. If a sharp bend is made over the edge of the anvil, the compression of the steel on the inside of the bend causes the bar to become a little wider in the vicinity of the bend. This is easily rectified by laying the bar on its side and hammering the edges back into line while still hot.

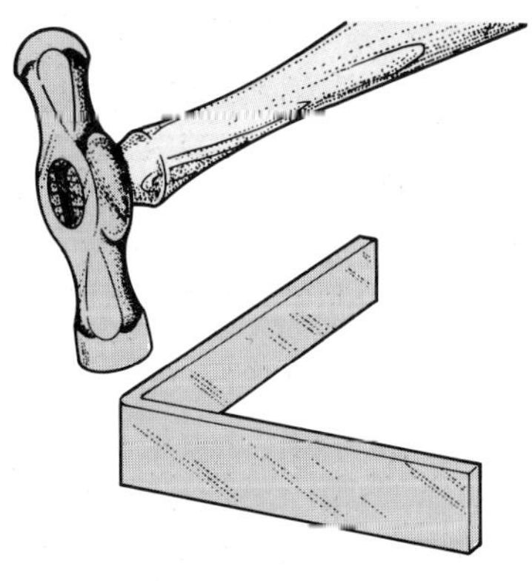

A steel bar is laid on its side and the edges hammered while it is still hot.

Drawing down to a point

This is a useful technique when using a steel rod. You may wish to reform the point of a fine poker or make a gate or fence railing.

The steel is heated to orange heat and a short, blunt point is hammered out first. This is to prevent a hole or 'pipe' forming up the middle of the point. Then the point is progressively tapered to the required shape by holding it at the correct angle on the anvil and hammering, reheating as necessary.

Drawing down to a point

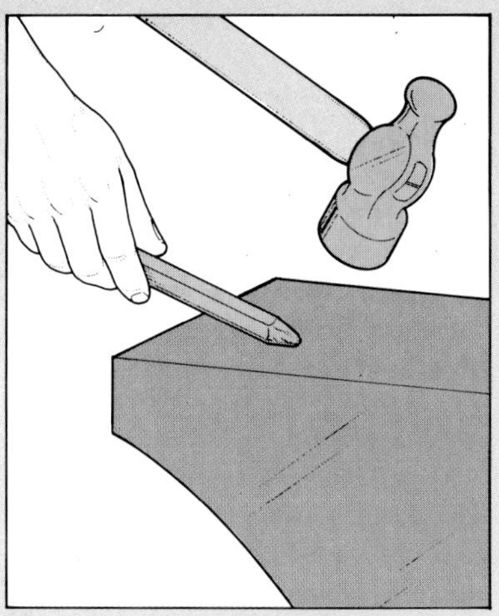

1. *Hammer out a short, blunt point.*

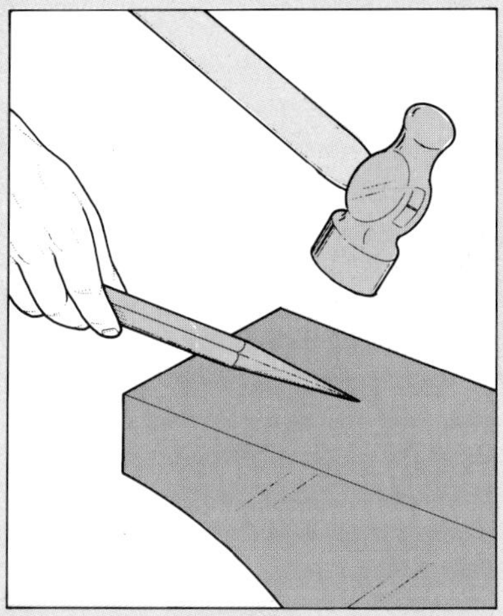

2. *Taper to the correct shape by drawing out the point.*

Scrolls

Scrolls are the traditional decoration used in most wrought iron objects such as old style light fittings and chandeliers. Even in modern homes they make attractive decorations for shelf supports and other brackets.

The true forged scroll has the thickness of the steel tapering during the scroll, with the inside of the scroll down to about 2mm (3⁄32in). The forging also causes the width of the bar to increase, with the result that the inside of the scroll stands out from the rest of it.

To produce a scroll, first draw out the desired shape full size, preferably in chalk on the floor where the figure can be used as a template to shape the work to.

Take a piece of wire, bend it into the required shape and cut it to length. Next, straighten out the wire and measure it. The measurements will give you the correct lengths to which your steel strip should be cut. Heat the end of the steel strip to orange heat and hammer down the thickness in a long, slow taper to about 2mm (3⁄32in). As you proceed, the strip will become wider as the thickness reduces. Reheat the end and bend it to 90 degrees for a length of 10mm (3⁄8in). Turn the strip over and gently tap the upturned end over into a 'U' shape. Reheat, if necessary; place over the edge of the anvil with the 'U' down and gently start to curve the centre of the scroll.

In the probable absence of a blacksmith's scrolling iron tool, the scroll is made by careful hammering over the beak of the anvil until the desired shape is obtained. If more than one scroll is to be made, as long as you work slowly and take great care, the first scroll may be used as a scrolling iron to form the other scrolls. Watch very attentively when reheating the scrolls; because

How to make a scroll

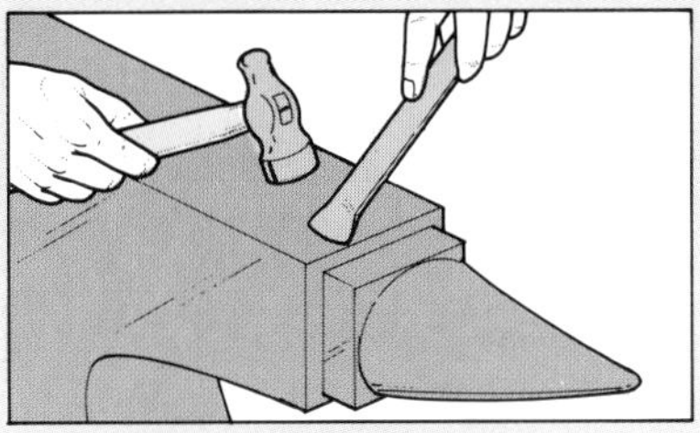

1. *Hammer down the thickness of the metal to form a long, slow taper.*

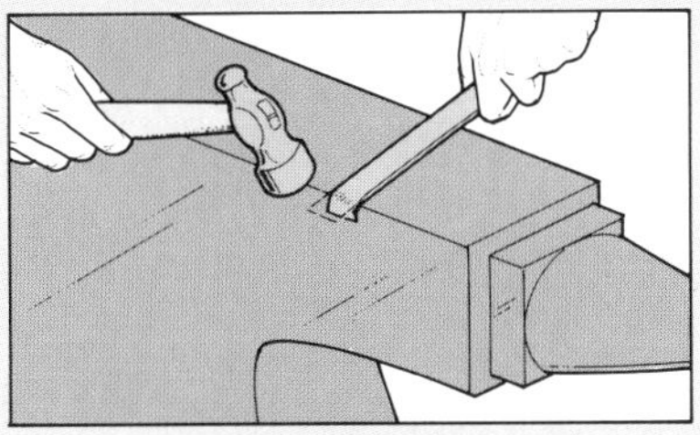

2. *Hammer 10mm (3/8in) of metal over the anvil edge to a 90 degree angle.*

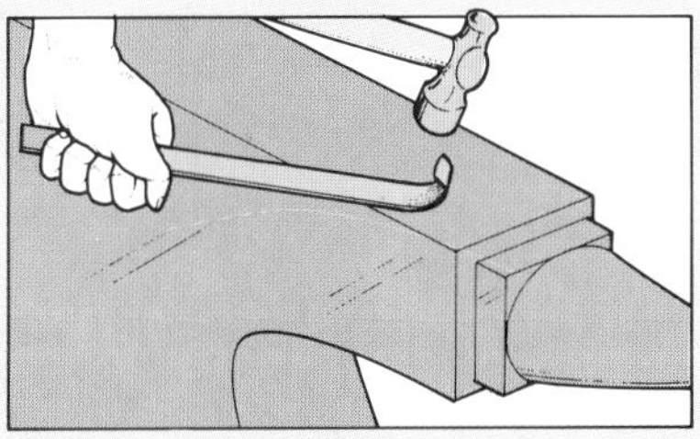

3. *Turn the strip over and hammer it into a 'U' shape.*

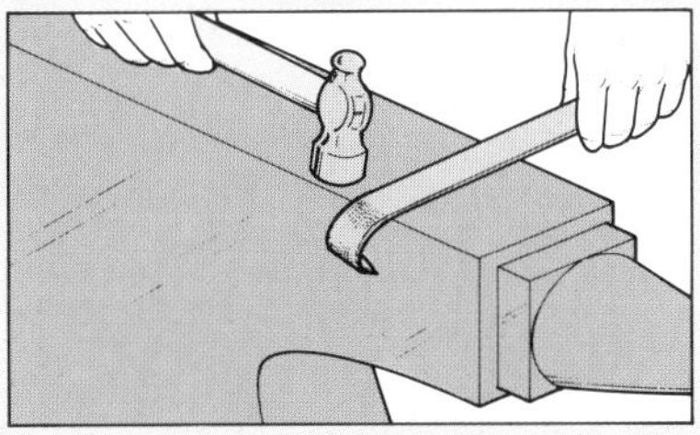

4. *Turn the tip of the metal over the anvil edge.*

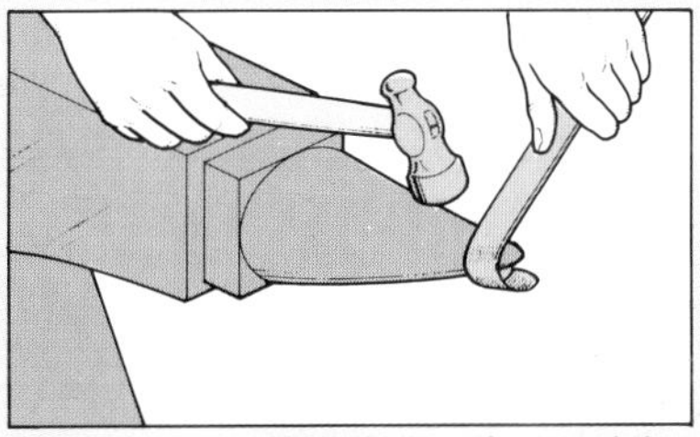

5. *Continue rolling the scroll around the beak of the anvil.*

This wrought iron gate combines scrolls and latticework. Less ornate gates can be purchased for a reasonable price.

the end is thinner than the body of the scroll it will heat up much more quickly and could easily melt.

Forge welding was a process used extensively by blacksmiths, and can be seen on genuine wrought ironwork. The most common example is where one scroll is seen to grow out of another. Two pieces of metal were heated to bright orange in the forge; a sprinkle of silver sand acted as a flux; and the two pieces were hammered together to become one piece of wrought iron work.

Joining steel

When restoring an old house, or even extending a new one, you may need to join steel. Steel may be joined in two ways, providing either a temporary or permanent fix. Using nuts and bolts is normally regarded as a temporary method; alternatively, if the steel is thick enough, a thread may be cut into one piece and a setscrew fitted through a hole in the other piece. For more permanent application, use riveting (see page 112) or one of the joining methods using heat. Hard soldering (see page 112) and brazing give a reasonably strong joint. Welding gives the strongest joint.

Brazing

Brazing is a relatively modern jointing process which may be used for joints in all steel items around the house. However, it should not be used on any joint vital for safety, such as a car chassis or cycle frame repairs, unless you happen to be a very competent metalworker.

You are likely to need to use brazing to repair non structural but heavy duty items, such as water tank brackets or gate and fence supports. And it is relatively easy to braze a security grill for a window, using a simple grid design.

A blowtorch, bronze brazing rods and borax flux are all required. See the box below.

Brazing is essentially a capillary jointing process, so no gap should be present in the joint before it is brazed together. If gaps have to be filled with a brazing rod the joint will be weak and difficult to make. A properly brazed joint, however, is very strong. Do not forget to boil off the excess flux after making the joint to prevent corrosion.

Welding

Welding is the process of joining together two pieces of steel using a steel filler rod. When skilfully carried out, welding produces a joint as strong as, or stronger than, the steel that it is joining. However, it is important not to use the method for structural repairs or alterations unless you are confident of your ability. The two main methods used today are gas and electric arc welding.

Gas, or oxy-acetylene, welding requires considerable skill and is probably best left to professionals. However, electric arc welding is worth mastering as it uses small, inexpensive welding sets. A low voltage, high amperage current flows through a flux-coated electrode and the arc produced when the electrode approaches the work melts both the work and the electrode. The resultant molten metal fills the gap and joins the pieces together. This is an easier process to use than gas welding, especially on thin metal sections. It is very important, however, to take note of one particular danger: the light emitted by the arc is so intense that it can damage the retina of your eye, leading to a painful temporary eye condition. To prevent this, use the full face shield provided with the equipment – and only this. Dark glasses are not sufficient. Anyone standing nearby who may glance at the sudden light is also required to use the face shield.

Detailed instructions on the use of the equipment are provided by the manufacturer and, after a few hours' practice, quite good welds may be made by the inexperienced amateur enthusiast.

Older houses often have cast iron fittings which are liable to break if they receive a sharp impact. Cast iron can be welded and this is recommended if the damaged area is adjacent to direct heat as in a fire surround, or is in an area where stress is applied. However, if neither of these situations apply, the crack can be repaired using an appropriate adhesive. The joint must be thoroughly cleaned and the pieces carefully bedded together. They should then be tapped into position and, when dry, the back can be strengthened with the fibreglass used for auto repairs.

How to braze

1. *Clean the ends to be joined back to bright metal with emery cloth or a coarse file. Flux with borax.*

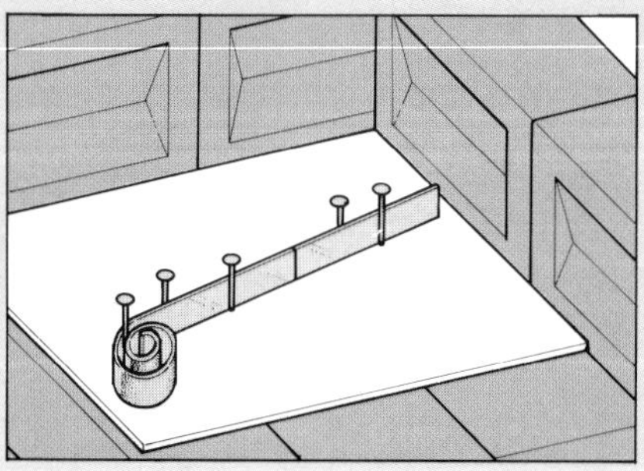

2. *Surround the pieces with fire bricks and place on an asbestos mat. Clamp the pieces together and heat the area around the joint to bright red heat.*

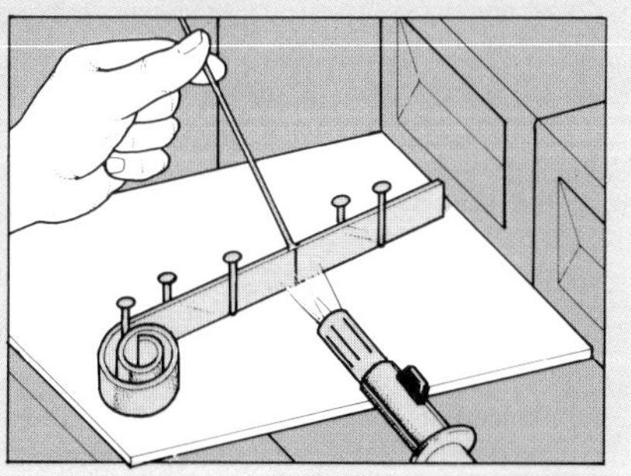

3. *When the correct temperature has been reached, hold the brazing rod on the joint. When it melts the molten brass flows into the joint.*

Copper and its alloys

Copper was one of the first metals to have been used, dating back to before 5000 BC. The material has been used for centuries for domestic items, including cooking pots, kettles and drinking vessels. The great popularity for collecting copper articles is undoubtedly due to the rich, warm appearance of the well-polished surface. Old pieces often use brass rivets to attach handles and join seams. When polished, these make a beautiful contrast which enhances the appeal of an old kettle or bed pan.

The green patina, known as verdigris, on copper is extremely poisonous, so the metal has to be coated with tin if liable to come into contact with food and drink.

Although copper is used in its pure form in the electrical industry and for some decorative metalwork, copper alloys are cheaper and more commonly used today.

Bronze, an alloy of copper and tin and brass, an alloy of copper and zinc, are used mainly for decorative purposes. The glorious gold appearance of brass makes it extremely attractive in the home. It is often seen in conjunction with copper. Copper troughs that can be used as plant holders often have brass feet and the alloy makes very attractive house numbers and name plates.

Gilding metal is a special type of brass which contains 80 to 95 per cent copper. This alloy is very malleable and can safely be heated to red heat. It is a brassy yellow and is frequently used for decorative metalwork.

Nickel silver is an alloy of copper, zinc and nickel. The metal contains no silver but has a similar colouring. It is commonly used in articles such as tankards and cutlery which are silver plated after manufacture. It is then known as electro-plated nickel silver (EPNS).

Buying copper and its alloys

Should you wish to construct or repair an item, copper, brass and gilding metal usually come in 1,200 × 600mm (4ft × 2ft) sheets, although larger sheets are available. Nickel silver is manufactured in a similar range of thicknesses, but the sheet dimensions are normally 1,800 × 300mm (6ft × 1ft). Of these metals, nickel silver is the most expensive, followed by copper and then gilding metal. If you feel like tackling the task, a copper cooker (range) or fire hood is relatively easy to make, using riveted copper sheet. Design your own or study an old one for construction details.

Annealing

Initially, the metal may be too hard to work. This difficulty is easily overcome by the time honoured method of annealing the metal.

Annealing is a process of softening metal to counteract the strain which is set up by cold working – which makes the metal brittle.

The annealing process is best carried out after the blank piece of metal has been marked out and cut to shape. When carrying out any decorative metalwork, take great care not to scratch the metal; any scratches will have to be polished out at a later stage and this is a time-consuming operation.

If you are thinking of repairing a damaged object in copper or gilding metal, the metal object should ideally be annealed. However, if more than one piece of metal has been used to make the object they will have been hard soldered together and these joints may separate during the process.

It may be possible to anneal a local area well away from a joint but great care must be taken with the blowtorch.

The annealing process requires the use of a blowtorch and a pickle bath.

These days, the normal propane-fired DIY blowtorch is suitable, but do not try to use an oxy-acetylene blowtorch as the flame is too hot and the metal will melt. The pickle bath must be both big and deep enough to completely contain the object being annealed. If a pickle bath is not available, the metal object being worked on must be quenched immediately after heating by immersing it in cold water. If, however, you are going to use a pickle bath, remember that it should contain a 15 per cent solution of sulphuric acid mixed with water. If you mix this yourself, *always* add the acid to the water, *never* the water to the acid, otherwise the solution may boil and spit at you.

A simple copper firehood, such as the one shown here, can be constructed using copper sheets riveted together. The brightness of the copper will complement the fire beautifully.

To anneal a blank piece of metal, lean it against a firebrick and heat until it is cherry red. Allow it to cool until it is black and then pick it up in wooden or brass tongs and quench it in the pickle bath. Leave it for about five minutes and then wash it thoroughly in cold water. The blank will now be soft and ready for shaping.

Shaping copper and its alloys

There are two basic methods of shaping or forming metal: sinking and raising. These techniques are well worth mastering as they are used to make simple items and generally to shape new metal. The methods have been in use for thousands of years and hand beaten items can often be bought in markets and bazaars in parts of the world where hand crafting of metal is still commonly practised. The finish is very attractive to the eye if properly executed, and mastering the technique is satisfying, although the domestic applications are a little limited.

Sinking

If simple bowls or saucer shapes, for example, ashtrays or small dishes, are being made, sinking is the easiest way to form the metal. A sinking block is first made by hollowing out the approximate shape required in a block of wood. (A leather sandbag may also be used for this operation.) Start at the outside edge and rotate the piece beneath the bossing mallet, gradually forming the rough shape of the bowl. If a flat rim is required, this may be formed after the sinking operation is finished, using a flat block of wood and a hide mallet.

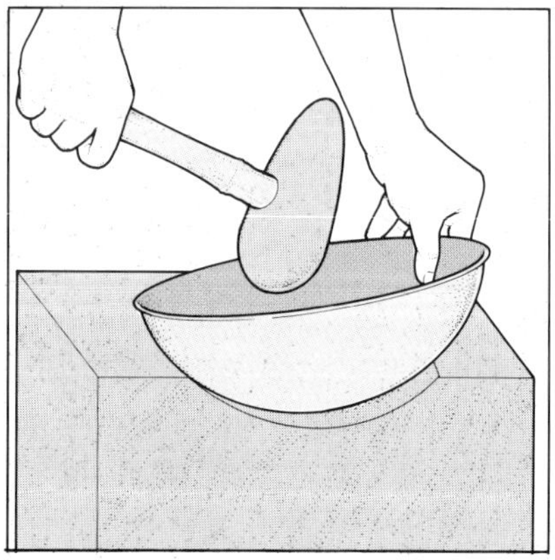

Rotating the workpiece beneath the mallet.

If a deep bowl is needed, it may be necessary to anneal the blank two or three times during the sinking process to enable a deep enough profile to be formed. After sinking, the bowl is ready for trueing and planishing.

Raising

Raising is a much more difficult forming process in which the metal is held against a steel raising stake and is hammered over it, using a raising hammer. The process is used for forming deeper shapes such as vases or tankards which are to be made from one piece. The blank piece of metal is slowly rotated so that the deflection runs all around the blank. It is then annealed again and the deflection deepened. As the edge is being raised above its centre, it is apparent that its diameter is being reduced; consequently the edge gets thicker. Frequent annealing is necessary as is accurate and continuous hammering. You are not recommended to try raising in any metal other than copper as the metal is severely treated during the process and very good malleability is essential.

When raised sufficiently into shape, the blank will look somewhat battered and will have the marks of the raising hammer all over it. These marks can be removed by trueing and planishing.

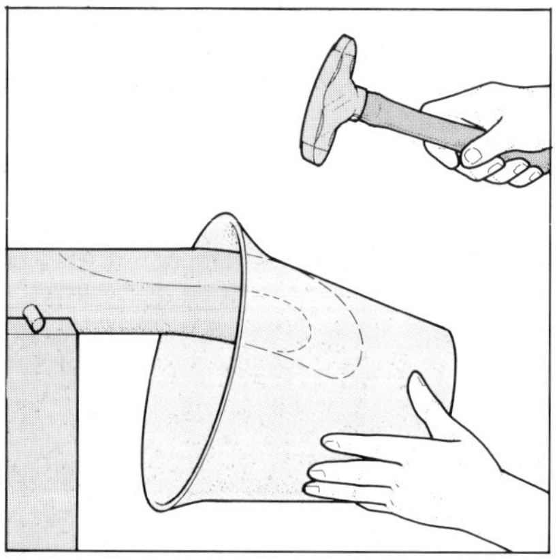

Hammering the metal over the steel stake.

Trueing and planishing

Trueing and planishing are the final shaping operations for forming the metal and for removing all dents. A steel stake of a suitable shape is used, which must be highly polished. This is done to ensure that the inside surface of the bowl will have a similar finish. The stake may be held in a vice or other suitable rigid support. The bowl is placed upside down over the stake and the initial trueing is done, using a hide mallet hitting the outside of the bowl against the stake while it is slowly being rotated.

Planishing, which is the process of evening out irregularities and rehardening the metal, is carried out in a similar manner, using a planishing hammer which also has to have a mirror finish on the head. The secret of this operation is to position yourself comfortably – sitting down is preferable – so that the head of the hammer falls easily and is always square to the surface of the stake. Ensure that you can comfortably use the hammer in this position for a large number of strokes without tiring. Now position the bowl so that the hammer is over the centre and, using the rounded head, start hammering. The correct sound

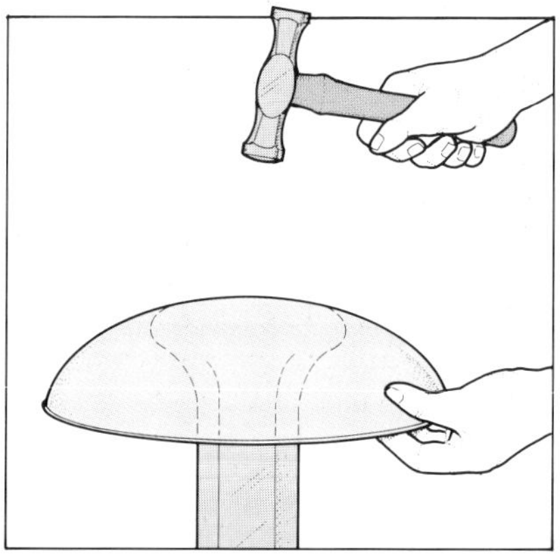

(above) *Start hammering at the centre of the bowl.*

(below) *Each blow should overlap the next.*

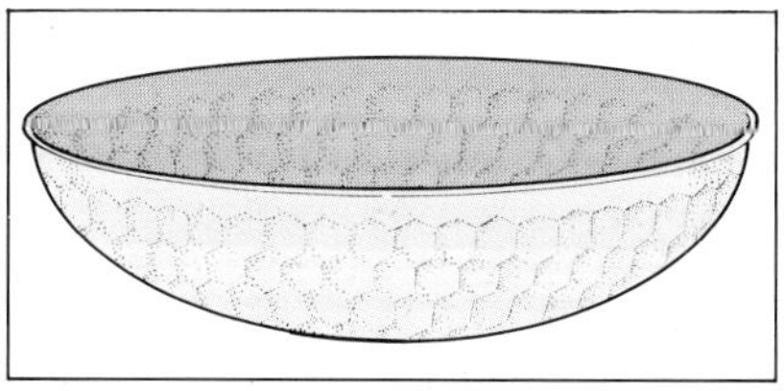

to aim for is a firm click, not a muffled blow. This indicates that the work is sandwiched between the stake and hammer. Slowly rotate the bowl below the hammer, keeping the hammer blows in the same place over the stake. This will cause the hammer blows to trace a spiral path working out from the centre to the edge of the bowl. Each hammer blow should overlap the next and each row should overlap the preceding row. You will see from this that a great many blows are needed to completely planish an object.

When you have finished planishing, the item should be true and have a very slightly faceted appearance. No scratches or raising hammer marks should be visible.

Removing dents

Many old items made from copper and brass can be bought at reasonable prices because they have dents in them. This, of course, makes the item concerned less valuable than it would be if it were in perfect condition. Taking some considerable care, it is quite possible to remove the dents and restore the item to its original shape. Most dents have to be removed from the inside. It is, however, normally impossible to use a mallet in the confined space inside the object being worked on. The best method of removing dents is to make up a suitable stake or dolly – a specially shaped block used for support – for the interior of the item and to use a hide mallet to cure the depression on the outside. The stake must be made from steel if the item is to be properly planished afterwards. However, a hardwood stake can be used when repair work is being undertaken and only a hide mallet is used. The stake must be an exact fit into the correct shape of the dented area; this can usually be achieved by making the stake fit an undamaged portion of the item.

If the item is made from one piece of copper it should be annealed, but if it is formed from several pieces soldered together, or is made from brass which might melt at red heat, it is probably safest to try to remove the dent without annealing.

The stake is held in a vice or other suitable rigid support and the artefact held over it. Using gentle blows with a hide mallet, start at the outside of the dent and work towards the centre. When the dent is removed, the area around the dent should be lightly planished with the mallet. If the stake is made from steel and has a mirror finish, the whole area can then be planished using the proper hammer.

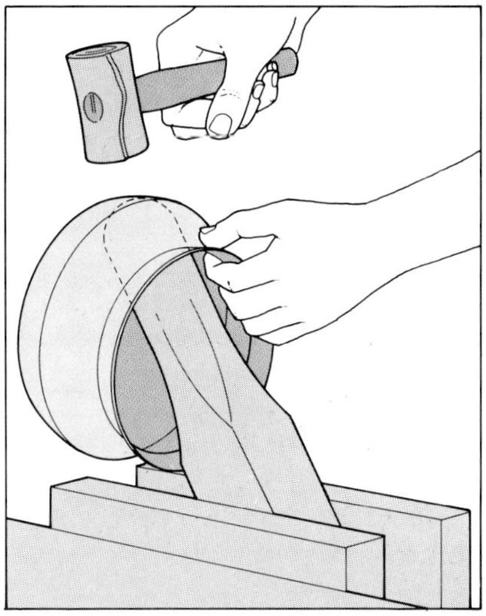

Removing a dent with a hide mallet.

Copper is very suitable for kitchenware and is used for cooking pots, decorative jugs and kettles. The metal is a good conductor of heat and is resistant to corrosion. Frequent polishing is required for pots in constant use, but decorative items can be lacquered.

Joining copper alloys

Seaming is the technique whereby two sheets of metal are joined together with the edges overlapping. Although you may only find occasional use for this technique around the home, it will help to understand the technique when repairing seamed metal articles such as copper tanks, coal scuttles or fireplace hoods. The basic, but weakest, seam is the simple lap joint. In this, the edges overlap and are sealed together by soft solder (see below). A folded and grooved seam is stronger, where the edges of both sheets are folded into a 'U' shape and are then hooked together. A grooving tool (hand groover) is then hammered down over the seam which locks the edges together. The seam is then sealed using soft solder.

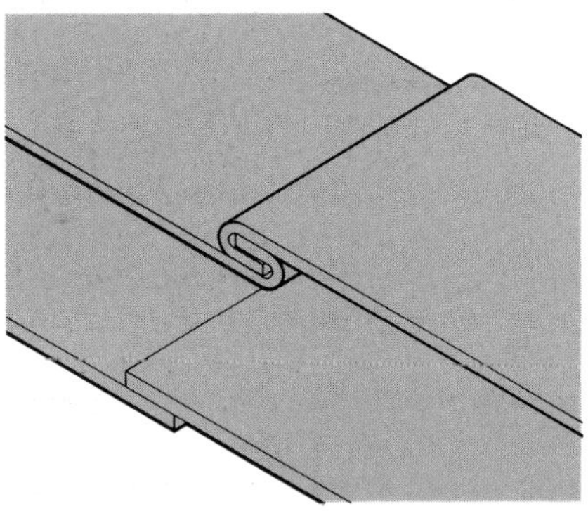

A folded seam and a lap joint.

Soft soldering

Soft soldering is the weakest method of jointing copper alloys and can be used with care on lead. It is normally used to seal joints such as the grooved seam which is already strengthened by its method of construction. The process may be used on small, inexpensive copper or brass ornaments to hold handles on, and can be used for mending solder joints in tinplate toys and small containers.

To make a soft soldered joint, first thoroughly clean the parts to be joined with emery cloth. Position the work so that the joint is in metal-to-metal contact and is resting on a wooden surface. Apply killed spirits (a solution of zinc chloride) to the joint. Clean up a soldering iron with a file and heat it with a gas flame until the flame is green. Remove from the flame and dip it quickly in and out of killed spirits. Now coat (tin) the iron with soft solder. Position the tinned iron against the joint and hold it in this position for a few seconds. The solder will flow onto the work when sufficient heat has transferred. Hold a stick of solder against the iron and move it along the joint at a speed slow enough to allow the solder to fill the joint. Reheat the iron when the solder stops flowing. Do not remove the joint until the solder has a matt finish, which indicates that it has solidified. Then wash the joint in hot, soapy water to remove any surplus flux.

Hard soldering

Hard soldering – also known as silver soldering as the solder used contains silver in addition to copper and zinc – is used extensively in beaten or decorative metalwork and normally joins the seams in tankards or kettles, and so on. Handles are also fixed on by this process. Many metals may be joined using hard solder, including copper, brass, steel and solid silver and gold where special high purity solders are used.

The solder is available in many grades, the difference between the grades being the melting point of the solder. The lowest melting point normally available is known as 'easy', which melts at about 610 degrees C (1,130 degrees F). Two other grades in common use are 'medium', which melts at about 750 degrees C (1,382 degrees F) and 'hard', which melts at about 820 degrees C (1,508 degrees F). The 'easy' grade contains the most silver and is therefore relatively expensive. (It also contains a small amount of cadmium which produces potentially dangerous fumes, so it is advisable not to use it in confined spaces.)

The parts to be joined are filed or beaten into the correct shape so that metal-to-metal contact takes place all along the joint. The contact surfaces must then be cleaned either by emery cloth or by chemical means, such as 50 per cent nitric acid solution washed off with clean water. After cleaning, do not handle the joint as this will contaminate it.

Borax flux is now liberally applied either as a paste from a cone or in powder form which is mixed with water to give a stiff cream. The joint is heated with a blowtorch which causes the flux to bubble until all the water has evaporated. It then settles down and melts so that the joint can be seen. If easy solder is used, the joint would now be nearly at the correct temperature – medium, however, needs dull red heat and hard needs bright red. The solder rod is now applied to the joint and is held there until the rod melts and flows along the joint.

If copper alloys are being soldered, they should be quenched in a pickle bath and washed in water after soldering to remove the scale. When all the joints are made, the item should be immersed in boiling water for five minutes to remove any surplus borax. If a hard soldered joint has been well made, it will be invisible on the finished item.

Riveting

The technique of joining metal using rivets has been in use for many years. The rivet, which is a short rod with a shaped head, is made from a malleable metal such as soft iron, copper or brass. A hole is made in each piece to be joined and the holes aligned. The rivet is placed through the two holes and the end opposite to the head is flattened so it cannot be removed. If properly done, the fixing is tight.

Within the home, rivets can often be seen in wrought iron pieces where they might be used to attach, say, a scroll. Copper fire hoods or log boxes might use rivets; often a join between two sheets of copper will be marked with a parallel row of copper or brass rivet heads. The riveted joint may be invisible in some cases, due to the use of countersunk rivets of the same metal which cannot be seen after the joint has been cleaned up. Examples of this can be seen in antique scientific instruments or an engineer's set square (try square).

Two specialized tools are needed which can be made from odd pieces of steel: the set and the snap. The set is a piece of metal with a hole drilled in it, exactly the diameter of the rivet shaft. The snap has a hole the shape of the rivet head. The set is fitted over the shank and hit with a hammer to bring the pieces to be joined together. The snap forms the hammered rivet shank into the required shape.

To make a riveted joint, the rivet is fitted through the two holes and the head rested on a flat steel block if the head is flat or countersunk. With a snap head it is rested in a snap held upside down in a vice. The set is then placed over the protruding end and given one or two sharp taps with a hammer to ensure that the pieces are a close fit. The rivet shank should protrude about one-and-a-half times its diameter, so that just enough metal is available to form a snap or countersunk head.

Using the ball pein of an engineer's hammer the end of the rivet is peened over, which is the process of swelling the end of a rivet by hammering. If a snap head is needed the snap is fitted over the end before it is completely peened over and hammered home to form the head. With a countersunk head, the peening over continues until the countersink in the component is filled with rivet, the surplus is then filed off flush with the surrounding metal. This filing process is then repeated on the other end of the rivet so that both ends are invisible.

Copper saucepans need a lining of tin to prevent contamination by verdigris.

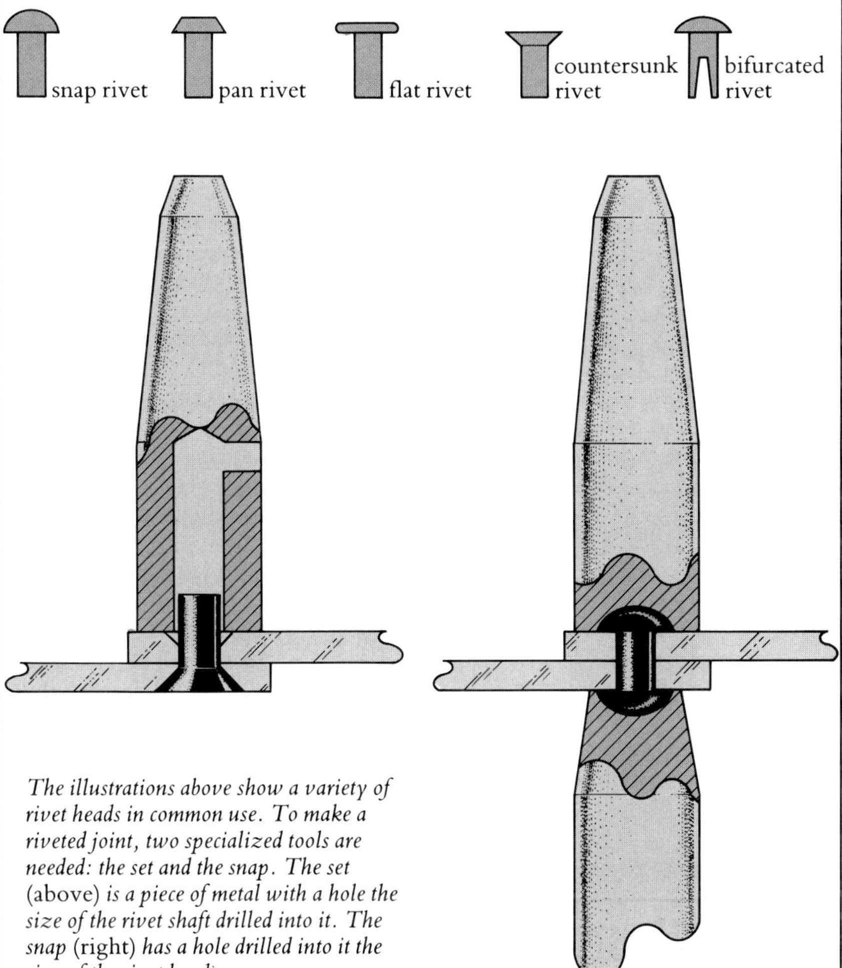

The illustrations above show a variety of rivet heads in common use. To make a riveted joint, two specialized tools are needed: the set and the snap. The set (above) *is a piece of metal with a hole the size of the rivet shaft drilled into it. The* snap (right) *has a hole drilled into it the size of the rivet head.*

The above techniques apply to all traditional rivets in all metals. A more modern type is known as the 'pop' rivet, which is very useful as it can be installed from one side of the component only, using special rivet pliers (gun), Pop rivets are easy to use and have many DIY uses. Unfortunately, they all have the same head shape and the back side of the rivet is rather untidy looking, which normally rules them out for use with decorative metal work.

If you wish to make a joint which is held together by a single rivet but which will form a stiff pivot – such as that used in a cupboard door stay – make the joint in the normal way but rivet a piece of paper between the two pieces of metal. The paper can then be removed by the application of gentle heat leaving a tight pivoting joint.

Lead and its alloys

Lead was extensively used in the past for domestic plumbing and roofing. Since the detrimental effects of lead poisoning have become understood, however, and the price of the metal has increased, it is now fast disappearing from the plumbing industry. Lead plumbing, for example, has been replaced by copper and plastics.

The DIY enthusiast is most likely to encounter lead today with the preparation of a wiped joint to connect a new brass fitting to the existing lead system.

A wiped joint

The step-by-step process described on the right is the traditional method of joining lead pipes to each other or joining brass end connections. The result is a bulbous lump or swelling in the pipe.

The joint is made using plumber's metal, which is a soft solder containing 60 per cent lead to 40 per cent tin which goes soft and plastic before it melts. This is wiped to a smooth profile using a plumber's mole, a cloth which used to be made out of mole skin but is now manufactured from a synthetic material. The cloth will have been heated and dipped in tallow.

How to make a wiped joint

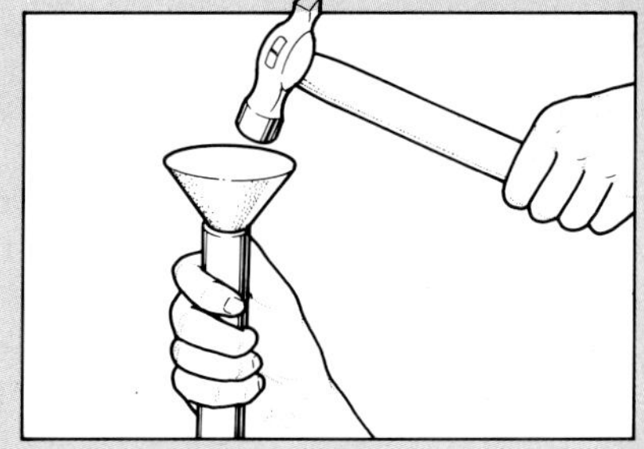

1. *Clean the component to be joined to the lead pipe with emery cloth or steel wool. Open out the end of the lead pipe to accept the fitting by driving a wooden cone into the end, twisting to prevent sticking.*

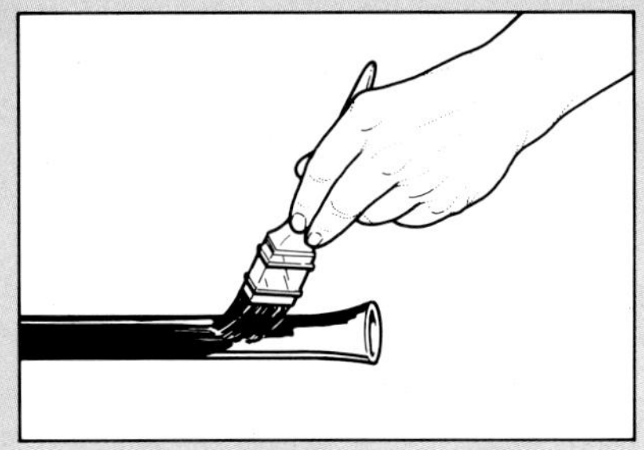

2. *Coat the outside of the pipe and the fitting with plumber's black – a black paste used to stop solder spreading.*

3. *Scrape off the black in the area to be jointed, leaving a bright surface for about 35mm (1½ in) on both the pipe and fitting.*

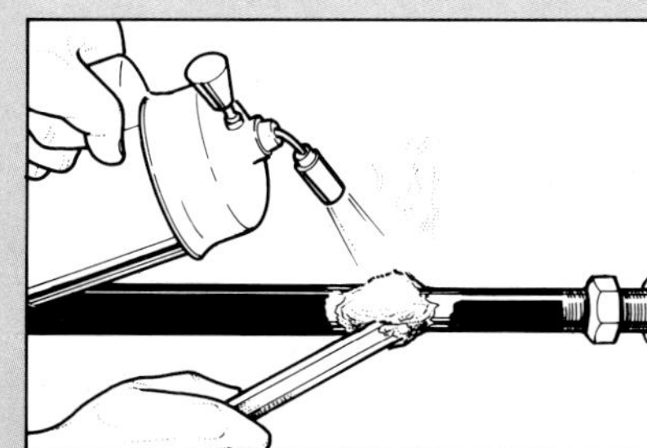

4. *Flux the joint with tallow. Heat up the fitting and tin the end with soft solder. Place the fitting into the pipe and gently heat it, keeping the flame on the move until the solder makes the joint.*

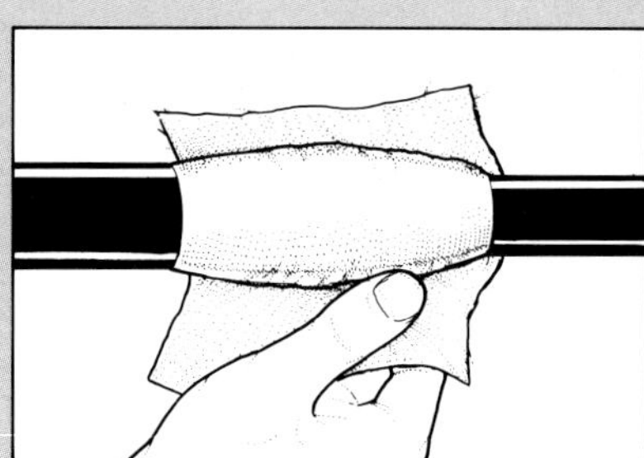

5. *Fill the joint with plumber's metal and wipe to a smooth profile, using a plumber's mole. Don't put any strain on the lead pipe or it may fracture.*

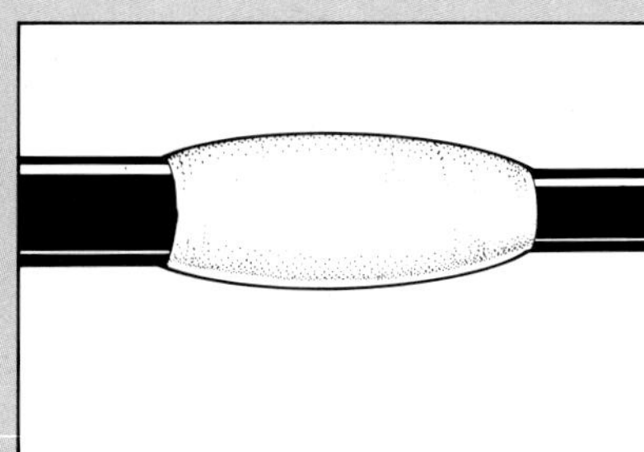

6. *Use as much plumber's metal as required until the joint takes on a smooth, wiped appearance. Allow to cool before subjecting to use.*

Lead alloys

Pewter is an alloy of tin and lead, containing about 80 per cent tin. It is very malleable and ductile. Any damage to a pewter artefact can usually be carefully beaten out, but the use of heat is not advisable. Pewter is solid when cold, but if too much heat is applied – and this may be very little heat – it turns immediately to liquid and holes appear. Do not repair a pewter object with soft solder as it has a higher melting point than pewter.

There are two types of Brittania metal. The first – an alloy of tin and lead – used to be used for making such objects as teapots or cheap jewelry, which was then silver plated. It is now rarely used because unfortunately, after a while, the Brittania metal attacks the silver plate and corrodes it away. Frequent polishing helps to minimize the corrosive effect, but it is not normally economical to have the item stripped and replated.

The second type – an alloy of tin, antimony and copper – was used in the past for items such as cutlery handles. It is nowadays called modern pewter. It is lighter in colour than real pewter, does not darken with age, and is generally harder and more durable.

Etching

Etching is a process which can be used to form a design on the surface of a polished item. The complete article is first coated with a stopping agent, which is a substance that the etching medium will not attack. Wax used to be used, but nowadays the aerosol cans of cellulose paint are much more convenient. It is important to coat all surfaces of the article with the stopping agent. The desired picture or pattern is then scratched through the stopping agent with a suitably pointed tool, and the article immersed in the etching medium until its chemical action has engraved the design into the parent metal.

Various mediums are available, but two are more common than others. All etching mediums are essentially corrosive, so very great care must be taken with them. Nitric acid in concentrations of up to 50 per cent is the quickest medium normally used; this works in a few minutes but leaves a coarse finish. Ferric chloride is much slower and therefore more controllable; this is available as a solid product in lumps. To prepare the solution, place the chemical in a plastic container and just cover the lumps with water. Leave the solution for a day and it will then be ready for use. When immersing the article, be sure to wear rubber gloves and check it frequently for the depth of the etching.

When the etching is completed, the stopping agent may be removed using cellulose thinners. Disposal of the chemicals must be carried out carefully; it will almost certainly be in breach of local laws to pour these down drains.

To make this card case it was covered in wax and the pattern drawn through it with a sharp, pointed instrument. The case was then immersed in a suitable etching medium.

Etching name or number plates using 'instant' lettering

1. *With a polished, chemically clean piece of copper or brass, set out the name or number plate using black 'instant' lettering.*

2. *Immerse the plate in ferric chloride, keeping a careful watch on the progress. When etching letters do not use nitric acid as this will lift them off the metal.*

3. *The result will be an attractive nameplate with polished letters on an etched background.*

Finishing techniques

Once you have repaired or restored a household item manufactured in metal there remains the highly satisfying job of finishing prior to polishing. This is done by using progressively gentler abrasives to make finer and finer scratches. Eventually, the marks left by the abrasives are removed until the surface is smooth.

Abrasive cloths and paper come in many grades – from coarse to fine – and should be used in that order. Emery cloth is very harsh and only the finest grades should be used – then only with great care – to remove deep scratches or blemishes.

Fine abrasive papers, coated with silicon carbon or aluminium oxide, can be used dry or, preferably, wet, as this will keep the metal particles from clogging the cutting edges of the grit. They are known as wet and dry papers. The fineness of the abrasive is dictated by the size of the grit particles.

You can also use pumice as a medium to fine grade abrasive. This can be used in powder form, on a damp cloth, or as a pumice stone dipped in water.

Water of Ayr stone (called 'Scotch' stone in the US) is a very soft slate which is used wet for the final smoothing. It comes in short sticks which can be shaped to reach into awkward corners.

Do remember that all blemishes and scratches must be removed before polishing. Polishing only enhances faults and the higher the polish the more starkly will blemishes stand out.

The buffing wheel

The buffing wheel consists of a series of calico discs spinning at high speed coated with buffing soap. This soap, which is the polish, comes in various grades: coarse, medium and fine – sometimes called tripoli, crocus and rouge. Various grades and sizes of wheel are available, including the finishing mop, known as swansdown, which is

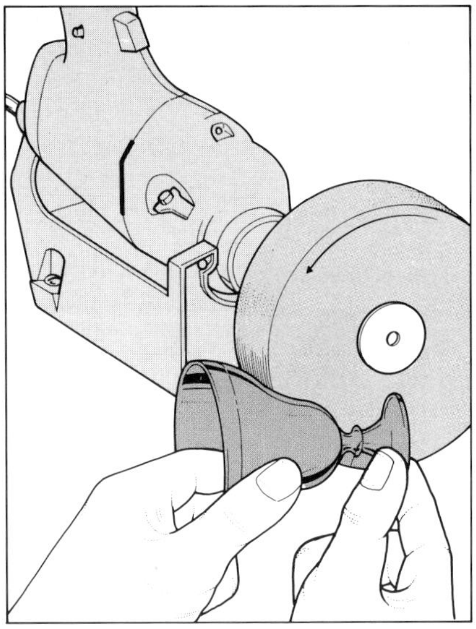

Using the buffing wheel.

made from a very soft cloth. Buffing is a dirty process and safety glasses should always be worn. The piece to be polished should be held in bare hands just below the centre of the wheel. Press hard and the soaped wheel will remove all minor scratches and discoloration, leaving a clean, greasy-feeling surface. If the work comes away from the wheel with a shiny surface the wheel needs more soap on it or the polishing action will be slowed down. The work will get hot whilst buffing but do not hold the work in a rag or gloves because this is potentially dangerous.

Metal polish

Various types of metal polish are available to suit different metals. Some form of abrasive is included in the polish to remove the dirt and oxide coating, together with a brightener to give the metal a lustre. Some of the more modern polishes include additives to retard the oxidation of the metal, thus lengthening the period between polishes. Use only the mildest of polishes to give a good shine; this will prolong the life of the item which would otherwise be polished away unnecessarily (similar to some old door plates which are polished every day). An old silversmith's recipe for a very mild but effect polish is a mixture of gin and cigarette ash.

Lacquering

To avoid the need for continual polishing, many items are coated with a transparent lacquer after an initial polish. This is a wise precaution, particularly with silver plated items, as it is easy to polish right through the silver to the base metal.

Various lacquers are available which can be brushed or sprayed on, but the best method with small articles is to immerse them in lacquer and then withdraw at a very slow but even rate. This will provide a mark-free, even coat.

Hang the item on a thin thread, so that all surfaces slope down to allow the lacquer to drain. Wrap the thread several turns around a pencil. Hold it above the lacquer container and unwind the thread, lowering the item into the lacquer gently. Leave it there until all the air bubbles stop, then very slowly rotate the pencil to withdraw the item from the lacquer evenly. Depending on its size, this should take up to 30 seconds. When completely removed, allow to dry in a dust-free area.

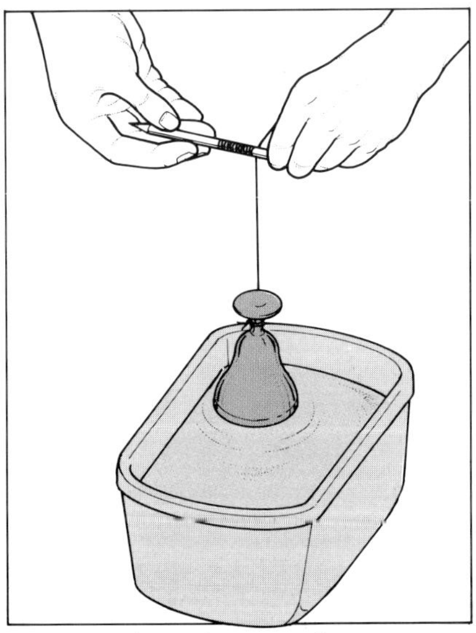

Immersing the workpiece into lacquer.

Cleaning

Before starting to clean a piece of domestic metalware, make sure you have a soft cloth available on which to rest it as some metals such as pewter are very soft and will be easily marked.

Find out the type of metal or metals used in the article to be cleaned. To do this, search for a portion of the metal which is not normally seen and gently remove the surface dirt with very fine wire wool (steel wool), metal polish or even a finger nail. Also look for the maker's marks.

Many pieces of metalware are coated with another metal. Copper may be coated with silver as a decorative feature as well as with tin as a protection against the patina. Sheffield plate used to have silver fused to one or both sides of a copper article. Later, electroplating techniques simplified the process. If you suspect the piece under examination to be made of a solid precious metal or coated, take extra care when removing dirt. Beware of fake or deceptive 'hallmarks'.

Having established what the item is made from, the dirt should be removed. Take care with the cleaning agents: if the item is made from, for instance, a mixture of metal and wood or bone, staining may result. Start with a strong solution of household detergent in hot water, applied with an old toothbrush. This will remove the top dirt. If the article has been lacquered, take it outdoors and remove the lacquer with cellulose thinners or petrol (gasoline).

With brass articles, the application of paraffin (kerosene), applied by vigorously scrubbing, will remove the ground-in dirt. Commercial impregnated wadding (batting) can also be used; if this is not successful use a solution made from a level tablespoon of salt and tablespoon of vinegar in half a pint of hot water. Rub with a very mild abrasive such as the finest wire wool (steel wool). Care for copper in a similar manner but treat more gently when applying mechanical pressure. Silver should be carefully washed in soapy water and cleaned with a commercial polish. Bronze items only need careful washing.

Iron and steel usually corrode badly if stored in wet conditions. If lightly rusted, soak in paraffin (kerosene) for three or four hours and then rub rusty areas with fine grade steel wool. If the rust is serious, use a rust remover.

If wrought iron is coated with paint, it can be removed with paint-stripper and sandblasted. Cast iron fireplaces can often be found coated with several, sometimes many, layers of paint and, if stripped to the bare metal, glorious relief decorations may be exposed. Ensure the item is thoroughly dry, then repaint, lacquer or simply wipe over lightly every so often with an oily cloth. Wrought iron should be repainted, preferably with specially formulated paint.

Dirty or discoloured pewter can be cleaned with a mixture of either rotten stone or pumice powder mixed with equal parts of linseed oil and turpentine.

Once the surface of the metal can be clearly seen, any minor scratches can be removed with water of Ayr stone (Scotch stone) and the polishing processes carried out. If a buffing wheel is used, ensure that fine decorative details are not removed by prolonged buffing.

Some specialist treatments are available for specific metals (for example, silver dip) which dissolve away the dirt. These are very effective, but should only be used in accordance with the manufacturer's instructions.

Glossary

Alloy: Mixture of two or more metals.

Annealing: Process of removing the hardness from metals.

Dolly: Specially shaped block of wood or steel which supports the object being worked on.

Flux: A substance used to prevent oxidization during the soldering process.

Killed spirits: Solution of zinc chloride used as a flux when soft soldering.

Peening: Process of swelling the end of a rivet by hitting it with a ball pein hammer.

Pickle bath: Mixture of sulphuric acid (15 per cent) and water. Used for quenching.

Planishing: Process of evening out irregularities and re-hardening the metal by hammering against a curved stake.

Plumber's black (carbon black): Proprietary black paste used to stop solder spreading when soldering lead joints.

Plumber's metal: Special type of soft solder which goes soft and plastic before it melts. An alloy of 60 per cent lead and 40 per cent tin.

Raising: A process whereby metal is formed hammering over a metal stake; see *Sinking*.

Sinking: Process of forming metal by hammering into a sinking block or leather sandbag.

Stake: Shaped block of steel with mirror finish against which metal is beaten to the required shape.

Tempering: Removing the brittleness from hardened steel, which is heated to the correct temperature and then quenched.

Trueing: Finishing the shape of beaten metal artefact, removing all dents and bumps.

Glasswork

Light shining through coloured glass creates one of the most beautiful effects in architecture. One of the reasons why tourists flock in such numbers to great cathedrals such as Chartres in France or York Minster or Canterbury in England is to see the glowing, vibrant colours in their windows.

Although it is normally associated with the Middle Ages and beautiful places of worship, coloured glass is also found in quite ordinary domestic interiors, particularly in houses of the late nineteenth century. While not in the same class as ancient stained glass, such pieces can be surprisingly valuable and very pleasing to look at, so they are well worth maintaining and restoring.

Stained glass is still made according to the same basic principles as laid out in the Middle Ages. Various oxides, depending on the colour required, are mixed with the sand, soda and lime which are the components of ordinary glass. Glass in this state can be bought from a store. At home it is then cut to the shapes desired and held together with strips of grooved lead.

The medieval glazier generally designed windows to tell a story in a simple and direct manner. A craftsman would then take up a piece of glass, cracking it in half with a red hot iron rod and subsequently shaping it by cutting small bits off at a time – a process known as grozing. Faces, hands and drapery were painted on with a vitreous enamel paint and the glass fired in a wood kiln.

Silver stain was discovered in the fourteenth century which completely changed the design of stained glass. Yellow paint, the basic ingredient of which is silver stain, could now be used to paint on figures and fabrics.

The craft of the glass painter reached its peak in the fifteenth century but was subsequently lost in the mid-seventeenth century when enamel colours and yellow stain were painted on white glass instead – usually proving to be unsatisfactory substitutes.

The nineteenth century saw a revival in stained glass production – mostly comprising imitations of previous styles, using inferior glass which was thin and crude in colour. Fortunately, however, the medieval techniques of making glass were rediscovered after a number of experiments and the antique glass used today is the result of this work.

No particular skill is required to replace a pane of ordinary window glass, although there are procedures to be followed which are described later on in this chapter. Leaded lights and stained glass, however, require constant maintenance and special skills for repair work. It is very likely that if you are restoring a house which is over 50 years old you will come across some lovely old coloured glasswork or bullions (bull's eyes) which you will find very rewarding to look after.

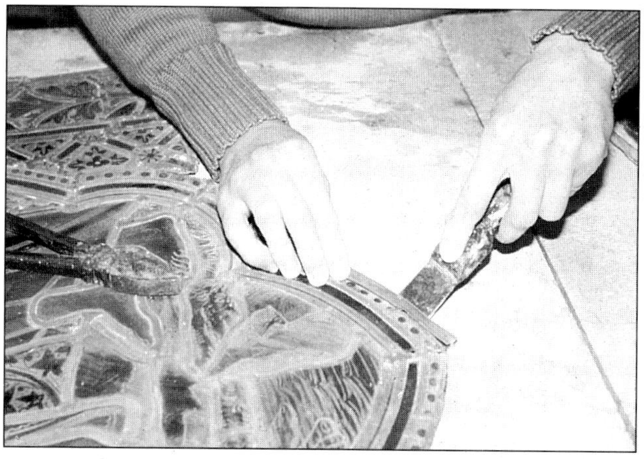

(left) *The entrance hall is given added elegance by this magnificent stained glass door. The changing effects of light on the glass panels offset the cream walls, bringing colour to the hallway and a warm welcome to every visitor.*

(right) *Leading up a splendid stained glass window. Tools for this craft should be used with care and a steady hand.*

Tools, equipment and materials

Annealing kiln or lehr
A kiln which controls the rate at which the glass cools after it has been blown into a cylinder, thereby releasing stresses. If the glass cools too rapidly there is a likelihood that it will break when cold.

Bat
A bat is a high-fired ceramic shelf on which glass is fired in a kiln.

Blowpipe
This implement is a hollow metal tube, about 1.8m (6ft) long, used by a glass-blower.

Brushes

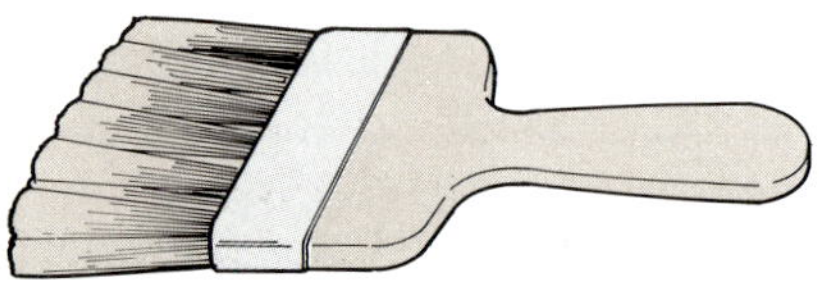

A *badger* is a large, long-haired brush made from badger hair, used for spreading the paint.

A stiff *hoghaired* brush is used for taking out highlights.

Liners, for line work, are long haired, fine and preferably sable.

A *mop* is a large, soft brush, used for putting on a flat wash.

Cleat (lead stretcher)
A cleat is a small vice about 75mm (3in) across, comprising two jaws on swivel pins. The end of a lead came (see *lead*) is inserted between the jaws; the harder the lead is pulled, the tighter the jaws grip.

Glass cutting easel (light table)
This is a sheet of plate glass raised horizontally above a table. A light is placed under the glass so that the cut-line can be seen.

Glass muller
A glass muller is a bell-shaped piece of solid glass with a perfectly smooth base. The implement is used for grinding paint on a sheet of plate glass or a tile.

Glass painting easel
A piece of glass is placed vertically in front of a window. The glass is cut and mounted onto the easel and painted in this position.

Horseshoe nails
Horseshoe nails are used for holding glass in place when leading up a stained glass panel.

Knives

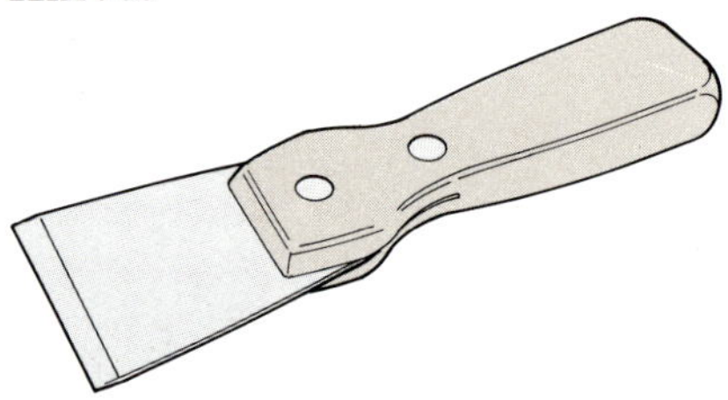

A *lead cutting knife* can be made from an old paint scraper, cut down and sharpened; the blade should be rigid, not flexible.

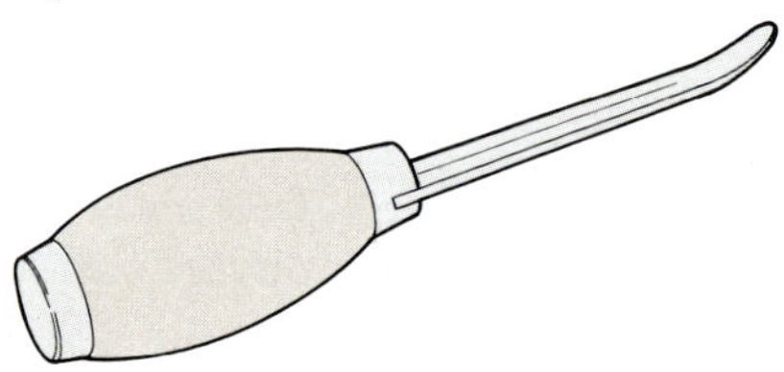

An *oyster knife*, a tool with a wooden handle used to open oysters, is adapted for use by the glazier by heating, casting and fitting a piece of lead to the handle. The blade is used for straightening lead flanges; the handle is used for tapping pieces of glass into place and hammering in glazing nails. Also known as a *stopping knife*.

Lathekin
This is a sharpened piece of hard wood, used to open up a groove of lead or spread down the edges of the lead when inserted in the glasswork.

Lead

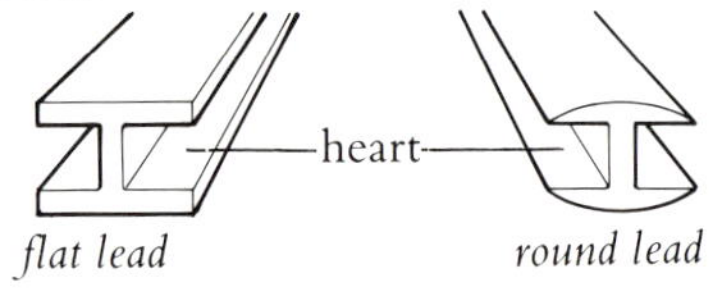

Lead comes in 2m (6ft 6in) lengths called cames, and in various widths and thicknesses: 13mm (½in), 10mm (⅜in), 8mm (5/16in) and 6mm (¼in). The lead is either 'round' or 'flat'. The height or heart of the lead is either 5mm (3/16in) or 6mm (¼in).

Platepliers

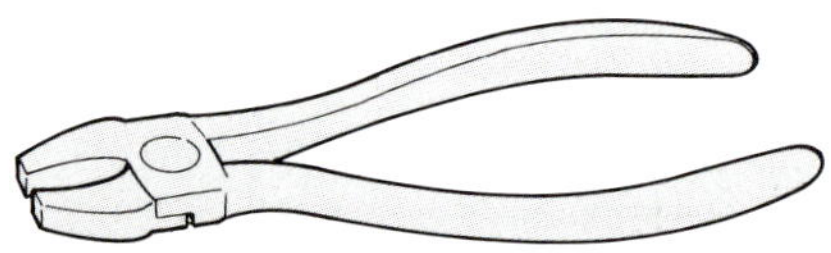

Platepliers are similar to ordinary pliers but with smooth jaws about 25mm (1in) wide. Very useful for breaking off thin strips of glass.

Saddle bars
Saddle bars are bars of iron or, preferably, non ferrous metal, used to support a stained glass window. They run across the front of the window and are set into the frame at either side.

Solder
Solder, a mixture of lead and tin, is applied to the joints of the leads with a hot soldering iron, firmly bonding the joints together. Soft solder only is used for glasswork.

Soldering irons
Either gas or electric soldering irons can be used. The thermostatically controlled variety are the best.

Steels
Steels are thin rods of steel, about 1.8m (6ft) long, 4mm (⅛in) wide and 2mm (1/16in) thick, for inserting into a came of lead for added strength.

Wheeled glass cutter
This implement is a small, hardened steel wheel, mounted in a holder, used for cutting sheets of glass.

Making a stained glass panel

The first three stages of making a stained glass panel

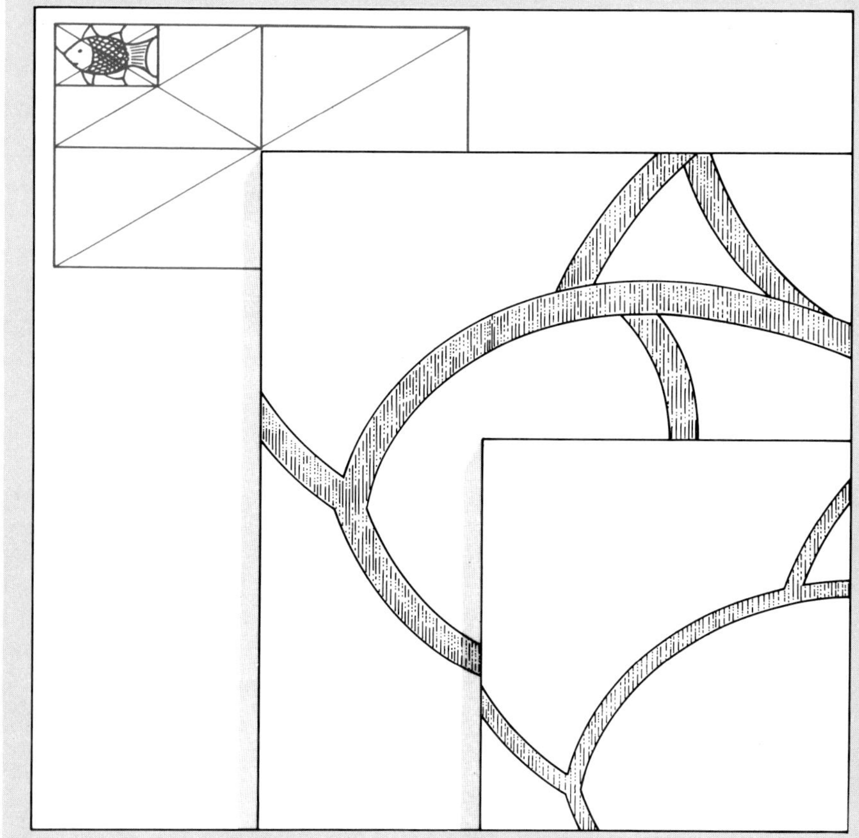

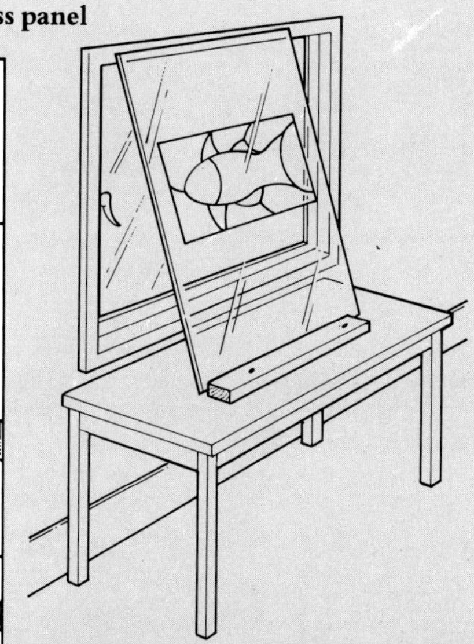

(above) *An improvised glass painting easel, showing the cut-line painted on the back of the glass.*

(left) *The illustration shows the first three steps necessary for constructing a glass panel. The first step is to draw a sketch of the proposed panel and the next to square-up and enlarge the design to the required size – known as a cartoon. The final step is to make a cut-line by tracing over the cartoon.*

Stained glass panels, very popular 100 years ago, are once more becoming desirable features of many homes today, particularly in the United States where great interest is being shown in making them.

Once constructed, a panel can be hung up against a window, or against a wall with a light behind it.

The following pages set out how to make a completely new panel. It will not be necessary to understand all the processes outlined for small repair work.

Before starting to construct the panel, it is first necessary to draw up a small-scale design on paper, using pencil for the lines representing the lead cames, and colouring in with water colour, gouache or pencil crayons. (1/10 scale is a suitable size.)

Square up and enlarge the design to the required size, known as a cartoon. It is essential to do this to ensure the glass work is accurate. If the panel is to be a square or rectangular shape it is easier to square up by drawing lines in a grid pattern over both the design and paper for the cartoon. The smaller rectangles thus formed can be subdivided and the design enlarged within these marks. This eliminates the need for any measuring. Don't be too ambitious to start with. Let the size of the panel be about 300mm × 400mm (12in × 16in). Make the lines of the cartoon black. They correspond to the width of the lead (see page 127). Do not design any piece of glass that will have to be cut smaller than 25mm × 25mm (1in × 1in) as small pieces of glass are very difficult to handle.

The next process is to take a piece of tracing paper, lay it over the cartoon and pin it down securely so that it will not slip. First, trace over the perimeter of the cartoon with a fine line, using a straight edge. Then trace over the middle of all the other lead lines with a black felt-tip pen, making sure that the resulting lines are no more than 3mm (1/8in) and no less than 2mm (1/16in) thick. This is known as the cut-line. The thickness of each line corresponds to the width of the heart of a piece of lead.

Next, take a sheet of 4mm (1/8in) glass or plate glass, larger than the panel that is to be made. Using sticky tape, fix the cut-line face upwards onto the sheet of glass. This is known as a glass painting easel. Turn the glass over and trace the pattern of the cut-line which can be seen through the glass onto the back of the pane with black powder paint or a felt tip pen.

Glass

The coloured glass used in stained glass windows is hand-made. The traditional method used in England is to dip a blowpipe into a vat of molten coloured glass and then to blow out a long cylinder which is cut off at either end and allowed to cool. It is then split open with a glass cutter, reheated in an annealing kiln and spread out. The resulting sheet of glass measures approximately 660mm × 400mm (26in × 16in) and is known as antique glass. Similar glass is made in France and Germany, but in these countries a much bigger cylinder is blown which means the glass sheets are bigger. This method is known as the muff process.

Another way of making hand-made glass is using the crown method. In this, the glass-blower gathers a lump of molten glass on the end of the pipe and spins it. Centrifugal force forms the glass into a large disc, as much as 1.5m (4½ft) across. The centre of the glass formed in this way is called a bullion or bull's eye, and it used to be discarded or used as a cheap means of glazing. Now, however, bullions are especially cast for use in the home.

There is one other method of making hand-made glass known as Norman slab. A bubble of molten glass is blown into a cast-iron box so that a glass box is formed inside. After cooling, the sides are cut to form four rectangular slabs, a fifth, smaller one being produced from the base. The centre of these slabs can sometimes be as much as 10mm (⅜in) thick, tapering to 3mm (⅛in) at the edges. The usual size of these slabs is 250mm × 180mm (10in × 7in) or 190mm × 140mm (7½in × 5½in). This glass has a lovely scintillating quality and comes in many colours. Unfortunately, however, it is seldom made nowadays.

Stained glass panels often depict a detailed scene or tell a simple story. The panel on the left has been stained with rich colours to give a striking effect.

(above) *A simple but effective panel such as the one shown may be found in domestic houses, perhaps above the front door. It is made using stained Salisbury glass.*

(right) *A fine example of a staining technique known as streaky colour. White glass and similar toned colours are used.*

Antique glass has uneven thicknesses and bubbles which give it its crystalline quality which cannot be matched by machine-made glass. However, it is considerably more expensive. An important difference between hand-made and machine-made glass is that the former is transparent, that is, rays of light are transmitted without diffusion so that bodies behind can be clearly seen; machine-made glass, on the other hand, is usually translucent, which means that the light transmitted is diffused.

Colours

Chemical ingredients are added to the basic materials which comprise glass to produce the wide variety of colours obtainable: cobalt for blue; copper and chromium for green; iron and selenium for yellow; copper and gold for red; magnesium for brown-pink.

The colour of the glass varies according to the length of time it is held in a molten state. The processes involved in staining glass are highly skilled and very technical.

There are three types of colour:

Pot colour: glass which is coloured throughout in a pot filled with molten glass.

Flash colour: a thin layer of one colour on top of another. For example, ruby on white or ruby on blue solid ruby glass would be too dark for the light to pass through. The glass-maker first dips the blowpipe into molten white glass and then into molten ruby glass, so that, when the cylinder of glass is blown out, the resulting sheet is a layer of ruby glass 'flashed' on to white glass. Areas of the flashed glass can be removed with acid to reveal the colour underneath.

Streaky colour: the blowpipe is dipped into more than one colour apart from white glass, so that several streaks of colours are found in the one piece of glass.

Cutting glass

Glass is cut with a glass cutter which has a small steel wheel set in its handle. Before attempting to cut the glass you are going to use for your restoration work, practise cutting on ordinary sheet glass first.

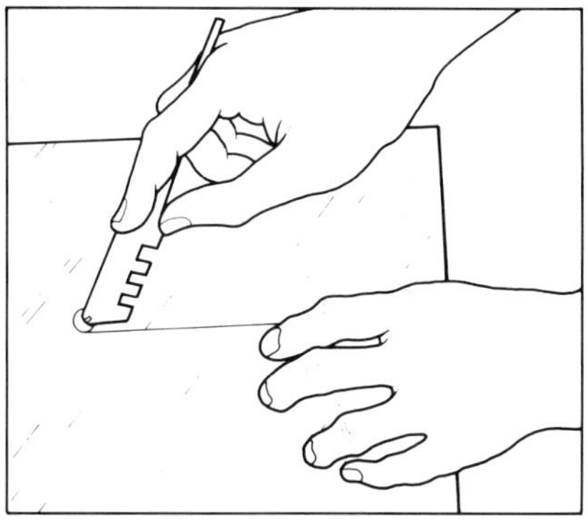

Using a glass cutter.

To cut the glass, hold the cutter between the first and second finger, with the thumb underneath at an angle just off the vertical. A firm, steady pressure should be used to make a white line on the glass surface, starting and finishing at the edges of the glass. Hold the glass firmly with one hand while cutting with the other, and don't go over the line twice as this will damage the cutting wheel. Avoid too much pressure because this produces what is known as an 'angry white line' which makes the glass almost impossible to break. Practise cutting straight lines on ordinary sheet glass first. Push the wheel; do not pull it or your hand will obscure the cutting line. A sharp tap underneath the line at the edge of the glass will start a crack. Now hold the glass on either side of the line, between the fingers and thumbs of both hands, and break sharply down and outwards. The piece of glass will split neatly along the line.

Breaking glass with a straight cut.

Once straight lines have been mastered, try curves. This time, tap all the way along the underside of the score-line, making sure the glass cracks from one end to the other. Scored lines must always run off the edge of the glass.

Uneven bumps and sharp 'whiskers' of glass are often left along the edge after it has been cut. These should be nibbled or grozed clear with a pair of pliers, or with the notches on top of the glass cutter.

When satisfied that your cutting is accurate to at least 2mm ($^{1}/_{16}$in) you will be able to start cutting glass for the panel. It should be cut flat or on a glass cutting easel – also known as a light table – which has a light bulb underneath, unless it can be seen through when it is lying on a table, in which case a table will do. (A simple glass cutting easel can be made by supporting a piece of sheet glass on two bricks.) Place the cut-line on the glass easel or table and lay the piece of glass which is to be cut over the cut-line. Cut out the shape, taking care to keep within the black line. Overcutting or undercutting will make the leading-up very difficult.

As each piece of glass is cut, put a small blob of modelling clay in each corner and then place it in its position on the large glass painting easel. It is now possible to see how the whole panel is building up and how one colour looks against another.

An alternative, traditional method is to set the glass painting easel horizontally across two tressles. Each piece of glass is cut, laid in place and a drop of molten beeswax placed at each corner to hold it in position.

Cutting circular shapes

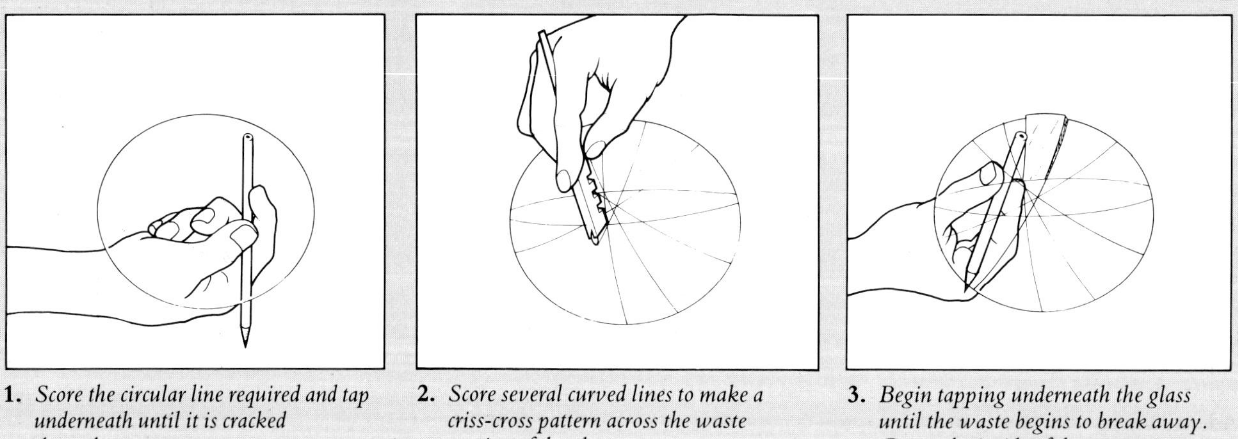

1. *Score the circular line required and tap underneath until it is cracked throughout.*

2. *Score several curved lines to make a criss-cross pattern across the waste portion of the glass.*

3. *Begin tapping underneath the glass until the waste begins to break away. Groze the inside of the curve.*

Glass painting

Glass painting is an integral feature of stained glasswork, used for portraying features, details and textures. It would be difficult to produce figurative work using only coloured glass as portraying the delicate features required in such work would be almost impossible.

A vitreous enamel paint is used which varies in colour from red-brown to black. After it has been applied it is fired at about 630 degrees C (1,166 degrees F) and is fused with the glass surface.

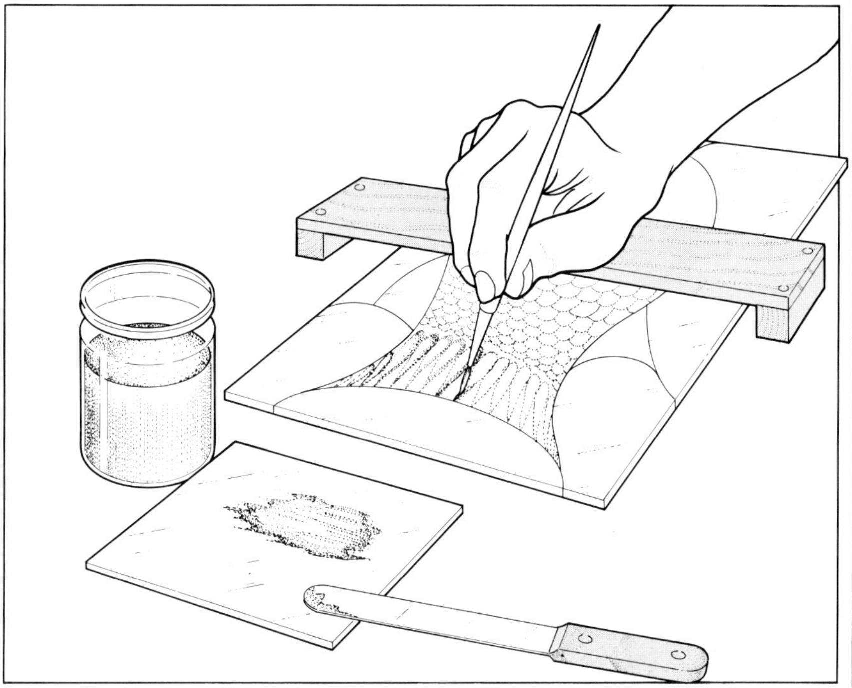

Line painting is made easier with the help of a simple hand rest.

Mixing the paint

The paint basically comprises powdered glass and iron oxide, ground to a fine powder and bought by weight from specialist suppliers.

It is either ground on a square of plate glass (or tile) with a pallet knife or glass muller, or with a small mortar and pestle.

To a tablespoon of glass powder, add a very little water, then enough gum arabic to cover a fingernail. Too much gum will make the paint blister when fired in the kiln. Add more water to produce a thick, fluid paint, the consistency of whipped double cream. Mix with water as required to make the paint flow.

Line painting

Begin by painting in the lines. Lay the glass face up on top of the cartoon which has been laid flat on a table or light-box. Trace the lines from the cartoon onto the glass with the paint. The line should be a solid, dark line, unless a washy effect is especially required. If it is too 'washy' it can be darkened with more paint while it is still wet; if a second layer of paint is added after the first has dried, air will be trapped between the two layers and the paint will blister when fired. If the paint is too thick and does not flow easily, dip the brush in clean water and then back into the paint, giving the brush a jerk downwards to remove excess paint. Any spreading of the line or unevenness can be tidied up with a needle point when the paint is dry. Do not add matt washes (see below) to unfired lines as they will be washed away.

When the lines have been painted in, the pieces of glass are put into the kiln and fired (see page 127).

When the firing has been completed and the glass has cooled down the pieces are reassembled on the large glass painting easel. If the lines require a further firing it is done at this stage. When the lines are considered satisfactory, matt washes and textures are applied and the glass fired again.

Matt washes

Matt washes, that is, glass paint diluted with water, are used to darken the glass and to build up shadows. They can be obtained by applying paint to the front of the glass with the mop brush and 'drifting' or stippling (see page 79) with the badger over it. When the matt wash is dry, brush out any highlights with the hoghair brush. Fire in the kiln. Further painting may well be necessary.

Silver stain

The use of stain allows tinted white or clear glass to be coloured yellow. Stain was first used at the beginning of the fourteenth century and enabled glass painters to produce, for example, a head with yellow hair or a halo in one piece of glass.

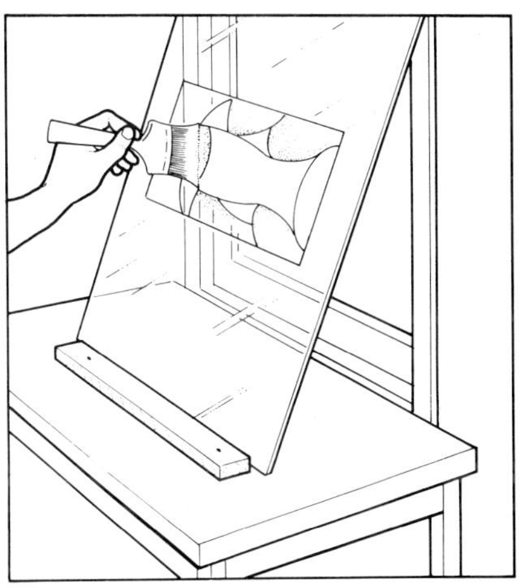

Applying matt paint with a badger.

(above) *This modern piece of stained glass depicts a dream sequence.*

(right) *Different shades and strengths of colour add realism to this rural scene.*

Stain is bought as silver reduced to a powder and is mixed with a little gum arabic and water in a similar way to mixing paint. Only a small amount of stain should be mixed as it is very expensive – a teaspoon of stain to a drop of gum arabic is sufficient. Stain is applied to the back of pure white or tinted white glass in the form of a wash the consistency of milk.

When applying stain put it on with a soft brush and then brush lightly with the badger before it is dry. This spreads the grains of the stain, resulting in an even yellow. The badger brush should be washed and dried before it is used for stain. Never use the same utensils, particularly the same brushes, for paint and stain.

When stain is fired in the kiln it produces a clear yellow of different tones. This is a stain and not an enamel; the silver actually penetrates the glass and is not just fused with the surface. Success with stain depends on trial and error. If it is fired at too high a temperature the result will be an opaque brown.

Pure white and yellow tinted white glass will take stain hard and can be fired at the same temperature as paint. This means that the paint and stain can be fired at the same time; the paint on the front and the stain on the back of the glass. Green tinted glass is soft and the stain should be fired at a lower temperature and at a separate firing to the paint. Alternatively, stain should be put on as a thin wash only.

Firing the glass

There are special kilns designed for the stained glass trade but these are expensive and, fortunately, not essential. A pottery or enamelling kiln will suffice – which can be used at nightschool. The temperature required is comparatively low, – 620-630 degrees C (1,148–1,166 degrees F). Whiting or builder's plaster is sprinkled on a ceramic bat or a metal tray to a depth of 6mm (¼in) and the pieces of glass taken from the painting easel and pressed firmly into it; the whiting should be smooth under each piece of glass. If several trays are to be fired they can be placed on top of one another with spacing ceramic beads separating them.

If a pottery kiln is to be used the tray should be placed in the centre of the kiln because most pottery kilns are uneven in temperature at 600 degrees C (1,112 degrees F); the top half of the kiln reaches the desired temperature long before the bottom half.

Once the temperature reaches 630 degrees C (1,166 degrees F), switch off and allow the kiln to cool down thoroughly. Glass can be taken out of the kiln once it is cool enough to hold in the hand. Beware of cracking the glass by taking it out too soon. The pieces of glass should now be assembled in their correct order on a board or tray, ready for leading up.

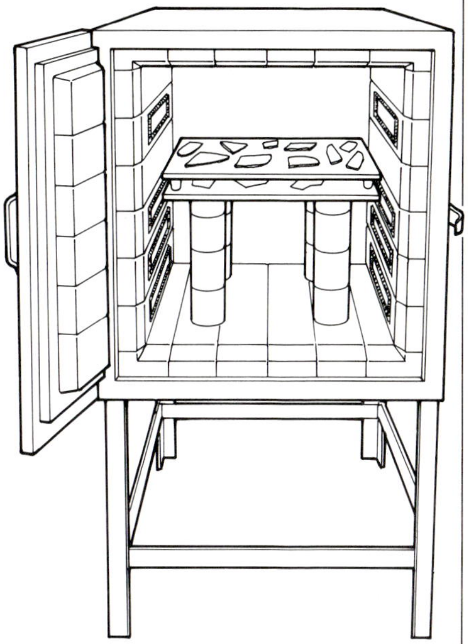

(right) *Pottery kilns are very often used for firing stained glass. This one is loaded with glass on trays which are separated by ceramic beads. If a pottery kiln is used, the trays must be placed centrally to ensure that the glass is fired evenly.*

Leading up

Having cut and fired the pieces of glass, you need to assemble them together. To do this you have to join the pieces with lead strips, a process known as 'leading up'.

Before leading up can begin, the lead must be stretched to straighten it. A lead vice or cleat should be firmly screwed to a rigid base. One end of the lead is placed in the vice; the other end held with pliers. Stand, one foot behind the other, and tug hard on the lead until it is stretched a few centimetres (fractions of an inch).

Another method of stretching lead is to put one end beneath the leg of a chair, stand on the chair and tug the lead vertically.

Use 13mm (½in) or 10mm (⅜in) flat lead to edge the panel and 6mm (¼in) flat lead between the pieces of glass being used.

The sweeps and curves of the lead, together with the fine shades of colour in the glass, call to mind the movement of a flowing river. Note the richness of the shades of blue.

When you have completed the procedures outlined in the step-by-step captions below, you can carry on with leading up the whole panel as described below.

Using 6mm (¼in) lead, cut a length to fit between the first and second pieces of glass, slotting it over the first piece of glass. Make sure it is 2mm (1/16in) short of the adjacent edge of the glass to allow for the flange of lead that will run along that edge. Slot in the second piece of glass and hold it firmly with a horseshoe nail. Continue in this way for the rest of the panel.

The black line of the cut-line should always stand clear of the pieces of glass. If necessary, groze the pieces with pliers or a glass cutter. Lead should be cut so that it butts neatly against the next piece. If flat lead is used, one flange can be tucked under another, and if a gap occurs because of inaccurate cutting, fill it up with a small sliver of lead. Where a piece of glass is too thick for the lead, it can be split and opened up.

The remaining two outside leads are fitted when the inside of the panel has been leaded up. To do this, remove the nail at one end of the panel, slot the outside lead over the glass and hold it in position with the nail. Remove all the other nails in turn, slotting the lead over the glass, and replace one or two nails outside the lead to hold it in place.

When both outside leads have been fitted, place two wooden slats next to them at right angles to each other. Hold them in position with nails. Push the outer leads against the slats of wood so that they are truly straight and at right angles to each other.

When fixing outside leads, make sure that they are perfectly straight.

Soldering

The joints formed where the leads meet must be cleaned with wire (steel) wool or a soft brass brush. Tallow or flux is rubbed onto these joints to enable the solder to fuse with the lead.

Hold a stick of soft solder against the joint and apply the hot soldering iron. Wait until the solder melts under the heat and then gently lift the iron away. A neat, clean sol-

Leading the panel

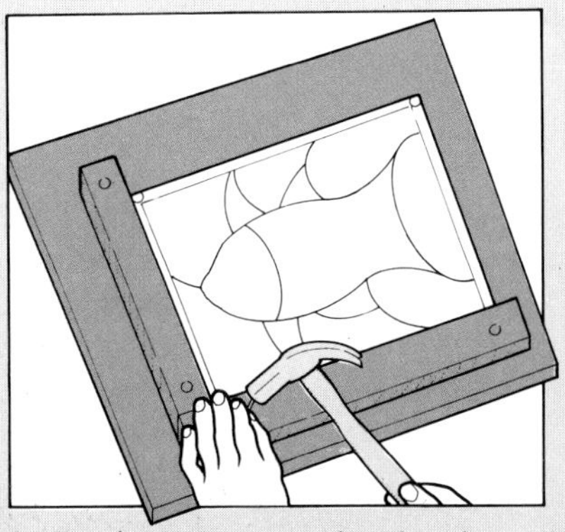

1. *Pin the cut-line onto a board or glazing bench. Lay two slats of wood – approximately 13mm × 40mm (½in × 1½in) – at right angles to each other over the cut-line so that they run along two adjacent edges of the design. These slats must be the width of one flange, plus the heart of the lead from the outline of the cut-line. Nail the slats to the board or bench.*

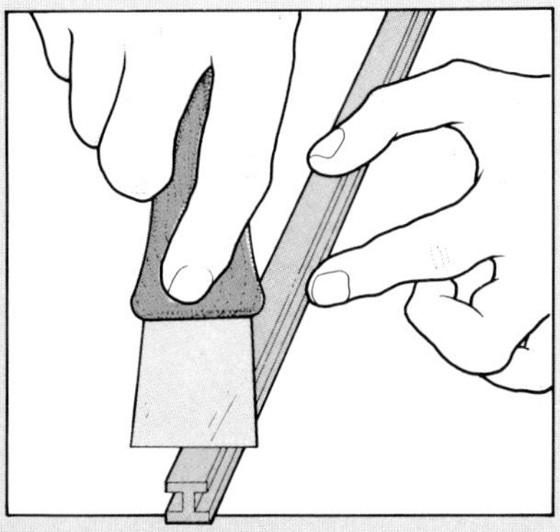

2. *Using the lead cutting knife, cut two lengths of lead to make two adjacent sides of the panel, making each about 6mm (¼in) longer than needed. Cut vertically through the lead, rocking back and forth. Keep the blade of the cutter sharp.*

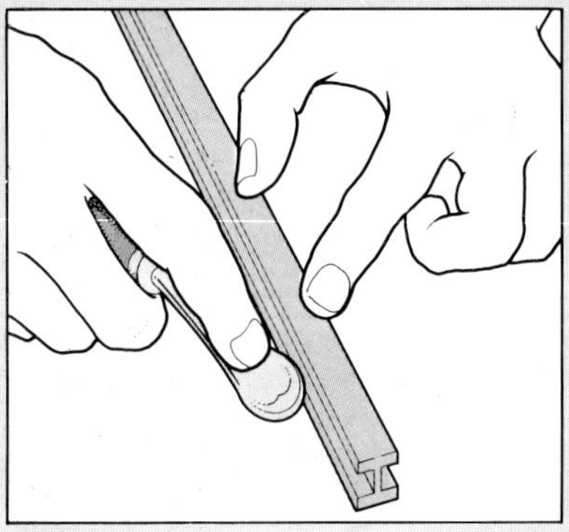

3. *Run the stopping knife along the inside of all four flanges of the leads, smoothing out any creases and wrinkles and opening them slightly.*

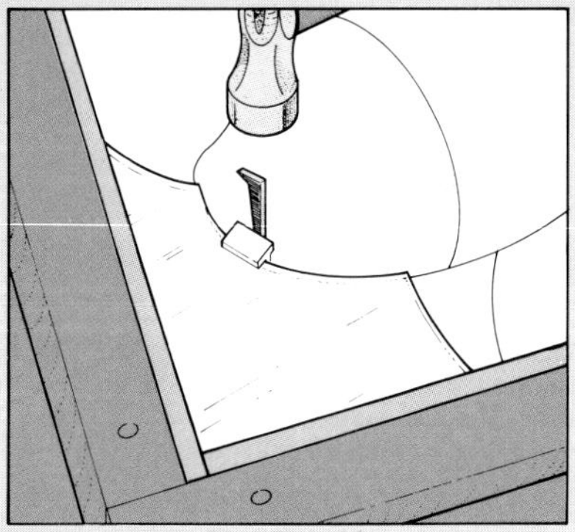

4. *Place the leads on the cut-line. Butt hard against the edges of the wooden slats. Take the piece of glass that fits into the corner you have made and slot into the open flanges. Place lead against the glass and hammer a horseshoe nail into the board against the lead.*

dered joint should be the result. Do not pad the solder about or jerk the soldering iron sharply as this will make the solder lumpy. Work with smooth, slow movements.

If the solder does not flow over the joint, the lead may be dirty or greasy. Clean it up again with wire wool or scrape it with a knife. If the solder still will not flow, examine the soldering iron tip, which should be shiny with solder. If it is not, scrape it clean with a knife or file and apply more solder when the iron is hot. If an electric soldering iron with an iron tip is being used, it should be sufficient to wipe the tip on a wet sponge. However, if the tip of the soldering iron is copper, it will probably be necessary to file it back to reveal the copper surface. Dip the tip in flux and tin it. Use the soldering iron to melt a few drops of solder onto a lid from a can. Dip the tip of the hot soldering iron into flux and then rub it into the melted solder until a thin layer adheres to the tip. When the first side of the panel has been soldered, turn it over and solder the other side.

Cementing

The final stage of making a stained glass panel is to cement it. The cement used is a fluid putty which is scrubbed into the leads so as to make the panel waterproof and, when set hard, strong and rigid.

Making the cement and cementing the panel are very messy jobs, so put some newspapers down and wear an apron. It is advisable to wear some head covering as well.

Put about six handfuls of whiting – or builder's plaster, which is cheaper and easier to obtain – into an old bucket or large can. Add a teaspoonful of black powder paint, or the black powder used by builders for colouring cement. Mix together equal quantities of boiled linseed oil and paint thinner in a jar. Then add this to the whiting of plaster and stir vigorously until it is the consistency of thick porridge.

Using the cement

First, cut a scrubbing brush in two and number the halves 'one' and 'two'. Then, ladle some of the cement onto the panel.

Using the number 'one' brush, scrub the cement into every nook and cranny of the leads, making sure that it goes under the flanges of the outside leads. Open them up where necessary, especially where the glass is thick, as it may be difficult to force the cement in. Clean off as much cement as possible from the panel with the number 'one' brush. Close up any of the flanges that have been opened with the lathekin or stopping knife.

Sprinkle whiting or plaster over the panel and continue scrubbing with the number 'two' brush. This should clean the panel completely of surplus cement.

Take a nail or thin stick of wood and run it round the inside edges of all the leads to remove any last traces of cement. Make sure that no cement is left sticking to the lead or the glass as it is very difficult to clean off when it has set hard. Continue in the same way for the second side.

Allow the cement to harden for an hour or two and then clean up both sides again with the number 'two' brush and a stick or nail.

Finally, take a soft shoe brush and brush the leads vigorously on both sides. This gives a nice polished look to the panel.

Hanging the panel

If the panel is to be hung in a window, solder two hoops of copper wire at each corner, making sure that the copper wire has been tinned first by dipping it in flux and melting on a thin layer of solder.

Great care and a lot of manual dexterity are necessary for successful leading up.

Making new leaded light windows

Diamond quarries which are pieces of diamond-shaped glass leaded together, and the most usual shape to use, are generally 150mm (6in) high × 100mm (4in) wide. Before starting to cut the glass it will be necessary to make a cut-line as follows.

Take accurate measurements from rebate (rabbet) to rebate (rabbet) of the window frame. On a sheet of paper large enough to cover the whole window, draw a thin outline of the window opening, using these measurements. This outline agrees with the exact outside dimensions of the window when leading up is complete.

Draw another line parallel to and inside the outline. The distance between the two should be equal to the width of one flange and the heart of the edging lead. The glass is cut to this inner line.

Divide each vertical inner line into equal portions. Make these 150mm (6in). Divide each horizontal inner line in the same way, making the sections 100mm (4in).

Joint up the marks diagonally across, one to the other with a felt-tip pen, to make the cut-line.

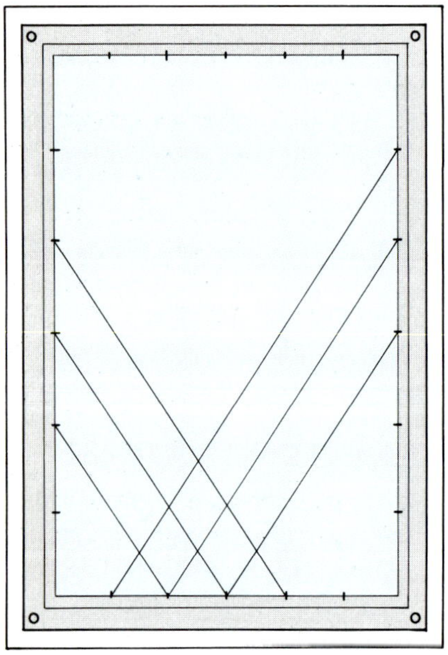

A cut-line, showing marking up for diamond quarries. The heavier outer lines mark the overall window size. The glass should be cut to the finer, inner lines.

Diamond quarries look very attractive.

Cut the glass into strips, the width of the quarry, and then cut them into the required sections. Use a straight edge and hold the glass cutter towards you, making sure the straight edge is held firm with the other hand. It must not swing off line. Cut these strips of glass into the individual quarries and place them in convenient piles near the cut-line. Proceed with leading up and cementing.

Rectangular quarries are made in the same way but are simpler to cut.

If a light is more than 1.2m (4ft) high it will be necessary to make it in two sections. With the exception of the very top and bottom leads of the light, which will be inserted into the window frame, fit a 6mm (¼in) wide lead at the top of each section. At the bottom of each section, fit a 13mm (½in) flat lead with an extra wide heart. This is called a division lead and its heart is wide enough to slot over the other leads. The flanges on one side are wider than those on the other, the wider flanges slotting over the top lead of the lower section.

Strengthening windows

If a leaded light is 450mm (18in) or more wide and more than 600mm (2ft) high, it will need strengthening with saddle bars. These are made of iron or a non ferrous metal 10mm (⅜in) thick, which are fixed across the inside of the window and into the window frame. The leaded lights are attached to the bars with copper ties, which are lengths of copper wire, about 70mm (3in) long, soldered at their centre to strong joints in the lead. About four, evenly spaced, ties will be required across a 450mm (18in) wide light. Make sure that plenty of solder is used so that they will not break off when tied to the bars.

For a leaded light of 450mm (18in) width, a saddle bar will be needed for every 450mm (18in) of height.

Leaded lights can be further strengthened by the insertion of thin steel rods (steels). Using 13mm (½in) or 10mm (⅜in) wide leads, run the rods along one or both sides of the heart of the lead.

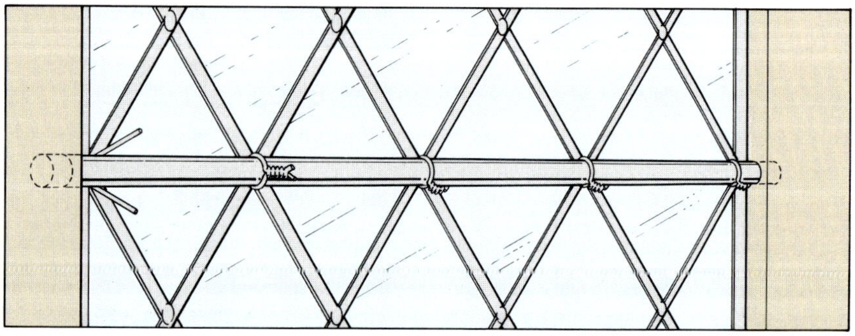

Saddle bars are attached to windows using copper ties. The ties are twisted around the bar and then tucked underneath it, as shown on the right of the illustration above.

Fixing a window into position

This circular wooden-framed window set in stone is situated in New Lanark in Scotland. To insert a circular window, a template of the casement should be made to ensure that your measurements are accurate.

A wooden-framed window is fixed using the following techniques. First, chisel out all the old putty or cement which was left in the window frame when the window was removed. Try the window for size and mark the positions of any saddle bars (if required) on the inside of the window frame. Allow enough room for the thickness of the outer came and the putty between the saddle bar as well as the outer edge of the rebate.

Drill or chisel out the holes for the saddle bars. They are inserted about 6mm (¼in) into the window frame on each side. So one hole should be slightly more than twice this depth to allow the bar to be slotted into it fully and to clear the opposite frame before being eased into the 6mm (¼in) deep hole in that frame. Cut the saddle bars to the required length: the width of the window opening, plus 6mm (¼in) at each end for insertion into the frame. Put the bars into position.

Put a layer of putty all round the inside of the window frame rebate (rabbet) and fit the window into position, pressing firmly all round. Twist the copper ties tightly round the bars with the pliers. Cut them short and tuck them underneath the bars. Replace any beading. Otherwise, hold the window in place by tapping panel pins (glazier points) into the frame and apply putty, using a putty knife for a smooth finish.

There are rare occasions when a domestic window is set in stone, similar to church windows. In this case, there is a groove all the way round the stone window for the leaded light.

Cut any copper ties holding the window to its saddle bars and chisel the mortar away to free the window. If the window is to be kept, great care must be taken not to crack the glass. When the window is quite loose in its grooves it can be levered out without too much difficulty. Chisel out the saddle bars if they need replacing.

If the window is badly damaged and a cut-line is necessary, take the measurements from one window edge to the other. This is called the sight size.

The repaired window, or the new one, should slot into the grooves in the same way as it came out. The groove on one side will be deeper than on the other. This allows one side of the light to be pushed in far enough for the other side to clear the edge of the window frame and be inserted into its own groove. When the window is positioned correctly, an equal amount of the outer leads will be visible on each side.

The next job to be done is to insert the saddle bars and tie them to the window with the copper ties. Wedge the windows up against the bars from the outside with small pieces of lead so that they do not rattle when shaken. Damp down the stonework and 'point' (see page 183) round the edges of the window, inside and out, with mortar made from three parts sand, two parts lime, and one part cement, plus water as required.

Casements are not always perfect rectangles, so accurate measurements must be taken of the opening between the frame's metal flanges. Draw the cut-line 3mm (⅛in) smaller all round to allow for the heart of the lead when fitting. When the leaded light has been made, open one flange of the outer leads at right angles so that the light can be slotted into the casement. Fold the lead down. Push putty underneath the flange and press firmly down, all the way round.

When making the leaded light the four corners of the outer leads should be mitred (see page 21).

If a window is not rectangular but is curved as, for instance, in an arched or pointed window, you will have to make templates of the shape to get an exact fit.

Use cardboard or brown paper to cut out a shape which will fit the window exactly. Base the cut-line on this. With stone windows, the outside edge of the lead will be the inside edge of the groove and the centreline of the outer leads will be the sight size measurement.

On windows with a rebate (rabbet), the outside edge of the lead fits into the rebate and the centreline of the outer leads will be level with the inside edge of the rebate.

Leaded light and stained glass repair

If a quarry – a diamond-shaped piece of glass – is smashed or badly cracked and needs replacing, it is possible to replace it *in situ*, provided the lead cames are undamaged and still firm. To do this, take a tracing from the inside of the lead surrounding the broken pane. Remove the broken glass, wearing thick gloves to avoid being cut. Cut the lead flanges at the joints and then fold back the flanges, using a pair of pliers if necessary. Clean off all the old cement or putty.

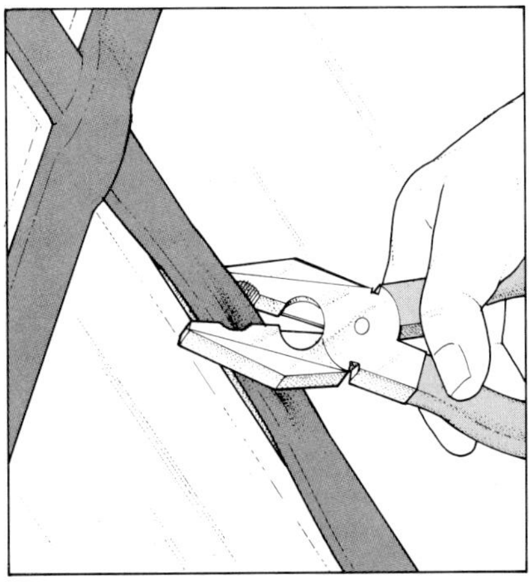

Folding back the lead flange.

Cut the new pane of glass, using the tracing as a guide, but making it 2mm (1/16in) larger all round. The extra will slot under the flanges but the new piece of glass should still be smaller than the original piece, otherwise it will not go back easily.

Add some black powder paint to some glazing putty to make it grey in colour, and press it into the open flanges of the leads. Fit the new piece of glass back into position and press back the leads.

If the stained glass window of the leaded light is badly damaged, the whole window has to be removed for repair. This can be done using the following techniques. Cut the copper ties if the window has been strengthened with saddle bars. Gently lever up any wooden beading that is holding the window in position. (If there is no wooden beading, the window will be held in position with panel pins and putty.) Gently chisel out the putty and pull out the panel pins with pincers.

Using a lead cutting knife, insert the blade between the lead and the wooden frame and lever carefully. Work the blade all the way round until the window comes away from the frame.

Levering out a window from the back.

To repair a buckled window, lay the window on the workbench and examine it. It may only need to be pressed flat with firm, hard pressure. Alternatively, lay a heavy weight on the buckled part and leave it for a day or two. It should gradually flatten itself out. If neither of these methods work, it will have to be re-leaded.

Examine the leads very carefully for damage. If they are broken, it is usually sufficient to solder over the cracks. The lead will have to be scraped thoroughly clean before it will take the solder.

Sometimes, whole sections of lead will have to be replaced. When removing old lead, cut through the flanges on both sides, using the lead knife. Cut through the heart of the lead with a sharpened horseshoe nail. Then proceed in the same way as for leading a panel (see page 127).

If a piece of glass has just one or two cracks in it, they can usually be repaired with a strap. First, cut one flange from a strip of lead with the pincers. Cut this lead to the correct length to fit along the crack. It can be butted up to the leads which surround the piece of broken glass, or, if possible, inserted underneath them. Solder the joints. Repeat the procedure on the other side of the glass and push some putty under the lead flanges to secure them.

Badly damaged glass cannot be repaired with straps. It must be replaced or completely re-leaded. For re-leading the window: measure the window from rebate (rabbet) to rebate (rabbet) before taking it out – this is a precaution in case the window is so badly damaged that it falls from its original shape as it is removed. Take the window out of the frame and place it on the workbench. Now, place a piece of tracing paper over the whole window and take a rubbing of the leads. Make a cut-line from the rubbing and proceed as for leading a panel.

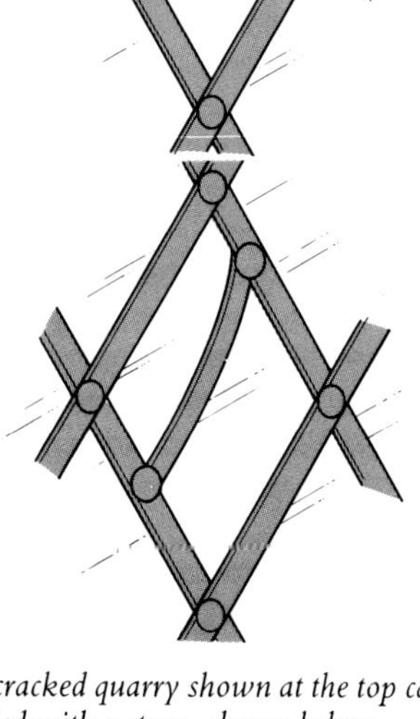

The cracked quarry shown at the top can be mended with a strap, shown below.

Repairing a bullion (bull's eye)

A bullion (bull's eye) is a large disc of solid glass, made by being spun round rather than being blown into a cylinder by a blowpipe. It is the centre of crown glass. Bullions are sometimes used in rectangular leaded lights, but are more often used on their own, set in small openings. The centre may be as much as 13mm (1/2in) thick, but the edges will always be fairly thin. In the UK, bullions are often found in the windows of old houses.

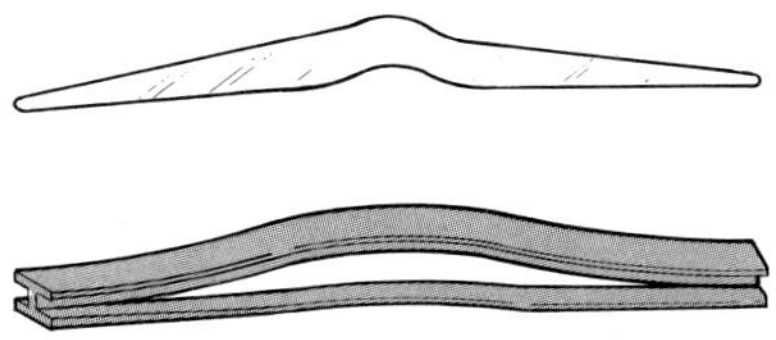

The illustration above shows a section of a bullion (bull's eye). Below it is a piece of split lead. On the right is the bullion slotted into the split lead.

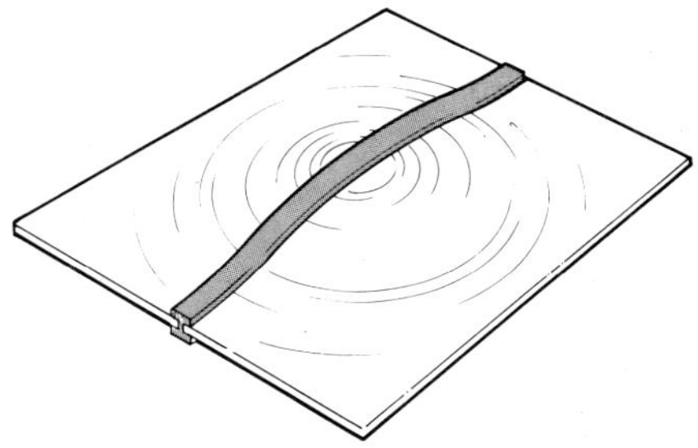

If the bullion is cracked in half through the centre it will be necessary to repair it with a lead strap. In this case, take some lead the width of the bullion and use pincers to split a section of the heart long enough to accommodate the centre of the bullion. It may be necessary to narrow the bullion by cutting or grozing both sides, to allow room for the heart of the lead. Lead up and solder.

If there is no lead around the bullion and it fits into some other material, wood for example, it may be necessary to surround the bullion with lead before it is reinserted, so that the lead strap may be soldered in place. This method of splitting the lead also works for any piece of glass that is too thick for the heart of the lead being used. It can also be used for 'plating', a method of laying one piece of glass on top of another to obtain a special colour. This is useful when trying to match colours in a repair job.

Glossary

Angry white line: a very clear white line made by applying too much pressure to the glass cutter. It is very difficult to break the glass when this happens.

Antique glass: hand-made glass, produced by either gathering a blob of molten glass at the end of a blowpipe and blowing it into a cylinder, or spinning into a large flat disc.

Bullion (bull's eye): the centre of crown glass which is left when the circular sheet of glass is broken away from the punty rod used for making glass artefacts.

Came: strips of lead, used to join pieces of glass in stained glasswork.

Copper ties: lengths of copper wire soldered to the stained glass sections and wound round saddle bars to hold the stained glass firmly in position.

Crown method: a method of producing a circular sheet of glass by spinning a 'blob' of molten glass gathered at the end of a solid steel rod.

Cut-line: a tracing made on tracing paper from a cartoon, or full-sized drawing of the stained glass panel, and used as a glass cutting guide.

Diamond quarries: diamond-shaped pieces of glass leaded together.

Division lead: a came of lead with core or heart off centre and greater in height than the rest of the lead used in the window. It is soldered to the bottom of the upper section of the window so that it can be fitted over the section beneath it.

Flange of lead: the edge of a came of lead.

Flat lead: the flanges or edges of a came of lead which are flatter and more malleable than those of round lead which has bevelled flanges.

Flux: a compound which enables molten solder to stick to the lead.

Glass powder: glass finely ground to the consistency of flour and used as a basis for glass paint.

Grozing: 'nibbling' or 'chewing' the edges of glass with pliers to obtain the required shape.

Heart of lead: the central core of a came of lead, linking the top and bottom flanges. It is about 3mm (1/8in) thick; the height varies.

Iron oxide: an oxide obtained from iron and mixed with glass powder to make glass paint.

Muff process: a method for making glass by gathering a 'blob' of molten glass at the end of a blowpipe and blowing it into a cylinder.

Quarry: *see* diamond quarry.

Score-line: the line made with a glass cutter on the surface of a piece of glass.

Sight size: the width and height of a window, excluding any rebate (rabbet) or groove.

Silver staining: specially treated silver for painting onto white glass, which will stain the glass yellow when fired in a kiln.

Spacing ceramic bead: a small ceramic cube used to separate the metal or ceramic trays which are used for firing glass in a kiln.

Whiting: chalk ground to a fine powder.

Tiles and tiling

It would be an unusual home indeed that had no ceramic tiles. Their ability to withstand water and other liquid penetration, and their hard-wearing qualities, make them the first choice for surfaces in the bathroom and kitchen and for whole floors. Without them, the home would be much less interesting because they provide colour and decoration.

Made of clay with a hard, shiny glaze finish, tiles come in a variety of shapes and sizes. The glaze protects and accentuates the pattern and colours with which the tile is decorated.

It is the versatility of tiles that has made them a popular feature since ancient times – and the modern tile is no different in essentials from its predecessors.

Tiles have been found in the remains of palaces built by the ancient Persians 2,500 years ago, while the Romans made exquisitely beautiful mosaics for quite ordinary homes. Their durability, which was one of their main attractions, has been proved by their survival in often very unpromising conditions.

Such was the cost of making tiles that in the Middle Ages they were limited to the floors of churches, cathedrals and the palaces of the rich but, despite the ravages of time and vandalism, fine examples of medieval tiles can still be seen both in museums and *in situ*. It was only in the seventeenth and eighteenth centuries, however, with English and Dutch hand-made Delftware that the tile again came into popular use.

In the second half of the nineteenth century, the introduction of mass production techniques produced a cornucopia of tiles in a seemingly endless variety of styles and designs. Some of the leading artists of the time lent their skills to the new fashion. Designs ranging from gothic to oriental motifs by famous names such as Minton, Wedgwood, Pugin, Wyatt, Millais and Temple abounded.

A meticulously hand-painted tile depicting blossom.

Note the fine detail of this rose design.

The decorative and hard-wearing qualities of tiles were appreciated and admired in the late nineteenth and early twentieth centuries and tiles were used extensively in kitchens, bathrooms, fireplaces and on furniture. Certain stores, particularly those belonging to butchers and fishmongers, were tiled throughout for hygiene, while entrance halls and rooms of public buildings were tiled for easy maintenance and to add a touch of splendour. Even the most modest house boasted some ceramic gem to lighten the drabness.

After World War 1 the vogue for tiling diminished and, with the fashion for art deco styles, became less ornate. Now, however, even these tiles have a tremendous following.

The photograph on the right shows a superb specimen of a nineteenth century fireplace. The inlaid tiles are designed to withstand the fairly rough treatment a fireplace receives in terms of both heat and constant cleaning.

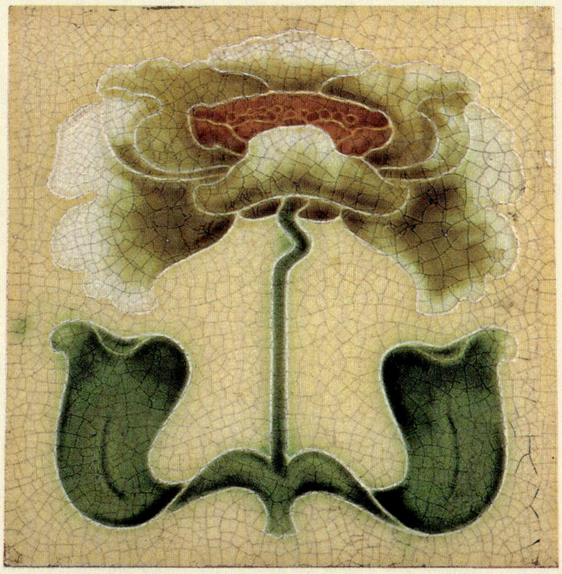

A crazed tile showing an art-nouveau lily.

A reproduction tile with a traditional design.

Collecting old tiles

A number of different tiles have been incorporated into this floor, adding variety and interest.

Vandals and the demolition contractor's hammer sadly have destroyed millions of these ceramic treasures. But such was the original plethora of tiles that fine examples can still be found literally on our own doorsteps.

Until relatively recently, it was possible to pick up some fine old tiles from demolition sites at little or no cost. This is now almost impossible. Nevertheless, the really determined collector can still pick up a number of tiles in this way which will be far less expensive than obtaining them from an antique dealer – and there is the added advantage of being able to date the tiles by the age of the building as well as knowing the original use to which the tile was put. It might have been, for example, to create a fire surround, or to grace the sides of a bath or tub. To acquire tiles this way you will have to move in quickly when the demolition men appear so that you can be in the right place at the right time.

Prices from antique dealers' markets and salesrooms depend on many factors. Dealers may ask more for tiles bearing such names as Minton, Maw or Wedgwood, not necessarily because they are better tiles but because these names command respect in the trade. By all means bargain, if you think the price is too high. You will certainly have to pay considerably more for a complete set with a special subject theme such as a Minton set of Shakespearean scenes, but there are many specimens of ordinary yet richly-coloured floral patterns, for example, which are much less expensive and equally satisfying for the collector.

Some dealers will look out for

special tiles for regular customers, so do not hesitate to let them know of your interests.

A number of specialist dealers not only stock nineteenth century tiles but can also supply a wealth of information and give excellent guidance to the serious collector.

Sale rooms usually sell tiles as part of a mixed lot. Sometimes, however, you may come across a whole box for sale and, if there are a few duplicates, these can be swopped for others. Swop two mediocre tiles bought at an auction for one fine specimen in an antique shop, if the dealer is willing to do this.

There are many ways to build up a collection of tiles. If you are determined, discerning and, above all, lucky, it is amazing how quickly the collection will grow.

Reproduction tiles

There are a small number of manufacturers who reproduce a variety of reproduction tiles to exact specifications which adhere to traditional manufacturers' techniques. These tiles are expensive as the quality is very high.

There are a number of specialist stores which cater for both old and reproduction tiles. Most reputable dealers can speak authoritatively on technical problems such as surfaces and fixers. Failing this, they can usually put you in touch with expert help.

Bearing in mind the practical and aesthetic benefits offered by ceramic and allied decor products, it must be appreciated that tiling represents an important investment. The selection of the right tiling scheme is, therefore, very important. Take your time selecting the tiles you want, and do not be afraid to ask questions. If the retailer cannot help, by all means contact the manufacturer.

Most manufacturers pride themselves on their advisory service and the right advice at the outset can save considerable disappointment at the finish.

Tools for tiling

The tools needed for tiling are few, which will mean your financial outlay will not be excessive. The tools are also simple to use, which is an added advantage. However, most are tools which cannot be used for other home restoration work, so it might be a good idea to reserve a cupboard in your workshop labelled 'tile kit'.

Wooden guides and nails

Your true datum line will need to be established along the entire wall. This is done by fixing wooden guides to the wall with masonry nails in line with the lowest row of whole tiles. These must be attached strongly enough to bear the weight of the tiles while the adhesive is setting, but not so strongly that the wooden guides cannot be removed when they have done the job.

Bolster

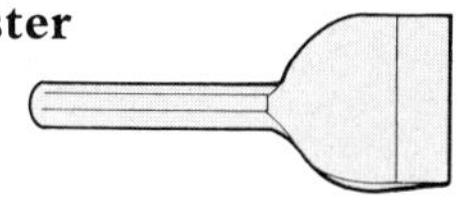

A bolster (a cold chisel with a broadly splayed cutting edge) is used, together with a hammer, for removing dried mortar from old tiles and also for cutting imitation brick or stone tiles.

Carborundum stone

A carborundum stone is useful for smoothing the edges of cut tiles.

Gauging stick

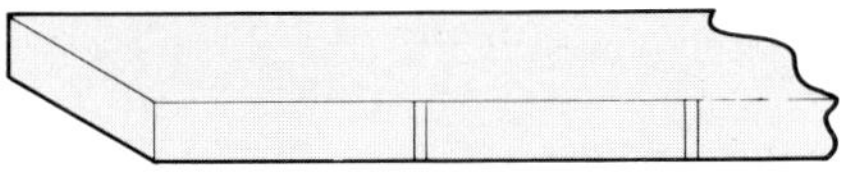

A gauging stick is best made on-the-job so that it conforms to the size of the tile you are using. Use a straight piece of wood about 2m (6ft) long, and mark off in tile widths, remembering to allow for space lugs or grouting joints.

Hammer

A hammer is used with a bolster chisel to remove dried mortar from old tiles.

Nippers

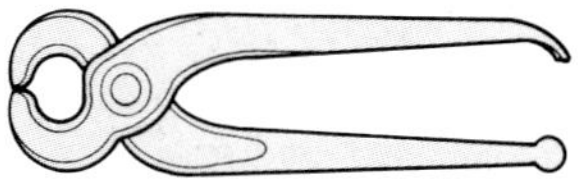

Special tile nippers may be bought, but ordinary pincers will usually do the job of nipping off pieces of tile quite efficiently.

Notched spreader

A plastic notched spreader is usually supplied together with most proprietary containers of adhesive. This is for ridging the adhesive at a uniform level from the surface to the tiles.

Notched trowel

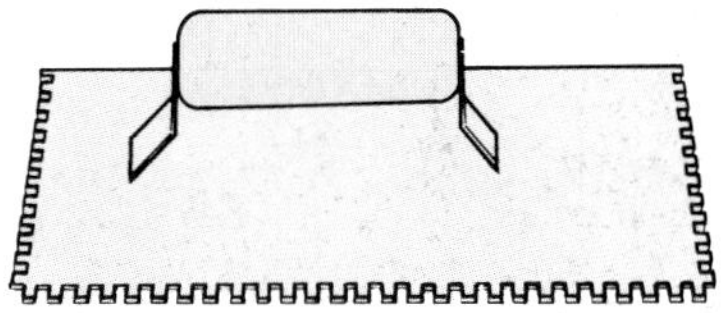

A notched trowel will both spread and ridge the adhesive. It is to be used only if you are tiling large areas when you will find the job much less time-consuming and tiring. For floor tiling, such a special trowel is essential.

Spirit level and plumb line

True vertical and horizontal lines, which are essential for well laid-out tiling, rarely occur without using a spirit level and plumb line.

Straight edge

A straight edge is a length of wood with a verified straight edge which ensures that all the tiles over a surface are lying flush, thus forming a flat surface.

Tile cutter (scriber)

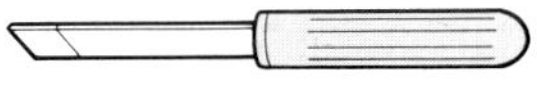

A tile cutter, or scriber, is an instrument with a tungsten carbide tip and is the most efficient tool for cutting tiles. A glass cutter can be used, but unless it has a diamond edge it will blunt quickly.

Restoring old tiles

The late nineteenth century in Great Britain witnessed the introduction of a seemingly endless variety of ceramic tiles in the most exquisite colours and designs. It is no exaggeration to say that the ceramic tiles of the period were, at best, an art form in their own right. Their restoration and, of course, the restoration of all tiles from an earlier period should therefore be carried out with all the care and attention normally devoted to *objets d'art*, with the added knowledge that they are extremely fragile.

Regardless of whether your tiles come directly from a long-neglected demolition site, or have been purchased from an architectural salvage specialist or an antique dealer, they will probably require a certain amount of renovation.

The renovation of antique ceramic tiles is essentially straightforward. The extent of restoration, however, depends very much on the use to which the finished product will be put.

Old tiles were commonly used as fire surrounds, splash protectors for baths or sinks, or as decorative inserts on washstands and kitchen ranges. Nowadays, they are often seen mounted in wooden frames as trivets or pot stands or hung on walls. (For more ideas, see page 145).

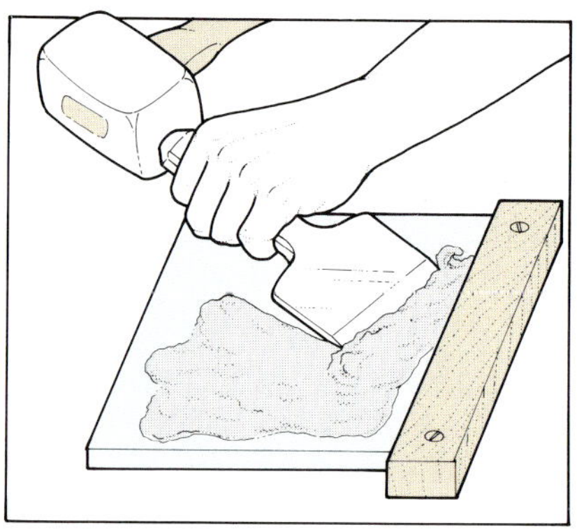

(above) *Tiles fixed to a kitchen wall near a work surface not only prevent plasterwork from being damaged by splashing liquids but also make the area look attractive.*

(left) *Removing mortar by hammer and chisel.*

Restoration techniques

The glazed decorative face of the tile and the unglazed back pose different problems for the restorer.

The back and sides will almost certainly have a firmly set layer of mortar attached which will have to be removed. This is best done on a traditional wooden bench rather than on one of the modern collapsible types. Remember that the tile will be lying glaze side down, so it is absolutely essential that the bench surface is both flat and clean. (It may be necessary to make sure of this by laying a piece of heavy cardboard or plywood between the tile and the bench.)

First ensuring that the tile is firmly anchored, gently remove the mortar with a hammer and cold chisel (preferably of the splayed bolster type). Bear in mind that tiles, particularly the thinner varieties, are very fragile. Keep the angle between the tile and chisel as shallow as possible and make sure that the edge is attacking the mortar and not the tile itself.

Cleaning agents

Should a hammer and chisel fail to achieve results, immersion in a strong solution of caustic soda, or one of the proprietary alternatives, should loosen the mortar sufficiently to allow its removal. (The caustic bath will not affect the glazed face of the tile and, in fact, will remove any cement on the tile face.) Any remaining tile mortar can then be removed using a cold chisel, sand paper or sanding disc. When using caustic soda or other strong cleaning agents it is as well to remember that they are extremely corrosive and can seriously damage both eyes and skin. Use them very carefully, following the manufacturer's instructions to the letter.

The glazed face of the tile may be covered with an age-old accretion of dirt and grime, but this can generally be removed quite easily with warm and soapy water or an ordinary household cleaner. Ingrained discoloration usually responds to household bleach. Tiles which were used as fire surrounds will often have acquired an accumulation of grate black (blacklead). This can be removed with a solvent such as paint thinner, using a fine wire wool and then rinsing with warm soapy water.

Crazing

Crazing in the surface glaze can either be seen as a problem or as a quality of old tiles. A good example of surface crazing is shown in the photograph below. Craze lines are literally splits in the surface glaze brought about by poor firing or by expansion and contraction of the tile due to temperature changes. Over the years, these cracks become ingrained with dirt. While this can be easily removed by the bleach treatment outlined above, you may prefer to retain the antique effect given to the tile by the crazed patterns.

An example of crazing accentuating the leaf and flower pattern.

Paint removal

Removing paint from the glazed surface of ceramic tiles is relatively easy as the non-porous nature of the glazing offers little key for the paint to stick to. Simply apply a proprietary paint stripper and remove the paint with fine wire wool. Multiple layers of old paint may require further applications of stripper which may be time-consuming. However, you do have the satisfaction of knowing that, over the years, the paint has provided a protective layer on the tile surface!

Do not use a paint scraper or coarse abrasives on the tile face. Surface glazes are often soft and easily damaged and, once damaged, are virtually impossible to reinstate.

Broken tiles

To a certain degree, even broken tiles can be reclaimed. Follow the cleaning procedures outlined above and dry off the tile pieces. Then assemble the pieces in the correct shape and apply a fast-setting, clear, synthetic adhesive (but not cyanoacrylate glues).

When assembling, make sure to lay the pieces face down on a perfectly flat surface so that, once assembled, the face is flush. Be sparing with the adhesive in order to minimize seepage onto the glazed surface. A sheet of newspaper beneath the tile will avoid the embarrassment of the tile irrevocably stuck to a nice table or work top. Any traces of newspaper or excess glue can be removed from the glazed surface with a craft knife or sharp chisel when the glue has dried but while it is still supple. Exercise extreme care to avoid carving lumps out of the tile surface.

Despite the apparently rough and ready nature of this technique, the resulting joins will be virtually undetectable to all but the closest of examinations.

Replacing damaged tiles

One of the advantages of ceramic tiles is the ease of general maintenance. In the unlikely event of a tile being damaged, its removal and replacement are relatively simple.

You may have difficulty in matching the colour of the tile you are removing, in which case you might consider it worthwhile to remove a number of tiles at random and replace these with decorative insets to give your surface a completely new look.

Replacing a damaged tile

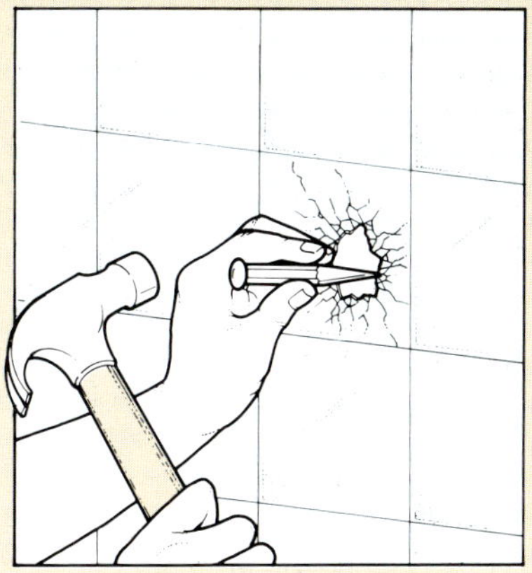

1. *Starting from tile centre, with hammer and cold chisel gently chip off small bits of damaged tile, working to the edges.*

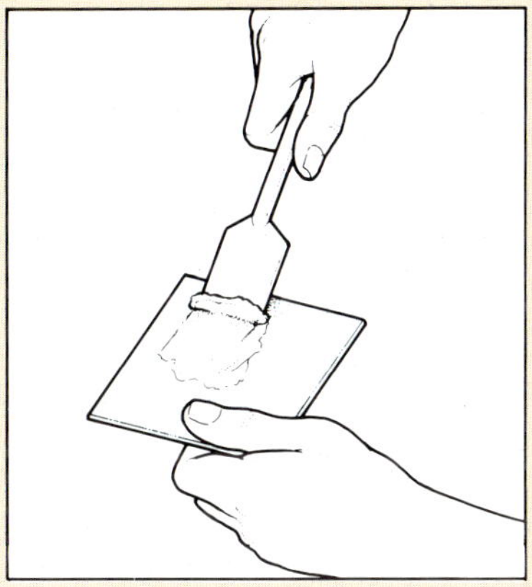

2. *Clean out recess to accommodate tile replacement. Apply adhesive to new tile. Press into position.*

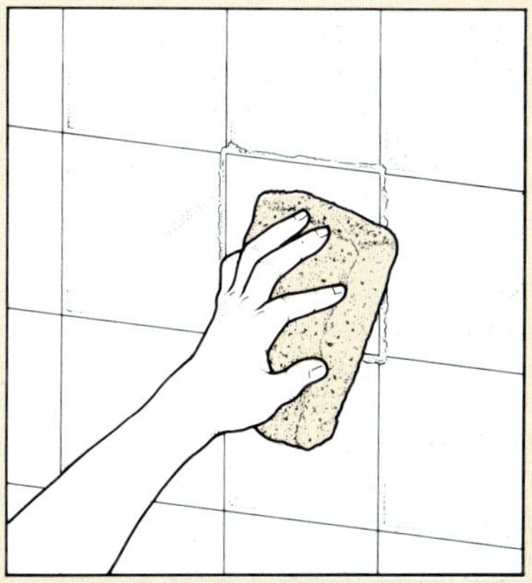

3. *Grout according to the manufacturer's instructions.*

Fixing materials, surfaces and movement

With the advance of modern tile technology, strict international standards have been introduced relating to quality, performance and fixing techniques for wall and floor tiles.

Tiles are classified according to methods of production, such as dust-pressed, extruded or cast, and are tested and graded according to such qualities as porosity (water absorption), tensile strength, abrasion resistance and thermal expansion.

Fixing materials

From around 1850 until 1949, mixtures of sand and Portland cement were used. In 1950, the first ceramic tile adhesive was marketed under the name of 'Richafix' and was the forerunner of the adhesives known today.

In 1959, the first water-based mastics and cement-based adhesives came on to the market. There are now two broad groups of adhesives available for fixing tiles. The first is cement-based adhesives, based on Portland cement, modified by the addition of various chemicals and fillers. These come in powder form and have to be mixed with water on site. The second is organic-based adhesives, which are usually mixtures of rubber, polyvinyl acetate and similar materials in either organic or water solvents. These are normally ready-mixed and can be used straight from the container, although some consist of a separate powder and a liquid catalyst which has to be mixed on site.

Sand-cement fixing methods are still quite widely used, but adhesives now by far predominate for tile fixing for the following reasons:

1. In most situations they offer greater adhesion.
2. Using adhesives, tiles are quicker and easier to fix.
3. Mixing errors, which contribute to installation failures, are avoided.
4. There is no need to soak the tiles.
5. Individual adhesive formulas are available to suit different surfaces.

Wall structures and surfaces

Wall structures comprise materials such as brick, concrete, concrete block, wood or studding. On top of the basic structure there may be an intermediate covering (of sand/cement rendering – finishing) and over this a finish of plaster or wallboards such as plywood, hardboard, blockboard, plaster boards (gypsum wallboards) and fibreglass.

Usually, the tiling surface will be sufficiently flat to allow fixing with a 'thin bed'. This is a setting bed of adhesive up to a thickness of 3mm (⅛in). However, irregularities in the surface may preclude this. Before applying the adhesive, check the trueness of the surface by using a 2m (6ft) straight edge. Any gap under the straight edge should not exceed 3mm (⅛in) in depth. If large gaps are apparent, correction will be necessary.

Alternatively, a 'thick bed' adhesive (that is, up to 13mm – ½in – thick) can be used.

Structural movement

There are three main categories of structural movement. Setting movement is the change in size which occurs as the materials used in the actual building set and harden as they dry out. This change may continue over several years, although normally any major setting takes place within four to eight weeks. Once it has occurred, it is irreversible. Sufficient time must therefore be allowed before tile fixing is attempted, especially in new houses.

Moisture movement is an expansion and contraction of the foundation, according to the amount of moisture in the atmosphere. Different materials vary in the extent of their movement. Stresses can be set up which can lead to 'movement failures'. For example, if plaster is applied to damp lightweight breeze blocks which have a relatively large moisture content, the movement of the wall in drying out, relative to that of the plaster, could set up a stress which might cause plaster failure. This would inevitably result in the tiles failing to adhere, even though they were properly fixed onto what appeared to be a viable plaster surface. If in doubt, allow sufficient time (at least two weeks) to elapse prior to fixing.

Thermal movement, as the name suggests, is caused by temperature variation. Except in unusual situations, such as fireplaces and boiler rooms, it is not of very great significance. When thermal movement does occur, a special flexible heat-resistant adhesive should be employed. Advice on this should be available from any reputable tile supplier.

As a rough guide, the table below illustrates the relative setting and moisture movements of materials most commonly encountered.

Structural movement of materials

1. **Relatively small amounts**
   Well-fired clay bricks
   Hollow clay bricks
   Wall tiles
   Calcium sulphate plaster
   Plaster block and slabs
   Some calcium silicate bricks
   Concrete bricks
2. **Moderate amounts**
   Dense concrete
   Sand and cement mortars
   Some calcium silicate bricks
   Concrete bricks
3. **Large amounts**
   Wood and cement materials
   Fibrous slabs
   Asbestos-cement sheeting
   Plywood and wood
   Most building boards

Preparing the surface for tiling

Before preparing any surface for tiling, thought should be given to the suitability of the surface for the tiles. You might be faced with a number of problems. Setting tiles in an antique table, for example, may well be pleasing to the eye, but will scarcely enhance the value of the piece on the market! Also, ceramic tiles are relatively heavy, so the surface to be tiled should be both thick enough and strong enough to bear the added load without stress.

A number of tile types are listed in the glossary on page 145.

Preparing surfaces	
Wood backing	**1.** The boards must be backed by a rigid framework and, in the case of hardboard, covered with a stiffer medium such as plywood. **2.** Natural wood expands and contracts as its moisture content changes. This may mean a special flexible adhesive will have to be used.
Painted surfaces	**1.** Ensure that the surface is clean and free from grease or other contaminants. **2.** Organic or solvent-based tile adhesives are not suitable for painted surfaces. **3.** Old water-based colours or old wall coverings should be removed. **4.** Good quality water-based or gloss (oil-based) paint may provide a sufficiently sound base. However, check the adhesion of the paint. To do this, press a strip of self-adhesive tape firmly to the surface and then rip it off quickly. If paint comes off the surface, it is not sound and should be removed entirely. Adherence will be improved if paint surfaces are scored with a wire brush or coarse sand paper.
Sheets and boards	**1.** Make sure the surface is perfectly dry and firm. **2.** Check that there are no bumps or hollows on the surface. **3.** Apply a primer according to the manufacturer's instructions. **4.** Exterior boards must be of marine ply.
Rendered (finished) brickwork and concrete blocks	**1.** The rendering (finishing) must be flat, dry and clean. **2.** With new rendering, allow at least 14 days for it to dry out before fixing. **3.** Allow new concrete blocks to dry out for at least one month before rendering and two weeks for rendering to dry.
Exteriors	**1.** Care should be taken to protect the surface to be tiled from adverse weather conditions and climatic extremes, both during tiling and for as long as possible after grouting. **2.** Where possible, use the solid bed fixing method, making sure that no voids occur between the tile and the bedding. **3.** When using frost-resistant or special types of tile, always seek the advice of the manufacturer concerning special fixing recommendations that may apply.
Plaster (stucco) surfaces	**1.** Make sure the surface is clean and grease-free. **2.** Allow new plaster four weeks to dry. **3.** Tile only onto a finished coat, not on to a bonding coat (finishing plasters have a fine texture; undercoats are normally coarser). **4.** Check the condition of the plaster – if dusty or friable use a primer.
Old tiled surfaces	Old tiled surfaces provide a flat firm base and can be tiled over with few problems. Make sure the old surface is clean and replace any tiles that are loose or missing.

If in doubt, seek the advice of a reputable tile dealer.
Mistakes can be costly and are usually irreversible.

Setting out the area to be tiled

Setting out the area to be tiled is crucial. All the extensive preparatory work, and the most skilful dexterity in fixing, will come to nothing unless great care is taken in setting out before a single tile is fixed. Planning is essential for the maximum aesthetic effect. You would be very lucky to find a surface to accommodate an exact number of whole tiles. Almost invariably, there will be a need for narrow strips of cut tile to fill out the gaps. A golden rule of tiling is that these strips should be distributed symmetrically around the edge of the area to give the area visual balance. If the wall is only half tiled, the cut pieces should be at the skirting board level, whereas if you are tiling a complete wall the border of cut tiles should run along the ceiling and skirting board (baseboard).

Where a wall is broken by a door or window, it may not be possible to centre the tiles on the wall without having to cut awkward pieces of tile to fit around the opening. In this case, a good rule of thumb is to regard the door or window as the focal point of the room and to centre the tiles on the opening.

Setting out the tile array is achieved by using the gauging stick to gauge exactly how many tiles will cover an area, and thus how many tiles will lie on a wall. The gauging stick will also give you the width of the cut border that will be needed at the end of each horizontal row. If this width is less than one-third of a full tile, accurate cutting will be difficult. This problem can be overcome by reducing the number of tiles in the row by one. Each border piece will now be between one-half and two-thirds title width.

At window openings, use the gauging stick to assess the width of the cut pieces on either side of the opening. Again, adjust the number of whole tiles in a row to avoid narrow strips. Where there is a window opening, apply the same principal to the area below the window, making sure there is an equal border of cut tiles both top and bottom. The next step is to establish a level datum line. Never trust a skirting board (baseboard): this will probably be out of true. Rather, mark a line right round the room, using a guide and spirit level to coincide with the lower level of whole tiles. Along the line, pin – don't drive home – slim wooden guides to the wall with masonry nails. Next, using a plumb line, draw a vertical line where you intend to start your whole tiles. Fix wood strips along this line to act as a vertical guide.

Check the angle of the intersection of the two guides by placing some tiles loosely in position.

(above) *Tiling large areas can only be achieved by meticulous advanced planning, as shown in this fine bathroom wall.*

(right) *Correct (**1**) and incorrect (**2**) ways to tile a window recess.*

(far right) *To check wood guide intersection is correct angle: tiles placed loosely in position should sit perfectly square.*

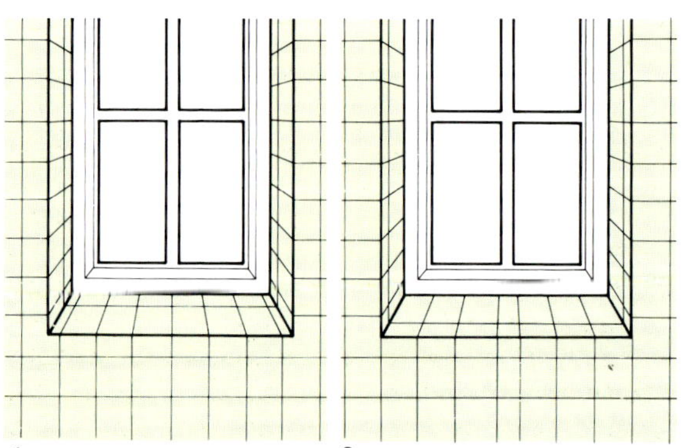

1 2

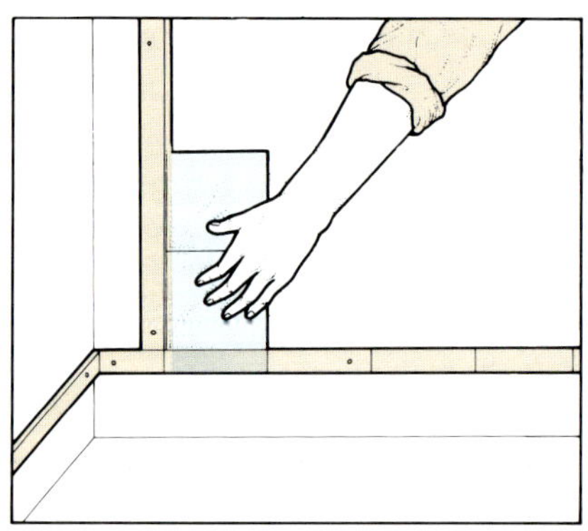

Tile cutting

Until the advent of modern cutting equipment, tiles were cut using a hammer and sharp chisel. Traditional tile cutting was an art in itself but tended to be very time-consuming and somewhat unpredictable, as success or failure depended very much on the strength of the tile being cut.

Specially developed tile cutters are available today in a wide variety of shapes and sizes. They are simple to use and extremely effective for all cutting except for some floor tiles when heavy duty cutters may have to be used.

Measuring for tiles to be cut is easy. Place a tile back to front over the space it is to fill and mark the edge to be cut at two points on the back. Transfer these marks to the face of the tile and score a line across the glazed surface with a cutter. Place a matchstick under the tile so that it runs back from the edge along the line of the cut. Press down gently on the corners of the tile with your thumbs and the tile will break cleanly. Apply adhesive to the back of the part of the tile you want to fix and fit it into the vacant space.

Where special shaped cut tiles are required, for example for fixing around light switches, pipes, and windows, they can be successfully achieved using a combination of tile cutters and tile nippers. The shape required should first of all be drawn on to the surface of the tile and scored with the cutter. Then use the tile nippers to carefully nibble away at the shape required. Work very slowly and take small bites to make sure you succeed. And remember! You can always nibble a bit off – you can't nibble a bit back on again!

How to cut a tile

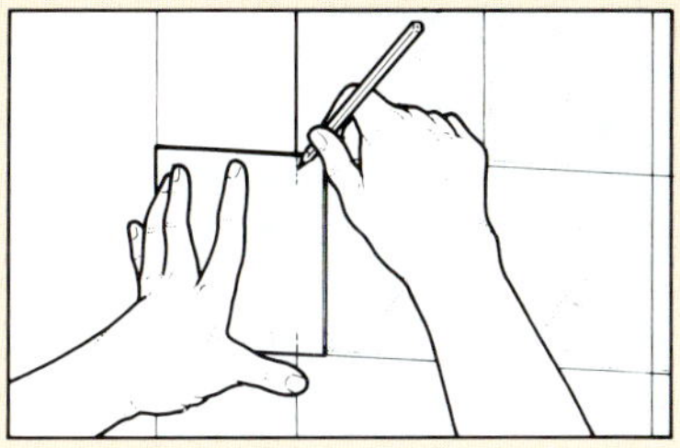

1. *Measure and mark a tile back at a wall. Transfer marks to tile face.*

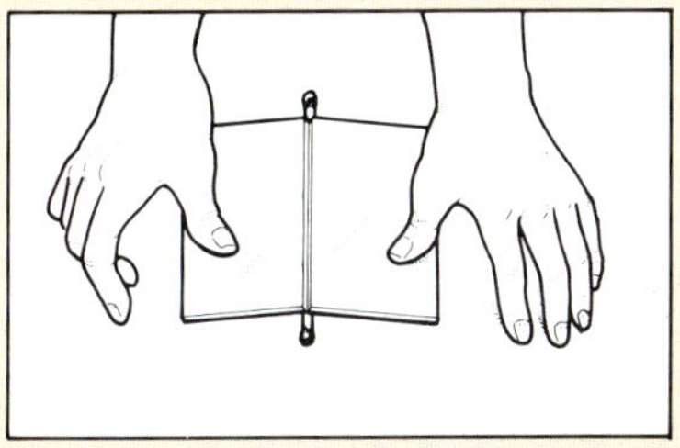

2. *Breaking a tile over matchsticks will ensure a clean cut.*

Cutting old tiles is very difficult unless a wet cutter is used. This can be bought or hired; otherwise tile stores often provide a cutting service at a reasonable price.

Fixing wall tiles

Sand and cement mortar is the traditional method of fixing ceramic tiles and is still used by some professional tilers. However, it has generally been superseded in the DIY world by modern adhesives.

Sand and cement mortar

For those interested in using the sand and mortar technique there are instructions set out below on how to fix tiles using sand and cement mortar, assuming that all necessary preparatory work has been carried out correctly.

A bedding mix, comprising 3 to 4 parts sand to 1 part cement, should be mixed thoroughly in sufficient quantity to allow for the complete job to be undertaken. This will also ensure a consistent quality of bedding mix throughout the work, which is essential. The amounts of ingredients in the mix must be accurately measured, using graduated measures – it is impossible to measure accurately with a shovel. Sufficient water should be added to the mix to make the mortar just workable. Only mix sufficient mortar at a time to last about two hours; any left over after this time should be discarded and another batch made up.

The tiles must be soaked in clean, cold water for at least half-an-hour before use. After soaking, stack the tiles tightly together on a clean surface to drain. After they have drained, use the tiles at once while they are still wet. Do *not* try to fix dry or semi-dry tiles.

Before tiling, damp down the coating sufficiently to prevent it absorbing moisture from the bedding mix.

Butter the tile evenly with mortar and then tap it firmly into position, making sure that the mortar bed is solid over the whole of the backs of the tiles. It is not enough just to place the tiles into position.

The bed behind the tile should thus be between 6mm (¼in) to 13mm (½in) thick. Where the tiles do not have inbuilt space lugs, uniformity of grouting joints can be attained by using matchsticks as spacer pegs. Frequent use of a straight edge will ensure a flat, even surface. Any adjustments should be made within 10 minutes of the tiles being fixed. Do not attempt to clean off the tiles until at least two hours have elapsed after the last tile has been aligned.

How to fix tiles with adhesives

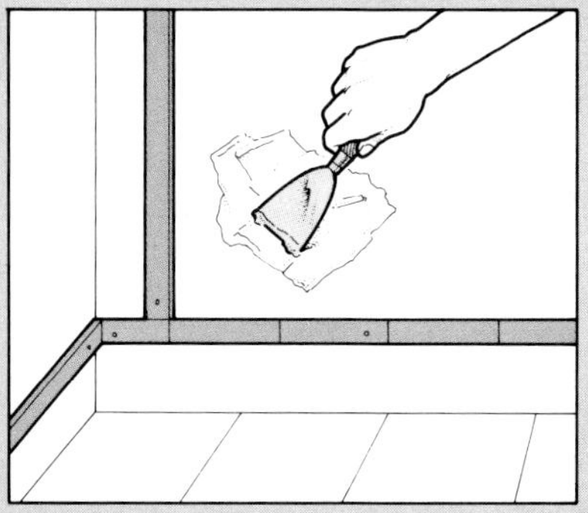

1. *Use a trowel to spread your adhesive over approximately 1 sq m (1 sq yd) of the wall.*

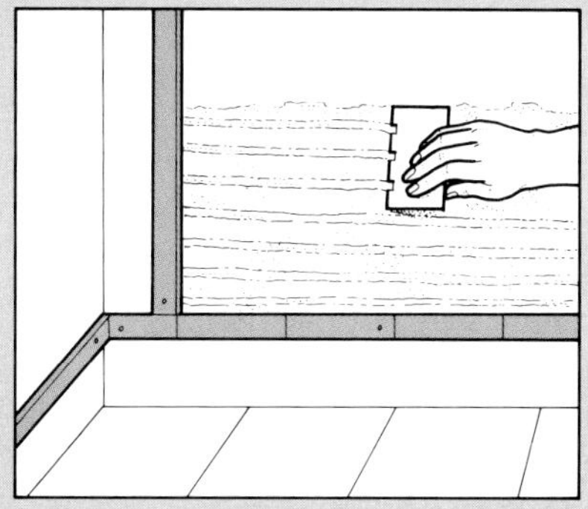

2. *Using notched spreader, form ridges in adhesive, pressing hard against surface so ridges are same height as tool notches. In confined areas, adhesive is best applied to tile backs.*

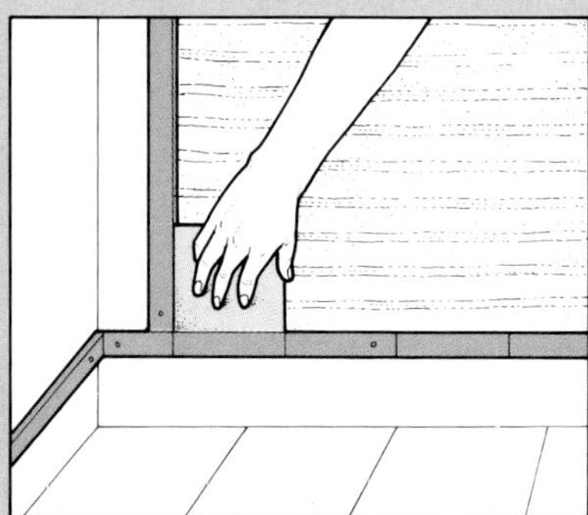

3. *Tile intersection of wooden guides, working horizontally. Press (not slide) tiles into adhesive. If tiles are self-spacing, ensure edges touch; if non-spacing, insert spacer pegs.*

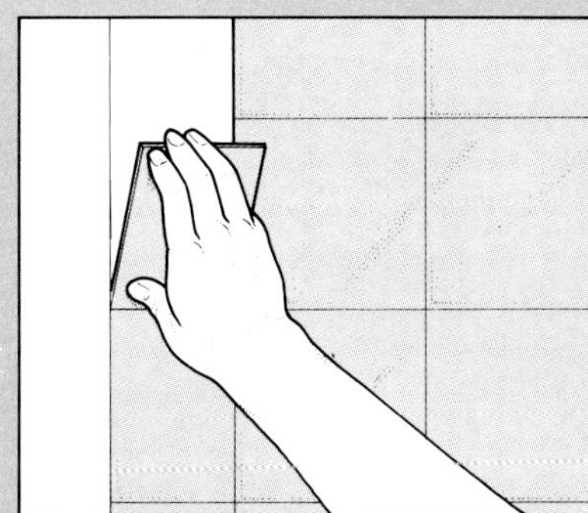

4. *Remove surplus adhesive from tile surface and joints without altering alignment. Finish off tiling main area before filling odd spaces at row ends.*

Using adhesives

Patience is a necessary virtue when fixing tiles and attention to detail is of paramount importance, never more so than when using adhesives. You must remember to make regular checks on the vertical and horizontal edges of the tiled area with a spirit level to make sure they are true throughout the time you are installing the tiles.

When tiling over sinks, baths, window frames or other fixtures it is a good idea to fix a wooden guide strip at the height of the nearest line of tiles above the fixture to act as a horizontal guide. Such fixtures are seldom level and the space beneath the wooden guide can invariably be best filled with cut tiles. Leave these and the main support guides near the skirting board (baseboard) in position until the adhesive has set, which will take 12 to 24 hours. If you remove the support too soon, the tiles might slip down under their own weight.

If your adhesive has to be mixed, read the manufacturer's instructions carefully and follow them when mixing.

Grouting

Grouting is the process of filling the gaps between the tiles with a quick setting mixture called grout. The purpose of this is to prevent water or other foreign substances from penetrating the gap and attacking the tile mortar/adhesive. It also enhances the appearance of the finished product. Grouting should be done 24 hours after fixing. Mix the grout and rub it well into the joints with a sponge. When it starts to dry out, remove any excess with a damp cloth and run a piece of rounded wood along each joint to finish it. Allow the grout to dry out completely – at least 24 hours – before polishing the tiles carefully, and not too roughly, with a soft cloth.

Ideas for tiles

It is very exciting to mount a display of tiles. The method used will depend on the size of the collection and the amount of space available.

The simplest method is to arrange the tiles along a shelf or ledge, which, besides being decorative, can serve a practical purpose. For example, laying tiles along a bathroom wall will help to prevent water affecting the wall.

A very effective way of showing tiles – particularly where four or more comprise a single design or picture – is to mount them, either in or out of a frame. It is even possible to inlay tiles into existing furniture, such as table tops or cabinet doors. Bear in mind, however, that furniture inlay requires considerable woodworking expertise and, once embarked on, any damage caused will probably be irreversible. Unless you are reasonably adept, it might be as well to leave such work to a professional cabinet maker.

The splash protectors in this bathroom are both functional and decorative.

Glossary

Bedding: refers to the layer of adhesive which is interposed between the tile and surface to be tiled. There are two techniques: *thin bed*, which is applied where the surface to be tiled is relatively flat and even and *thick bed* which is used to compensate for irregularities in the surface. Using the latter method it is difficult to achieve uniformity of thickness.

Biscuit: an unglazed tile.

Buttering: spreading a layer of mortar or adhesive directly onto the back of a tile, rather than to the surface to be tiled.

Brick and stone tiles: wafer-thin pieces of compressed stone aggregate. Can be fixed with either adhesive or mortar.

Crazing: tiny cracks in the glazed surface of a tile.

Delftware: tiles which have been dipped into thin glaze at the biscuit stage and then hand painted.

Field (spacer) tile: tile with four straight edges used to fill the surface to be tiled.

Firing: process of baking a tile in a kiln or oven.

Gauging tiles: measuring exactly how many tiles will cover a given area. A gauging stick is used to estimate the number of whole tiles needed for a specific surface.

Glazing: smooth, vitreous non-porous surface.

Green tile: un-fired tile.

Grout: cement-based material for sealing joints between tiles.

Low tiles: tiles first produced over 100 years ago in America. Their name was taken from John Low, one of several manufacturers of these tiles. Their superiority was due to the artistry of Arthur Osbourne whose exquisite relief artistry designs are still much sought after as collector's items.

Pit: excavation into the surface of furniture or wall, etc., to accommodate a tile which is intended to lie flush with the surrounding surface.

Quadrant tiles: thin strips of tile, either concave for corners or convex for finishing tiled areas (compare RE tiles).

RE and REX tiles: tiles having one or two rounded edges. Used for window sills or for finishing tiled areas.

Rendering (finishing): process of covering a rough brick or concrete surface with mortar and/or plaster to attain a flat, smooth surface.

Reproduction tiles: tiles made to traditional specifications.

Space lugs: small projections from the edges of a tile to maintain a standard in space between tiles to receive grout. Where they are lacking, an even joint can be achieved by sticking matchsticks between the tiles when fixing them.

Flooring

Floors must above all be functional but beauty and decorative effects have, from very early times, been very important attributes, as anyone who has seen the intricacy of Roman mosaics or the patina of a medieval wood floor can testify. Natural materials, such as stone and wood, have for many centuries faithfully served as flooring in homes both rich and poor, and it is only over the last hundred years or so that synthetic floorcoverings have begun to displace loose woven carpets and rush mats as overlays for the various flooring materials beneath.

During that time there has been a plethora of novel floorcoverings, from Elija Galloway's kamptulicon (an amalgam of rubber and cork, invented in 1844), through linoleum (patented in 1860) and congoleum (a printed felt-based sheet) to the many plastic materials in tile and sheet form that have been developed since the late 1940s.

There is no doubt that these modern floor coverings offer excellent wear and a constantly changing range of up-to-the-minute designs. However, there is a growing desire for a return to traditional flooring materials. Present-day manufacturers' ingenuity in copying travertine marble, cork or hardwood strip in plastic cannot match the look, texture and durability of a natural material that in most cases actually improves with age and use.

Traditional floorcovering materials can be divided up into four broad groups. These are woodblock (parquet) floors, planked wood floors, mosaic, terrazzo or granolithic floors and brick or natural stone floors.

Woodblock floors are usually laid as a decorative surface over a solid concrete sub-floor. The blocks themselves often comprise a decorative hardwood such as mahogany, teak or oak, although softwood (notably pine) may also be used. The traditional way of laying the blocks is in herringbone or basketweave patterns, and they are sometimes secured to the sub-floor with a thin layer of hot bitumen. (This method of laying a floor also provides excellent protection against rising damp.) Varnish or wax polish is the usual finish, and it is usual to lay carpet squares (area rugs), bordered by an area of woodblocks.

The beauty of an old planked floor is highlighted by careful cleaning and regular polishing and sets off some well-chosen matching furniture to perfection. A rug is the only adornment needed.

Planked floors are a structural flooring in most cases, with the planks spanning the floor joists. If good quality wood is used (such as beach or maple), the upper surface is varnished or highly polished to show off its attractive grain pattern. Carpet squares (area rugs) are often laid in the centre of the room leaving an exposed area of boards round the perimeter.

Mosaics (small pieces of stone, glass or fired clay set in a fine mortar bed), terrazzo (stone chippings set in mortar and ground smooth to expose the aggregate) and granolithic floors (granite chippings mixed with Portland cement) are continuous floor surfaces laid over concrete sub-floors. Mosaics and terrazzo floors were (and are) comparatively expensive to lay, and so are likely to be found in entrances and hallways. Granolithic flooring is rather less attractive and used to be laid in service rooms where it was turned up walls to form a matching skirting (baseboard).

In older houses, stone floors are very attractive and at the same time very durable. They are believed to keep out penetrating moisture. In this respect slate is most certainly a very reliable material. All damp stone floors can be rescued by modern damp proofing techniques.

Brick is less commonly found as a floor covering indoors, with the notable exception of service areas and conservatories.

Floor construction

If repairing or refurbishing an old floor, the treatment you carry out will depend to a certain extent on the way the floor has been made. There are two main methods of floor construction.

The most common type is the suspended floor, so called because it literally hangs from the walls surrounding it, and can be used for the ground and upper floors in houses. Wood (or more rarely iron or steel) joists are fixed to span the gap between opposite walls, and upper floors may also be supported partway across by intermediate structural partition walls. The joist ends may rest on wooden wall plates on protruding ledges of brickwork, or be set into gaps in the masonry (metal joist hangers are a comparatively recent introduction). At ground (first) floor level, where the heaviest loads are expected, small 'sleeper' walls are built up from the ground beneath the floor to give extra support to the joists. Because of the risk of moisture penetration in wooden ground floors, the joist ends are usually cut back just short of the walls, and the wooden plate between joists and sleeper walls rests on slates. These are effective ways of stopping moisture penetrating wood.

The floor surface of a suspended floor is usually solid wood planks nailed to the joists. The boards were square-edged for centuries; tongued and grooved boards became commonplace after World War I, and had the advantage of preventing draughts and dirt passing between the boards. In modern homes, where floorcoverings of one type or another are certain to be laid, sheets of plywood or chipboard are now often used rather than solid wood which is very expensive.

With suspended wood ground (first) floors it is very important for the space between the floor and the ground to be well ventilated so the wood stays dry and does not rot. For this reason, air bricks or grilles are set into the exterior walls just below floor level to allow air to flow into the underfloor space, and the sleeper walls supporting the joists are usually constructed like a honeycomb so that air can circulate freely to prevent damp.

It is now usual for the ground beneath a suspended wood ground floor to be covered with a layer of concrete (the 'oversite' concrete). In addition to keeping the underfloor space dry this layer prevents the growth of vegetable matter beneath the floor – a common problem in older buildings with bare earth beneath the floor.

The other main type of floor construction, the solid floor (otherwise known as direct-to-earth floor), is once again popular in the home. In earlier times, humble homes had a ground floor consisting of hard packed earth; their wealthier counterparts may have had stone flags or bricks. Then (as now) the main drawback of a direct-to-earth floor was penetrating moisture; with plenty of wood available for house-building, suspended floors meant dry feet, and it was only the comparative scarcity of wood after World War II which led to the almost universal return of the solid ground floor. Such floors now incorporate efficient moisture barriers, and the suspended wooden ground floor is now fairly rare (except in houses on sloping sites, where excessive backfilling would otherwise be necessary).

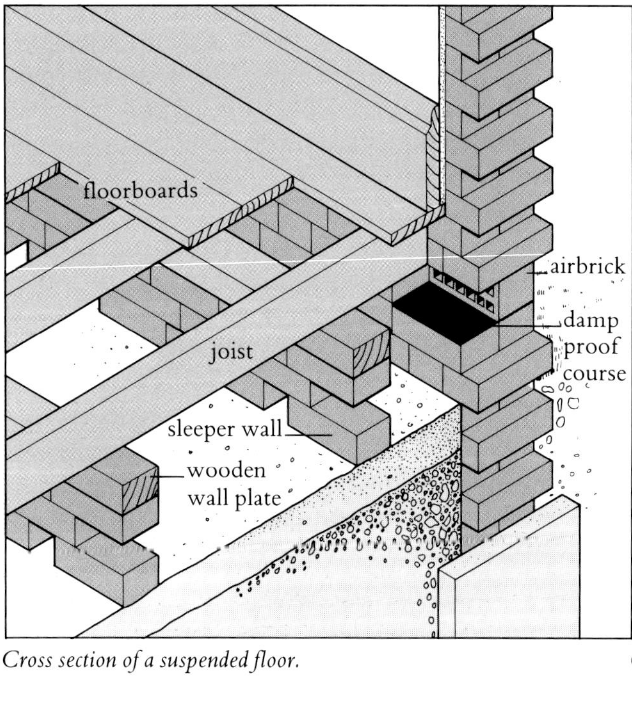

Cross section of a suspended floor.

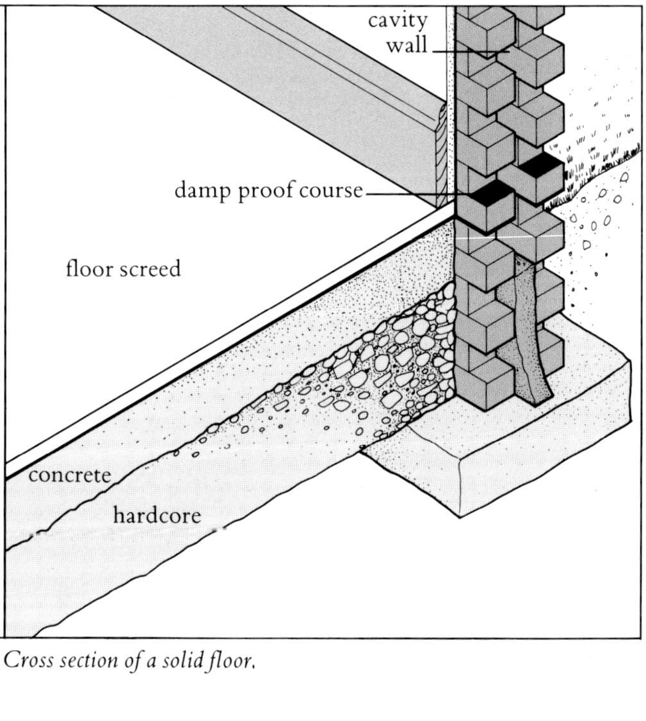

Cross section of a solid floor.

Faults in floor structures

With suspended wooden floors, the most common problem is rot. Rot is usually found only in ground (first) floors, but can affect upper floors too if structural or plumbing faults result in wet wood. The most serious enemy is dry rot, which can spread unseen extremely quickly beneath wood floors and can ultimately lead to complete collapse of the floor structure. Outbreaks can usually be eliminated completely with the aid of chemical fungicides, but all infected wood has to be cut out and replaced. Wet rot is less serious and easier to eradicate than dry rot.

Note that in North America very little rot occurs. That which does occur is almost always wet rot.

Insect (woodworm or termite) attack can also be a problem, marring the look of wooden floors, and in serious cases leading to the possibility of structural weakness too. Chemical insecticides can kill present infestations and discourage future ones, but visible damage (in the shape of the flight holes left by the emerging insects) will remain and can be difficult to camouflage, if extensive. As long as the wood is not weakened by the attack, it may be best to accept the holes as part of the 'aged' look.

The third problem, less common than the other two, is sagging. This may be caused by overloading – with heavy furniture, for example – or, in the case of ground floors, by subsidence of the bearing wall due to ground movement or inadequate foundations beneath the wall brickwork. In the former case the floor will have to be strengthened, if the loading is to continue, by the addition of stronger joists. In the latter case rebuilding of the sleeper walls will be required. In both cases, the floor may have to be jacked up into its original position before remedial work can begin.

Moisture penetration is the major trouble with solid floors. There may be no damp proof membrane (dpm) – vapor barrier – present (likely in houses over about a hundred years old), or the membrane, if fitted, may have become defective. With some floor finishes such as stone, brick and clay tiles, evaporation may be fast enough to keep the floor surface comparatively dry, and trouble arises only when another floorcovering, such as carpet or smooth sheet material, is laid on top, thus trapping the moisture. If moisture persists, the only long-term solution is to lift the flooring completely and re-lay it over a new dpm (vapor barrier) – either heavy duty polyethylene sheeting or a brush-on bituminous or pitch-epoxy compound. In such a situation it is important to ensure that the new dpm is linked to the damp proof course (dpc) – not known in the US – in the surrounding walls. There are four methods of damp proof coursing, all of which require specialist treatment: silicone injection; siphonage, electro-osmosis or insertion of a new damp proof course. Whatever treatment is provided, in most cases a guarantee of up to 20 or more years is given.

The tell-tale fruiting body of the dry rot fungus (top), well entrenched on wooden panelling; beneath the floor the spread of the tendrils is self-evident.

Floorcovering types

Floor type	Faults and remedies	Cleaning and care	Durability
Woodblock (Parquet)	*Stains:* strip and refinish *Cracks:* fill with stopper (plastic wood) or wood strips *Unevenness:* lift and re-lay *Loose blocks:* lift and re-lay *Severe damage:* replace blocks	*Finish* with wax polish or varnish *Maintain* with regular sweep/ mop and polish	Generally good, soft woods may indent
Planked	As for woodblock floors, plus *Gaps:* re-lay boards to close gaps *Damage:* lift boards and re-lay top side down	As for woodblocks	As for woodblocks
Mosaics	*Stains:* blot out, try acid cleaners (not on marble) *Loose stones:* chip out and re-bed *Severe damage:* have floor relaid professionally *Cracks:* seal with silicone mastic	*Sweep* and *wash*, but do not polish	Very durable
Terrazzo	As for mosaics, plus *Chips:* patch with epoxy-resin filler	*Sweep* and *wash*, but do not polish	Fairly durable
Granolithic	*Dusting:* use clear sealer or floor paint *Cracks:* patch with mortar *Lifting:* have floor re-laid professionally	*Sweep* and *wash*	Very durable
Stone/brick	*Stains:* scrub with strong floor cleaner, try dilute hydrochloric acid *Cracked pointing:* rake out and repoint with fresh mortar *Loose units:* lift and re-bed in fresh mortar, then repoint *Damp:* lift floor and re-lay over damp proof membrane (vapor barrier)	*Sweep* and *wash* (treat slate with linseed oil/turps, polish marble with water-based sealer). *Seal* if preferred	Generally very durable, though soft stone/brick may wear unevenly

Woodblock (parquet) floors

Woodblock (parquet) floors consist of regular shaped blocks of wood, sometimes softwood but usually hardwood, stuck to a suspended or solid sub-floor with adhesive. To minimize problems of expansion and contraction caused by changes in the moisture content of the blocks, they are usually laid in patterns with half the blocks at right angles to the other half. The blocks are usually laid with the grain direction parallel to the floor surface, but occasionally they may be cut and laid as endgrain blocks – a wood mosaic that is extremely durable.

A woodblock (parquet) floor is the perfect background for carpet squares or rugs.

Stripping old finishes

Even if you are lucky enough to have a woodblock floor in perfect physical condition, it will benefit from being stripped and refinished to enhance the beauty of the wood. Wear and random stains may have marked some areas, and dirt will have accumulated in the finish over the years.

The traditional (and one of the best) methods of stripping old floor finishes is to use a strong solution of washing soda in hot water. Swab the surface repeatedly until the finish softens and can be removed with a broad-bladed scraper. Then rinse thoroughly with clean water and leave to dry out. It is best to work in small areas – up to about 1 sq m (10 sq ft) – to reduce the job to manageable proportions.

An alternative to soda that will lift most old polishes and varnishes is 0.880 ammonia, available from pharmacists. The drawbacks are a pungent smell, the fact that it darkens most hardwoods and its irritating effect on skin. If you use it, wash yourself and the floor thoroughly with clean water afterwards.

Modern solvents may be required if these treatments fail. Polishes may respond more quickly to white spirit (paint thinner) or a proprietary wax remover, while varnishes may lift more easily with a paint or varnish stripper. If you are using the latter, make sure that the room is well ventilated, and remove the residue according to the manufacturer's instructions. Make sure you do this thoroughly, as any traces of stripper will mar the new finish.

Sanding (by hand or machine) should be very much a last resort, taken because either other methods have failed or the floor is in such poor condition that only by exposing new bare wood will an adequate finish be achieved.

Stains and burn marks

Dark stains in the wood indicate that water has penetrated the finish. When the finish has been removed, treat the stains with oxalic acid or a proprietary wood bleach, brushing either of these carefully onto the stained area only and rinsing off as soon as the stain disappears.

Burn marks must be scraped out carefully to expose bare, clean wood. If this leaves a noticeable hollow, fill it with a matching proprietary wood filler, or experiment with melted beeswax, coloured to match the surrounding wood with vegetable dyes.

For further information on stains and burns, see pages 61-62.

Filling cracks and holes

There are almost as many traditional recipes for wood fillers as there are cracks and holes in the average floor. Most involve mixing various proportions of ingredients such as beeswax, rosin and flaked shellac with traditional aniline dyes such as Vandyke brown. With the enormous range of modern plastic wood fillers, available in shades to match almost any wood, the effort hardly

Relaying blocks

1. *Using an old chisel, remove dried adhesive. Spread fresh adhesive, taking care not to mark the surrounding blocks.*

2. *Tap the lifted blocks down into place, using a mallet or a hammer and a softwood block to protect the surface.*

3. *Sand or plane the new blocks until they sit flush with their neighbours.*

4. *Fill any gaps round the perimeter of the block with a matching wood filler.*

seems worthwhile nowadays, unless you must have an authentic 'period' repair to your floor. (For more information, see pages 63-64.)

Uneven, loose or damaged blocks

You may find that some of the blocks are not sitting flush with their neighbours. This may be due to the adhesive failing to hold the blocks in place, in which case it should be a relatively simple matter to prise up the affected blocks using a sharp chisel tapped into the end or side face of the block. Don't split the first one as you ease it out. Check that you have raised all loose blocks by tapping the floor all over: a hollow sound indicates failed adhesive.

If individual blocks are badly damaged, prise them up, or chop out carefully with a mallet and chisel if securely bedded. If you cannot get hold of a good match, buy a paler wood and stain it to match instead. Cut the block down carefully to fit the recess, and set it in place in fresh adhesive. When this has set, sand down and refinish the new block to match its surroundings.

If large areas of blocks have bowed upwards, expansion due to moisture penetration is probably the cause and the whole floor will have to be lifted and re-laid over a new dpm (vapor barrier). This will probably be less difficult than it sounds, since the moisture will have caused widespread failure of the adhesive. Prise the blocks up row by row and allow them to dry out in another room in the house. Then brush on a new pitch-epoxy or bitumen dpm over the whole floor surface and re-lay the blocks.

You can help to avoid this type of expansion fault in new wooden floors by finishing off the perimeter of the room with a cork expansion strip; it will be nearly hidden by the skirting board (baseboard), which should be fixed with its lower edge a fraction above the block surface.

Refinishing techniques

The first step is to give the entire floor surface a light sanding with fine grade abrasive paper; the stripping treatment will have raised the grain of the wood if water was used, and other filling and repair work is sure to need a careful smoothing. Vacuum clean the floor thoroughly to remove as much dust as possible, and then wipe carefully all over with a tack rag – a clean lint-free cloth dipped in white spirit (paint thinner) – to pick up any dust.

Wax polish is the traditional finish for all wooden floors. However, it does not give a durable finish. The best method is first to seal the floor with a clear varnish and then to wax and polish up to a perfect sheen. Modern polyurethane varnishes and floor sealers have the edge over traditional oil varnishes in terms of ease of application, speed of drying and long-term durability, although you will get excellent results with the traditional finish if you prefer your restoration to be authentic.

Apply the first coat of varnish, thinned with white spirit (paint thinner) (for polyurethane varnishes) or linseed oil (for oil varnishes). The thinning helps penetration and provides a better key for subsequent coats.

The first coat is usually 'rubbed' into the wood with a clean cloth; two further coats are then applied by brush, with a light sanding between coats (and a wipe down with the tack rag) to key the surface and to remove any flecks of dust or other foreign bodies that land on the surface while it is still wet.

When the varnish has dried absolutely hard, the polish can be applied either by hand or with an electric floor polisher. Use a good quality wax polish and *apply sparingly*.

You need only to sweep or mop regularly. Occasionally apply polish.

Planked floors

Solid wood, well looked after, will last for years and its appearance actually improves with age, acquiring a character all of its own.

Old, suspended wooden floors are, by definition, planked floors. Whether square-edged (most likely in older buildings) or tongued and grooved, they are invariably nailed to the joists beneath, although on a good quality floor the nails will have been punched below the surface of the wood and the holes created plugged with filler.

Stripping and filling

The methods outlined in detail in 'Woodblock (parquet) floors' on page 151 apply equally well to planked floors, especially hardwood. Softwood floors in good condition can be treated in the same way but are more likely to have been seriously disfigured by the fixing of successive floorcoverings or by border staining as a surround to carpet squares (area rugs), and so forth. However, if you want exposed planking, some fairly drastic action is more likely to be needed to remove surface blemishes off this type of flooring.

It is possible to do this by hand sanding, but a mechanical floor sander makes the work much easier. It uses wide belts of abrasive paper to sand away the floor surface. It will remove deep stains and other blemishes and will also level off ridges between boards caused by shrinkage and curling of damp or poorly-seasoned wood, which can only be otherwise cured by extensive refixing of the warped boards. However, this machine is rather coarse in action, even if successively finer grades of abrasive paper are used, and score marks are certain to remain in the wood however carefully you work.

If you want a perfect finish you can either tackle the job by hand, or lift all the boards and re-lay them the other way up. The undersides may carry slight marks where they crossed the joints, but these will be comparatively easy to remove. The major part of their surfaces will probably be free from stains and marks altogether.

This lift-and-lay technique is also the ultimate answer to closing extensive gaps between square-edged floor boards. As each board is laid against its predecessor, use an old broad-bladed chisel dug into the top edge of the joist as a lever to wedge each successive board up tightly while it is nailed in place.

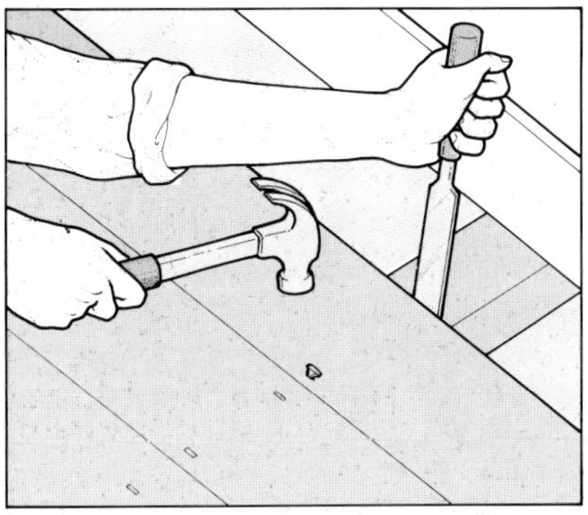

Wedge boards up tightly; nail in place.

When the last board has been re-laid, it is likely that a length of new wood will be needed to fill the space left by the closing up of the gaps. Plane or saw this to the required width and nail it in place, ready for finishing.

Loose individual boards should be fixed down securely. Check beneath the board for any pipework or electrical circuits that may have been run beneath it – you don't want to pierce them with an ill-placed nail. If the loose board is warped, secure it with screws rather than nails, which give a better grip and allow easier lifting of the board if required for maintenance of the plumbing or electrics. Check that all other nail heads are punched just below the surface of the boards.

Occasional gaps between boards can be best filled with long, thin wedges of wood cut from the edge of a matching board. Apply woodworking adhesive to both edges of the strip and tap it into the gap carefully with a mallet, leaving it slightly above the surface so it can be planed down perfectly flush when the adhesive has set. This method gives much neater and less conspicuous results than the alternative time-honoured technique using papier maché.

Replacing damaged sections

If an individual strip of any planked floor is so badly damaged that only complete replacement can be considered, the first job is to prise it up. Try to locate the fixing nails first, and drive them through into the joist below with a nail punch and hammer. Next, use a long, thin-bladed knife poked down between the board edges to ascertain whether they are square-edged or tongued and grooved. If the former, you should be able to prise up the plank easily; if the latter, you will have to cut through the tongue on each side with a padsaw (compass saw) or a special floorboard saw.

With the old board raised, use it as a template to cut a new piece from matching wood and nail it securely into place.

Replacing entire floors

If the existing floor has been badly damaged by rot or insects, you will have to consider complete replacement. Since the joists will probably have been affected too, the job will involve quite a lot of structural woodwork. It is essential to ensure that all wood used for the new floor has been treated with preservative and to renew all the damp proof courses (not known in the US) on which the wall plates rest. Build up the new floor structure to match the old, and nail on the new floorboards. Make sure they are all tightly fitting as you work across the floor, and butt join cut ends neatly over the centres of joists. Take care not to mark the new boards as you fix them, and punch in all nail heads and disguise them with wood filler.

Finishing techniques

Much the same considerations apply to finishing planked floors as were outlined earlier for woodblock (parquet) ones. Staining is an additional decorative option which can enhance the grain pattern dramatically on softwood planks. They sometimes look rather bland unless the wood is close-grained.

The traditional method is first to stain the bare wood with either a water-based or a spirit-based stain and then to seal the surface with three coats of clear varnish. The stain is applied to one board width at a time, using a clean lint-free cloth. Aim to avoid overlaps between successive bands of stain, which will result in a greater depth of colour at the overlaps. It is safer to go for a too weak stain to start with, since a second application is easily carried out if greater colour depth is needed. Leave the stain to dry; if a water-based stain has been used, it will have raised the wood grain slightly and a light sanding will be needed before the varnish can be applied to finish the job.

Modern varnish stains can be used instead of separate stain and varnish to reduce the scale of the job. They give generally good results, but they cannot give the same depth of colour as separate stain and varnish treatments.

Once your planked floor has been sealed, you can polish and maintain it using the same methods as for sealed woodblock (parquet) floors.

Ceramic and quarry tiles

Ceramic floor tiles are made from natural refined clays and other additives, compressed into whatever shape is required and fired at high temperatures. The coloured glaze is then applied and designs added (nowadays usually by silk-screen printing, although in Victorian times they were often hand-painted). Finally the glazed tile is fired again to harden the glaze. Most tiles are around 12mm (½in) thick – appreciably thicker than wall tiles, with which they are not interchangeable. A range of sizes is available.

Quarry tiles get their name from the French word *carré*, meaning square – they are not quarried! The tile shapes are extruded from unrefined clays which give the tiles their attractive colours – mainly natural browns, buffs and dark reds, occasionally dark blues. They are unglazed, the firing process giving them their smooth surface texture. Old tiles may be 25mm (1in) or more thick; common sizes for old tiles were 300mm (12in) and 215mm (8½in) square. Modern quarries are usually smaller though. The 150mm/6in square is the most popular size today – and it is also thinner (usually around 15mm/⅝in).

Both types of tile are extremely hardwearing, and unaffected by water, grease and heat. They are, however, cold and rather noisy underfoot, and they may need sealing.

Cleaning and repairing

Ceramic and quarry-tiled floors need very little cleaning – just regular washing (polishing can make them very slippery). Grout lines may become discoloured with age; in the long run re-grouting is the only way to restore their appearance fully. Localized re-grouting may be needed to deal with cracks between individual tiles.

Where individual floor tiles are cracked, the only remedy is to chisel the cracked pieces carefully out of their mortar bed with a small, sharp

Terracotta quarry tiles, with small inset ceramic tile squares, provide a flooring that is immensely hard-wearing, yet easy to clean and a surface that will look good for years. Such a floor can be rather noisy in use, however.

cold chisel. (Work from the centre of the tile towards the edges to avoid damaging the neighbouring tiles.) Then bed a replacement tile if one is available. (For further details see page 139.)

Suitable surfaces

Ceramic and quarry tiles can be laid over almost any surface, provided that the floor to be tiled is rigid, flat, dry and free from dirt, grease and polish. Wooden floors are sufficiently strong to support the tiling without excessive deflection and have adequate ventilation underneath. When tiling over existing thermoplastic or quarry tiles, ensure that they are securely bonded before starting to lay the replacements.

Wood surfaces or thermoplastic tiles should usually be primed with a PVA bonding agent before using adhesive. Brush the bonding agent liberally over the whole surface to be tiled and allow it to become touch-dry or tacky before starting to lay the tiles.

With cement/mortar bedding (usually used for quarry tiles) allow at least four days for the adhesive to set before grouting.

Setting out the floor area

When setting out the floor area, make sure that any awkward cuts are placed in unobtrusive places. Lay the tiles so that they are square to the doorway. When you enter the room, the line of tiles should run squarely from you towards the back of the room.

Methods of laying ceramic and quarry floor tiles

If you are going to use adhesives you must bear the following points in mind.

a) Make sure that the floor to be tiled is flat and firm. If there is a wood base, nail down any loose boards. Very uneven or rough wood floors can be lined with 12mm (½in) plywood (exterior grade) which must be very firmly screwed down at 300mm (12in) intervals.

b) Using a notched trowel, spread the adhesive over the first square

Setting out the floor area

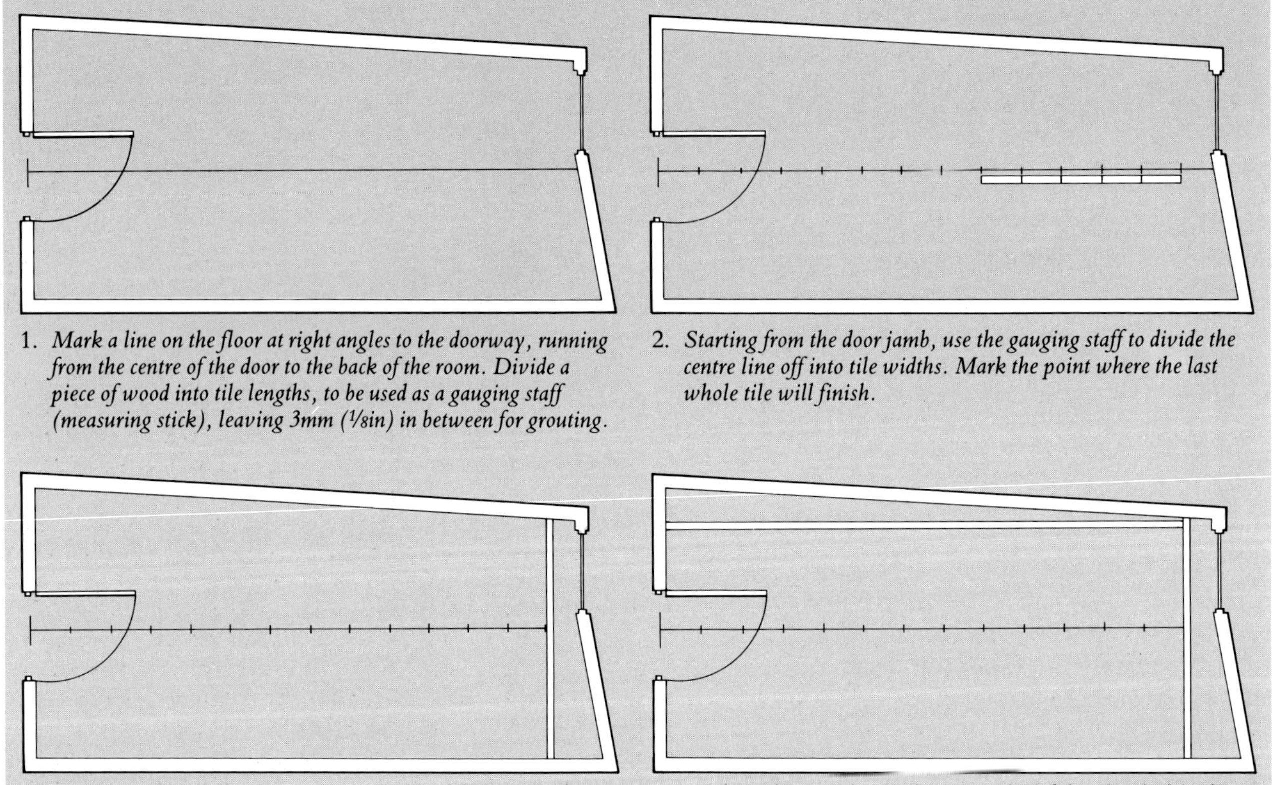

1. *Mark a line on the floor at right angles to the doorway, running from the centre of the door to the back of the room. Divide a piece of wood into tile lengths, to be used as a gauging staff (measuring stick), leaving 3mm (⅛in) in between for grouting.*

2. *Starting from the door jamb, use the gauging staff to divide the centre line off into tile widths. Mark the point where the last whole tile will finish.*

3. *Nail a wooden guide strip across the width of the room at the point where the last whole tile finishes. The wood strip must be at right angles to the centre line.*

4. *Nail another wooden guide strip at the left hand end of the first strip to give you a perfectly square corner. This is where tiling will start. It is imperative that the angle between these wood strips is a right angle.*

Plain ceramic tiles offer a flooring that is simple and dignified in appearance.

metre (about 1 square yard) of floor in the corner where you have laid the wooden guide strips.

c) Tiles must be fixed dry. Each tile must be placed firmly into position, using a slight twisting action to bed the tile in properly. Make sure that each tile back is in total contact with the adhesive bed so that no voids are left underneath the tiles. About every 1 or 2 square metres (square yards), you should pull a tile up a few seconds after you have fixed it to see that you have adequate adhesion.

d) Work in small areas of approximately 1 square metre (1 square yard) at a time, leaving approximately 3mm (⅛in) joint around each tile for grouting.

e) Before the adhesive sets, clean off any surplus remaining on the face of the tiles or on the adjacent floor area. Also clean out the tile joints in readiness for grouting.

f) When the main area of the floor is complete, remove the wood strips and cut tiles to fit into the spaces around the edges of the room.

g) Leave the floor for at least 24 hours for the adhesive to set ready for grouting.

Laying floor tiles in a sand and cement mortar bed is the traditional method, still extensively used professionally, for laying ceramic floors. The setting out of the areas to be tiled is the same as that for adhesives, but there are three very different and demanding methods of application which are probably too difficult for anybody except the most proficient handyman.

The first method is an application of mortar over a separating layer of non-bonding paper or film installed over the backing or base. This method is not recommended for exterior tiling. The surface which is receiving the separating layer should be clean, sound, true and smooth. The separating medium should be laid flat in a continuous layer over the base with 100mm (4in) lapped joints between adjacent sheets. It must not be stuck down.

The bedding mix should comprise 1 part Portland cement to 3-4 parts sand by volume. Sufficient bedding mortar should be used for about two hours' work only. Tiles must be soaked in water and allowed to drain afterwards. The tiles are then placed into position and firmly tapped down into the mortar to the required level.

Another technique is to apply mortar directly to the concrete or screeded base. This is suitable only where the base is so mature that no risk of further movement exists, or where a damp proof membrane (vapor barrier) is incorporated between concrete base and screed. This fixing method is suitable for heavy traffic.

Finally there is the semi-dry mix procedure which is also suitable for heavy traffic and applicable to exterior and interior situations. If a screed is to be applied, the concrete base must be at least four weeks old before a 1 part cement to 3 or 4 parts sand and mortar screed is laid. This screed must then be left for at least another two weeks before fixing is started. This method is designed to prevent stresses from affecting the floor finish without the need to lay a separating layer.

Mosaic, terrazzo and granolithic floors

An intricate mosaic design like this would form the centre-piece of an entrance hall or similar room, its grandeur reflecting the status of the original owner. Careful maintenance will be needed to keep it in good condition over the years.

Mosaic floors are made up from small pieces of coloured stone, glass or ceramic tile bedded in a fine mortar, with the individual stones laid in abstract, geometric or pictorial patterns. They are most likely to be found in small areas such as porches; a larger mosaic – in an entrance hall or living room, for example – would have been an expensive investment for the average dwelling house.

Granolithic and terrazzo floors are essentially concrete floors incorporating mineral aggregates for decorative effect, and both would have been laid originally by a specialist contractor. Granolithic floorings contain finely-graded granite chipping (hence the name), and have a fairly coarse but extremely hard-wearing surface. Terrazzo contains multi-coloured aggregate, and here the surface is ground down after it has been laid to leave a perfectly smooth polished surface with the cut aggregate exposed. It rarely occurs in jointless form in domestic premises, but terrazzo tiles up to 25mm (1in) thick and 305mm (12in) or 410mm (16in) square are occasionally found.

Cleaning the surface

Since all these floorings have extremely hard surfaces, cleaning methods can be fairly coarse. Scouring with a household abrasive cleaner should remove stains from mosaic and terrazzo floors; you may need to experiment with stubborn stains. For example, oil stains can sometimes be lifted by spreading clean white blotting paper soaked in white spirit (paint thinner) over the stain and leaving it to draw the oil out as the spirit evaporates. Diluted hydrochloric acid (from pharmacists) can actually etch away larger blemishes. Modern proprietary concrete cleaners are always worth trying if localized cleaning leaves the rest of the floor looking dirty; they are simply scrubbed into the surface and then rinsed off, following the manufacturer's instructions.

Superficial damage

With mosaic floors, loose stones can be re-laid in a strong mortar. Prise up the stones carefully with a sharp pointed tool – an old screwdriver or a small cold chisel, for example – and chip away as much of the old mortar as possible from the recess. Clean up the individual stones in a similar fashion; holding them in a vice allows you to use a small cold chisel; otherwise grind away the mortar using a masonry cutting disc fitted to a power drill. If you are using this last technique, grind down the thickness of the stone by

1-2mm (1/16in) to allow not only for a thicker bed of mortar underneath it, but also to make it easier to tap the stone level with its neighbours as you replace it. Wipe away excess mortar when the stone has been bedded, at the same time leaving a neat line of grouting round it.

Terrazzo flooring is extremely durable, and only severe pressure is likely to crack or chip it. Such damage can only be patched, using a modern epoxy-resin based filler in preference to mortar.

The most common problem with granolithic flooring is dusting off the surface, usually caused by poor laying – too weak a mix is the likeliest fault. The best treatment is to brush on a solution of sodium silicate, in which case it will be necessary for reapplication to take place every year or so. Alternatively, you could treat the surface with a proprietary floor sealer or even a chlorinated rubber floor paint; the former, widely used on dusty concrete floors, is clear, while the latter is available in a restricted range of colours and provides a very distinct surface film.

Laying new mosaics

1. *Apply grout to the back of a sheet of mosaic with a trowel. Press the grout well into the gaps. Do not allow the sheet to soak for long before laying it.*

2. *Position the sheet of mosaic on the adhesive; place other sheets around it at the same distance apart as individual mosaics. Tamp the sheets down hard to make sure the tiles have been bedded properly into the adhesive, and remove excess grout.*

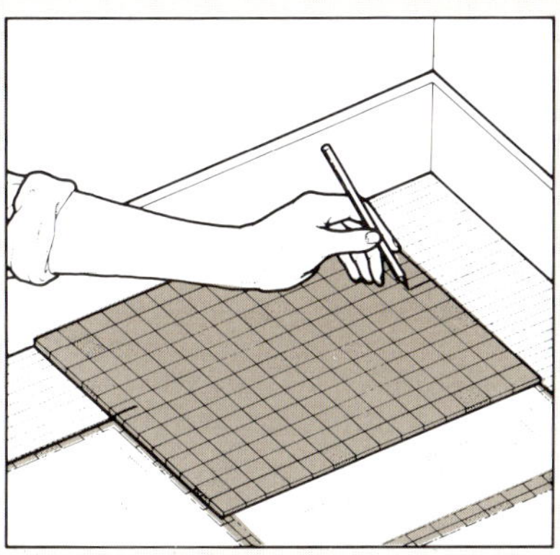

3. *Remove wooden strips and cut tiles to fit the gaps around the edges. Complete mosaics may fill the gaps; if not, score and break the individual tiles with a pair of pincers. Carefully spread the adhesive on the floor and tamp down the mosaics.*

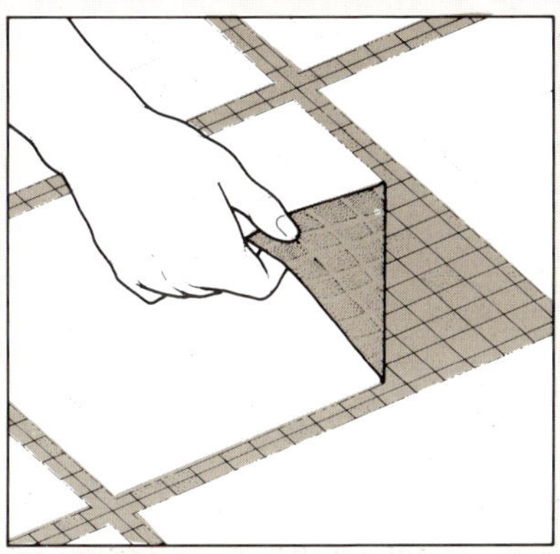

4. *Allow the paper to soak for a while and then peel gently off the tiles. Apply more grout to fill gaps where the sheets meet.*

Laying new mosaics

It is possible that you will be laying new mosaic tiles over a large area, in which case it will be much easier, and certainly much faster, to use adhesives – especially if you previously have not had very much experience in laying mosaics. It is important to note that mosaic tiles are sold in paper-backed sheets to help ease application.

Resanding terrazzo and granolithic floors

It is possible to refurbish terrazzo and granolithic floors by abrading the surface with an industrial floor grinder, but this is a job for a professional flooring contractor and not for the amateur. Properly done, the sanding exposes a fresh aggregate surface, but over-zealous use of the machine can simply tear up the surface. Such treatment is worth considering only for large expanses of floor that are in good physical condition but are stained or marked superficially.

Refinishing techniques

Mosaics need no finishing treatment, although you can seal the grouting with a silicone sealer to stop the dirt collecting. Regular washing is all that will be needed to keep them in good condition: polish should not be used.

With granolithic floors, clear floor sealers are the only finishes that enhance the aggregate and keep dusting to a minimum. Terrazzo, with its glassy smooth surface, should not be given any finish – in particular, it should not be polished, or it becomes dangerously slippery.

Natural stone and brick

Natural brick is the perfect flooring for this traditionally furnished kitchen area.

Natural stone, the most durable flooring material, is usually identified by the area where it was quarried. In Britain, for example, common sandstones are York stone, Darley Dale stone and Forest of Dean Blue stone. Limestones may be known as Portland, Hopton Wood or Ashburton, while granite is usually identified merely as Scottish or Cornish. There is a great colour variety, from the soft yellow warmth of York stone to the flecked grey of Scottish granite. Slate varies in colour from green (Westmorland) to dark blue (Welsh). For all these types of stone, broadly similar repair work and maintenance treatments are required.

In marble there is an almost infinite variety of colour from white Sicilian to yellow Travertine and a range of browns, greens, greys and even black. Slightly different techniques are needed to clean and restore marble because of its crystalline nature and – usually – polished surface (the name marble originally derives from the Greek *Marmaros*, meaning shining stone).

The best way of appreciating the range of colours and textures available is to visit a good stonemason; he will also be able to give advice on specific matters like size, thickness, availability and price (an important consideration, mainly dependent on delivery costs from the stone's source).

Bricks, laid flat or on edge, are less common for interior floors. Many local varieties occur, in shades ranging from dark brown through deep red to pale yellows, and the only requirement for successful use as a floorcovering is a hard brick with a comparatively smooth surface that will be durable and easy to keep clean. Local building suppliers are the best source, guaranteeing a choice of bricks which will be appropriate to your area's architectural traditions.

Cleaning stone

How you tackle the problem of cleaning up a stone floor depends mainly on the nature of the stone and the degree of soiling present. With soft, porous bricks and stone flags, your first treatment should simply be to scrub the surface with a stiff bristle brush and clean water. This will lift general surface dirt from the pores of the stone, and give you a chance to pinpoint and treat stubborn individual stains.

Minor stains can be tackled with a dilute solution of oxalic acid – the same treatment as for water stains on wood floors – or diluted hydrogen peroxide to which a drop of ammonia has been added. Oily stains can be lifted, as for terrazzo and granolithic floors, with a pad of white blotting paper soaked in white spirit (paint thinner), or with a poultice of kaolin (china clay) and benzene (from pharmacists) which should be left on the stain for about a minute before being wiped off.

If you have marble floors, clean only with soap and water with half a cup of ammonia added to each bucket; avoiding any acid floor cleaners as they will pit the surface. Restore the surface shine with a water-based floor sealer.

Repairing pointing

Pointing is the thin line of cement mortar trowelled into the gap that is left between individual stones or bricks when they are bedded into place. Where the mortar pointing between individual stones or bricks is cracked or crumbling, rake and brush out all the loose material; the nozzle of a cylinder vacuum cleaner is useful for removing any dust that remains. Then brush some polyvinyl acetate (PVA) bonding agent along the recess to improve the adhesion of the new mortar, and repoint carefully with a fairly dry mortar mix. Take care not to get any mortar on the face of the stone; on smooth stones you could protect the surfaces on each side with masking tape. Finish off the new pointing to match the style used elsewhere on the floor.

Rebedding loose stones

Where individual stones or bricks are clearly loose, lever them up carefully with a cold chisel and chip out much of the hardened mortar beneath – at least to a depth of 12mm (½in) or so. Also, cut away the old pointing round the recess, chopping inwards so you don't damage the surrounding stones. Clean off any mortar adhering to the back of the stone you have lifted, working with the chisel at a shallow angle to the stone and pointing towards the centre to avoid splitting.

Next, brush PVA bonding agent into the recess, and spread a shallow bed of mortar in it. Wet the back of the stone, lay it in position and tamp it down carefully level with its fellows. If it is above the surface, lift again and scrape out some of the mortar bed before setting it back in place again. If it sits too low, lift it and trowel in some more mortar. Finish off by pointing round the stone as already described.

If the stone or brick is cracked, you have to decide whether to put up with the crack or attempt to obtain a matching unit to bed in its place – perhaps by lifting one from an inconspicuous part of the floor. You may well have to do some careful trimming of the replacement piece to match the recess into which it will fit. Use the cracked pieces to fill the hole where the replacement stone has been lifted.

You may be lucky enough to have a local stonemason who could provide a matching unit; take the cracked pieces with you so he can attempt to identify the stone and suggest possible replacements. If he can do so, ask him to trim the new stone to roughly the size you require, and bed it in mortar as described for rebedding loose slabs. Try to match the existing mortar colour when you come to reinstate the pointing.

If you cannot find a matching unit, either trim the cracked unit to create two smaller ones and bed and point them as described above, or lift a whole unit from a less obtrusive part of the floor and use that instead of the cracked unit. Fill the hole left with the cracked pieces.

Tackling damp stone floors

If your stone or brick floor is very damp, there is obviously no damp proof membrane (vapor barrier) underneath it. You can (if you are strong enough to face the work) lift the whole floor and re-lay it over a bituminous or pitch-epoxy dpm, but this is really worth considering only if your floor is a particularly fine specimen and thorough damp proofing is thought to be essential. Even then, you risk damaging the stones when you prise them up, unless the moisture has already weakened the mortar bed in which they were laid, and you will still have a laborious job cleaning them up ready for re-laying.

An alternative 'chemical' treatment is available, using the clear damp proofing sealants widely used nowadays for holding back penetrating moisture in basements. These sealers actually cure chemically in the presence of moisture, and offer the only realistic way of treating such floors without lifting them... there is simply no traditional remedy here. The sealer will alter the appearance of the stones and bricks, however, changing the colour and highlighting shade differences in the surface.

As a last resort you could, of course, cover a stone floor with a new concrete screed laid over a new dpm – if you can cope with raising the floor level by about 75mm (3in) and you are prepared to consign your stone floor to the archaeologists. Unless your floor is in a really bad condition, this drastic action can only be viewed as ultimate defeat, but at least you will have created both a dry and usable floor surface from the ruins.

Maintaining stone floors

Regular washing and sweeping will keep most restored stone floors in good condition. You can seal brick and flagstones with a clear floor sealer, which will change the colour and look of the surface but will stop dirt from getting into the stone. Remember that if you seal marble it will become slippery and, very probably, dangerous. Treat slate occasionally with a 1 to 4 mixture of linseed oil and white spirit (paint thinner) to help it keep its lustre. Avoid polishing slate which, like marble, can then become slippery.

Plasterwork

The technique of plastering has been practised for a very long time. For instance, around 200 BC in Egypt the craft was already highly skilled. A plastering material was used, based on lime stucco and burnt gypsum, which differed very little from the plaster of Paris used today. Around 500 BC, the craft was common in Greece and was subsequently adopted and improved on by the Romans for many centuries.

With the advent of the Dark Ages, however, plasterwork fell into disuse. During the late thirteenth century, with the evolution of wooden-framed buildings, the 'wattle and daub' technique evolved. Vertical wooden staves, fixed between the wooden frames, were interwoven with wattles (reeds or osiers). These were daubed inside and out by a plaster of clay or dung, mixed with a horsehair binder.

During the fifteenth century, ornamental work was introduced which meant there were far more potential creative opportunities for the craft, which no longer had to be used simply as a base for decorative purposes. Mouldings and figures were formed, which were often reinforced with metal or wooden prongs. At this time, the materials used were either 'stucco', which was a mixture of sand and lime, or 'stucco duro', a stucco made firmer by the addition of gypsum plaster.

As the craftsmen's abilities and ingenuity increased, ornamental plasterwork developed rapidly. Plasterers produced curved, angular and interlacing panels, enriched with floral designs. Designs were cast with wooden or lead moulds, carved in reverse, and the casts pressed in a soft state to the ceiling. From this, the running mould developed (see page 172). Cornices and friezes also became fashionable.

The beauty of the ornamental plasterwork is the highlight of the stairs and hallway and is a fine feature of decorative relief which offsets the arch and doorway.

Ornamentation became very complex and included flowers, fruit, birds and fish.

Changes in plain plasterwork have been gradual, mainly involving the materials used. Wattle was replaced by split, subsequently sawn, pieces of wood known as laths, which were still being used up until the early twentieth century. Modern plasterboard and expanded metal lathing have only recently become popular. The plaster used has undergone a very slow development from river mud to the modern, bagged, pre-mixed products. The actual techniques used in plain plasterwork have changed surprisingly little.

This chapter is fairly technical because it attempts to teach a very skilful craft, using techniques which have been handed down through the ages. There is no easy way and there are no short cuts that can be used to apply plaster. Plastering has always been a complicated craft, and one which many DIY enthusiasts find daunting. Certainly, major jobs such as replastering a complete room or house would be best left to professionals. However, with patience and practice and the correct materials, there is no reason why a capable amateur should not attempt minor repairs and projects such as the following: repairs to cracks or chips in plain plasterwork; replastering small areas of walls and ceilings; repairs to angles; simple plain moulding repair; fixing of fibrous plaster mouldings, ceiling centres and producing a new cornice. All these processes are set out in this chapter.

Two critical factors related to successful plasterwork are the quality of the materials used and the suction, that is, the propensity to absorb moisture, of the background. The success of any plasterwork depends primarily on these factors. Otherwise, the type of job which should be attempted depends on individual confidence and level of competence.

Tools and equipment

Brush
A water brush, a good quality bristle brush 150mm (6in) to 200mm (8in) long, is used to splash the wall surface for the 'trowelling up' process (see page 167) and for all wetting. Other small brushes will also be useful when working small areas or mouldings.

Comb scratcher

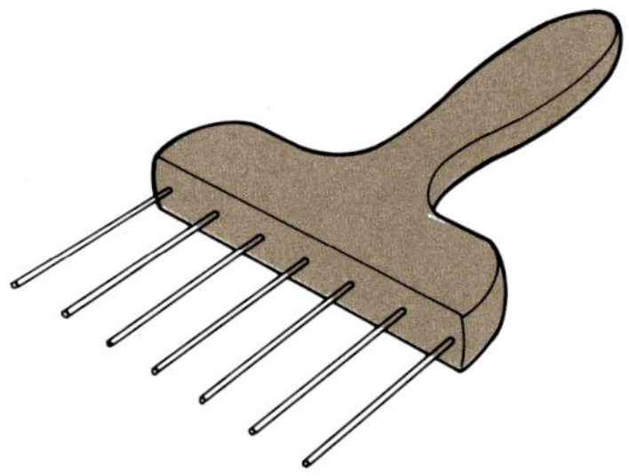

A comb scratcher comprises a plain, wooden handle with thin, metal prongs approximately 75mm (3in) in length, spaced 9mm (⅜in) apart. The tool, made by the plasterer, is used to scratch an already plastered surface to key it in preparation for another heavy coat.

Float

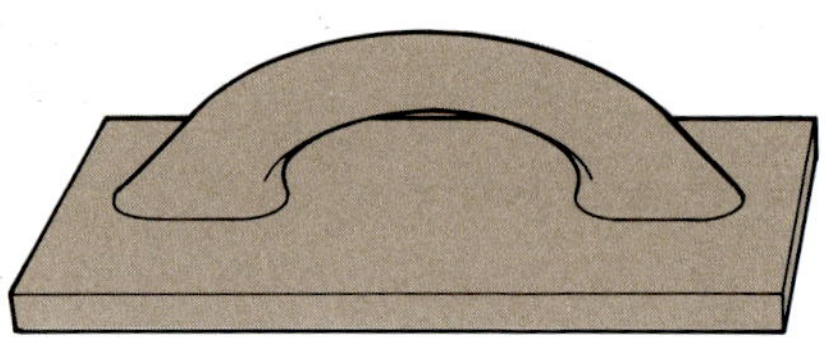

Traditionally, floats were made by the craftsmen themselves, the best comprising yellow pine. A float is made from a hand-curved handle attached lengthways to the back of the smooth float face. The face is straight grained with a grain running lengthwise, the edges of the face being slightly rounded. The size can vary but is generally in the region of 280mm × 100mm (11in × 4in) and 9mm (⅜in) in thickness. This tool can be used for a number of tasks; for example, to apply the finishing coat or to rub up plain face cement finish to produce a sand-faced texture, or to scour up a coarse surface. It is customary for plasterers to own a number of different shaped and sized floats to enable them to carry out complex cement finishings and mouldings. Plastic floats are available on the market but they do not match the individuality of the wooden floats.

Hammer
The lath hammer was the traditional tool, with a blade at one side like a hatchet, used for splitting wood for laths. An ordinary claw hammer will, however, be sufficient for most woodworking operations.

Hawk

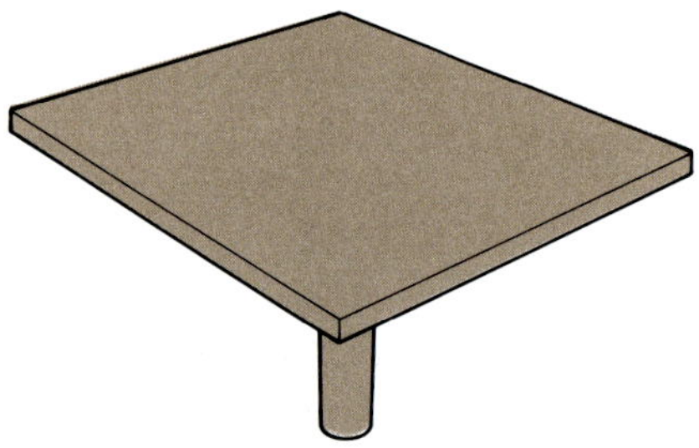

The hawk or hand board is a square board made from wood or aluminium, varying in size from 300 to 340mm (12 to 13½in) square, and having a handle attached to the centre of the underside. It is used to carry plaster from the spot board to the point of application. The hawk is normally carried in the left hand.

Joint rule
A joint rule is a flat piece of steel with a 45 degree angle end with the longest edge bevelled. Traditionally, sizes ranged from 12mm (½in) up to 600mm (24in). Only two main sizes survive today: 100mm (4in) and 300mm (12in). They are difficult to obtain, but can be easily made using ordinary metalwork procedures. (Not available in the USA.)

Mixing tub or trough
A mixing tub or trough can be used as a container for the plaster. Any flat, clean area can, however, be used, provided there is no concern about permanent staining.

Small tool

A small tool is not unlike a spoon, with ends which can be leaf- or square-shaped. It is mainly used for moulding work but is also useful for all small areas and delicate applications. (Not available in the USA.)

Spot board and stand
The plaster to be used is put on the spot board at the working area. A long, flat board, it is made out of 19mm (¾in) resin-bonded plywood 900mm (36in) square, supported by a wood or metal framework at hip height. Size is not critical but it should be made to make working comfortable. Factors such as ease of transport and lightness in weight should be taken into consideration.

Straightening rules

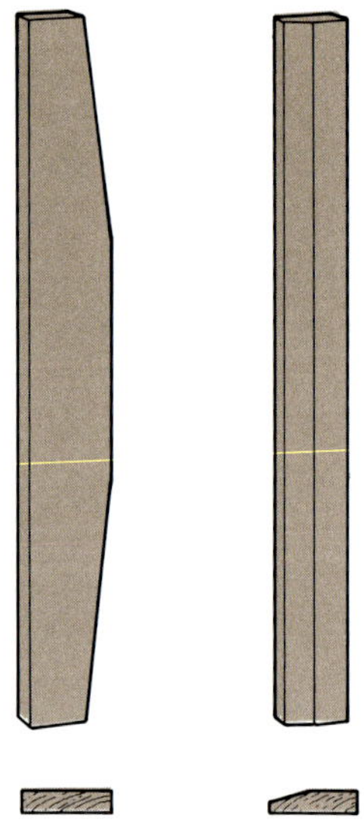

Straightening rules, as the name suggests, are used for straightening or ruling out plasterwork while it is still in a malleable state. Two kinds are used: a floating rule and a feather-edged type. The *floating rule*

should ideally be 2m (6ft 6in) long, 150mm (6in) wide and 25mm (1in) thick. The *feather-edged rule*, while the same length, is narrower – 100mm (4in) – and thinner – 18mm (¾in) – with the straight edge bevelled to a taper.

Trowels

Gauging trowel

The gauging trowel has a long, triangular blade which tapers to a rounded end with a handle attached to the other end. Such trowels vary in size from 152mm (6in) to 200mm (8in). They are used for both mixing small quantities of material and for spreading the plaster in very awkward places.

Angle trowels (corner tools)

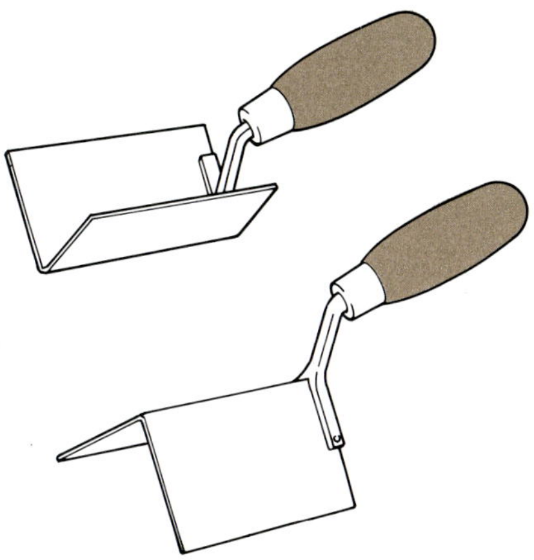

Angle trowels have handles attached – on the outside of external and on the inside of internal trowels (corner tools). They are used for forming angles.

Laying trowel

The laying trowel, which has a thin, rectangular blade of highly tempered steel, varies in size from 280mm × 115mm (11in × 4½in) to 408mm × 115mm (16in × 4½in). This implement is used for spreading and flattening the plaster after it has been taken from the hawk.

Woodworking and metal cutting tools will be used from time to time. Other equipment includes shovels, buckets, steps and basic scaffolding, stirring stick and mechanical mixers for large quantities of plaster.

Materials

Cement

Portland cement is commonly used as a hardener and is mixed with coarse lime plastering because of its weathering qualities. Cement and gypsum should never be incorporated in the same mix as the material will then set very rapidly and become unworkable.

Gypsum

Gypsum is found in most parts of the world. When burnt, it is used to produce plaster in the form of plaster of Paris or to act as a hardening and setting agent when mixed with lime and/or sand.

Lime

Lime, in the form of slaked lime, is a major component of plaster. Quicklime used to be produced from quarried lumps of limestone or chalk. The lumps of limestone were fired and then immersed in water-filled slaking pits or drums. Water was added until all chemical reaction had ceased. The resulting product formed slaked lime. Its setting properties varied according to various factors such as its natural composition and the firing process. Today, hydrated lime is produced under controlled conditions or as a by-product of other manufacturing processes. The function of lime in the plastering mix is to act as a plasticizer and setting agent.

Plasterboard

Plasterboard comprises two sheets of heavy paper enclosing an aerated gypsum core and was designed as a base for plastering to replace laths (strips of wood). (In the USA, plasterboard is not skim coated; the joints are filled and the plasterboard then decorated.) To begin with, it was rejected by most craftsmen and only achieved general acceptance after about 1930. However, during World War II, plasterboard really came into its own in war-torn Europe as it was a method of making good war damage. Today, it is in common use throughout the world.

Plaster

The main constituent of plasters is gypsum (calcium sulphate) which has been partially or wholly dried in a kiln. The addition of various aggregates and additives determines the types and grades of plaster, which have different setting and hardening times. Because of the critical importance of the mixing proportions, it is advisable to use pre-mixed plasters. Your dealer can probably advise you as to the type of plaster required if you specify what work you are going to undertake and provide fairly detailed plans.

Remember to store plaster in a dry place – the material chrystallizes with water and can never be reconstituted.

Sand

Sand, which is the bulk or filler of the mixture, should meet three criteria: it should be very clean, well graded and reasonably sharp and angular.

The best sand for plastering is dredged river sand or certain types of pit sand. A good test of whether or not it is suitable is to squeeze some in your fist. When you open your hand, the sand should cling together and not stain unduly.

Plastering techniques

The white plastered walls of the alcove contrast with the rough wooden beams.

Before attempting to embark on any plastering, whether repairs or major jobs, it is vital that you fully understand the nature of the work. This is particularly important when you are dealing with plasterwork in a house built over 60 years ago. In such houses, the plasterwork will most probably be lime-based. Lime plaster falls into two categories. First there is course stuff, which is a mixture of sand, lime and a binder, such as horsehair, used as a base coat. There is also setting, which is a mixture of lime and washed sand, mixed with gypsum plaster to increase its strength, and used as a finishing coat.

Plaster mixes

Selecting the correct plaster for the particular job in hand is most important if you are going to produce a good finish. If you are unsure about what plaster to use for the surface you intend to work on, it is best to ask a plastering expert. Note that if the wrong mix is chosen it can affect the finish.

The plaster mix should be selected for compatibility with both the original surface and materials. Select the finishing coat first – and this is particularly important if you are patching for a repair, as you must end up with a matching surface. Once the finishing coat has been decided, the undercoat can be selected. It is important to ensure that the finishing and undercoats are compatible, that the mixed plaster can be spread according to the recommended mix proportions and that the strength of the mix is adequate. Here it should be noted that it is best to aim for a weak rather than a strong mix. Many more problems have arisen from plasters having too strong a mix than too weak a one. There are many traditional lime and sand mixes which, although they are relatively weak, are still in place hundreds of years later. For more information on mixing, see page 167.

Three-coat method

Traditionally, all large plastering jobs employed the 'three-coat method'. This technique was used a great deal in old houses which had lath work as a plastering surface. Laths are thin strips of rough wood which are attached to the wooden frame of the wall to provide a surface to which plaster can grip. It was also useful for covering up irregular brickwork or stonework.

The first two coats are undercoats. The first is called the render (base) coat. It performs three functions: first to form a background to work from; second to even the base and third to even the suction of the surface. The second layer, called the floating coat, provides a level surface or undercoat for the third, thin finishing coat. The surface of the finishing coat should be flat and ready to receive the decoration provided by painting or wallcoverings.

Two-coat method

Modern house construction methods provide a reasonably good surface for plaster, so if you are plastering a new building the render (base) coat can almost certainly be dispensed with and only the floating and finishing coats need be applied.

With the two-coat method, the floating coat is usually referred to as the undercoat

One-coat method

Some repair jobs and finishing off plasterboard only require one coat of plaster. In this case, the finishing coat is used.

Plaster constituents

The render (base) and floating coats use a mix involving plaster and a coarse-grained additive, known as an aggregate. Finishing coats can be made using only plaster.

Recommended thicknesses

It is very important to bear in mind the recommended thicknesses for each coat which are 6-9mm (¼-⅜in) for the render coat, 9-11mm (⅜-7⁄16in) for the floating coat and 2-5mm (1⁄16-3⁄16in) for the finishing coat. Remember that each coat can be, and usually is, built up using more than one application.

Mixing

There are several ways in which plaster can be mixed. The method chosen depends upon the types of material used and the quantity required. Undercoats are usually mixed on a flat, clean surface such as a board. Pre-mixed plasters are more conveniently mixed in a trough or tub. If a large job is to be attempted, it may be worth hiring or borrowing a mechanical mixer. It is very important to remember not to mix more than the quantity that can be used in half-an-hour. This is, of course, because the plaster will start to stiffen and will become unworkable.

If you are not using pre-mixed plaster, make a layered sandwich of the necessary constituents. This helps to mix them properly and prevents the powder being lost. Thoroughly mix by turning the outer portions into the middle with a shovel at least three times. Form a large ring with the constituents and pour some water into it. Turn the dry material into the water and mix. Make another ring from the wet material and add more water. Continue until enough water is added to produce a pliable, workable consistency. If you are using pre-mixed plaster, add plaster to the water. If you only require a small amount of plaster, it is best to use a bucket. First fill the bucket three-quarters full of water. Add the plaster by hand, breaking the lumps as you go. Fill until dry powder shows above the water and allow the mixture to settle. Then mix with a stick until it is a heavy cream. Thoroughly clean the containers after use.

For mechanical mixing, first pour in the water and then part of the aggregate. Add the binding powder and finally the remaining aggregate. Ensure the mix does not become too dry – add more water if necessary. Water is the catalyst that allows the setting to take place.

Applying plaster

The mixed plaster is transferred onto the spot board from whence it can be moved with a trowel onto the hawk. Using a dragging, rather than cutting, action to transfer the plaster from the hawk to the laying trowel and press it to the wall. Keeping the upper edge of the laying trowel away from the surface, work it up the wall, exerting slight pressure. This is an important technique, ensuring that the plaster is 'fed' to the wall a little at a time. The method is quite difficult to manage. You could practise beforehand, however, with a non-setting material, such as sand. Remember to remove this practice coat before you begin plastering.

Taking plaster off the hawk.

Working above your head on a ceiling is much more difficult. Make sure you are not spreading directly overhead as you will then have very little control over your movements. Rather (if you are right-handed) position yourself so that the trowel is to your left and you are spreading to the side.

Ruling out

To ensure that the finished wall is both flat and even, the render (base) and floating coats should both be ruled out, using a floating rule. The rule is worked in a zig zag, either horizontally or vertically, over the coat. Any hollows which appear can be filled with further material until the surface is even. A feather edged rule is used in the same way as a floating rule, except that the movement is more of a dragging action.

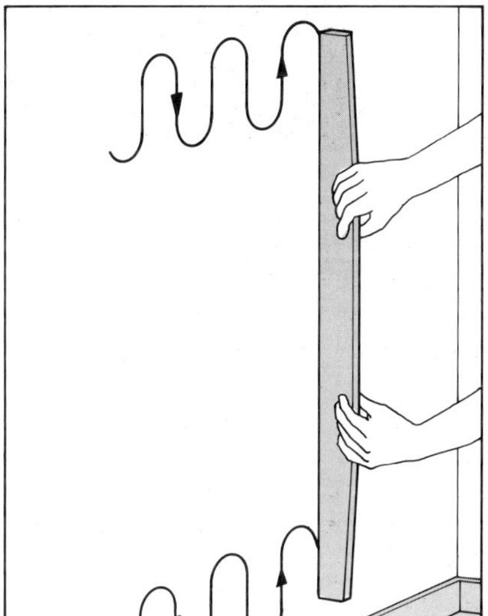

Ruling out with a floating rule.

Trowelling up

When the finishing coat has been applied, to ensure a perfectly smooth finish, a trowel is passed over the surface and every now and again is lubricated with water. This process is known as 'trowelling up'. It is a very important part of the plastering process.

Repairing plain plasterwork

A detail of exposed wattle and daub on a wooden-framed house. Internal lath and plaster is basically similar, although it was introduced later into house construction.

To start with, find out the extent of the repair. The first indications of a problem are cracks or bulging plasterwork. Cracks can often be quite sound and only require cutting out and filling. To test the condition of the plasterwork, the area should be tapped. Sound plasterwork will give a dull thud if the background is solid brick, block or concrete. Hollow plasterwork, that is, plasterwork which has lost contact with its base, will, when tapped, give out a higher pitched sound, indicating that it is a hollow. If hollow plasterwork is discovered, it should be carefully removed with a club hammer (small sledge hammer) and bolstered down to a solid surface. For plasterwork on lath or board it is best to cut through it with a knife before removal; this ensures the extent of the repair is contained. The edges of the repair should be straight and slightly undercut. If there is a large repair to be carried out to plasterboard, it should be cut back to the centre of joists or studs. Small holes should be cut as regular rectangles to allow for easy board patching.

Testing for suction

The period during which plaster is malleable – that is, before it has set hard – is known as the working time and can, unlike the setting time, be affected by the rate of absorption of water by the base. For example, a plaster which has a setting time of one-and-a-half hours could have its working time reduced to 15 minutes by a base with a high suction. To test the base, splash it with water. If the water soaks in quickly, the base needs further wetting. In extreme cases the base can be treated with a stipple coat (see page 79) or a diluted bonding agent. The edges of the repair should also be wetted and, if damage to decoration is to be avoided, should also be sealed.

It cannot be over-emphasized that the two most vital factors affecting a satisfactory job are suction and set.

Matching the materials

The character of a room is partly determined by the type and shape of materials used. Many traditional buildings have irregularly shaped plasterwork with different surface textures. When repairing, the original shape should be followed to avoid aesthetic loss and the original materials used should be matched as near as possible. Often, much greater thicknesses of plaster are found in old buildings than in the conventional modern two-coat work. When this is the case, the plasterwork should be built up in layers of no more than 10mm (3/8in) to 13mm (1/2in), making sure that preceding coats are comb scratched to provide a key. To obtain the best results you should follow the same principle as traditional craftsmen and let each layer dry properly before applying the next. When horsehair was used as a binder for undercoats, the plaster dried out progressively. This meant that the surface had to be comb scratched to form a key, allowed to dry out, then wetted before the next coat.

Small repairs

Small repair work, other than very minor jobs such as hairline cracks, should use a minimum of two coats of plaster. The floating coat is applied so that it is flush with the surface of the wall, then cleaned up so that the old and new plaster are flush at the edges. Finally, the surface of the repair receives a key ready for the finishing coat. When the plaster sets it will shrink back from the surface, leaving space for the finishing coat.

Dents and chips

The size and depth of a dent in a plaster coat determines how it should be repaired. Shallow or small dents can be soaked with water and filled without trimming simply by trowelling flush with the surface. Deeper dents or hollows, however, will have to be cut back and trimmed. Corners or projections are prone to chips. On corners, each side should be worked from the flat wall surface by damping, filling flush with the flat surface and scraping back with the trowel on each face. The chip is finished by filling in any remaining depressions and then trowelling up (see page 167). If chips appear on a plain wall or ceiling, however, they are treated in the same way as dents.

Hairline cracks (crazing)

Crazing is the name given to hairline cracks in a surface. Test the plaster for soundness (see page 168). If unsound, treat as a normal repair job. If sound, drag a knife through the cracks to remove any grease or loose particles. Dampen the surface and fill with a fine plaster or all-purpose filler (spackle). Scrape the surface with a trowel and refill, ensuring it is kept sufficiently damp to control the suction. Repeat until all the plaster has completed its shrinkage back from the face and all of the cracks are filled and flush with the surface.

Major repairs

Repairs to large areas should be carried out in the same way as for plastering a complete wall, that is, by cutting back to the original base and starting again using the two- or three-coat method.

It is important to prepare the base correctly because of the problems of suction and setting.

Brickwork

New brickwork only needs wetting before plasterwork is applied. Old brickwork, however, should have the joints raked out, brushed down with a stiff brush and then wetted.

Wooden lathwork

Broken laths should be removed and replaced with new ones. The joints between the laths should be cleaned out and the whole area brushed down dry and dampened ready for the render (base) coat. Alternatively, a base for plastering can be provided by plasterboard, tacked over exposed laths, depth permitting, and the nails used for fixing the board allow for the thickness of the laths. Or all laths can be removed – though this is not advisable for patchwork.

Concrete or dense backgrounds

Concrete should be brushed down and keyed. The key can be formed by hacking or by applying a stipple coat (see page 79) with a brush of one part cement to two parts sand, mixed to a slurry. Cracks that may previously have occurred can be covered with expanded metal lathing before plastering.

If the surface is very uneven – and it will be with materials such as laths, for example – it is best to use the traditional three-coat system.

Applying the plaster

The render (base) coat is spread with a laying trowel, ruled out with a feather-edged rule, and a key produced with a comb scratcher. On lathwork, ruling out is often omitted so that the key is not disturbed.

When the surface is quite even as regards surface height and degree of suction, use the two-coat method.

The original method of applying the floating coat is known as dot and screed. A dot is actually a small piece of wood 75mm × 25mm (3in × 1in) which is 6mm ($\frac{1}{4}$in) thick. The dot is embedded in a newly applied patch of plaster and the distance from the surface of the dot to the base surface is adjusted so that it represents the desired thickness of the finished plaster.

Initially, dots are applied to the four corners of the wall needing repair, with a plumb line used to help to locate them. Additional dots are placed between the first four. A strip of plaster, known as a screed, is then applied to join the dots, using the ruling out method (see page 167) to ensure the correct thickness is maintained. Once the screed is hard, the area between them can be filled in. The dots can then be removed

How to repair a crack

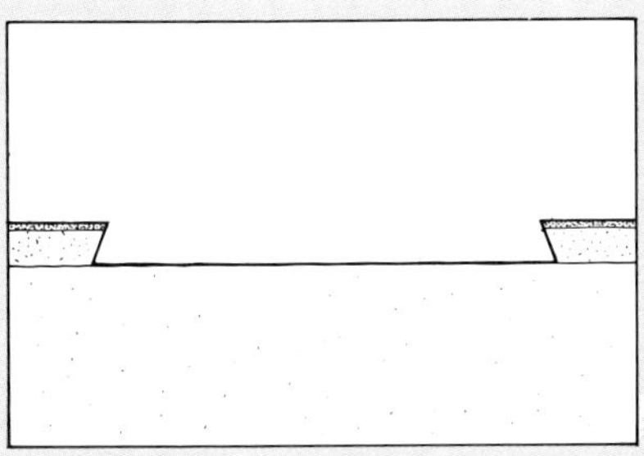

1. *Cut back on both sides to sound plaster to provide an undercut dovetail key. Trim the edge and brush clean.*

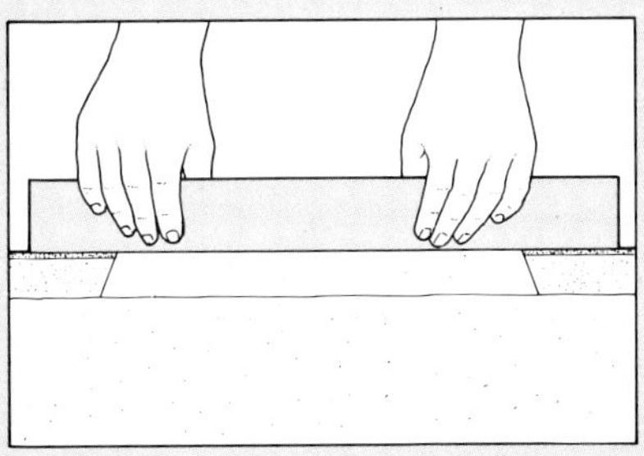

2. *Damp with water to control suction and fill with plaster. Smooth off flush to the surface.*

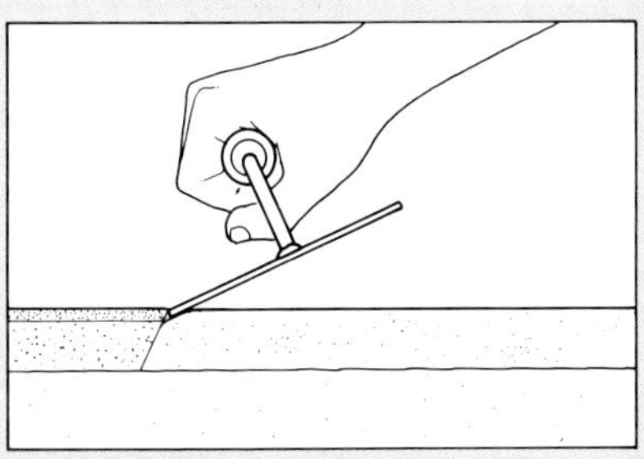

3. *Cut back the edge with a trowel so that the finishing coat can be applied flush.*

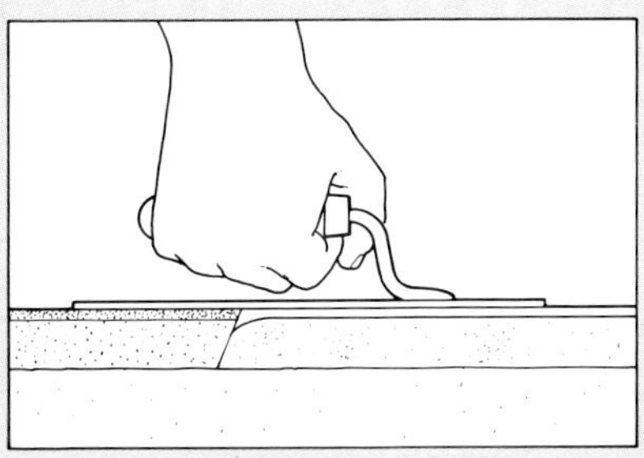

4. *Apply the finishing coat, making sure it is flush with the surface either side of the crack.*

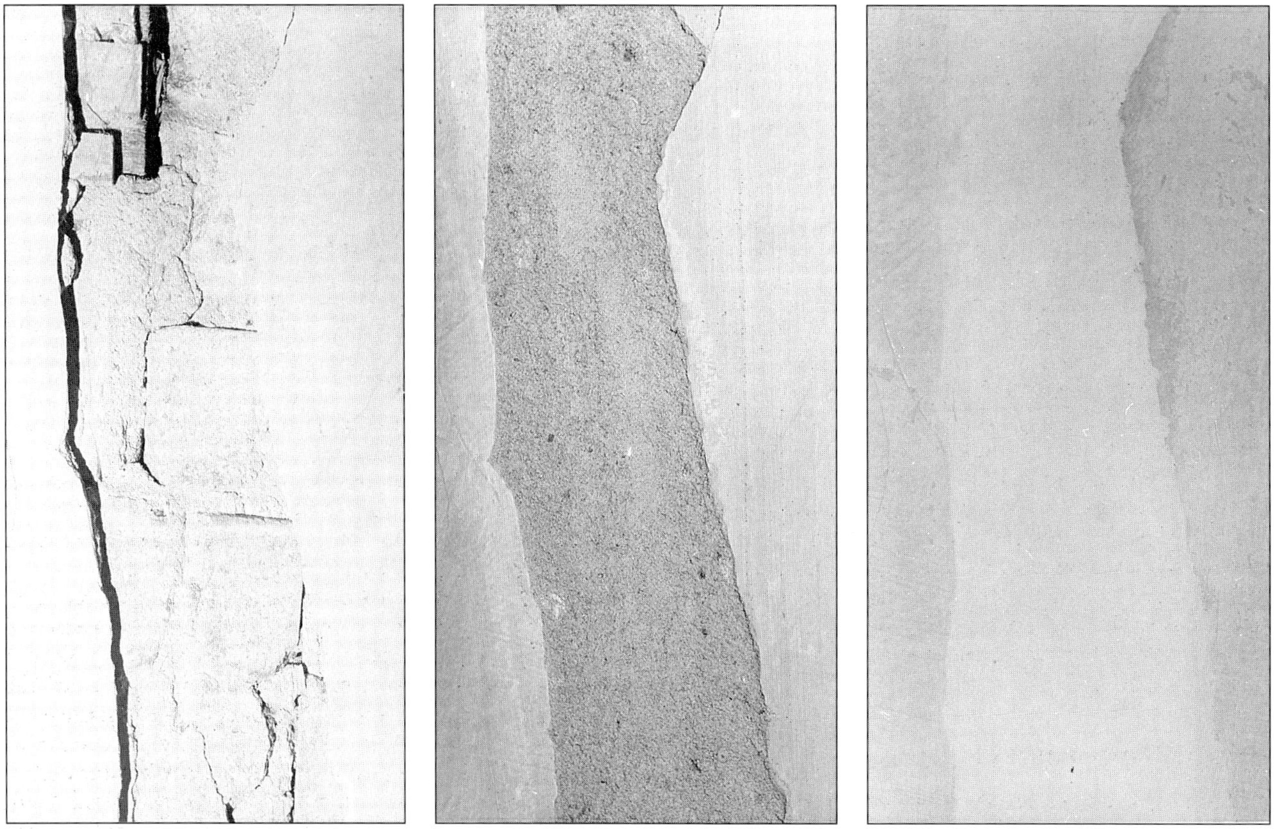

Repairing a wall crack: (above) *crack cut out;* (above right) *floating coat applied to crack;* (far right) *finished coat applied.*

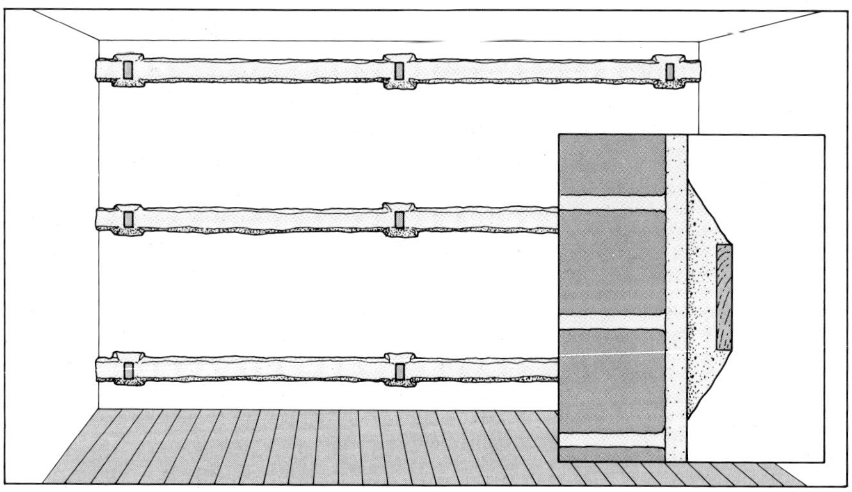

A wall showing dots lined and plumbed, and screeds ruled out.

and the holes filled in. The whole surface should then be keyed, using a float.

Many short cuts using the dot and screed system have been developed. The system used to work on the principle of narrow screeds which were allowed to harden. Then the broad or box screed which used much wider screeds was developed, which dispensed with the dots, with the whole being ruled out while the plaster was still soft.

The freehand technique was developed from the broad screed method which did not require either screeds or guides. It was commonly used in simple dwellings.

As the finishing coat is so thin, the work of levelling the surface is done by the floating coat. The first layer of finishing coat is applied with a trowel, the second a float and the third with a trowel. The finishing coat provides a finish suitable for decoration. Working from right to left, a very thin and well-worked coat is spread over the whole wall, which picks up the selvage or excess plaster left by each trowel stroke. The finishing coat is applied using the float, which helps to flatten the surface and produces a fine lined surface. The final application, known as laying down, is applied with the trowel. After the surface has stiffened, the trowel should be passed over the surface, working from left to right.

Mouldings and ornamental plasterwork

Before the introduction of modern fibrous materials, almost all moulding was produced on site, mainly from sand/lime mixes reinforced with horsehair. The best work used conventional mixes, gauged with plaster of Paris.

By the sixteenth century, plasterers were producing single moulded plaster ribs, sometimes with curved, angular or interlacing panels, enriched with floral designs. Cornices – mouldings running between walls and ceilings – were developed, and wider moulded ribs, using ornament consisting of hop vines, laurel, and guilloche and scrolls, were also made. Ornament was produced using a revolving press in addition to the reverse carved wood and lead moulds already in use. Moulds were cast which were pressed to the ceiling where they were wedged in position until set.

Repairs to cornices

Minor chips, cracks or holes can be repaired relatively easily, using a mixture of lime putty and plaster.

It is best to fill large holes with a sand/lime/plaster core, allowing 6mm (¼in) for the finish. Be sure to wet the background and surrounding plasterwork frequently to make sure that suction does not affect the finish. The material is spread into the hole with a gauging trowel or small tool and, then ruled off flush with a joint rule.

Small pieces of ornament can be replaced by making an impression from an original ornament, using clay, modelling clay, or stiff linseed putty. Rule off the plain moulding, key the surface, and fit and bed the cast ornament with plaster.

Where a simple repair cannot be carried out, or a large section of the cornice is missing, another section must be made matching the original. First, a template must be made up, either from a drawing or from an impression of the original. If a section of moulding can be removed, make a straight cut with a saw and draw a cross-section of the cornice on a piece of card or paper. Alternatively, a cut can be made through the existing cornice to the wall and ceiling. A sheet of card can then be slotted into the cut and a profile of the moulding drawn on it. Make sure that the depth of the cornice is recorded to give a true cross-section of the outline.

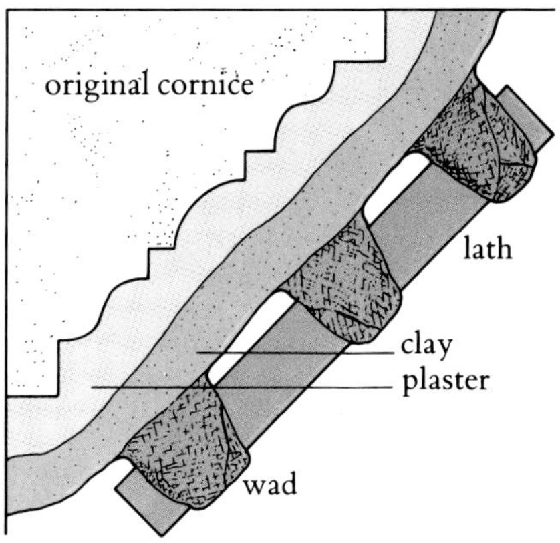

Taking a squeeze from a plain cornice.

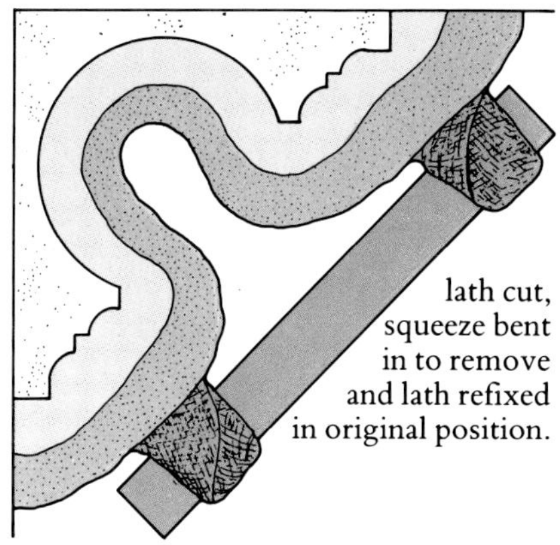

Squeeze from cornice with re-entrant curve.

If you think you might damage a cornice, it is advisable to take an impression of it. This is known as taking a squeeze. The materials required are a pliable substance such as modelling clay or putty and plaster of Paris, French chalk or talc and a small strip of wood.

Work the squeeze material (that is, the modelling clay or putty) to the correct usuable consistency and form it into a strip that is not less than 13mm (½in) thick and both long and wide enough to cover the cornice section. To ensure that the surface of the squeeze material is perfectly smooth, press it into a piece of glass.

Dust the cornice with French chalk and squeeze the clay firmly into the moulding. The plaster of Paris mixture can now be laid over the back of the clay. If the cornice moulding is undercut, that is, overhangs or returns into itself within its own projection, a strip of wood can be attached to the back of the plaster by means of strips of plaster coated bandage (wads) wrapped around the ends. When the plaster has set, the squeeze is removed. On an undercut cornice the wood will have to be cut as the squeeze has to be broken so that it can be removed.

Remove the squeeze and lay it on its back. Mix the plaster of Paris and apply it lightly to the clay with a soft brush, building it up until the rough depth of the cornice is formed. This process is known as casting. When set, the plaster cast of the cornice is both removed from the clay and cut through with a saw. Finally, the section is drawn round the cut end.

Taking a squeeze can also be done when the cornice contains ornament. The ornament should first be blanked out with tissue or thin paper to ensure that the clay does not get trapped in the face. The same process can also be used for producing a small amount of ornament when repairing. Traditionally, a small length of ornament 300mm (12in) in length is fixed to a board or moulding ground and a reverse mould poured in plaster or moulding wax – using equal parts beeswax and resin by weight and melted down. Only ornament with no undercut can be used.

When removing old ornamental cornices it will be found that the ornament attached is in small lengths or individual pieces, such as a single leaf. If care is taken, these traditional pieces of ornament can be cleaned up and then rebedded in a new cornice.

Producing a new cornice

Producing a new cornice is difficult, but not impossible, for the amateur plasterer enthusiast, provided meticulous attention is paid to the detailed instructions. The best way of learning how to do this is to learn on-the-job with a professional in charge. In any event, a professional should be left to fix any ornament required for the cornice.

First, a paper outline of the mould is made and transferred onto a sheet of steel or zinc, which is then cut and filed to produce a template. This is attached to a wooden stock. Both the stock and the template are attached at right angles to a wooden board, called a 'horse', and secured by a strut which also acts as a handle. The complete assembly is known as the running mould. A shoe – a piece of metal – is clipped over the top, or nib, of the mould. Beneath the horse is a wooden rebate (rabbet), set back to fit over the running rule, which is a length of smooth wood attached to the wall to ensure an even run. A metal muffle can be fitted to project 6mm (1/4in) in front of the template to run the core of the moulding (the backing or main part).

Any damage to the ceiling or wall should first be repaired before work on the new moulding is carried out. Make sure that the running mould is in an upright position. Mark the position of the tip of the shoe of the mould on the ceiling and the position of the underside of the horse on the wall at each end of the required length. When these marks have been made, join them with a straight position line. This can be done by snapping a chalked string line joining the points on the ceiling where the moulding is to be run. Cut the wood for the running rule to length. This is made of smooth wood approximately 10mm × 50mm (3/8in × 2in). Hold the running mould up in place on the position line and mark and place it in position on the wall. Position the running rule under the horse and behind the rebate. Fix the rule with a nail. Move the running mould and repeat the process at the other end. Fix the whole rule by sliding the mould along, making sure it is no more than just touching the chalk line.

The core of the moulding

Place sufficient coarse undercoat on the spot board. Open up in a ring, pour in water and gauge with plaster. Using the hawk and gauging

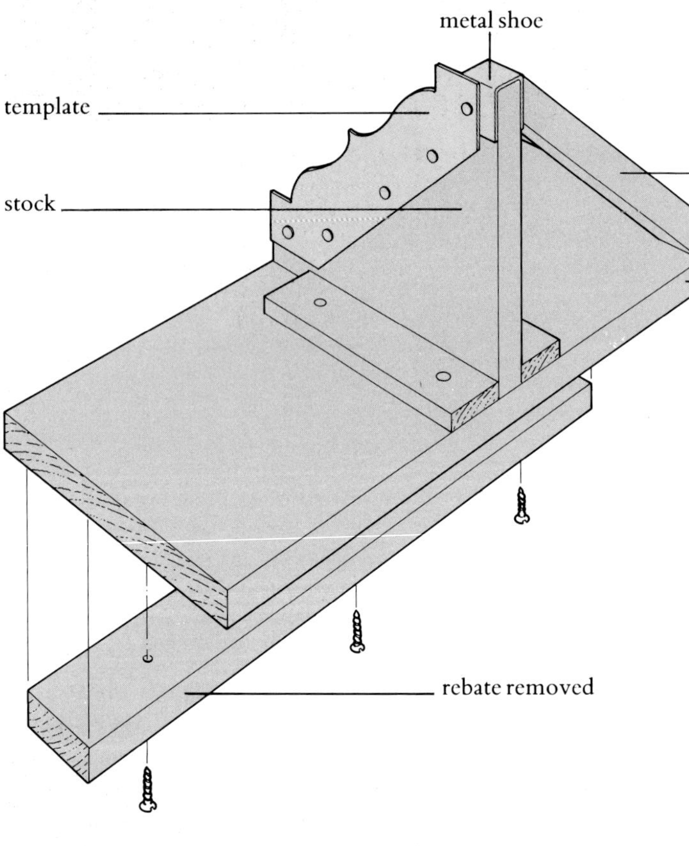

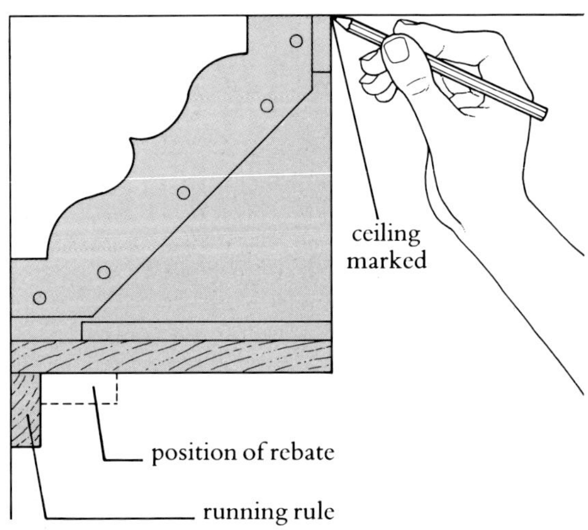

(above left) *A running mould is used to produce a new cornice.*

(above right) *Marking the tip of the running mould shoe on the ceiling.*

trowel, push the mixed coarse stuff firmly up in the corner. With the muffle in position, place the running mould at the right-hand end of the running rule and, with firm pressure, run through the mould. Continue this operation until the core has been built out. Further batches of material may be necessary to complete it. Remove the muffle and clean the area, tools and equipment.

Prepare to apply the finish coat and place the lime putty, water and plaster of Paris in clean buckets. Pour lime putty on the spot board, make a ring and pour in water. Sprinkle in plaster in the hole until level with the lime putty ring and quickly mix. Break down the lumps with the trowel and use the hawk to control the material on the board. As an alternative to mixing on the board, the lime and plaster can be mixed in a bucket like ordinary finish. If alternate two handfuls of lime are mixed with one handful of plaster, the mix proportions will be correct and it can be stirred up soft. Size water, that is, glue size plus water, can be used to delay the setting; this should be tested on a small sample first to get the timing right. The mixed material is applied to the core with the gauging trowel and the running mould passed through. Further material is applied to the cornice and the mould again run through.

A steady pressure has to be applied on the mould which should not be allowed either to come off the running rule or away from the ceiling. Sometimes considerable pressure is needed when expansion of the plaster starts to take place. A number of plaster gauges may be required until the finish has run out. The ceiling and running mould can be wetted but not the cornice which is being run. The running mould, spot board and tools should be

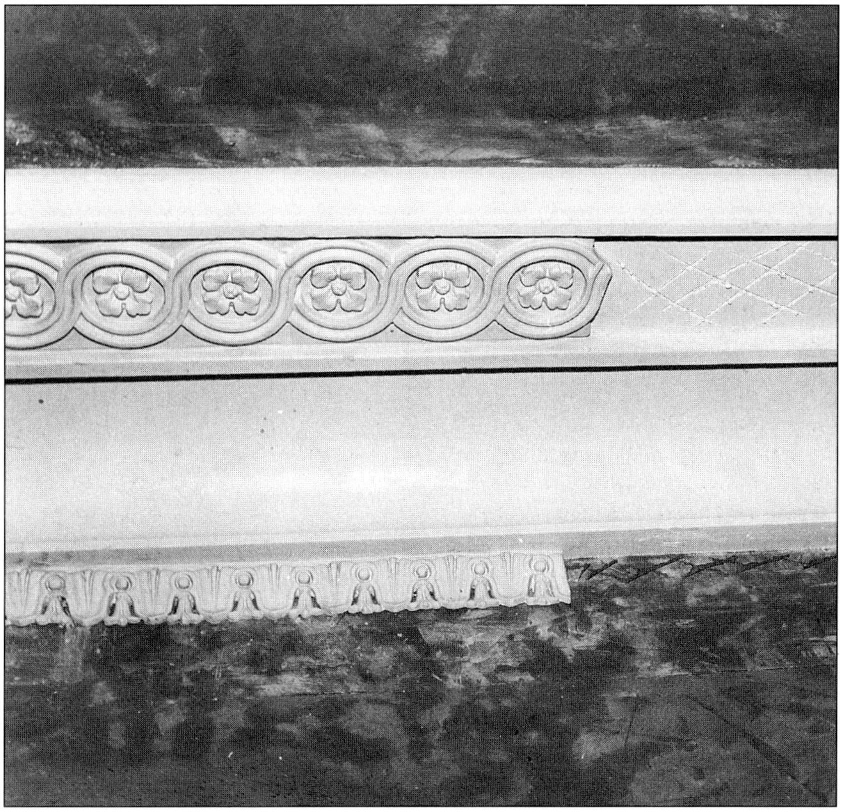

(above right) *A cornice undergoing repair. Notice that the plasterwork has been keyed.*

(below right) *A corner of the same cornice which has been completed.*

cleaned between each gauge. Make sure that the running mould has been run through completely once before each application of freshly gauged plaster to remove the plaster from the previous gauge.

When the cornice is complete, the rules are removed, any selvage trimmed off and holes made good.

Running down

Short lengths of cornice and small pieces can be produced away from the surface on which they will be attached. The cornice is made on a horizontal surface which acts as the ceiling and a board which acts as the wall (see the illustration right). A running rule is attached to the horizontal surface and grease applied to all surfaces.

The cornice can be built up on plasterboard which will reinforce it and cut down the amount of material to be used. Only plaster of Paris is used for producing the shape of the cornice. As for work *in situ*, run out until complete and remove from the boards for cutting and fixing.

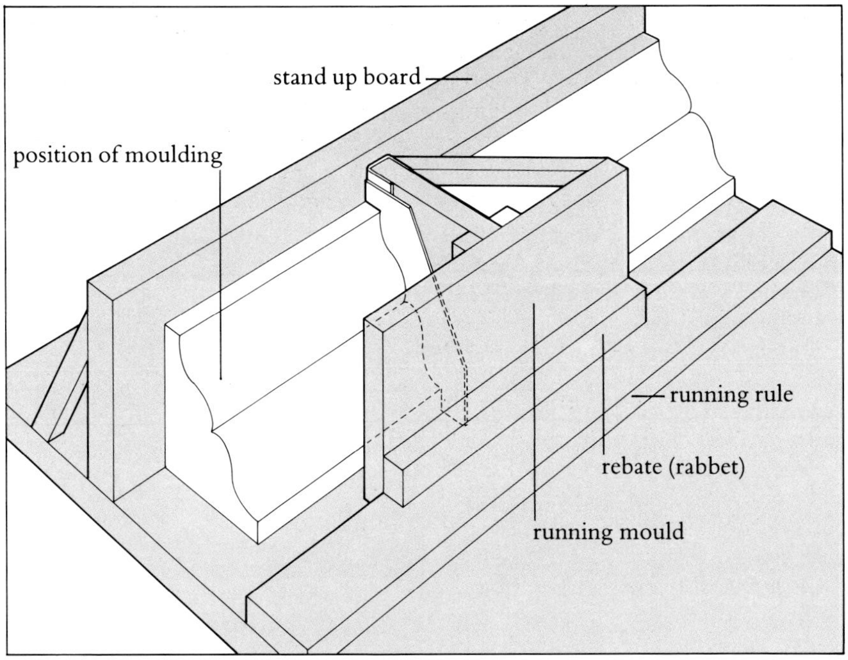

The equipment which is necessary for running down a length of cornice.

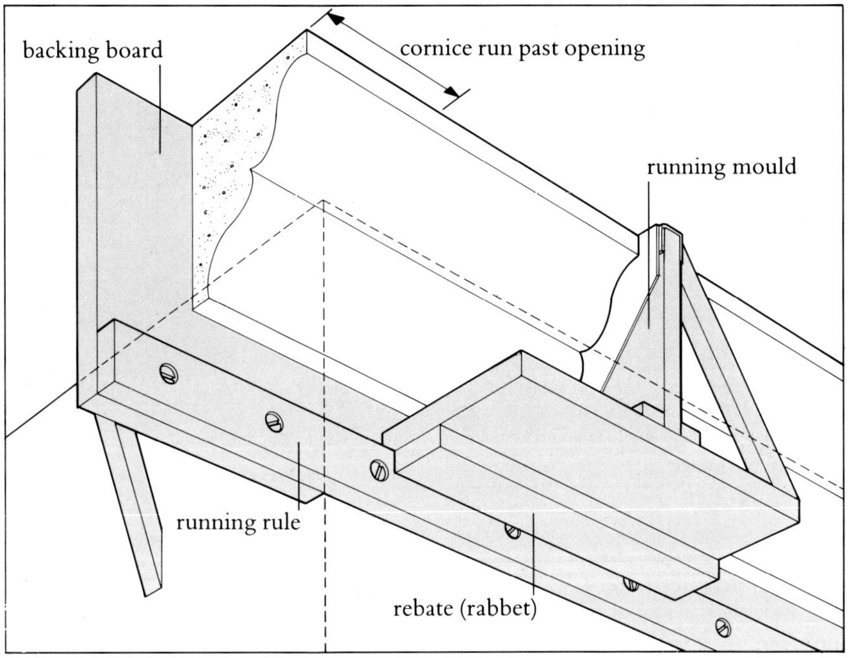

The running angle is taken past the end of the wall to form an external mitre.

Forming the mitres and joints

Internal mitres are formed by continuing the run from the original cornice. It is important to ensure that the material matches the original lime putty and plaster. A small tool is used to place the plaster and the joint rule used to form the shape by hand. The joint should be kept moist all the time you are working by continually soaking it with water. When complete, it should match the existing moulding and finish with a sharp corner, which is normally a 90 degree angle but which may, in certain circumstances, comprise a wider angle.

External mitres can be formed by continuing from the original cornice using the running mould. The running rule is taken past the end of the right-hand wall and supported to ensure no movement. A piece of board can be fixed up behind the rule and the cornice run past the end of the wall. The backing board is carefully removed and the rule reversed to run the other length. The running rule is run past the edge and the gap between the existing cornice and the projecting cornice moulded. When the new length is run, the mitre is formed and any selvage can be cleaned up or filled in with the joint rule as the running proceeds.

Very short returns are run down and planted individually.

Fibrous plaster

If you do not need to match and repair the original mouldings but simply want to add an attactive feature, cast fibrous plaster is recommended for decorative mouldings. Fibrous plasterwork is universally available.

Fibrous plaster is designed to be fixed to finished walls and ceilings, although in some cases it may be necessary to design the background to accommodate the new features, for example, when fitting a niche or arch. The niches require depth behind the wall face to allow for the size of the cast. Most flat walls cannot accommodate the depth, so the niche needs to be fixed across a corner of a room or a false wall made. Ready-made arches are made to standard sizes and an opening, therefore, would need to be adjusted to suit, unless a special order can be made. Fibrous plaster casts are either fixed with nails or screws or stuck in position, sometimes using a combination of these methods.

Fixing

Temporary fixing blocks can be nailed in position, ready to accept the cast. All necessary adjustments for size should take place before fixing is attempted. The cornice should be cut to length and mitres cut, preferably using a mitre box. Fibrous plaster can be cut with a hand saw – the blade being lubricated first with water. The back of the casts should be roughened and the fixing positions marked.

Casts can be fixed with plaster, tile cement or metal fixings. If plaster of Paris is used, both casts and background should be soaked with water. Care should be taken to make sure that any wet plaster coming into contact with finished surfaces is removed without delay.

All mitred joints should be soaked with water, filled in and worked with the joint rule to finish. Strands of scrim (canvas or bandage), soaked in plaster and squeezed in with a small tool, will help to reinforce the joint.

Glossary

Aggregate: the bulk of any material being mixed; the infill can comprise sand and stones.

Binder: the part of a mix which holds the material together.

Casting: the process of producing an item from a mould.

Core: the bulk of material in a moulding.

Cornice: a moulding which runs between a wall and ceiling.

Dot and screed: dots are small pieces of wood in coatings of plaster which are lined, plumbed and levelled. Bands of plaster, flush with the face of the dots, called screeds, are used together with the dots to produce a lineable plumb wall or level ceiling surface.

Finishing or setting coat: final coat of plaster.

Floating coat: an undercoat of plaster.

Horse: a *member* of a *running mould* which runs against a rule and supports the stock in wood.

Laying down: the final layer of the finishing coat applied with a trowel.

Member: a large or small part of a moulding outline.

Mitres: the junction of two mouldings at a corner.

Muffle: a template in plaster, wood or metal, fixed to a *running mould* and projecting in front of the template, which enables the *core* of the moulding to be run out.

Ornament: decorative feature in moulding.

Render coat: the first undercoat of plaster.

Re-entrant or returning moulding: a moulding which turns into itself within its own projection.

Rule off: passing the rule over a surface, dragging off any projecting material.

Running mould: a shape formed and made out to run a moulding. A framework.

Running a mould: the process of moving a running mould along a rule to form a shape.

Running down: making a piece of moulding on a surface other than where it will finally be placed.

Scrim: a narrow band of canvas used for strengthening joints.

Selvage: surplus material left behind or overlapping.

Soffit: the underside; the term being generally used when referring to the plaster surface over a window or similar opening.

Stock: a part of the *running mould* which supports the *template*.

Strut: usually a piece of wood which ties the *stock* and *horse* of a *running mould* together to strengthen it.

Stucco: plaster or cement used for coating an external wall surface or moulding into decorative features.

Stuff: plaster mix.

Taking off: removing plaster from the hawk ready for application.

Template: a shape cut in sheet metal and supported on a wooden *stock* which is used to form the outline of a *moulding*. Part of the *running mould*.

Trowelling up: the process of finishing a wall surface by passing a trowel over the surface, lubricating it with water and producing a smooth finish for decorating.

Undercut moulding: overhanging moulding.

Brickwork and Stonework

Before the advent of rail, buildings were constructed largely from local materials. In practice, this meant using materials which could be found within a five-to-seven mile radius, which accounts for the great diversity of buildings to be seen within a particular area of the countryside. Today, the type of building in any given district is still dependent upon the geology and geography of the region and the building style, too, may be determined by the local area, as it has been developed and passed on by the local craftsmen.

Stone is an invaluable building material which lasts for a very long time, as shown by the many ancient stone buildings, or parts of buildings, which can still be seen today. Some of the old stonework was very intricate – the Incas, for example, constructed a type of drystone wall in which the stones were cut so accurately that it is difficult to insert a knife blade between the stones.

Because of its hard-wearing and aesthetically pleasing properties, stone is today still used extensively as a building material.

Bricks are easy to manipulate and have the advantages of being fire resistant and needing very little maintenance. They are also pleasing to look at. By using different bricks and bonds, a variety of effects can be achieved. The material has been used to construct buildings since Roman times. In fact, parts of St Albans Abbey in England were constructed from bricks or tiles taken from the former Roman town near Verulamium. Very fine, technologically advanced examples of Islamic architecture have been found concentrated around the Mediterranean. In some of these there are large panels of brick decoration which are actually constructed in the form of religious writing.

A cruck-framed building with square infill panels. The infill comprises brick and stone on the front elevation. The area below the window level is constructed with random rubble, with large stones at the corner.

Brick houses are built using various methods in different parts of the world. In colder climates (for instance, the UK and Northern states of the US) the wall is constructed as two leaves with a cavity between them. The external wall is of brick, while the inside wall is of lightweight insulating block. This method of construction reduces the amount of heat which flows through the fabric of the building. In warmer climates, however, this requirement is unnecessary, so the walls are solid. Houses are also constructed so that the external brick wall forms a face to the building, while the interior is a prefabricated wood frame construction.

Wood has also been used extensively as a structural material and many medieval wood buildings still exist throughout Europe. Today, wood, more than any other material, is used for constructing buildings in the US, which are known as balloon-framed buildings.

Traditional types of wood-framed building were the box frame and cruck. Many such buildings still survive today because of their very sound framework. In the box frame type the frame was constructed of vertical wooden studs built into a sill at ground level with the spaces between filled in a variety of ways – for example with brick, rendered stone slates, stone, cobbles and plastered panels.

Cruck-framed buildings were constructed from curved tree trunks, cut through their centres, with the two halves joined at their apex to form a support for the rest of the wooden frame.

In addition to the main construction materials, a number of finishes – known as claddings or facings – including stucco (exterior plaster) and tiles, can be applied to the face of a building to enhance its individuality.

Tools and equipment

When selecting tools which are to be used for brick and stone laying, buy only good quality tools. Cheap trowels and chisels, for example, are virtually useless and require constant replacement. It is also important to keep them scrupulously clean when they are not being used. Clean every scrap of mortar from the tools and lightly oil those made of metal.

Tools for brickwork

Boaster or bolster

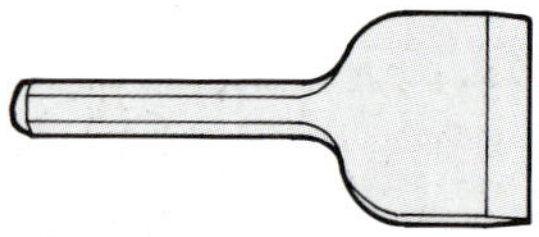

This resembles a very wide chisel and is used to cut bricks to size. Do not attempt to copy the bricklayer by cutting bricks with the trowel.

Cold chisels

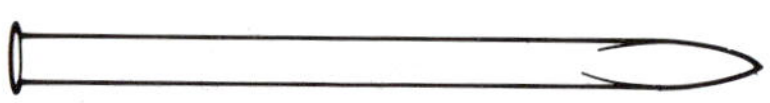

You will need a selection of these tools, one of which should be a plugging (cape) chisel for cutting out mortar joints in old brickwork.

Hand hawk

This comprises a flat piece of wood or metal with a round handle beneath it. It is used to hold mortar when pointing.

Jointer

This tool may often consist of half a bucket handle inverted to produce a rounded, slightly recessed, joint.

Lines and pins

A bricklayer's line is a length of string fixed to line pins which are

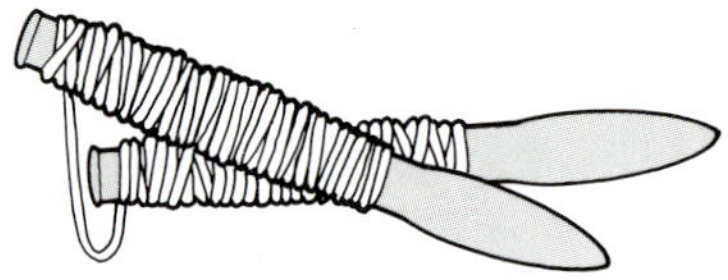

placed in joints at each end of the wall, tension being applied to the line to keep it taut. The bricks are then laid close to the line and are therefore straight. Many amateur brickworkers believe they can build a wall straight without a line; such confidence is always misplaced.

Lump or club (bricklayer's) hammer

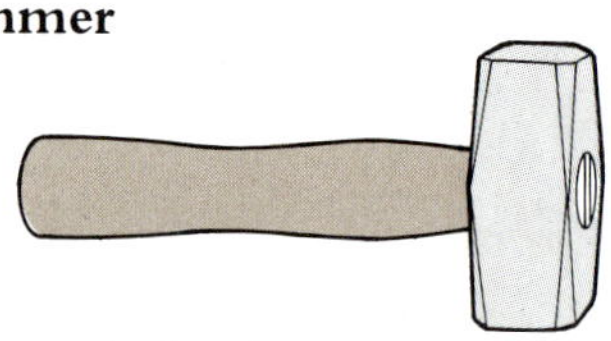

This tool should be heavy enough for cutting holes in brickwork.

Rule and Frenchman

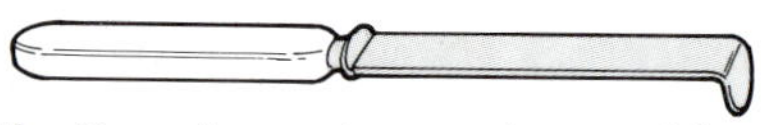

The Frenchman is a tool resembling a knife with a curved end. It is used to neatly trim surplus mortar when pointing. It may be used in conjunction with a rule which is placed against the wall to ensure that the joint is cut perfectly straight.

Skutch or comb hammer

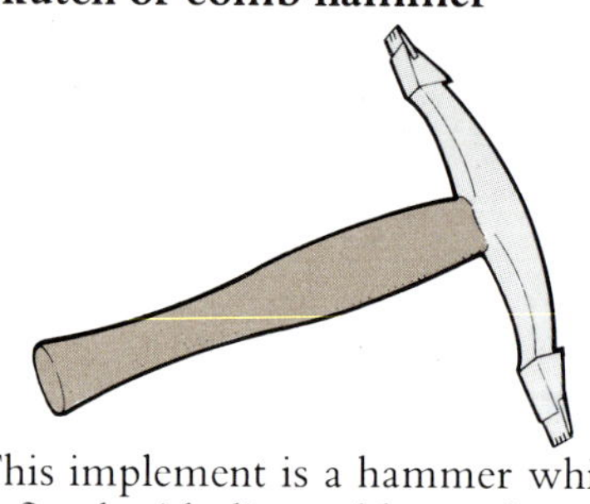

This implement is a hammer which is fitted with disposable combs and/ or blades and is used for trimming second-hand bricks. When the blade is worn down it can be replaced with a new one.

Spirit levels

Spirit levels come in assorted lengths and are used for checking for levels and verticals.

Trowels

Ordinary trowels are manufactured in various shapes and sizes, varying from 225mm (9in) to 325mm (13in). *Pointing trowels* These vary from 75mm (3in) to 150mm (6in). One of each size should be purchased. The small sized are used for the mortar cross joints and the large sized for the bed joints.

Woodfloat

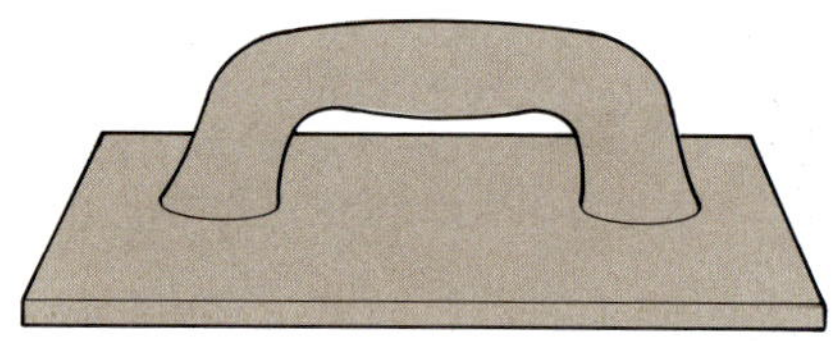

A woodfloat is a flat piece of wood with a handle, used to flatten and smooth cement rendering (smooth stucco finish) before it sets.

Tools for stonework

Tools used for stonework are similar to those used for bricklaying. They include two trowels of different sizes, a level, a straight edge, a hammer and bolster and a number of chisels for cutting and dressing stones.

To enable the stone to be laid reasonably straight, bricklayers' lines may be used as a guide. Except when laying ashlar, it is not necessary to lay the stones to the same degree of accuracy as for bricks.

If the stones are to be cut at an angle, a bevel may be used. This tool comprises two arms, the angle between them being adjustable.

Brick types, mortars and bonds

The appearance of brick buildings is determined by a number of devices which include type and colour of mortar, size and regularity of joint, bond of brickwork, the inclusion of the design of 'string courses' which are courses different in appearance to the rest of the wall and the use of headers and stretchers (see page 180) of complementary colours. The main elevation of a building may be constructed of brick with stone dressings at the openings. Conversely, in Britain brick is often used as a dressing and backing to a wall built from cobbles and knapped flint.

Bricks are manufactured to a variety of shapes and sizes and usually made so that they are not too heavy to handle and to fit a human hand. They are usually approximately 215mm (8½in) × 112mm (4½in) wide and 40mm (1½in) × 70mm (2¾in) deep, although many variations to these dimensions exist.

There are a number of different shaped bricks. 'Purpose-made' bricks are manufactured for use in different positions on the building. These include 'squints', which are used at a point where a wall changes direction by some angle other than 90 degrees; plinth bricks which form a satisfactory sloping finish at the point, usually at floor level, where a wall is reduced in thickness; shaped bricks, used to form cornices; and 'bull nosed' bricks, which are rounded on one corner and used at openings or in arch construction. A close inspection of older buildings will reveal other types of purpose-made brick.

The most common brick in use in the UK today is the Fletton, named after the village near Peterborough where it was first produced. The clay used to manufacture the bricks contains an oily deposit which burns by itself. As this greatly reduces the amount of fuel required to fire the bricks, and because the production of these bricks is highly automated, they are cheap to produce and therefore dominate the UK market.

Different brick types give style to this brick building.

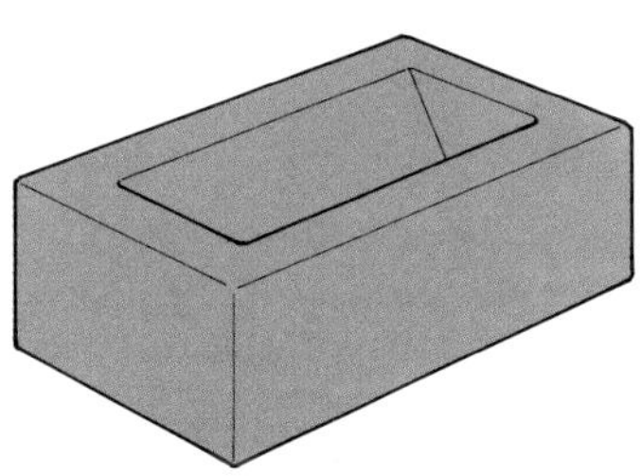

Standard brick.

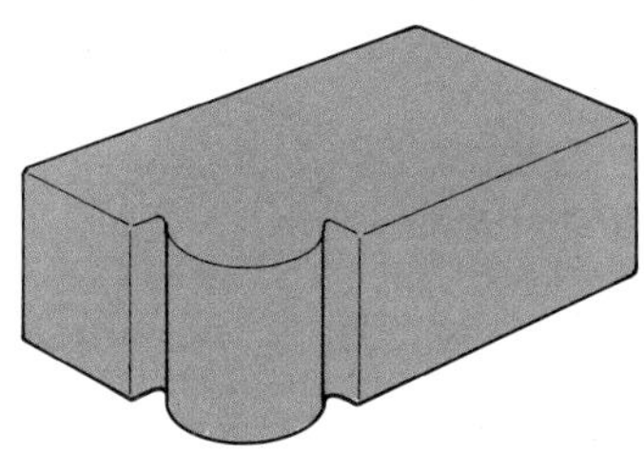

Staff bead or staff brick.

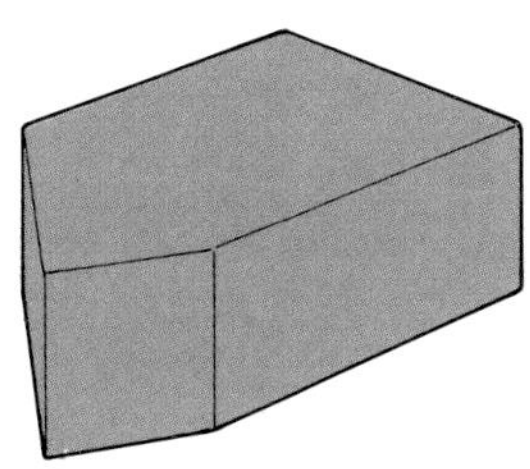

Squint brick.

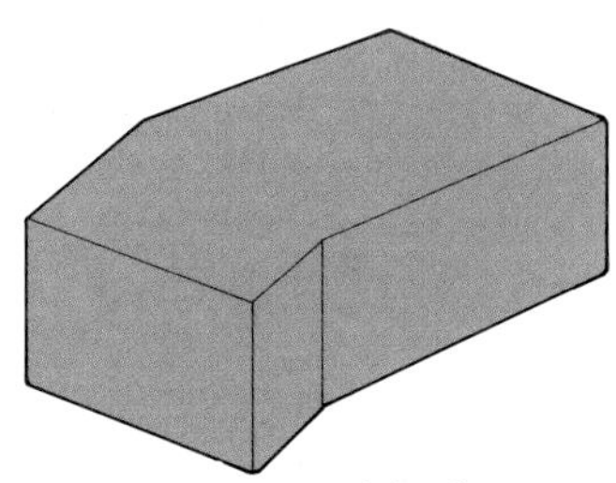

Birdsmouth brick.

Plinth brick.

Cornice brick.

When attempting to match up old bricks, which have probably not been manufactured for many years, there are a number of options open to the bricklayer. Some manufacturers produce bricks which are intended to appear much older than they actually are. There are a variety of such bricks on the market – 'hand-made' bricks made by machine – which as substitutes are not very satisfactory. Many old buildings were constructed with lime mortar. When demolition of the buildings takes place the mortar can be cleaned from the bricks and the bricks used again. Stocks of such bricks are often retained for re-use. In the UK, there are architectural consultancies available to provide a brick matching service to customers. Special shaped bricks are still obtainable and, although expensive, may be the only way to obtain the desired effect.

Mortars

When deciding on which mortar to use in the construction of a brick wall, a number of factors should be taken into consideration. These include: strength of brick, anticipated movement, amount of exposure to weather and load to be imposed upon the wall.

In general, the strength of the mortar is determined by the proportion of cement or cement and lime to sand. For example, a mortar containing one part of cement to three parts of sand will set very hard and be highly resistant to rain penetration, but, at the same time, will not be able to absorb any movement without cracking. Conversely, a mortar made with one part cement and one or two parts of lime to six parts of sand will be less resistant to bad weather conditions, but, at the same time, be less liable to crack. If a mortar is stronger than the bricks which surround it, it will not absorb differential movement (see page 182); the bricks will crack should any such movement occur. Therefore, the mortar should always be slightly weaker than the surrounding brick; this is especially important to remember when rebuilding old brickwork.

The main traditional brickwork bonds

When observing brick built houses or walls you may notice that the bricks which make up the walls are laid to a pattern. This is known as the bond. The bond helps to spread the load imposed on the wall and may also be extremely attractive.

Often, walls appear to contain whole, half and quarter bricks – known as stretchers, headers and closers, respectively.

The bonds used are usually half, quarter or random bond. For a half or quarter bond this means that the vertical joints occur at a distance of a half or quarter of a brick away from the joints in the course above and below it. With random bonds, of course, the vertical joints are at varying distances. A half bond is often used when modern houses are built with a cavity wall frame.

There are other, more complicated, bonds such as English bond, where the bricks comprise alternate headers and stretchers with a closer brick adjacent to the corner header, and Flemish bond which contains alternate stretchers and headers in the same course. With rat-trap bond, often used in the past for barns, bricks are laid on edge to reduce the number required. This bond only requires 64 bricks per square yard, compared with 96 bricks per square yard for a wall one brick thick in other bonds.

Different types of bonding

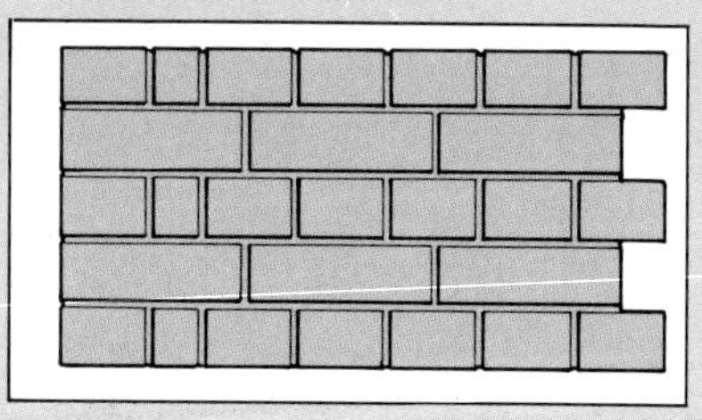
English bond.

English garden wall bond.

Whole or stretcher bond.

Flemish bond.

Flemish garden wall.

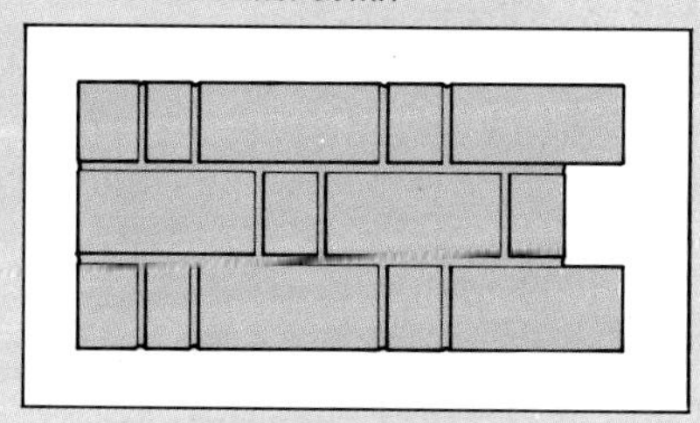
Rat trap bond.

Stonework

A beautiful stone house in Scotland.

The stone used in buildings is dependent upon the geology of the particular district. The following is a brief classification of the three principal types of building stone.

Sedimentary rocks were originally deposits of, for example, an accumulation of shells or other remnants of plant and animal life which were laid down under water on the beds of seas, rivers and lakes or on older land surfaces by wind or other agencies. These rocks vary considerably in composition and character. Within this category are calcareous rocks which contain limestone, oolite and magnesium limestone. These stones tend to be light in appearance. Some are almost white, but impurities in others give them a cream, yellow or grey look.

Arenaceous rocks are essentially sandy in grain size and texture. This group contains sandstones and gritstone. Small quantities of minerals produce the colour, which may be grey, green, yellow, brown or red.

Igneous rocks were formed by the cooling of molten rock, known as magma. The character of the rock is dependent upon the composition and rate of cooling of the original hot magma. Granite is the only igneous rock which has been widely used for both building and ornamental purposes.

Metamorphic rocks have been formed from existing igneous or sedimentary rocks by heat, pressure and chemical fluids acting separately or together. The only metamorphic rocks used in quantities are slates and marble. The slates may be used to cover the roof of a building or, like marble, polished and used for decorative purposes.

Cobbles, which used to be picked up in fields or taken from the beach, are still a cheap building material. Flint, an extremely hard form of silica usually found in chalk foundations, is also inexpensive. No cutting to size is required, although flints might be knapped – that is, split to produce one flat face. Cobbles can be laid in a mortar bed requiring only a backing and dressings in brick or stone.

Ashlar masonry, however, is expensive. It is characterized by its very accurately cut stones. The stones are also bedded very carefully, the joints usually being no larger than 3mm (⅛in).

When local stone is used in building, the thickness of the beds of stone in the quarry often determines the thickness of the courses of stone in the wall. Unlike brickwork, where all the courses are usually the same height, the stone may be laid randomly (uncoursed). There are many such types of stone walling.

Coursed rubble consists of stones of similar height but irregular length. With snecked walling, where coursed rubble is used, the horizontal joint is interrupted at intervals by a stone two or three courses in height. There is also rubble walling, whereby the corners of a building are built with large stones and the spaces filled with smaller ones. There are, of course, many variations on these basic types of masonry.

Nowadays when building a stone wall it is not necessary to cut stones to size as they can be bought ready cut. Reconstructed stone – crushed stone mixed with cement and recast – can also be bought.

Different types of walling

Uncoursed or random rubble.

Coursed rubble.

Snecked walling.

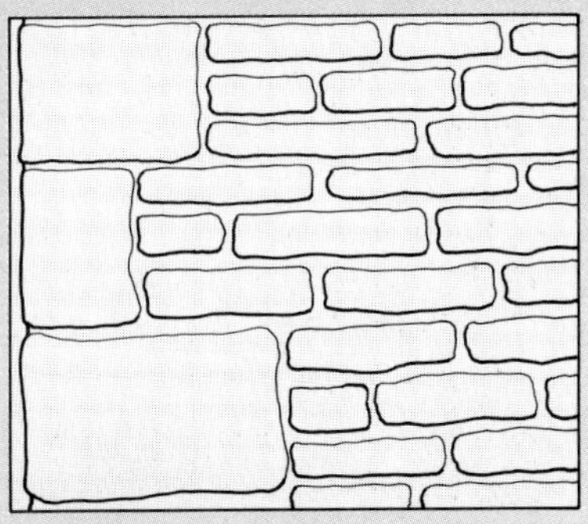

The corners of this wall are built with large stones and the infill constructed with smaller ones.

Repairing existing work

Repairs to brickwork or stonework are usually for two reasons: either the material has eroded and needs refacing or replacing, or cracks have appeared and have let water into the fabric of the building. This water may, by freezing and thawing over for a number of years, cause the surface to disintegrate.

When cracks appear in the wall, the cause may be due to differential settlement, which means that one part of the building has moved in relation to another. A simple way to determine whether the crack is old or new is to look inside it. If the bricks and mortar appear clean and new it is probable that the crack is new and may increase in size. This may be verified by fitting a 'tell tale', a piece of glass about 75mm (3in) long × 25mm (1in) wide, bedded in mortar or epoxy resin adhesive on each side of the crack.

Should any further movement occur, the tell tale will break which would suggest that whatever caused the crack in the first place is getting worse – in which case, professional advice should be sought. If no further movement occurs, the bricks on either side of the crack may be carefully removed, replaced with similar bricks and repointed.

Common faults occuring in brickwork are spalling, erosion and efflorescence.

Spalling, that is, splintering or chipping, often occurs in brickwork where the brick is in a fairly exposed position and is subject to a continuous freeze/thaw cycle. In the winter, moisture from rain and snow enters the brick through very fine capillary-like paths. The brick becomes saturated and, if freezing occurs, the water expands. If this is repeated a large number of times the brick will disintegrate, in which case the brick should be removed and replaced with one with low permeability so that water is excluded.

A brick wall, badly damaged by spalling and erosion, needing extensive repair.

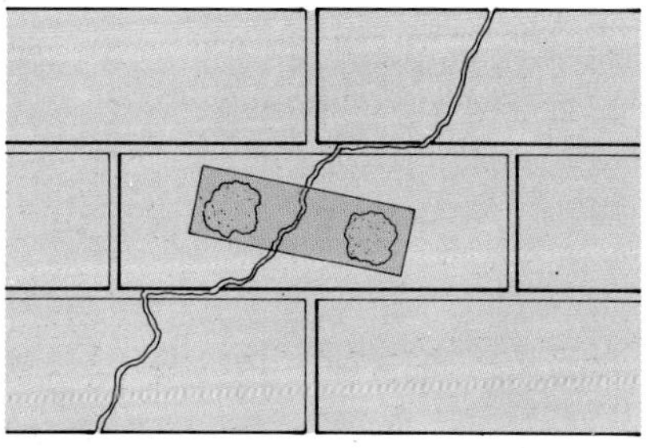

A tell tale is attached across the crack. If the two parts of the wall move, the glass will break. Then seek professional advice.

Erosion of brickwork frequently occurs in a wall below a faulty coping stone (see below) or gutter. Over a period of years, rain water gutters may fill with dirt or vegetation, and when this happens water from the roof overflows the gutter and runs down the wall. Initially this shows as clean marks where the concentration of water washes dirt off the wall. After a while the wall material will begin to erode. Before repairing the wall the cause should be sought and, if possible, rectified. The faulty brick(s) should then be carefully removed using a hammer and chisel. The resulting hole(s) should be filled using a similar material, mortar and bond to the existing brickwork.

Efflorescence takes the form of very unsightly white or bluish stains and often occurs on new work, especially where it faces driving rain. It is caused by rain entering the brick or stone in the wet season and mingling with salts present in the bricks and mortar. In the spring the water returns to the surface and evaporates, leaving the efflorescence on the surface of the wall. When the next wet season arrives this deposit will be largely washed away to be replaced by a new but smaller patch the following spring. This cycle repeats itself until the problem disappears. Although efflorescence appears alarming, especially on a recently built wall, it is probably best left alone or, at most, brushed off. Don't use a wire brush or anything which may damage the surface of the wall material.

Coping stones, which are those on the tops of walls, are often incorrectly jointed and the anti-capillary groove or drip stop not kept clear. This allows excessive water to run down the wall which will cause damage. When the cause of the trouble has been removed the repairs can be completed.

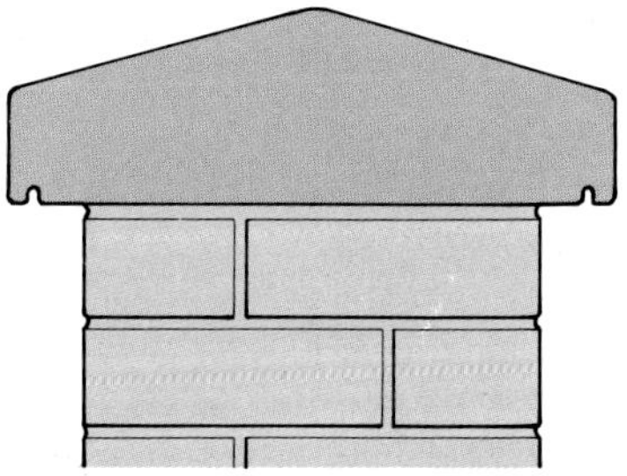

If mortar collects in the anticapillary groove, water will run across and down the wall, causing damage.

Repointing and infill

Repointing is the process of repairing the joints between bricks or pieces of stone filled with mortar. Ideally, the mortar should contain the same type of sand mixed with lime in the same proportions as the original and it is essential that it is approximately the same strength as, or weaker than, the bricks which form the wall. (If too strong a mortar is used, any movement in the wall will result in the bricks spalling, which will mean that the face will break off or the bricks will crack and allow water into the building.) When the lime and cement are being mixed they should be packed to the same density, otherwise the true amounts of these materials will vary between mixes and each mix will be a different colour.

Water used to mix the mortar should be clean and just enough should be used to bond the mixture. Too much water will result in the brickwork becoming stained and, because of shrinkage, the joint will crack when the mortar dries out.

Purpose-made colours may be added to the mortar to produce a variety of shades. When matching existing work, the mortar should be coloured to a slightly darker shade as it will lighten when drying out.

Types of pointing

The main types of pointing are: flush pointing, struck or weather-struck pointing, tuck pointing and the tooled (concave) joint.

Flush pointing may be carried out by scraping the surplus mortar from the brick, or by raking out the joint and filling with a different type of mortar. Struck or weather-struck pointing is formed by smoothing the joint with a pointing trowel to ensure water is deflected away from the brick below the joint. Tuck pointing was popular on houses in the nineteenth century and the method is still used today. When the bricks are laid, a flush joint is made, about the same colour as the bricks. A groove is filled with a lime putty, cut to about 3mm (⅛in). The tooled (concave) joint, popular since 1945, is formed with a rounded tool.

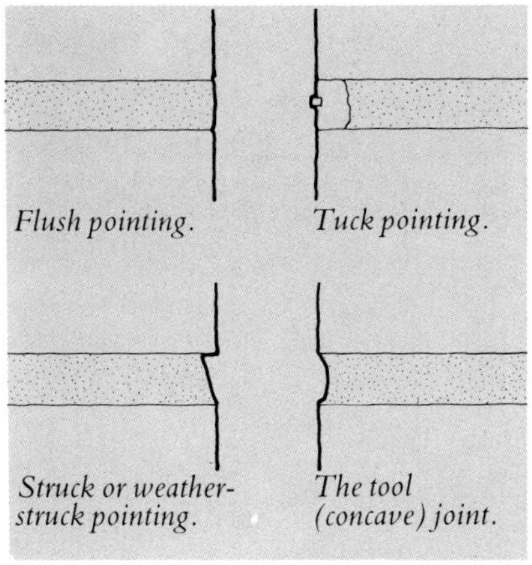
Flush pointing. *Tuck pointing.* *Struck or weather-struck pointing.* *The tool (concave) joint.*

When repointing, the old mortar must be raked out to a depth of approximately 18mm (¾in) using a plugging (cape) chisel and hammer. The joint should be brushed clean, well wetted and then allowed to partly dry. Semi-dry mortar is packed into the joint taking care to keep the face of the brick clean. The required finish is then applied.

Infill

Infill is a method of filling the walls between the studwork – the wooden framework – of a building.

The visible studwork surrounding the infill can be divided into two main types. The first is close studding, where the spaces between the studs are tall compared with their width. The second is small framing, where the panels between the studs are approximately square. The panels between the studs can be filled with a variety of infill materials, including brick, cob, rendered stone slates and plastered panels.

Brick nogging

Where there is brick nogging, that is, brick infilling to a traditional wood-framed building, a variety of patterns can be used, including random coursework, diagonal bonds and the herringbone bond.

To repair brick nogging, to start with, place a piece of plastic sheeting over the panel and trace the exact position of the existing bricks, stones and cobbles. The bricks may then be carefully removed and placed on the ground in the same position relative to the positions they occupied in the original wall. Bricks which can be re-used should be retained – the rest replaced with bricks which closely match the originals. They can then be built into the wall and their final position checked with the tracing on the sheeting. Care must be taken to ensure that the mortar is kept slightly back from the face of the wooden frame.

An enchanting old wood-framed building with brick infill.

Stucco (exterior plaster)

A house finished with stucco in excellent condition.

Stucco (exterior plaster) is a finish which is applied to a building to make it look as though it has been faced with stone. It is applied to the wall in two coats and, while the top coat is still wet, joints are cut into it to create the impression that the wall is made of ashlar stone blocks.

For stucco (exterior plaster), remember that the render (finish) should be weaker than the mortar in the supporting wall, otherwise any movement in the wall will result in cracking of the render and loss of adhesion. Before rendering the wall, it is important to 'dub' it out, that is, to fill all the holes. If this is not done, the render will sag. To ensure a smooth, flat finish, it is essential that the whole of the area to be rendered (finished) has a similar suction. The wall may be hosed down if it is very porous. This will reduce suction so that all the surface can be finished before it sets hard.

How to apply stucco

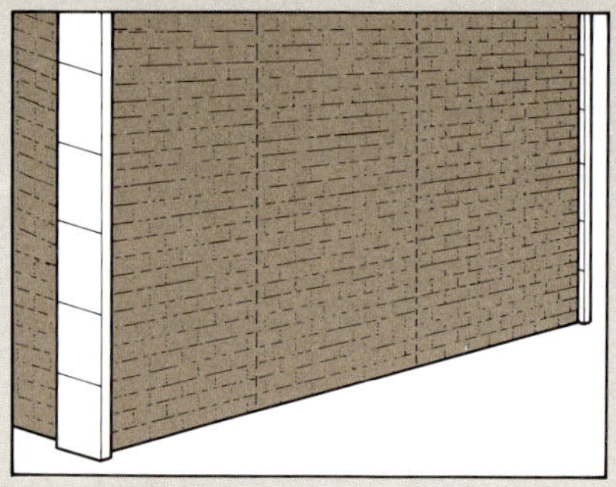

1. *Divide the wall into bays approximately 2m (6ft 6in) wide. Fix and plumb floating rules at the building's corners.*

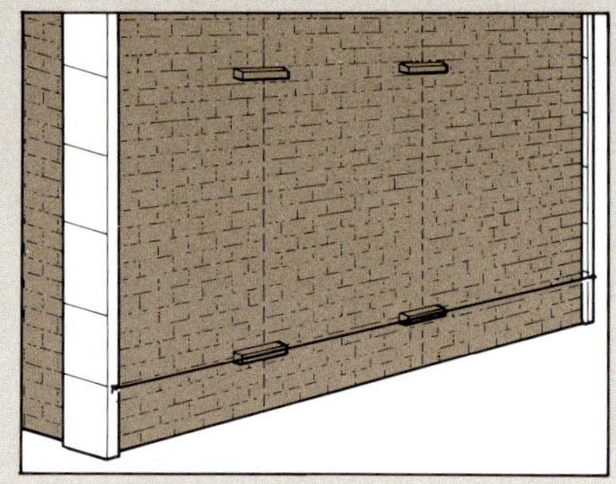

2. *Stretch a line between the rules; mark positions of screeds by attaching thin strips of wood to the wall. Place further strips above each. Plumb.*

3. *Using the laying on trowel and hawk, a vertical screed is laid between each two pieces of wood and straightened.*

4. *Apply and straighten the backing coat which is scratched to form a key for the second coat.*

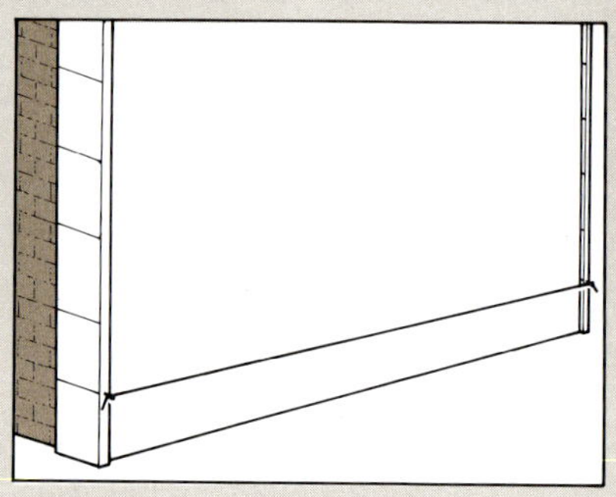

5. *When first coat is dry, apply second coat. Fix line, covered with powdered chalk or lime. Snap against wall to ensure a straight white line.*

6. *Incize joint marks with the jointer while the material is still soft.*

Repairing stucco (exterior plaster)

It is very difficult to make the repair work on damaged stucco (exterior plaster) invisible. This is because the material used may not match the existing material, and no two people will render (finish) the wall with exactly the same force.

All loose material should be removed and the edge of the damaged zone squared up. The render (finish) should then be built up in two or three layers and the final layer levelled off with a straight edge. When the render begins to set it should be rubbed over with a wooden float. Don't finish the wall with a plasterer's steel trowel, as this is too harsh a tool to use for this job.

Walls

Before a wall is constructed, it is usual to excavate a trench to a depth at which the subsoil is strong enough to support the load of the wall and so that the foundation is below the level likely to be affected by frost in winter.

To construct a brick wall, the trench should be excavated and pegs, small wooden stakes approximately 50mm × 50mm (2in × 2in), hammered into the bottom. The tops of the pegs are levelled with a straight edge and spirit level.

The concrete for the foundation is mixed in the proportion of approximately one part sand to about seven or eight parts by volume of aggregate, with enough clean water to mix the ingredients. The concrete is placed into the trench level with the top of the pegs and tamped down. It is important that the concrete is reasonably flat, or it will be difficult to lay the bricks level.

The usual way to build a brick wall is to construct a corner first and then, using a line as a guide, to lay the bricks in the main wall.

Retaining walls

Retaining walls built in a garden are usually of the gravity type. That is to say, the earth to be retained is held in position by the weight of the wall. The amount of soil to be retained is dependent upon the density of the soil, the critical angle and the amount of moisture present. A footing is excavated at the point at which the wall is to be built and the concrete foundation laid.

If the retaining wall is to be constructed of brick, the foundation can be fabricated with a slight transverse slope. The wall, when it is being built, can be battered – sloped backwards with the aid of a piece of wood cut in the shape of a wedge.

If the wall is to be built of stone, the foundation is laid level and the face of each course laid slightly back from the stone below it.

Water must not be allowed to build up behind the wall, so it is a

Building corners and walls

1. *Mark the position of the corner on the concrete foundation by spreading a thin bed of mortar and marking with a trowel and straight edge*

2. *Lay two bricks in either direction and check they are level. Raise the corner four courses, checking to ensure the wall is upright.*

3. *Lay enough mortar onto the previous course to form a joint approximately 10mm (3/8in) high when the brick is tapped into position.*

4. *Make a vertical joint – known as a mortar cross joint – by spreading mortar on brick end. Push brick against another already in position. Clean off surplus mortar with a trowel.*

5. *Extend the corner by half the number of bricks for the number of courses required. Continue building the corner as described in the previous steps. Then build the second corner in exactly the same way.*

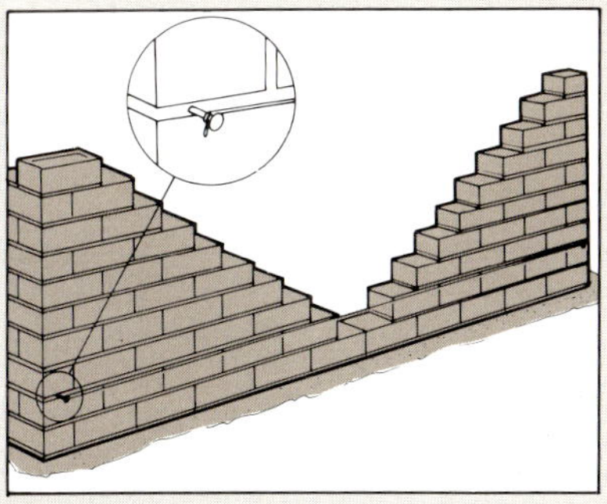

6. *For the wall, push line pins into the joints at the corners and stretch a line between them. Before laying bricks in mortar, lay them dry along the wall, adjusting the joints so that they fit without needing to be cut. Start building the wall, aligning the top of the bricks with the line and moving the line up as you complete each course to ensure each course is completely level.*

Cross section of a retaining wall.

good idea to place some large stones at the base. This is known as a French drain. A small piece of plastic tube should be built through the wall from the French drain to the outside of the wall.

Piers

A pier is an independent structure. When built between doors or windows it supports the load above them. Used in walling, it divides a long wall into a number of short lengths. The distance between piers is known as the effective length and generally it can be said that the smaller the effective length, the more stable the wall. A pier may also be used where a wall terminates, or where an opening is set into the wall. It can be built using traditional bonds.

If the pier is at a point where it is likely to be knocked by traffic, it can be filled with concrete in the following manner. Build the brickwork around the outside of the pier and allow it to set. Line the inside of the pier with corrugated cardboard or several sheets of newspaper. Then fill the pier as gently as possible with fairly dry concrete. The cardboard or paper will absorb any initial expansion in the concrete and eventually will rot.

The top of the pier is covered with a coping – the top course or covering – for protection. This may be made of stone, concrete or brick, although most bricks used in this way will disintegrate after a few winters.

If a gate is to be fitted between two piers, it may be stood on two piles of bricks, together with hinges, and the piers built in position.

Garden walls

A garden wall may be built using a number of materials such as cobbles or knapped flints. The piers are built, together with a small portion of wall adjacent to the piers. Bricklayers' lines are now stretched between the two corners and the wall constructed.

Drystone walling

Rough drystone walling has been constructed from time immemorial until the present day in areas where stone is freely available. In many parts of the world, sufficient quantities of suitable stone are found lying on the surface of the ground and used to construct walls for the purpose of marking boundaries or for restraining domestic animals.

As its name implies, drystone walling is built of stone without mortar joints. This makes the wall more difficult to build. However, it also means that the materials can be used more than once; whole walls can be demolished and built elsewhere.

Essentially, the wall is built laying large stones on the outside of the wall, with rubble in the middle and with the gaps being filled with small stones or large bonding stones.

Where the stones are shaped very unevenly, the face may be laid flush to the wall and the back supported by chinking, that is, small pieces of stone tapped into the space to support the space at the back.

At intervals of about 600mm (24in) a bonding, or through, stone is built through the wall for added strength.

The thickness of the wall should be less at the top than at the bottom; a 2m (6ft 6in) high wall being perhaps 600mm (24in) at the base and 450mm (18in) at the top. The style of the wall will be determined to some extent by the basic shape of the stone available, whether flat, triangular or wedge-shaped.

If the heap of stone is divided into piles of the various shapes it will be

A stone wall comprising different coloured stones built to a random pattern and framed by brick piers. The effect is striking and, at the same time, surprisingly orderly.

How to build a drystone wall

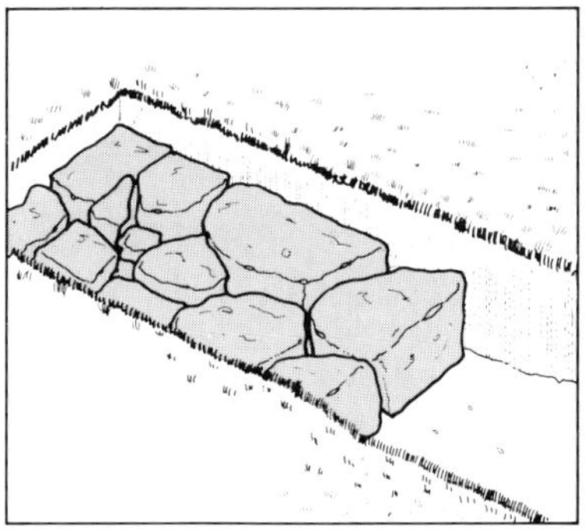

1. *Excavate a trench about 300mm (12in) deep and 600mm (24in) wide. Build the wall directly into the subsoil. Start laying large foundation stones in the trench.*

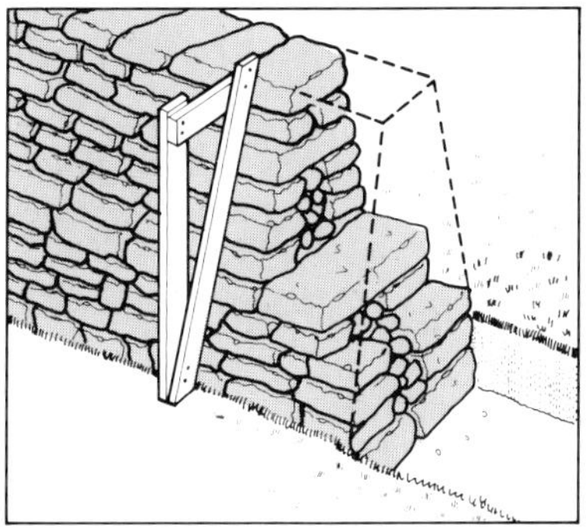

2. *Lay large and small stones along each course, using a wooden frame to help form a batter. Lay bonding stones at suitable intervals.*

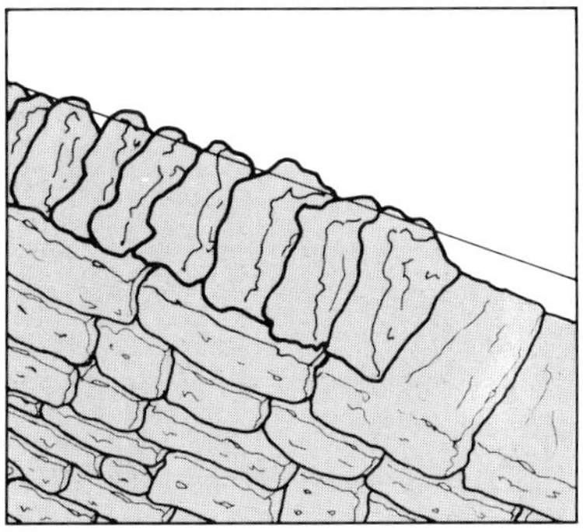

3. *When the correct height is reached, a mason's line should be stretched along the wall and coping stones laid to fit the line. Stones should be selected which will provide both an attractive and protective finish to the wall.*

A drystone wall under construction, using a bricklayer's line and a batter which is slightly different to the one shown in the drawing on the left. Such walls can continue to serve as boundary markers for hundred of years.

simpler to find the stone to fit the available space. Practice will enable the amateur to carry out this type of work fairly easily after a while.

Stones that have been dressed, that is, finished with a flat or textured face to a round or triangular shape, are laid along the wall, with the bedding planes – or strata – laid vertically.

Flint and cobble walls

Occasionally, flint and cobbles have been used as a facing to brick or stone walls; usually, however, walls containing these materials have been constructed of rubble.

When flints or cobbles have fallen out of the wall, they can be replaced, using a bedding of lime mortar. Remember to wet the area being repaired very thoroughly as it is most likely that the existing course will be very dry and the old mortar will tend to soak up the water from the new working, in which case it may well be difficult for the flints or cobbles to adhere properly.

Where the mortar is crumbling, scraping out the bedding and repairing should be carried out working in small sections at a time. Allow the pointing to harden before an adjacent area is worked on. A mortar of one part cement, one part lime and six parts sand will suffice.

Arches

Before the development of reinforced concrete and structural steel, both of which are able to carry loads in tension, the only other building material with this capacity was wood. The loads on walls over openings were carried either by a stone lintel, which was very cumbersome, or an arch which acted as a compressor, transferring the load to other parts of the structure. This principle operates in almost any church where arches transfer the loads of the walls, and sometimes even the tower, onto columns or other walls.

The arch must have sufficient height to resist the weight imposed upon it. On some types of arch, where the direction of the load is horizontal as well as vertical, it is necessary to construct a skewback or abutment at the end to resist this outward movement and to receive the thrust.

Brick arches are divided into two main types for constructional purposes. A rough arch is where the bricks are laid either as half brick rings with wedge-shaped joints or are cut slightly wedge-shaped to enable the joints to radiate from the centre or centres of the arch.

The second type is a gauged arch, which differs from a rough arch in that the bricks used are cut and rubbed very accurately to size, with the result that the joints are 2mm (1/16in) wide. The construction of this type of arch is highly skilled, time-consuming and expensive.

Arches on small houses are usually of the rough type; gauged arches usually appear on larger, more prestigious, buildings.

Arches are of six main types: flat, segmental, semi-circular, semi-elliptical, camber and circular. Both stone and brick arches are constructed in a similar way – the units forming the arch are built onto a temporary structure – the centre – which is removed when the arch has been built strong enough to support its own weight.

Segmental arch

The segmental arch is the most simple to construct and probably the most common of the 'true' arches. It is usually constructed as a rough arch.

The turning piece is set out as follows:

1. The line AB is drawn to the length of the span of the opening.
2. This line is bisected and the bisecting line continued upwards and downwards.
3. The rise – point C – is measured. This distance is approximately 1/6 of the span.
4. The line CB is drawn and bisected. The point at which this bisecting line crosses the vertical line through the centre of the arch span – point 0 – is the centre of the arch.

A semi-circular brick arch.

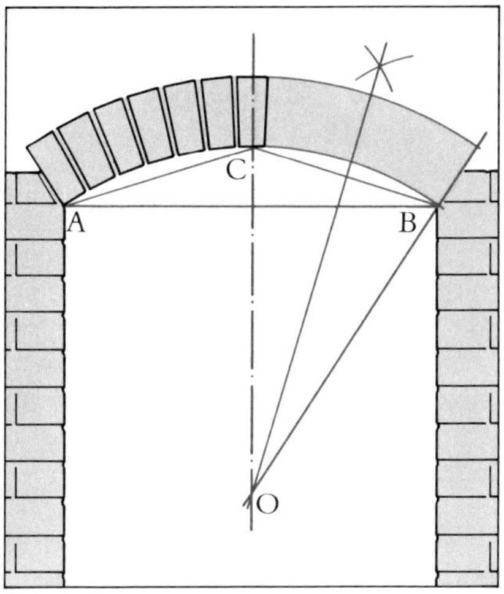

A segmental arch.

The bricks in the segmental arch are often laid in two or more rings as illustrated above.

Semi-elliptical arch

Most elliptical arches are not true ellipses but are compromises; usually three or four centred arches which are easier to set out and construct.

The three-centred arch may be set out as follows:

1. Set out the base line AB to the span of the arch and divide this line into three exactly even parts, giving points C and D.

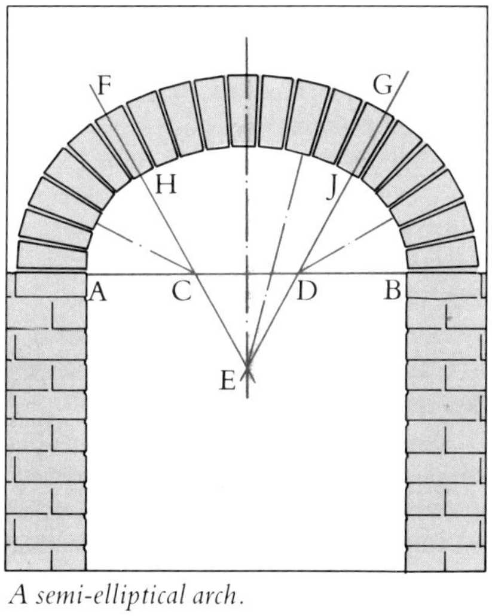

A semi-elliptical arch.

2. Set the compass or trammel to distance CD and strike arcs from C and D to meet at E.
3. The lines EF and EG are now drawn, cutting points C and D.
4. The compass point is now used to draw an arc from A to H, with point C as its centre and from B to J with point D as its centre.
5. The intrados, or inner concave surface, of the arch is now completed by means of an arc from H to J, with point E as its centre.
6. The points A and B can now be marked off to the face width of the arch and the extrados, or convex outer surface, drawn.
7. The bricks may then be set out as indicated.

Building the arch

If the arch has been set out on the board, and the shape and size of the template determined, the next step is to cut the voussoirs to shape. The voussoirs are the wedge-shaped, tapered bricks or blocks used to form an arch.

If the arch to be constructed is of a type in which the soffit is not at right angles to the arch, a bevel is used to set out the cutting angle. Transfer the marked and cut angle to the springing brick, that is, the first brick to be laid. Place the template on the brick with the setting out marks on the arch coinciding with the template.

Cut away the surplus brick with the hammer and bolster, but do not cut the centre of the brick square away from the point at which the bolster is used. Any surplus brick can be cut with a scutch hammer.

With arches where the intrados – that is, the inner concave surface, or soffit – of the arch is at right angles to the arch, only the last three steps are carried out.

These activities are repeated until all the bricks in the arch are cut.

Before the arch bricks are laid, the window, turning piece, or arch centre is fixed firmly in the correct position. The position of each brick in the arch is marked on the support. Note that it is important that the last brick laid – the key brick – is the first brick to be marked.

Folding wedges

Two pieces of wood are cut to the same angle and placed together. If the top wedge is tapped with a hammer in the direction of the arrow, the vertical height of the system will be increased while the top and bottom surfaces will remain level.

The main wall is built to the height of the arch and either a skew arch is cut (that is, bricks are cut back for the arch) or an opening is left in the wall to accommodate the arch. The bricks can now be carefully bedded.

The arch is built from each end, care being taken to ensure that each brick registers with the mark on the arch centre and that each joint radiates from the striking point of the arch. If the previous instructions have been carried out correctly, the key brick will fit into position exactly. The arch is then straightened with either a straight edge or a spirit level – if long enough, and pointed.

The framework for an arch template. The illustration shows both wall and arch while under construction.

Paving and pathways

This path, made out of natural stone (flagstone), provides a distinctive and decorative surface. Notice how the pieces with straight edges have been laid along the border.

There are many materials available for building paths, including gravel, bricks, paving blocks and cobbles.

The surface must be durable, self-draining, non-slip, pleasant to walk on and, above all, must not stick to the soles of shoes.

The main points to remember when laying a pavement are that it requires support and restraint at the edges to ensure that the paving units do not move sideways, and that the units must be solidly, but not very rigidly, laid.

Whatever surface used, ensure that it is laid onto a well drained, stable base. All topsoil should be removed and weeds prevented by a liberal application of suitable weed-killer beforehand.

Plan for effective drainage from the outset. Lay the surface with a camber or fall of at least 1:50 in order to prevent bad sinkage and rainwater puddles forming.

Edges

In order to ensure a neat appearance, prevent edges falling away and to avoid soil contamination, it is usually best to make retaining edges.

Edging material can take the form of boards, treated with preservative and set into the ground. The draw-back is that the wood can only be laid in straight lines.

For a more decorative and durable edge, it is preferable to use bricks which can either be laid flat or set upright into mortar below ground level so that they lean at an angle one upon another.

A more traditional edging can be made using edging tiles, but these are now rather difficult to find.

Traditional edging making a dividing line between path and flower bed.

There is also a variety of modern concrete edgings available.

Edging is always laid in concrete with the top edge to a line stretched between the level pegs. Always install edging before laying the path.

Materials for paths

Gravel is relatively inexpensive and easily laid. Curves are easy to form and changes in level are easily accommodated. An added advantage is that gravel can be taken up without difficulty and relaid if piping or other services need to be installed. It forms a ready-made base for other surfaces if they should become needed. Because it is loose, however, constant use means that the surface requires frequent raking. Stone may be thrown up onto an adjacent lawn which will affect the lawn mower.

Remove all the topsoil down to a depth of at least 230mm (9in). Grade the sub-soil to remove any unwanted undulations and set the edgings in concrete along the sides. Apply a weedkiller which will not leach into the surrounding planted area. Fill one-third to one-half of the depth with hardcore (rubble), comprising 35mm to 50mm (1½in to 2in) diameter stones or broken bricks, and tamp down well, using a rented vibrating roller. A camber of about 1:40 should be incorporated. The hardcore can now be filled in and lightly covered with some finer material such as quarry waste, sharp sand or ashes. Tamp this down and cover with about 25mm (1in) fine gravel mixed with sufficient sand. Once again, using the roller and watering occasionally, compact into a firm surfące. A *thin* layer of gravel – no more than 25mm to 27mm (1in to 1½in) may now be spread and raked level. Ensure the gravel is all one grade: a mixture of stone sizes settles in layers and looks ugly.

Of all the traditional paving materials, brick offers the most scope for creative design. The best bricks to use for paving should be hard, dense and impervious; they should be frost-resistant and not subject to efflorescence (see page 182). Before selecting the bricks it may well be worthwhile checking their suitability with a brick manufacturer.

Crazy paving (flagstone)

The challenge of crazy paving (flagstones) lies as much in the choice of materials as in the laying of them. Natural stone is the best choice, but because of its thickness and uneven surface it presents many more difficulties than, say, slate or broken concrete paving slabs. Some pieces may be considerably thicker in places than others. These can be split off by a stone mason. It is best to work on a bed that is flexible enough to accept the thicker sections while leaving the walking surface fairly even.

Excavate the path area topsoil to a depth that allows for the maximum thickness of the slabs, together with 150mm (6in) for hardcore (rubble) and a further 18mm (¾in) for the mortar bed. Consolidate the hardcore, blinding and just covering with a mix of one part cement to four parts sand to produce a flat surface. Leave the prepared base for one day before laying the slabs. Try to sort out pieces with straight edges to lay along the borders.

Having allocated the edge pieces, the centre of the path can be filled. First, use as many large pieces as you can fit in and fill the gaps with small pieces. Try to keep the joints to less than 25mm (1in) if possible. Starting at one end and working from the edge inwards, fix the slabs by laying them on three or more blobs of mortar. Tap them level with the trowel handle. Check the levels in all directions.

If the joints are grouted with mortar it should be pointed with a trowel for a tidy finish, or the mortar can be taken off at surface level with a trowel and a dry brush.

A crazy paving (flagstone) laid with slates alongside a stream.

Laying a brick path

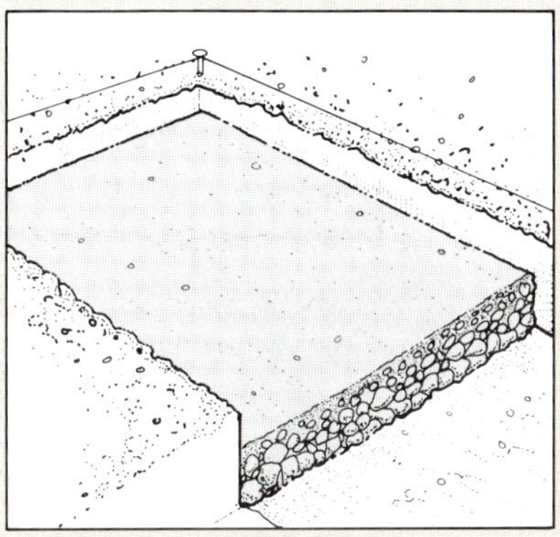

1. *Remove the topsoil to a depth of 200mm (8in) and prepare a bed 130mm (5in) of hardcore, well blended with a mixture of one part cement to four parts sand. Make sure that this base is completely flat and incorporates a 1:50 camber.*

2. *Dampen the bricks and lay them in a well-levelled bed of mortar 37mm to 50mm (1½in to 2in) in depth. Tap gently into position, making sure they are all flush. Allow a 10mm (⅜in) gap between each brick to allow for tolerance of brick sizes and grouting.*

3. *To avoid staining the bricks, use a dryish mortar tamped in with a stick. Finish the joints with a piece of bent rod so mortar is just below brick level.*

4. *Cement in edging bricks along both sides of the path.*

Steps

Stone steps laid in three courses. Note how the treads slope to allow for rainwater drainage and slightly overlap the other courses to protect the risers.

Steps constructed of brick, concrete slabs or stone are common in the garden. Before starting to build, consider the uses to which they will be put. If they are a vital means of access, for example, the material used should be hard-wearing and also slip and frost-resistant. Several varieties of brick and stone are suitable – advice can be obtained from building suppliers as to the best material.

Before starting construction work, some careful thought should be given to the basic design. The distance between the bottom and top of the steps, the number of steps required and the width have to be

How to lay brick steps

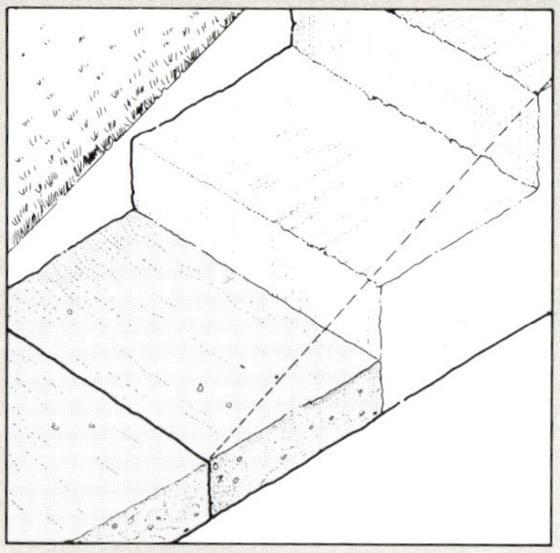

1. *Plan the number of steps to be built. Remove the top soil and lay a concrete base for the first step.*

2. *Lay the first tread by laying one course flat and the second course on edge. The second course can overlap the first course by about 10mm (3/8in).*

3. *Place concrete behind the first tread to provide the base for the second tread. Build the second tread as described in the previous step and repeat until the requisite number of steps have been built. Remove any surplus concrete or mortar with a trowel.*

calculated. The distance between the surface of one step and the one above is known as the rise and that portion of the step is therefore called the riser. To find the number of risers, measure the vertical distance between the upper and lower ground levels to be linked by the stairs and divide this into equal units. The number of steps or treads will always be one less than the number of risers. The width of the treads should ensure they are comfortable to walk on and safe. A suggested width is between 300mm (12in) and 400mm (16in).

When laying the steps it is good practice to tilt them very slightly down towards the edge to ensure that water drains off after rain.

Using bricks

Both the treads and risers can be built using bricks which must be laid on a mortar base. Always remember to choose frost-resistant bricks – many household bricks such as the Fletton brick mentioned on page 179 are unsuitable for garden work. The cement mortar mix should comprise one part cement to four parts sand, while the concrete foundation mix should be two-and-a-half parts sand, three-and-a-half parts aggregate, to one part cement. Hardcore (rubble) will be needed to pack behind the second and subsequent steps.

Glossary

Abutment: a structure receiving the thrust of an arch or wall.

Aggregate: the infill or bulk of the material being mixed which expands the volume of the *mortar* or concrete.

Bed: lower horizontal surface of a course of brickwork.

Bed joint: a horizontal joint, formed in the wall between two *courses* of bricks.

Bevel: a splayed surface, formed by cutting away a portion of a brick at the external edge.

Blinding: method of filling in spaces in hardcore with fine *aggregate* to form a flat surface.

Bond: a systematic, and sometimes decorative, way of arranging bricks in a wall to ensure that the vertical (cross) joints are broken throughout the work.

Bonding or through stone: a large stone built into a drystone wall at fairly regular intervals for added strength.

Brick nogging: brick infilling to a traditional wood-framed building.

Centre, centring: a temporary structure or frame, usually of wood, made for the purpose of supporting an arch during its construction.

Chinking: small stones used to support the back of a drystone wall.

Closer: brick cut to present a face on the wall, equalling one-quarter of a brick in length.

Coping: top course or covering of brickwork or stonework at the top of a wall.

Cornice: moulding(s) projecting from the face of a building, usually at the top; a moulding running between a wall and ceiling.

Course: layer of bricks between two beds of *mortar*.

Eaves course: last *course*, built under the eaves of a roof.

Efflorescence: stains on brickwork.

Extrados: convex outer surface of an arch.

Facing: also known as *cladding* is the finish applied to the exterior face of a building.

Gauged brickwork: brickwork in which the bricks are rubbed and gauged to precise dimensions.

Header: the end part of a brick, placed in a *course* of brickwork with the end facing out.

Intrados: the inner concave surface, or *soffit*, of an arch or vault.

Mortar: a compound of lime and/or cement and sand, mixed with water and used as jointing or bonding in brickwork.

Mortar cross joint: a vertical joint between two bricks.

Pier: a four or more sided detached construction, generally used for carrying a load; also a structure at the end of a wall, often used to support gates.

Rendering (finishing): covering an outer wall with a layer of cement and sand, or cement, lime and sand.

Repointing: filling in the joints with *mortar* after they have been raked out.

Rise (arch): the height from the *springing* line to the highest point of the *intrados*.

Rise (step): the distance between the surface of one step and the one above.

Soffit: the under surface of an arch.

Spalling: splintering or chipping of brickwork.

Springing block: the first brick in an arch.

Springing line: the horizontal line from which an arch springs.

Stretcher: a whole brick.

String course: a continuous horizontal *course* or moulding which projects from the face of the wall.

Turning piece: length of wood, cut to the shape of the *intrados* of an arch and used to support an arch under construction.

Voussoir: wedge-shaped, tapered bricks or blocks, used to form an arch.

Roofing

On a purely practical level, houses are built for shelter from the elements, and it is, of course, the roof of a house which receives most of the sun, wind, snow or rain. Roofing material therefore has to be hard-wearing and durable, and, above all, prove reliable as a protective covering.

Many roofing materials have been in use for a very long time and are still being employed today. Stone and slate, although heavy and difficult to fashion, have the advantage of being both non-flammable and durable. Lead has been used to cover important buildings such as churches since Roman times, while zinc and copper have been used extensively. Another traditional and picturesque material is thatch, which can consist of reeds, grass or heather.

A roof covering which is very widely used, particularly popular in the US and Canada, is wooden shingles.

In many parts of Europe, the clay tile has very largely replaced the shingle and thatch because it is much more fire proof. Originally, tiles were time-consuming and expensive to produce, but since the seventeenth century, when new and improved manufacturing techniques were developed similar to those used for bricks, they were able to be produced more quickly and inexpensively.

Older roofs need constant maintenance to ensure they perform the purpose for which they were constructed. Most repair work should be left to professionals, although the amateur can undertake certain tasks, the most important of which is constant searching for signs of decay. Any effort made to look after your roof will be very well rewarded.

House style

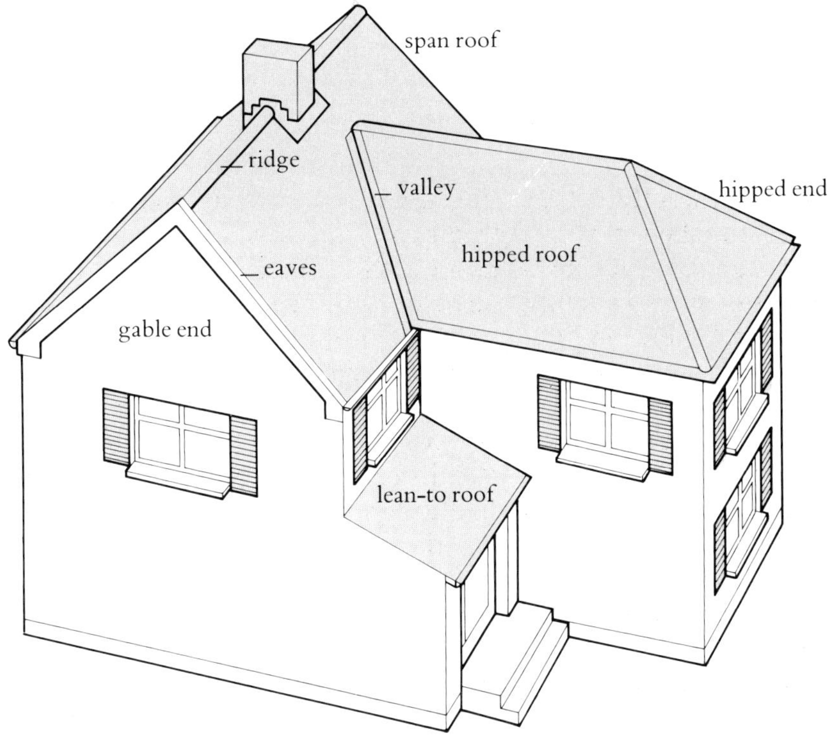

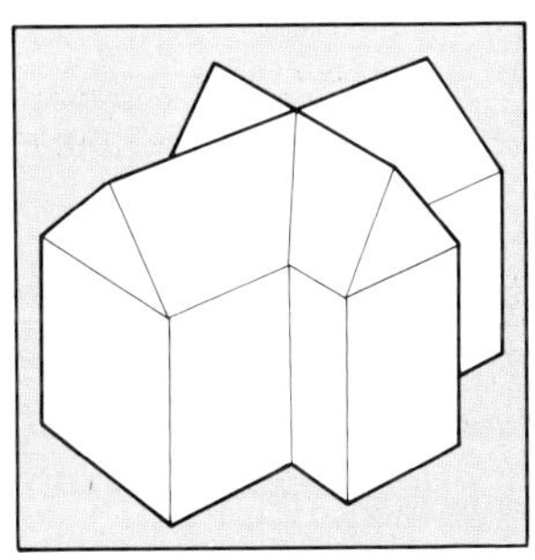

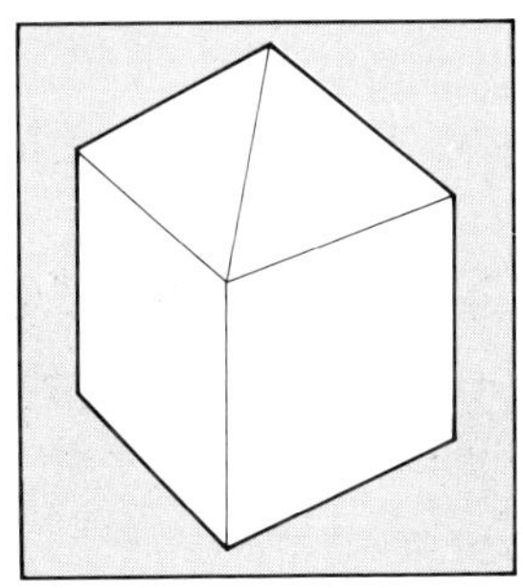

Various types of roofs are illustrated above, ranging from the lean-to, which covers the area between two parallel walls, to the gabled and valley roof. Two common roofs are the span (gable), where the building has two parallel walls of equal size which are covered by a roof built up in triangles (bottom left), and the pavilion where the sides of the roof rise as a pyramid of isosceles triangles (bottom right).

The style and types of roofing have, until recently, been largely dictated by the environment and materials to hand. As technology and the exchange of ideas progressed, however, an increasingly wide choice of both roof styles and materials have become available.

The primary function of a roof is protection from the elements, whether snow in the North or sun in the South. Traditionally, in Northern Europe and the Northern US, where heavy snow builds up in winter, roofs tend to be steeply pitched with overhanging eaves. This allows the snow to slip off the roof, thus avoiding the build up of intolerable weight. (The exception is Switzerland, where roofs tend to be almost flat with long overhangs to cope with the snow.) Steeply pitched roofs cost more to build, because the steeper the pitch the greater the roof plane area. The pitch tends to be less steep in the South and in some areas around the Mediterranean, for instance, roofs are almost flat.

The simplest style of roof is the shed or lean-to. This covers the area between two parallel walls. The wall of one of the sides of the building is carried much higher than the wall parallel with it to give the required slope.

A span (gabled) roof is where the building to be roofed has two parallel walls of equal size. The roof is laid on rafters, slope to slope, from the top of the walls up to the horizon. When the equally inclined planes meet they form an arris which is called the ridge of the roof. The end walls are built up in a triangle, above the eaves level, to support the ridge pole. These are called gable ends.

If a gable end is required on more than two sides of a building, then two roofs of equal slope or pitch will meet at right angles, or cross one another, giving rise to two ridges. The intersection of the slopes of the roofs, which will lie diagonally to the square of the building, will form valleys or flanks. This type is known as a gabled and valley roof.

When all the walls form a square (or a polygon) of equal height, it may be simpler to make the sides of the roof rise as a pyramid of isosceles triangles. The salient intersections formed by the slopes are called hips. This is known as a pavilion.

An oblong building can be covered by a hipped roof where the long sides of the roof are truncated by roofs of equal slope rising from the ends of the building.

Styles of roofing vary greatly, particularly in North America and Europe. The examples given, however, will form, either singly or in combination, the more common roofs likely to be encountered. The combination of roofs illustrated above shows the various styles and their individual features.

Some wonderful examples of natural slate roofs which have existed since medieval times in a town in Switzerland.

Safety

When attempting any roof repair, it is essential that safety precautions are taken and strictly adhered to. Working under safe conditions means that you can work in a relaxed state and are therefore able to concentrate on the work in hand.

When erecting an extension ladder against your house wall, get help from a friend or neighbour, who should stand on the bottom while you make the top secure. Always use two hands on the ladder. Grip the sides, not the rungs. *Never* try to carry anything up a ladder in your hands, especially tools. Wear a belt, and tie a small bag on it in which to put nails, tools, and so on. Larger tools can be pushed through the belt and hung by your side or behind you in safety, leaving your hands free to hold the ladder. Always make sure that wooden ladders are sound and not rotten. Aluminium alloy ladders must not be bent. Rent proper roof crawling ladders from your local hire centre for work on the roof slopes. They are designed for the job. Never use leather soled shoes for roofing work; always wear non-slip soles. For all work around chimneys and for larger repairs, scaffolding should be erected. You can put up a sectional scaffold tower yourself or have proper scaffolding erected. If it is over 5m (16ft) high the scaffolding should be tied to the building. *There is no substitute for safety*. Good scaffolding contractors will ensure a safe working platform is erected for the work to be carried out. They will also supply ladders and ladder access through the scaffolding for you.

Provided you are not afraid of heights, take sensible safety precautions and are of average ability, you should find very little difficulty in coping with the jobs described in this chapter. Any large repair job or re-roofing, however, would be better placed in the hands of a reputable contractor.

Tools

Tools used in roofing are very traditional and established. Roofing is one of the oldest crafts and the tools required have been designed over the years by practical people. In former times, the craftsmen would have had their special tools made for them by the local blacksmith. Today, carpenter's tools will suffice for most jobs.

However, if, for example, a broken slate has to be removed and replaced, you will find it almost impossible to remove the nails which hold it without the help of a slater's ripper (nail pulling tool). Listed below are some of the specialized tools that could be required for roofing jobs. Most can be hired from local hire centres – but only in the UK. Hardly any are available in the US.

If these tools are not readily available, do not worry; all that is needed to repair most roofs is an ordinary hammer, small panel (hand) saw, a hacksaw blade and a pair of pinchers (tile nippers). The hammer and saw are used as they are normally; the hacksaw blade for cutting off any nails left in the roof (in lieu of a slate ripper or nail pulling tool) and pinchers to shape the odd tile or slate to fit back into place.

Roof tile cropper

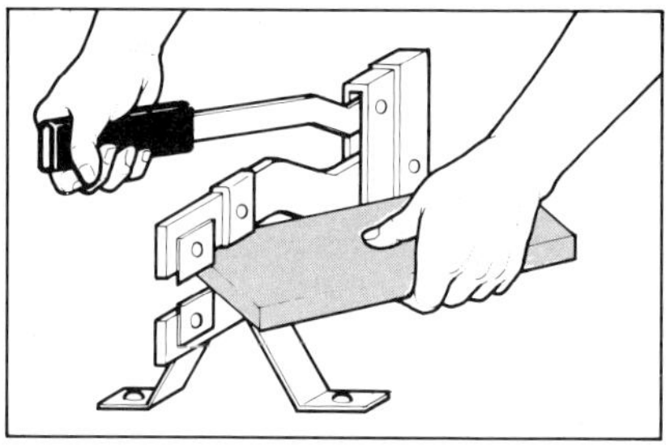

This implement quickly crops plain roof and cladding tiles to any shape.

Slate cutter

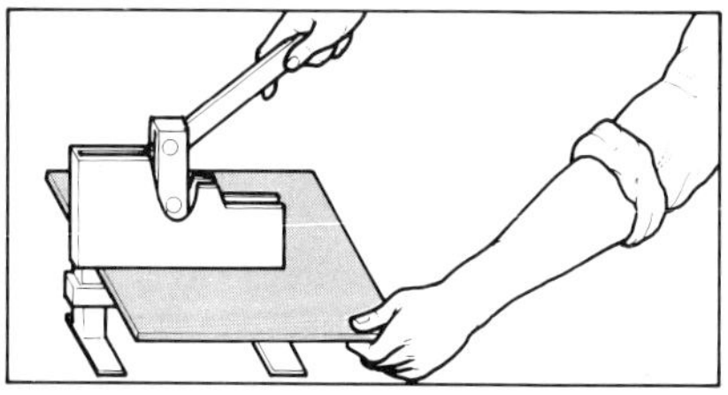

This is made from iron bars with a spike on one side for fixing onto planks of wood for stability.

Slater's bench iron

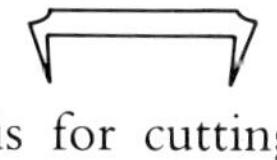

This tool is for cutting and trimming slates on the ground, usually on a bench. The spikes stick into the bench for support.

Slater's break iron

A slater's break iron is for cutting and trimming slates on the scaffolding.

Slater's hammers

One of these is used for trimming the battens (nailers) and any wood that needs trimming for the cover; another has a spike at one end and is used for making holes in slates prior to nailing down on the roof.

Slater's ripper (nail pulling tool)

This tool is approximately 600mm (2ft) long and 25mm (1in) wide flat tapered iron, with a hook formed at one end to enable nails to be removed from the broken slate.

Slater's sax

This is used for cutting and trimming slates on the roof, usually up a valley or hip.

Repairing roof structures

When inspecting the roof space, it is wise to use a small knife to test the wood for rot. If small rotting areas are found they can be cut out and new sections spliced on, working from inside the house.

However, rotten patches in roof coverings are usually inaccessible internally and need outside work. With tiles or slates, carefully remove the covering from the area, stacking them on one side. It is best to number each one before removal and then there will be no difficulty in subsequently replacing them. When the rafters and battens (nailers) are exposed it will be easier to see the bad problem areas.

If battens are rotten, it is a relatively simple job to cut them out and replace them. With rafters, look to see how deep the rot is: if less than one-third the width of the rafter, cut out the rot and insert a new piece of wood. Glue the new piece of wood well and nail into position. If treated well with a preservative, no further trouble will ensue. However, if the rot is deeper, the rafter should be removed. If this is not practical because of its position, fix a strip of zinc or aluminium along the side of the rafter and fix a new one next to it. The metal shim will stop the rot creeping into the new wood and causing damage.

If soffits and fascias are rotting due to continuous leaks, carefully remove enough of the roof covering on either side of the rotten area to expose two rafters. Cut the battens (nailers) away by angling the saw at 45 degrees to the run of the rafters. This gives more room to move the saw for cutting. Cut any felt down the centre of the rafters and remove. A view is now possible of the inside of the soffit and fascia. To prevent any possibility of the rot creeping into the new work, cut out the wood for a minimum distance of 600mm (2ft) either way from the centre of the rot.

With eave overhangs, which provide a wide soffit, affix a bearer across the rafter or, if there is one already there, fix one onto the side of the existing bearer.

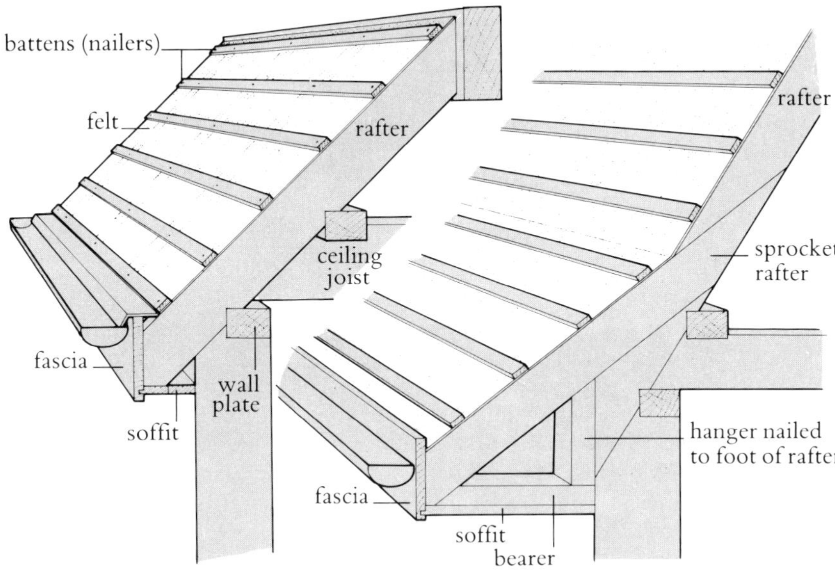

Shown above is the structure of a typical roof underlay. Ceiling joists support the rafters. Battens (nailers) are fitted horizontally over the rafters. At the right is an eaves overhang which clearly shows the fascia, an upright piece of wood at the end of the overhang, and the soffit which is attached to the fascia and bearer beam.

Cut new lengths of soffit and fascia to fit neatly against the remaining soffit and fascia. Prime or soak the new wood in preservative or wood primer for protection before fixing on the roof.

Ventilation

A problem can occur in roof spaces related to the area above the ceiling joists below the roof covering, when it has been insulated. This is condensation. The problem is caused by the insulation material stopping up all the air gaps in the roof space. The heat generated in the house condenses in the roof void and lies as water on top of the ceiling. Modern, low-pitched roofs are very prone to the problem. There are many ways to ventilate roof spaces and appliances are available on the market, from purpose-built slates and tiles with vents fixed on, vents that will fit onto fascia boards, special strips that fit onto the top of fascia boards to vents that will fit into the roof slope. All of these appliances can be fairly easily fitted.

It is vital that checks are made on the inside of the roof space for air movement. If it has been insulated and no ventilation ducts have been fitted, it is advisable to fit some, remembering to make sure that the air entering the roof void must arrive in the roof above the insulation material, otherwise the air will be trapped by the insulation and serve no purpose at all. If it feels drafty in the roof space and cold or cool, there is probably plenty of natural air for ventilation. If, however, it smells damp and is clammy, then almost certainly you should do something about ventilating your roof space, and the sooner the better. If you are unsure of what to do, consult a reputable roofing contractor or builder, who should be prepared to give sound advice free and will offer a competitive estimate for carrying out any work that may be necessary.

Roof coverings

When considering a suitable type of covering for a roof, the architect designing a house has to take many factors into consideration, such as the prevailing weather conditions, the natural materials available, how the covering blends in with the immediate surrounding area and the longevity of the material.

The different forms of roof coverings available today are many and varied. Most last well over 15 years, so there is no inherent danger of a roof suddenly deteriorating in a few weeks to a dangerous condition.

The roof coverings you are likely to encounter are wood and asphalt, shingles, concrete tiles, clay tiles, thatch, copper, sheeting made of lead or zinc, natural slate, stone and manufactured slate.

Modern concrete tiles and asbestos slate are very popular because they are easy to fix quickly. However, they are not nearly so long lasting as natural slate, a material which is extremely fire resistant and does not absorb water. Natural slates have been known to last for over 250 years without any maintenance, and it is a sad reflection of the present time that many such roofs are being replaced with a roofing material with a much shorter life span than that which has been removed. Concrete tiles will last well over 40 years without much maintenance; clay tiles and manufactured slate up to 35 years.

Tapered wooden cedar shingles are used extensively in the US and Canada. When treated with boiled oil they will last 30 years or more.

Signs of wear

It is usually fairly easy to detect signs of wear on roofing material – provided you are prepared to climb up a ladder. With natural slate or concrete tiles, tap gently with a small hammer. If they are unimpaired, they will ring with a hollow sound. However, if they are beginning to rot they will sound dull and will break easily. Slates will delaminate, that is, begin to flake. Manufactured slates will begin to grow moss and lichen. They will also show signs of colour loss. While the mosses can be cleaned off easily, the slates will begin to curl at the edges and become porous. This will eventually lead to leaks.

Clay tiles will show flaking pieces inside the roof and may start to crumble. Although at this stage the tiles are probably reaching the limit of their effective life, there is plenty of time to find a solution to the problem – it is as well, however, to start immediately to seek a solution.

Deterioration in shingles can be spotted by fungal growth showing on the roof or the shingles themselves will show black. They may also show splits and appear spongy. Defective shingles must be removed and replaced as soon as possible.

Leaks in roofs

Leaking roofs can be very costly. Not only is the roof at risk but also the internal decorations and plasterwork which can be ruined by prolonged water seepage. So it is best to mend a leaking roof as soon as possible after you have discovered the exact location of the leak. It is an advantage if it is raining, because you can quickly discover exactly where the water is seeping through. A long length of coloured electrical wire, pushed through the hole, will enable easy identification outside.

Anywhere where water is running in large quantities, for example in valley gutters, will eventually wear out. Holes will appear, allowing water to run through. The danger here is that the water, while gaining entrance through the outer cover, comes up against the valley or gutter boarding upon which the outer cover was laid. It can take years to rot the wood and this might not be detected until major damage has been done.

Loose ridge and hip tiles are another common cause of leaks. A loose ridge tile will allow water to penetrate between its two adjacent tiles as well as allowing water to soak up between the roof slope and ridge tile itself. If a roof has a dormer projection, or is part of a terrace where a number of soakers (flashing) have been used to finish off the roof between properties, there is a danger that one or two of the soakers may have worn away. (Soakers – flashing – are zinc or lead rectangles, bent at right angles, which link one course with another to prevent water penetration at the meeting place of tiles or slates and any upright member coming up from the roof.) Water will run in at these points and travel many feet before showing through the ceiling or wall, causing extensive damage.

A fine example of old slates on roofs which, having mellowed with age, blend into the surrounding landscape.

Shingles, slates and tiles

Shingles, slates and tiles have proved to be very effective materials for covering roofs. Used correctly, they provide not only adequate protection from the elements but also an extremely attractive appearance.

Shingles

Cedar shingles form an extremely light roof covering. They come in packs and are cut in random widths to give the roofer a chance to vary the bond. Usually 400mm (16in) long, lengthwise they taper from approximately 12mm (½in) thick to nothing in length. They are laid to an ordinary slate gauge (overlap) and usually nailed to thick boarding covering the rafters. (The gauge is found by taking the length of the shingle, less the lap divided by two.) If the roof is close boarded, the shingles can be nailed direct, in a random bond, and removed from the pack without sorting.

Copper nails must be used for nailing the shingles as anything else will stain down the cedar and look unsightly. Blunt copper nails are best, as sharp nails can easily split the shingles. The shingles are laid down course by course up to the ridge, which is formed by splitting the shingles lengthwise and laying two courses horizontally which overlap each other.

Shingles should not be used to cover a roof with a pitch of less than 30 degrees as rain is sure to work up between the courses and cause leaks. As shingles curl up in the sun, they should be laid with only one-third of their total length exposed.

Replacement of individual shingles is quite simple as the laps are quite close and new shingles can, therefore, be inserted into the gaps and nailed down with blunt copper nails. As they are tapered, they will wedge neatly into place. Only the fact that they are new allows you to see they have been repaired.

Nowadays, asphalt shingles are often used instead of wood shingles. They are not only more durable but also provide a very lightweight roof.

Slates

Slates sometimes fall off the roof or break as a result of high winds which cause pressure in the roof space, thereby lifting the roof covering in places. Objects landing on roofs from various heights, such as branches from overhanging trees, can also cause a lot of damage. Slates will often become dislodged because the nails they have been fixed with have become corroded.

When buying replacement slates, check to make sure that they are the correct size, thickness and colour and that they are not cracked or delaminated.

Slates are normally fixed to battens (nailers). Sometimes, battens only are fixed to the rafters; at other times, boards and battens are used; on other occasions roofing felt or asphalted paper is inserted before the battens are fixed and sometimes slates are nailed directly to boards.

The slates are laid on the battens (nailers), starting at the eaves. There must be no straight joints or rain will find its way through the roof. The first course of slating is double. Half-length slates are laid down first (called undercloak or under office). The first course proper is laid over these, using one-and-a-half width slates to give the correct bond.

When slates have to be removed, use a slater's ripper (nail pulling tool). This instrument is thrust up beneath the broken slate and the sharp hook-shaped blade brought up against the nail so as to sever and free the slate.

It will probably be quite easy to notice missing slates because the course lines will be broken up. Take a slater's ripper (nail pulling tool) onto the roof and push up under the slates above the missing ones. Move the ripper about from left to right, until contact with the nails are made. Pull out these nails and bits of half slate that may be trapped, it

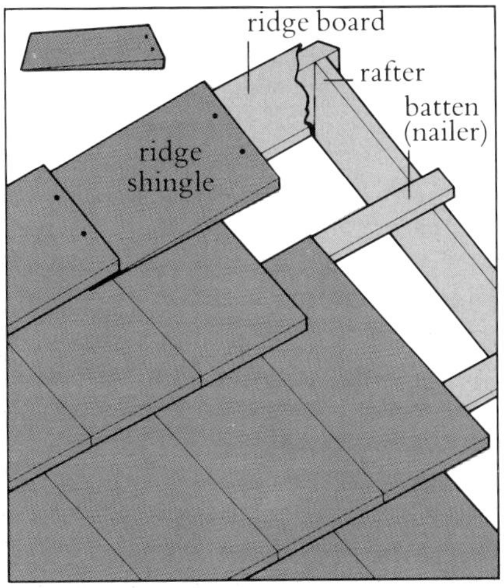

Shingles are laid from eaves to ridge.

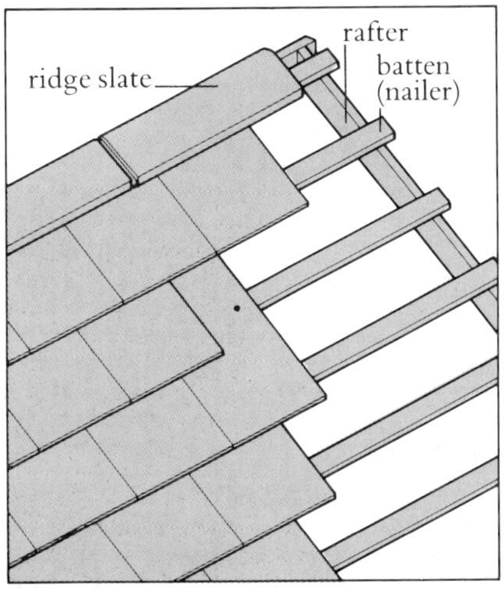

Slates should be laid to a random bond.

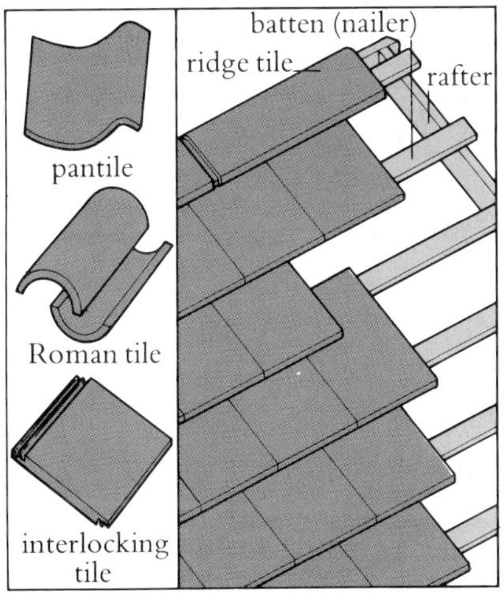

Tiles are available in many sizes.

(left) *The roofer is repairing the soaker (flashing) on a tiled lean-to roof.*

(right) *Houses with cedar shingle roofs.*

will be almost impossible to fit another slate in properly with nails or slate in the way. When contact is made with the nails, pull sharply downwards. The hook on the slate ripper will connect with the nail and remove it. Do the same with the fixing nail on the other side of the slate. A new slate can now be inserted into position. The method of holding these slates has for decades been a strip of metal approximately 230mm (9in) long which is nailed to the lower batten (nailer) and bent up over the bottom edge of the slate, after the slate has been pushed up into position. Holding slates in this fashion is not necessarily very effective as the metal strips bend back straight, allowing the slate to slide out again. There are better, more modern, fittings now available on the market to overcome this problem. (Adhesives can also be used, but in hot weather the glue becomes tacky and the slate tends to slip out of line.) Since the slate lies over three battens it is important to make sure that the slate rides up onto the batten at the top. To help, a long length of thin metal such as hoop iron can be pushed up under the roofing area first. The slate will, when pushed up, ride nicely up over the top and its correct position will be reached.

Tiles

Tiles may be made out of clay or concrete and appear in quite a number of colours.

When tiling a roof, ideally, it should first be covered with sawn boarding and then laid with roofing felt. Often, however, the boarding is omitted. The tile battens (nailers) are fixed to the correct gauge by nailing through the felt and into the boarding, thus keeping the roof water-tight and draught-free. If a tile should get broken or fall out, water will lie in the channels formed by the battens and felt, or snow could be driven up under the tiles. To prevent this, counter battening is sometimes carried out, whereby battens are first fixed over the felt in the direction of, and on top of, the rafters before normal battening takes place. If any water then finds its way through the tiles, it will run away down the felt and evaporate behind the fascia boarding.

The most common type of tile (plain tile) is that which has a slightly curved surface, two holes at the top for the fixing nails and (usually) two projections called nibs on the underside at the top edge to hook over the tiling battens (nailers). They are laid in a treble overlap. There are also special curved tiles, known as hip and ridge tiles, used to waterproof the valley.

Interlocking tiles are used on new houses and for roof replacement. They are laid in a single layer, with overlapping and interlocking head, tail and side joints for weatherproofing. They can be used on low pitched roofs down to 15 degrees.

As only every fourth or fifth course is nailed, it is quite possible that a broken tile is not nailed and removal in this case will be quite easy. There is no need to try to renail tiles, as odd replacements are quite safe. The tiles rely on the nibs to hold them in place. Raise the tiles in the vicinity of the damaged area; push up the broken tile and lift it over the battens (nailers). Replace with new tiles. The use of a proper roof board or some other method to protect tiles from breakage is paramount, otherwise more damage is likely to be caused to the tiles. The amateur should attempt only the simplest of replacements and preferably on a low roof. Apart from the likelihood of damaging the sound part of the roof there is considerable personal risk.

Thatching

The thatcher's craft is, perhaps, the oldest craft in the building industry. Today, some of the most popular materials for thatching are long straw and combed wheat reed. Another is Norfolk reed, which is usually about 150mm (6in) long is very durable and can last for up to a hundred years.

The best way to identify which type of thatch is used on the roof is to look at the gable ends and ridge. You will almost always find that the long straw method will be decorated with a pattern of liggers and cross rods fastened down onto the straw with spars. Liggers are split strips of hazel approximately 2m (6ft 6in) long and chamfered at the ends so that they lie horizontally along the roof slopes. Spars also consist of strips of hazel, 750mm to 900mm (2ft 6in to 3ft) long, and are pointed at both ends. They are twisted through 360 degrees and bent to form a staple. If looked at closely, a roof covered in long straw will appear as though it literally has been poured over the cottage that it covers. Combed wheat reed and Norfolk water reed, however, are laid and cut to show the holes in the ends of the reeds. They are laid in yealms – compact layers of straw about 450mm (18in) wide and 150mm (6in) thick – with both ends level, and dressed with a leggett.

A thatched cottage undergoing repairs. Note the yealms on the roof.

Preparing for thatching is basically similar for all materials used in the craft. The following is a description of long straw thatching. First the straw has to be built up on the floor and wet very thoroughly. This is very important for the finished job. When this process is completed, the heap of straw is known as a bed. The well soaked straw will be more flexible to use and will compress better when fitted to the roof. After wetting, the lengths of straw are made up into yealms and put into a yoke ready for transportation to the roof. The yoke is a forked hazel branch about 1.25m (4ft) long with string at the top to keep the ends tight when loaded up with yealms. For setting the eaves

Long straw thatching

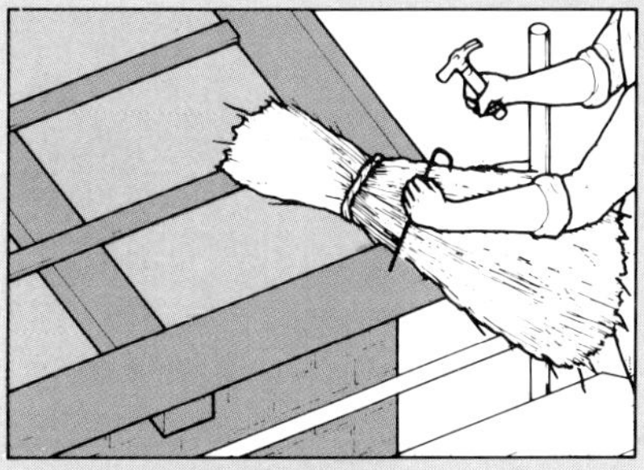

1. *Lay first bottle 45 degrees to angle caused by eaves and gable. Temporarily fix iron hooks.*

2. *Lay several bottles tightly together. Hold down with sways and drive hooks deep into the rafters.*

3. *Place yealms on top of bottles. Hold down with spars. (The sways and hooks are hidden by the course fitted above them.)*

and gable ends, larger lengths of straw are used called bottles. The first bottle for the eaves is laid down at 45 degrees to the angle caused by the eaves and gable. An iron hook is fixed on both sides to hold the bottle in place. This operation is repeated until several bottles are laid and held down with hooks. The method of holding down the bottle is either with tarred yarn or, preferably, with a hazel sway, which is a length of flexible hazel.

The sway is laid down at an appropriate position on the bottles and fixed with staples. The hook is driven down as far as possible into the lower part of the rafter. The sway is trapped down tight and also holds the bottles. As each bottle is laid along the eaves, it is levelled up against its neighbour to make a tight fit. The hooks are driven in at intervals to complete the course. Yealms are placed on top of the bottles and are held down with spars which look like 'U' nails in wood. The sways are hidden by the course fitted above them and held down with the spars.

Repairs

As thatching is very complicated it is recommended that all new work be done by a professional thatcher. However, small repairs can be undertaken by the amateur, provided safety precautions are taken.

The material used should be new and of good quality – whether reed or straw. When repairing a hole in a rotten piece of thatch, carefully remove the rotten portion, taking out the spars as you go. Try to remove the whole bottle or yealm where the rot has gained a hold. (A new bottle will be needed if the damaged section to be removed is near the eaves or up the gable ends of the roof. If, however, it is the middle part of the roof which is in need of repair it will mean a yealm is required.) Make up a new bottle and refit into the gap. The bottle is made up by gathering the material into tight bunches approximately 125mm (5in) thick and 550mm (22in) wide. This is larger than the average yealm and one of its ends is much larger than the other. The bottle is then folded in half to make it doubly thick. The narrow end is tied firmly with twine or a straw bond. The straw bond is a handful of straw twisted round and round to look like a rope. Two or three bottles may be needed to give sufficient cover for trimming. Trim off the overhanging straw with sharp shears; this will avoid unnecessary accidents with the thatcher's shearing hook, which is an extremely dangerous tool.

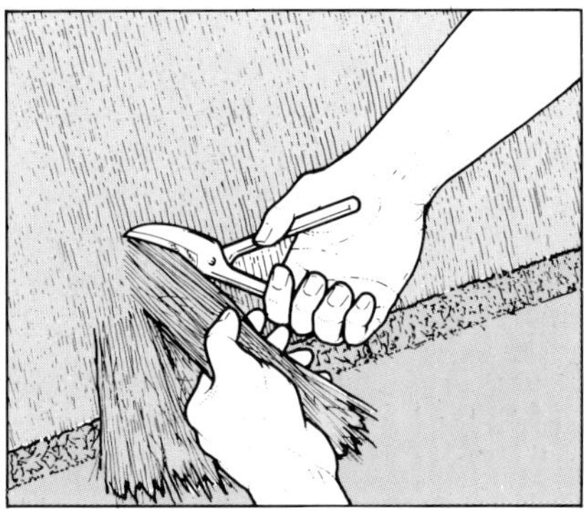

Shears trim off over-hanging straw.

Tools and equipment

Many tools are hand-made to the thatcher's own specification.

Eave's knife
This is used mainly when working with straw.

Hand shears

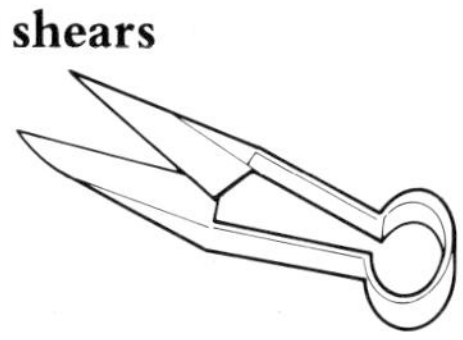

Hand shears are used for trimming the thatch when finishing off.

Iron thatching hooks

These vary in length from 180mm to 300mm (7in to 12in) and are used in conjunction with hazel sways to fix the thatch to the rafters.

Leather palm
This is useful for protecting the hand when pushing home spars while 'palming' the butts of reed.

Leggett

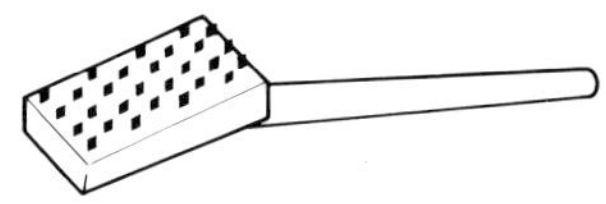

This tool is used for dressing the thatch material into position. It varies according to the material used and is usually made to the thatcher's own specifications and requirements.

Reed holder

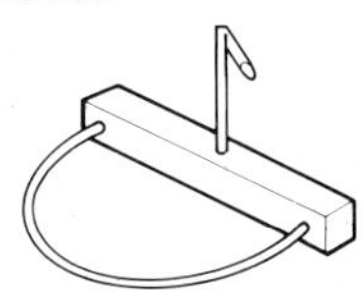

An implement which hooks onto the batten (nailer) with the reed held in the bow.

Side rake

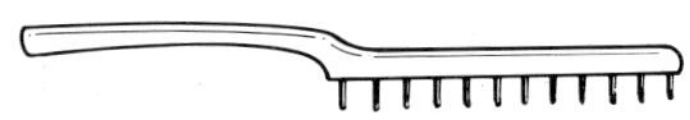

A side rake is used for long straw only, for raking out waste.

Spar hook
It splits and points hazel spars.

Thatcher's horse
This is a wooden frame with spikes which penetrate the thatch.

Thatcher's shearing hook
These are specialized shears for a dressing overhang of thatch. *Not* recommended for the amateur.

Yoke

This is a forked hazel branch which is laid on the roof after being packed with yealms.

Metal roofs and coverings

Metal coverings have been used particularly for irregularly shaped roofs such as domes and spires. Some church roofs are covered in lead sheets to good effect. Copper sheeting has proved very popular because of its versatility. It is hardly affected at all by changes in atmospheric conditions and has little or no expansion and contraction and after several years it changes colour to a beautiful shade of green, a from of patina. One such roof is the Planitarium in London. The whole dome was covered in copper sheeting well over 30 years ago, and it is still in very good condition. Zinc sheeting is very similar to copper; indeed, the only difference is in its longevity and workability (copper lasts longer and is better to work with).

Most domestic homes have metal coverings on such small awkward areas as valley gutters, gutters behind parapet walls and the valleys between roof slopes on balconies. Lead and zinc are used for flashings (metal cut into a wall) and soakers (flashing) around chimney stacks. There is often lead or copper work on flat roofs over bay windows. There are also wooden gutters covered with lead which are used in the hollows of 'M' shaped roofs and behind parapets, as well as over valley rafters.

If you have an area of copper roofing which fails, the fault will almost certainly be that the sheet has split along a fold, or else that it has just worn through. The same is true for zinc sheeting, and the remedy for both is the same. If splits are evident, acquire a strip 150mm (6in) or so longer than the split. Clean down both the roof and strip with wire (steel) wool. Fit the strip over the split and solder it into position.

If worn thin, acquire a sheet of the material to cover the worn patch, again larger by 150mm (6in) or so all round. Clean down, lay the sheet down over the worn area and solder. To stop the sheet patch from moving while soldering, lay a house brick on top. This will be sufficient to keep the material still.

Zinc soakers (flashing) tend to deteriorate quicker than lead ones. Usually, they fail after many years' service because they simply wear out. Remove the roof covering, allowing at least 600mm (2ft) either side of the damaged area. The soakers are now exposed and are seen to be overlapping with each other. Carefully remove the cement and sand rendering (finish) from the wall into which the top edge of each soaker is fixed. This is best done by tapping sharply about 50mm (2in) above the finished line of rendering. The rendering will crack along a line level with the top edge of the soaker. Remove any nail holding the soaker to the roof and sweep the area clean. Starting at the lowest course removed, replace the soaker and then the cover, each time laying a new soaker in place on top of the cover just laid down. Once all the soakers have been replaced, gently tap the upstand part of each soaker back against the wall with a hammer and a piece of wood. If necessary, nail into a brick joint to hold the soaker in place. Cover the area with a protective sheet before refinishing up the wall. A narrow board laid on the soakers will usually give a straight edge to the work.

For lead valley or guttering repairs, it is important to remember to mark the slates or tiles on both sides of the damaged area so that they can be replaced correctly. When both sides are stripped, it will be seen that the valley cover fits under both sides up to 100mm (4in). Lift the lead up carefully to expose the damaged section and push a short piece of wood under for support. With a sharp knife, cut out the damaged length. Lay the undamaged piece back on to the valley boards. Cut the new material at least 600mm (2ft) longer than the section removed. Lay in the valley, tucking the highest end under the existing end and the lowest end over the existing end. Use aluminium or galvanized nails to hold the valley material at each side. Replace the roof covering to complete the job.

Glossary

Batten: strip of wood used to span rafters to carry slates and tiles.

Eaves: the overhang of roof on gable ends and sides.

End walls: either end of a rectangular building, excluding any triangular top piece.

Fascia: board nailed to the end of *rafters* to which the guttering is fixed.

Gable ends: the triangular top to an end wall.

Hips: the joining of two roof slopes of equal pitch at the right angle of a building to form an excluded angle.

Hipped roof: a roof where all the external right angles are joined by forming slope to slope.

Hip tile: tile fitting over the hip to join the course on both sides.

Rafter: wood used to construct roof.

Ridge tile: tile used to cap off top of roof.

Shim: metal sheet washer.

Soffit: wood used to fit under *rafter* ends to finish off *fascia*.

Soaker: metal right angle for joining tile or slate courses at wall junctions.

Valley: included angle of roof.

Garden Crafts

The principles and design concepts of formal gardening offer great scope to the keen gardener: topiary, formal hedging and bedding present an exciting new challenge to gardeners in the 1980s.

Until 100 years ago, a gardener did not have the variety of colours to choose from that we have today. The modern gardener, however, has the advantage of being able to produce a truly distinctive garden, combining traditional features with the great diversity of plants that we now take for granted.

The chapter describes traditional methods of gardening practised in the United Kingdom on a limited scale which are, as yet, little known in the United States.

The ideal is to have an ancient garden to restore but in practice traditional features can look just as attractive in a newly created garden. Where applicable, we have indicated how these traditional crafts can be used in a modern setting. What you should try to avoid is mixing too many styles, periods, and materials within the one garden.

All these formal features are the legacy of horticultural evolution. Topiary goes back to at least Roman times and possibly earlier, and the extensive use of hedges and formal bedding have their origins in the development of early European gardens.

Enclosed gardens were a feature of monasteries and fortified gardens at the end of the Middle Ages, together with formal beds, perhaps containing herbs and bounded by straight paths, would have been common. As Europe became more settled and peaceful, gardens were extended beyond defensive walls. Gardens became larger, at the same time retaining their formal structure. Much more complicated designs, such as the English knot gardens, became popular with the flowering of the Renaissance.

Clipped trees, hedges and knot gardens shown here are characteristic features of formal gardens in many parts of the world.

The Italian Renaissance found merchants from Florence building villas and farms in the cooler surrounding hills, and the beauty of the landscape led to a gradual opening up of the enclosures. In the sixteenth century, gardens became more ostentatious with terraces and water features, including elaborate fountains which abounded. Hedges were used extensively, acting as architectural links between gardens and houses.

France followed the Italian style, but here most of the gardens were on the level. The style was still basically geometric without being so flamboyant. Nevertheless, in the seventeenth century a style evolved that incorporated more elaborate vistas, long pools, canals, and *parterres*.

The eighteenth century saw the influence of British landscape gardeners – in particular, Lancelot ('Capability') Brown who developed an open parkland style of gardening attempting to create a 'natural' style with the minimum of boundaries.

Many of the traditional skills associated with garden crafts in earlier times have gradually fallen into neglect because the cost of the necessary skilled paid labour became prohibitive. Topiary, for instance, required too much initial training time and maintenance; carpet bedding, though still carried on as a traditional part of public park gardening, is also succumbing to financial pressures and giving way to ground-cover shrubs or other low-cost and low maintenance beds.

None of these restraints apply, however, if you are gardening for a hobby. Employing these features in the private garden will help to preserve traditional skills and at the same time provide your garden with a touch of style.

Topiary

In 1925, Charles Curtis and W Gibson, head gardener of Levens Hall, one of Britain's most famous topiary gardens, wrote: 'Modern horticultural works . . . do not as a rule take any notice whatever of Topiary, and those in which it is noticed deal with the subject with such brevity that it is provoking insomuch as the student is little or none the wiser for any information given.' Things have not changed much in the intervening 60 years, and the subject is still shrouded in mystery, which is surprising for a garden craft with a long history.

Topiary has never been very well known or favoured, partly because, until recently, it was not very fashionable, and partly because the art of topiary takes many years of careful training before the results of one's labours are seen. In these days of 'instant' gardening it is very easy to see why topiary remains relatively unpopular.

When topiary is out of fashion it tends to be dismissed as either quaint or childish, yet it was certainly considered an important horticultural pursuit by the Romans. On the authority of Martial, a Roman author of the first century AD, the art of topiary was first introduced to the Romans by Gnaius Matius, a friend of Julius Caesar.

Pliny, the Roman Consul, had extensive topiary in his famous Tuscan Villa. In a letter written by Pliny the Younger, there is a description of the portico opening on to a terrace 'embellished with various figures, and bounded with a box hedge, from which you descend by an easy slope, adorned with the representations of diverse animals in box, answering alternately to each other: this is surrounded by a walk enclosed with evergreens, shaped into a variety of forms'.

From the gardens of wealthy Romans the taste for clipped trees spread throughout the Empire. It was later taken up by monks, who continued to spread the art throughout Europe.

This garden demonstrates the art of topiary, creating order and tranquility.

The sixteenth century was probably the start of the golden age of topiary. It almost certainly reached its height in Britain during the reign of William and Mary (1689-1702). William III, when he became king of England, brought with him from Holland a taste for clipped yews, and this is likely to have accentuated a prevailing taste.

Yew (*Taxus baccata*) has always been the favourite choice of plant for topiary. Parkinson, Apothecary to James I of England, who was made Botanicus Regius Primarius by Charles II, pointed out that yew was largely used for 'shadow and ornament', although he clearly had a predilection for privet (*Ligustrum ovalifolium*), which he thought had not received attention because it was such a widespread hedging plant. He suggested that it could be 'cut, lead, and drawn into what forme one will, either beastes, birds, or men armed or otherwise'.

Topiary today

You do not need a large garden to practise the art of topiary. Even a tiny plot, little more than about 6m

(20ft) square, could sustain perhaps 20 or more pieces if you keep to small subjects and choose a plant such as shrubby honeysuckle (*Lonicera nitida*) which will make for a very small piece of topiary more successfully than yew. Just a few isolated pieces in a small garden can look out of place – unless they become a focal point. It is possible that a tall, abstract shape, or a spectacular imitation of an identifiable figure, could be used in the same way as a garden ornament. Do not overlook the possibility of growing a clipped box in a tub – perhaps one on either side of an entrance.

If the lawn is large enough, and the setting suitable, a group of figures or shapes could make your garden look distinguished. They can also be very useful where a 'period' garden is being created.

Most modern gardens are small, however, and topiary pieces on a grand scale are inappropriate.

If you are not trying to create a particular classic garden style, and simply want to try your hand at topiary while keeping a traditional art very much alive, start with an existing hedge. This can save several years of growth – and time – that would otherwise be necessary to build up the 'plinth' (an item which is not essential, but recommended).

A Dutch garden

A Dutch garden (confusingly called an English garden by the Dutch!) is usually a compact rectangular area enclosed by tall hedges with simple symmetrical flower beds, filled with low-growing plants that will not detract from topiary and hedges. It will make an ideal setting for topiary, and it is quite feasible to use the whole of a small town garden for this. Alternatively, you could section off part of a larger garden, to make an 'open-air room'. Low, usually box, edging is used to emphasize the formality of the design, and, of course, topiary holds interest centre-stage.

The ground between the beds and around the edge should be paved. Grass is unsuitable because some areas would be subject to too much wear, and mowing round the beds would be extremely difficult.

Bricks, clay or concrete pavers will all look attractive, and a herringbone pattern will add interest.

A garden such as this will take perhaps a decade to look really good, but you will have constructed a feature that should endure for a very long time.

Making a start

There are three options for anyone starting from scratch:

1. Use an existing hedge.
2. Buy young plants and grow them on until ready for training.
3. Adapt an existing tree or shrub.

Using an existing hedge is probably the quickest way to see some results of your labours.

A good way to start is to build on a hedge. The base or plinth is there already, and because the plant is established, growth should be comparatively rapid.

Simply let several bunches of growth develop untrimmed. The hedge will look untidy for a while, but the reason you are doing this will soon become obvious to your neighbours!

Planting specially for topiary is the best method if you intend making several set pieces within the garden, or plan to have a topiary

(left) *This shows what can be achieved by clipping alone. No wires were used here.*

(above) *Formal beds and clipped hedges make good companions in a Dutch garden.*

garden. Because it will take perhaps five or six years to see whether or not the topiary has been successful, it is worth planting the maximum number of plants you are likely to need; it is better to discard unwanted plants later than to find you have to wait several years for another plant not planted at the initial stages to grow sufficiently.

Whenever possible, it is worth ensuring that all the plants come *from the same source*, in fact from the same parent plant if possible, as different clones may have different rates of growth.

For an ambitious project, where a lot of pieces the same height are required, it may be worth buying very young plants and growing them on in a nursery bed (a spare piece of ground) so that you can select the right plants for particular pieces. That is the way it was done traditionally. However, if you reckon you cannot wait for so long you should be able to go to a garden centre and select suitable plants with the right formation and so save yourself at least one year.

Bare-root or balled plants are best planted in mid-autumn. (They used to be planted right through to midwinter if the ground was suitable, though this is now considered unwise. It would be better to wait until spring.) Container-grown plants, not available to topiarists of the past, can be planted at any time (but from early spring to late autumn is still best).

To the enthusiast, when adapting an existing tree or shrub, size alone will not deter. However, such a transformation can hardly be tackled by a beginner. The smaller and the less woody the plant, the easier it will be to train initially. The best choice is an isolated bush that is about 1.5-1.8m (5-6ft) high.

Start by cutting the bush back hard, wherever the existing growth is in the wrong place. Hard pruning will stimulate growth in, say, one year, though some species may be less than ready to oblige. Make use of as much fresh growth as possible so that the plant can grow again quickly. Very little clipping should be necessary for the next year.

The traditional method used tarred string to tie young shoots into place, but modern plastic tying materials will do just as well. Thick, old stems will have to be held in place with copper wire (galvanized wire is thought to have an injurious effect on the plants). Always use a piece of cork or rubber between the wire and the wood.

Suitable plants

Although other plants are sometimes used – the very famous topiary at Tulcan in Ecuador is trimmed from *Cupressus arizonica*, for example – there are four firm favourites that have found popularity over the centuries simply because they work well: yew (*Taxus baccata*), privet (*Ligustrum ovalifolium*), box (*Buxus sempervirens*), and the shrubby honeysuckle (*Lonicera nitida*). All these plants have comparatively small leaves that look much neater when clipped than larger-leaved candidates such as holly (*Ilex* spp.) and sweet bay (*Laurus nobilis*).

Yew (*Taxus baccata*) is by far the best for large, isolated specimens. It clips well, is generally well clothed to the ground and, quite simply, looks good. It has a reputation for slow growth – quite undeservedly in fact as it is likely to grow as fast as most other hedging plants. There is a golden form of yew that can be used for contrast.

Privet is not worth planting specially for topiary because in cold areas it tends to shed most of its leaves in winter. Nevertheless, it is well worth trying topiary on an existing privet hedge.

Box has many varieties, but for topiary the hedging box (*Buxus sempervirens* 'Handsworthensis') is probably the best as it is extremely adaptable and clips very well.

The honeysuckle (*Lonicera nitida*) is a good choice to start with, and is particularly suitable for very small objects (for which yew may not be so suitable). Again, there is a golden form ('Baggessen's Gold') when variety is called for. The main problem with loniceras is their tendency to develop dead areas, and also to become bare at the base. Cold weather may cause some loss of leaves.

Box topiary.

Training the plants

The author of one ancient book on topiary (*The Book of Topiary* (1904) by C H Curtis and W Gibson) considered: 'fortunate indeed . . . the gardener in charge of a Topiary garden who can rely after a year or two on three or four men who are thoroughly trained and accustomed to the art of topiary clipping'. He went on to say that a beginner should only be let loose on 'trees of least importance and most concealed from view', and preferably those with a round or oval shape because these are the least difficult to work with.

Despite doubts about what beginners can achieve, many self-taught amateurs have managed superb results. However, the advice about shape is, for an amateur, worth bearing in mind.

Lonicera topiary.

How it is done

It is difficult to describe in detail how to produce a particular figure – just as it is impossible to teach someone how to paint creatively by numbers. Every tree is different, and there are many forms that topiary can take.

Some of the simplest forms of topiary to produce are created merely by clipping with shears over a period of years, as and when you fancy. No wiring, no framework and no special development of shoots are required. The plant is 'chipped away' with shears in much the same way that a sculptor might work with a chisel.

As errors can take several years to correct, it is best to cut away less than you reckon is necessary. You can always remove a bit more later; you cannot quickly put it back on.

The most popular and admired subjects, however, are traditional ones such as birds. The principles are demonstrated below, but you will have to adapt the details to suit whatever shape appeals to you.

If you are starting with new plants, do nothing in the autumn or winter of planting, and perhaps not even the following autumn. Be very careful not to remove any young shoots that could be used.

For quick results, put several plants together. If there is to be a centrepiece arising from a plinth, put a tall specimen in the middle and a smaller one either side.

Once pruning has started, be content with a height increase of about 75-100mm (3-4in) a year.

Watch out for small branches or shoots that are inclined to grow outwards (towards the outside of the bush), and remove them. If left to grow they will eventually become a nuisance and if you have to cut them out later the shape will become disfigured.

Making a peacock or cockerel

Whether you want a fan-tailed bird or one with tail closed, you will need at least two good stems growing from the point at which the bird is to sit. If there are more than two shoots, all the better – bundle several together and treat as a single stem.

Make a galvanized wire outline – fencing wire will do, but it must be firm and rigid – to form the two halves: the head and the tail. For the peacock, where the tail is to be in the fan position, the wire will have to form a loop against which canes can be tied to form the fan. If a cockerel is preferred, a single straight cane can be used to strengthen the tail section.

The wire framework and canes will need secure support by wiring to a stout stake.

Tie the shoots into position, and cut away any pieces that you are quite sure will not be required. For a fan-tailed peacock, tie in as many separate stems to the fan as possible. If there are too few, remove the tips on the existing stems to encourage more to branch out.

Fast-growing plants will need regular trimming in the first few seasons, with shoots being tied in whenever necessary to fill gaps and produce new detail. Once the framework is established, yew and box will need cutting only once a year.

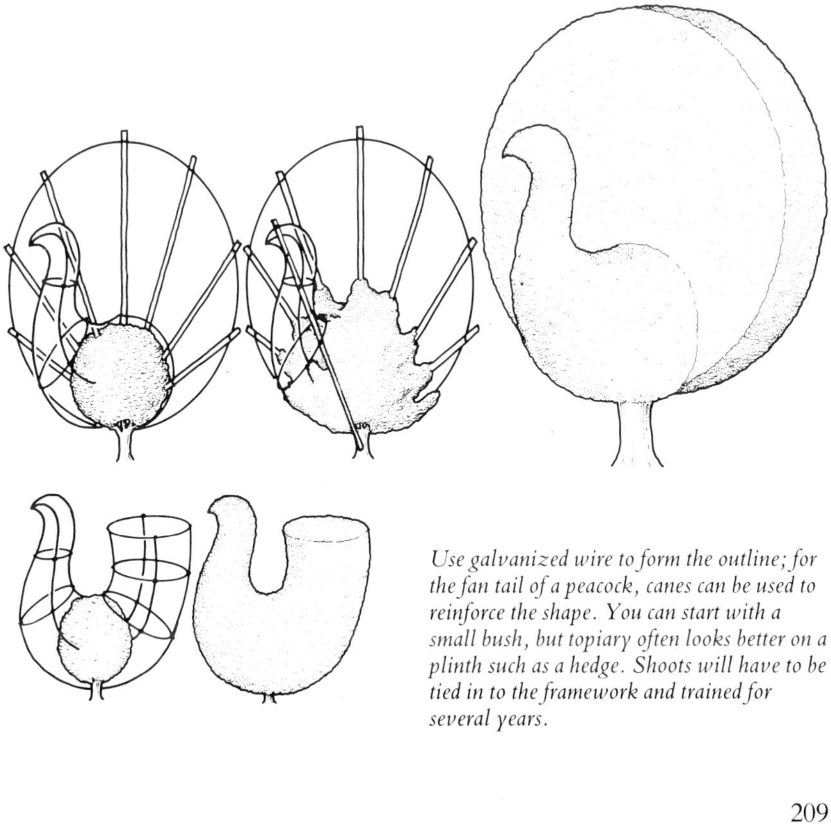

Use galvanized wire to form the outline; for the fan tail of a peacock, canes can be used to reinforce the shape. You can start with a small bush, but topiary often looks better on a plinth such as a hedge. Shoots will have to be tied in to the framework and trained for several years.

Pleaching

The effect produced by pleaching is that of a hedge supported on stilts. Pleaching can be achieved with a head as thick as a hedge, but the opportunities for finding a suitable position are few. A thin profile where the tracery of the branches is the main feature is probably a better choice for most gardens.

Before embarking on a line of pleached trees, it is important to consider the problem of pruning and training. It will be like cutting a 1.8m (6ft) hedge on 1.8m (6ft) stilts! In the past, special high trestles on wheels were used. Today you could use the mini-scaffold platforms which serve for many DIY jobs.

What you need

2.4m (8ft) stout stakes for the main tree supports (600mm/2ft will be buried).
Strong bamboo canes (those for the vertical stake extensions should have a diameter of about 50mm/2in).
Tying material.
Tree ties.

How it is done

Prepare the planting holes, working in plenty of compost or manure, 2.7m (9ft) apart and insert the vertical stakes, leaving 1.8m (6ft) above ground.

Plant the trees – you may have to turn the position of the tree several times until the most suitable profile aligns with the row – and ensure the stakes are firm.

Lash the bamboo canes to the top of the stakes to make vertical extensions. The height of the canes will depend on the desired height of the trees – 3-3.6m (10-12ft) is about right – but make sure there is sufficient overlap for strength. Take particular care with this job, otherwise the whole of the rigging will collapse in a gale. Eventually, the canes will rot but by the time they do so the branches should be strong enough to survive on their own without support. In the old days tarred string would have been used, but today, any modern rot-proof tying material will do.

Fix rows of horizontal canes 300-600mm (1-2ft) apart (see illustration). These canes can be thinner than the vertical ones, but they do have to be long. Overlap them adequately so that they can be joined and lashed together firmly. Be confident that the ties are secure (but if one slips it will not be as serious as if an upright collapses).

Start training by tying the branches lying in the right direction to the horizontal canes. Sometimes it is necessary to bring down a young branch to a lower level. If a thin profile-pleached line is required, prune off branches growing in the wrong direction.

Remove the top of the tree once the required height has been reached. The horizontal branches will need tying to the canes as they extend. Once they reach each other, let the ends intertwine.

Branches that grow out beyond the required profile will have to be pruned out annually, and any extension to height must be restricted in the same way as a hedge.

Pleached hedges look as though they are supported on stilts. They look superb, but clipping and training can be a problem.

The principle of pleaching

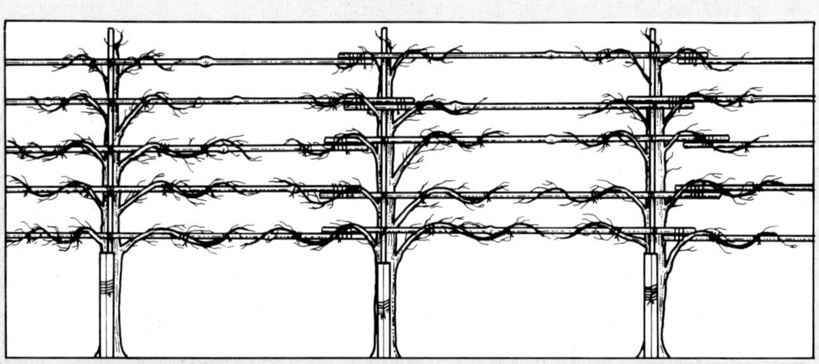

The initial framework looks inelegant and ugly, but is essential.

Suitable trees

Lime (linden) trees are the usual choice for pleaching, though other types have been used, including purple beech (*Fagus sylvatica*), a whitebeam (*Sorbus aria* 'Lutescens'), and hornbeam (*Carpinus betulus*).

Traditionally, the lime used was *Tilia* x *europaea*. Another lime, *T. platyphyllos* has also been popular, but perhaps the best choice today is *T.* x *euchlora* because it does not attract aphids (greenflies) so readily. Aphids produce a 'honeydew' – a sticky substance which they secrete – that drips from the leaves and causes a considerable nuisance.

Formal bedding

Knot gardens, characterized by complex interwoven designs comprising contrasting flowers, herbs or foliage, were popular in England in the sixteenth and seventeenth centuries. By the seventeenth century they had also become highly developed in other parts of Europe. *Parterres* were generally larger and more elaborate than the English knot garden, and became very popular in France and Italy during the seventeenth century.

Bedding with tender exotic plants is very much a product of the nineteenth century. It came about partly as a rebellion against the 'natural' gardening style of eighteenth century British gardeners such as 'Capability' Brown. In the first half of the nineteenth century, it became fashionable to grow 'exotics' and to use plants that were clearly imported.

Beds were changed seasonally. In the summer half-hardy and tender plants were used that had to be over-wintered under glass or raised afresh each year from seed sown in heat in spring.

Carpet bedding, an extension of ordinary bedding, was a product of the last half of the nineteenth century. The aim was to use dwarf foliage plants, trimmed if necessary, to provide a flat uniform surface, and to pick out the patterns or designs with the different plants, which were chosen for contrasting foliage.

With formal bedding, the *raison d'être* is the shape and rigidity of the designs and plants within them. The plants are chosen primarily to provide shape (often with the aid of clipping) or colour; they are intended to be looked at *en masse* and not to be appreciated individually.

Formal bedding needs to be very carefully thought out and positioned; the odd formal bed in an otherwise informal, or modern, garden will almost certainly look inept and incongruous.

Parterres and knot gardens

A *parterre* is an elaborate arrangement of beds in a geometrical design, usually edged with a clipped box. Sometimes the beds are covered with gravel, or even crushed brick or coal, which provide a contrast in colours accentuating the design.

The basic principles of *parterre* gardens, which were developed by French and Italian gardeners in the sixteenth century, are to use low-

Part of a large knot garden planted in Gloucestershire, England. Even a small part of a knot garden can look excitingly unusual, as is shown in this photo. The plants comprise traditional aromatic herbs.

growing plants to cover the whole of the ground within a bed, having only one or two types of plant.

A traditional *parterre* was usually a distinct area cut off from the main garden – in earlier times and in large gardens by a formal division, such as a stone balustrade. In a modern garden, which is likely to be fairly small, it is best to devote either the whole of the back, or the whole of the front, garden to *parterre*. Otherwise, perhaps, partition off a section of the garden with a hedge such as box (*Buxus sempervirens*) or yew (*Taxus baccata*) (see page 206). Topiary, formal hedges, and *parterres* all combine happily together and, once you have decided to design a garden in a classical style, it is usually possible to try not one but many of the traditional skills.

A knot garden is characterized by the geometrical interlacing design, each quarter usually being reflected in the other three. Some of the traditional designs for large gardens were extremely complex, and are too ambitious for a modern garden. For instance, in about 1520, the craze for effect reached such a pitch that sand and stones were used to the exclusion of flowers. The design for a knot garden really needs to be viewed from above, and at a distance, to be appreciated. In a small or medium-sized garden this is sometimes very difficult and a fairly simple interlinked geometric pattern will usually have more impact.

Early knot gardens generally used herbs such as lavender cotton (*Santolina chamaecyparissus* 'Nana', syn *S. c. corsica*), hyssop, or thrift (*Armeria maritima*), but, so that the design could be picked out, clipped dwarf box (*Buxus sempervirens* 'Suffruticosa') soon became the standard evergreen for the job.

The paths and spaces within the beds can be surfaced with gravel. These days, there is no problem in keeping gravel weed-free with modern herbicides. Make sure you use one that will not 'creep' and so affect the edging plants. If preferred, the paths and spaces can be filled with seasonal colourful bedding or maybe dwarf or carpeting evergreen shrubs.

Possibly the best example of a knot garden is at Hampton Court, England, which was constructed using sixteenth century records.

Making a knot garden or parterre

Clear the ground thoroughly – it is worth considering one of the modern herbicides to make sure that you start weed-free – rake it level and allow it to settle for up to two weeks while you prepare the plan.

Work out the design on graph paper, using a scale that is suitable for the area. One square might equal 300mm (1ft), as you do not need to bother about detail within the bed.

Mark out the ground round the edges of the bed, using pegs about 300mm (1ft) apart (or whatever intervals suit your plan). Stretch string between them, to make a criss-cross pattern which corresponds with your graph paper. Obviously this would take a lot of string for a knot garden or *parterre* of any size, but you can do it one section at a time. Then move the strings along to the next section.

Use other pegs to mark the shape to be formed by the edging plants.

If you have the plants ready, and you are confident that the design has been marked out correctly so far, you can plant, say, a quarter of the design before you peg out the next quarter. (Use *small* plants.) Or you can mark out the whole design first, drawing lines between the pegs with a stick.

If you are using gravel for either beds or paths, lay it down once the edging plants are in position. (For gravel paths, see Chapter 10 Brickwork and Stonework page 190.) If using gravel or other coloured chippings within the bed, it is worth laying down a sheet of thick polythene (black plastic) first to help suppress perennial weeds and to keep the gravel relatively free from soil contamination.

If you intend to have plants within the beds, these can be planted straight after the edging plants. If, however, you wish to spread the work and the cost over a couple of seasons, you can wait a year, because it will take several seasons before the edging plants look substantial.

Trim the tops of the edging plants as soon as they are planted, removing only enough to ensure they are

Designs for knot gardens

Knot gardens are based on geometric designs using contrasting flowers, herbs or foliage. The two plans above are from layouts for a proposed restoration in Wales.

all the same height. Allow only a modest increase in height each year, as this will encourage stocky plants, well clothed at the base.

Suitable plants

Dwarf box (*Buxus sempervirens* 'Suffruticosa') is the plant to choose to pick out the design for a conventional knot garden or *parterre*. You can, however, consider other plants, especially if size or a particular situation calls for something on a different scale or with a different scent and appearance. Thymes are an obvious choice: they are quick-growing and will soon meld into each other if planted close enough. Be sure to buy the upright bushy type, however, not the carpeting thyme. For contrasting colours you could try *T. vulgaris* 'Silver Queen' (silver) and *T. v.* 'Aureus' (yellow).

Dwarf lavenders (*Lavandula officinalis*) are very good in their prime, as they have evergreen aromatic foliage, but they can become straggly with age. The well-known lavender flowers in mid and late summer. Lavender cotton (*Santolina chamaecyparissus* 'Nana') with its grey evergreen leaves and yellow flowers in summer is also attractive in its

Formal bedding in a park. The design can be adapted to suit private gardens.

prime, but it needs careful pruning, and the shape is easily damaged by pressure.

Formal bedding

There are still a few bastions of the art of formal bedding left. Many local government authorities are trying to retain some annual bedding schemes, though these are generally under threat of being reduced because they are much more expensive to maintain than grassed over areas or, say, areas planted with roses.

Not only is summer bedding labour-intensive; it can also be costly because two sets of plants have to be bought each year – or raised at home, in which case you will almost certainly need a heated greenhouse.

Colour schemes

Getting the colours right is as difficult as choosing the right plants. Colouring is perhaps made more difficult because many bedding plants are available in a wide range of vivid colours and are often sold as mixtures by the nursery trade.

If you can grow your own plants, there is much to be said for growing separate coloured plants whenever possible. This will give you more control over colour schemes. A mass of one single colour can often look better than mixed colours in a formal bed. Mixtures are at their best in beds of a single type, or where plants do not form part of a larger pattern.

Do not use too many colours. Two, or at the most three, are usually enough. Avoid clashing colours and aim for harmony, or else concentrate on contrasting colours.

Beware of associating colours such as magenta or pink with scarlet.

Grey-leaved plants are particularly useful for separating plants with different colours. They also generally help to blend a bed together, even if only used as 'dot' plants (see 'Shape and form' below).

Shape and form

Three or four different types of plant should be enough for your formal bed – too many will make the bed look fussy. If the bed is large and can take a lot of variety, try using the same type of plant with a different colour – perhaps a red-flowered, bronze-leaved begonia (*Begonia semperflorens*), together with a white-flowered green-leaved variety. This way, you will create interest and variety without any confusion.

The design should be as simple as possible, especially for a small bed, although if the plants are small and compact, a more complicated design might work.

Make good use of 'dot' – sometimes called 'spot' – plants. These are tall plants 'dotted' about the bed – but arranged very carefully, not randomly – to provide height or contrast.

Classic dot plants are standard fuchsias (*Fuchsia magellanica*) and heliotropes (*Petasites fragrans*). These will take several years to train and you must have the facilities to over-winter them as large plants. It would be difficult and costly to buy these plants each year.

There are cheaper, more 'instant', alternatives. Some taller-growing annuals (or perennials treated as bedding plants) have the necessary qualities for dot plants: kochia, ricinus (which might be too big for some schemes), and amaranthus are some examples.

Carpet bedding

Carpet bedding has certain features in common with *parterre* or knot gardens: the pattern is picked out with plants, and the spaces in between are filled in with blocks of colour. Masses of low, compact-growing plants with coloured leaves, and sometimes coloured flowers, are grown. It is usual to have plants of one colour as a background and to run plants of other colours through this in stripes or ribbons, or as bold sheets of colour. Traditional beds had very elaborate designs full of scrolls, swirls and fancy designs, rather like those found in Turkish carpets.

For it to work, carpet bedding requires commitment and dedication. Even a small carpet bed takes a lot of plants, and many of them are quite difficult for the amateur to get hold of at a local garden centre in spring. This means that you may need to plan at least one year ahead, so that you can propagate your own plants to bulk up the numbers. Even then, it may take several years to build up a good stock of suitable plants, so it is a good idea to start with a small, simple scheme and then gradually to progress to larger, more complicated designs, using a greater variety of plants.

A frost-free place to over-winter some of the tender plants is really essential, unless you confine yourself to the more hardy varieties and those that can be bought as bedding plants in spring.

Carpet bedding design

It is worth spending some time drawing designs on graph paper before you order seeds or buy plants. Use coloured pencils to fill in the various colours so that you can visualize the design more easily. The table on page 216 contains suggested plants.

The design chosen will eventually have to be marked out in sand or some similar material before you start planting. The first priority, however, is to ensure that you have sufficient quantities of each type of plant. Ignore the normal spacings recommended for the various plants; for carpet bedding they have to be very close together. You must use some discretion when actually planting; usually, professionals calculate on the basis of one plant taking up a 25mm (1in) square! Even if you allow twice this amount of space for each plant, it will soon become clear how many plants are required. If you have drawn the plan on graph paper, it will be a simple job to calculate the number of each type of plant required. This factor may affect your design.

It is possible you may be considering a very grand outline for your carpet bedding design – something spectacular such as a coat of arms, or letters to spell out the name of your house, but be warned that

Floral clocks need very careful choice of plants and regular maintenance.

Carpet bedding depends on contrasting colour and texture of foliage.

this type of design is much more suitable for a public place than a private garden! And the smaller the area, the simpler the design should be. However, if you absolutely must include lettering or dates, choose bold, contrasting colours – silver letters against a red background, for instance.

Before starting to plant, make sure that the ground is firm and *level*. Ups and downs that would not normally be noticed will show up conspicuously with carpet bedding. However, if the bed is large it will improve its appearance if the soil is gradually banked up towards the centre, which could then be about 150-300mm (6-12in) higher than the edge. To give the soil time to settle, it should be prepared about two weeks before planting – and this will have to be after the risk of frost has passed because some of the plants used will be frost-tender.

Only apply fertilizer if the ground is in really poor condition; too much fertilizer will encourage lush growth which may make the plants difficult to keep under control. You want tight, compact plants with little surplus growth.

Plants for carpet bedding have to be used with both care and precision. The areas will have been marked out with sand or some similar material first, which means that you will not be able to walk over the bed. Starting at one corner or side of the bed and working methodically to the next also presents problems, because it is rather like making a tapestry, involving constant changes of colour and position. Trying to create a carpet bed like a knitting pattern – so many of one plant, then two of another, for instance – will rapidly become a planting nightmare, and the chances are the lines will not 'flow' neatly.

The easiest way to start is by planting any 'ribbons' or 'threads' which separate areas, or simply to go along each block, planting the edges where two blocks join up, and fill in within the blocks afterwards.

The major problem is how to plant the area without treading on it. One solution is to work squatting on a stout plank of wood, placed across the bed and supported by bricks or blocks.

Trimming

Some of the plants used for carpet bedding (fibrous-rooted begonias, *Begonia semperflorens*, for instance) have neat, compact habits and should not need any attention other than weeding. Others may need pinching and trimming to keep them in shape and within their alloted space. Pinching and trimming will prevent the design being spoiled by strong growers running into, and perhaps smothering, the weaker ones. The effect of carpet bedding is lost if the outline becomes ragged, the plants straggly, or the bed full of weeds. You need to be prepared to go over the bed at least once every two weeks at the peak of the season, using the supported plank to reach the plants and the weeds. Hoeing is impossible because, of course, the plants will have knit together. Using a hoe would damage the plants and thereby upset the symmetry of the overall design.

The plants

In the past, a vast range of different plants was used for carpet bedding. Many of these plants are now rare or very difficult to buy. The small selection of plants listed below (and even some of these are not widely available at garden centres) should be enough for all but the most ambitious schemes: they are used regularly by local authorities for modern carpet bedding.

Some of the plants listed can be raised from seed as half-hardy annuals; others are normally regarded as greenhouse plants; and some are hardy alpines. The footnotes will tell you which group a plant falls into, to help you to track it down from specialist suppliers if you are unable to get hold of it from your local garden centre.

Other plants to consider

Many of the plants listed below are grown for foliage and they will withstand the necessary clipping. You may prefer, however, to cheat a little and use more of the readily available half-hardy annuals. These will produce the desired effect with flowers rather than foliage. The results, of course, can be equally, if not more, impressive and you can achieve results in the first season with no problems of availability or building up stocks. Many professionals use half-hardy annuals in a modified form of carpet bedding.

Normal flowering bedding plants will be somewhat bushier so you will need less of them. If you choose suitably compact plants, little trimming should be necessary.

Besides the half-hardy annuals already listed, consider lobelia (*Lobelia Urens*) (blue), French marigolds (*Tagetes patula*) (yellow – choose very small varieties), and ageratum (blue – choose compact varieties). The important thing to remember is that they should be compact and almost mound-forming. Bear in mind that begonias (*Begonia semperflorens*) come in a wide range of flower colour and leaf shade. These can be used extensively to produce a long-lasting display with a fine range of colour effects.

Suitable plants for carpet bedding

Red	*Alternanthera bettzichiana* [1] *Begonia semperflorens* [2, 3] *Iresine herbstii* [1] *Sedum spathulifolium 'Atropurpurea'* (a stonecrop) [4] *Sempervivum spp* (houseleeks) (some) [4]	**Silver/ grey**	*Echeveria glauca* [1] *Raoulia australis* [4] *Santolina neapolitana (S. rosmarinifolia)* [5] *Sedum spathulifolium* 'Cappa Blanca' (a stonecrop) [4]
Yellow	*Pyrethrum aureum* 'Golden Moss' or 'Golden Ball' [2]	**White**	*Alyssum maritimum (Lobularia maritima)* (sweet alyssum) (white flowers) [2, 6] *Antennaria dioica* [4] *Sedum dasyphyllum* (white flowers early summer) (a stonecrop) [4]
Green	*Herniaria glabra* [4] *Sedum acre* (a stonecrop) [4, 7] *Sempervivum spp* (some) [4]		

Notes
[1] Tender perennial; may be available from supplier of greenhouse plants.
[2] Can be raised from seed as a half-hardy annual.
[3] Some have red leaves. There are varieties with flowers in shades of pink and white as well as red. Some have green leaves.
[4] Rock or alpine plant.
[5] Dwarf shrub.
[6] Choose very dwarf, compact variety such as 'Snow Carpet' or 'Snow Drift'. Some are too tall.
[7] May be invasive if all traces not removed at the end of the summer season.

Formal hedges

This formal garden at Hall Place, Bexley in England makes use of two traditional hedging plants: yew (Taxus baccata) *at the back, and dwarf box* (Buxus sempervirens *'Suffruticosa') for the front edging.*

Look down almost any street and you will see hedges in abundance. They grow easily and are widely planted – so what is the traditional skill required?

Apart from that most traditional of hedges the privet (*Ligustrum ovalifolium*), not many of them will be the classic hedging plants which formed the backbone of so many earlier gardens, when hedging was a feature of the garden rather than a boundary marker. Beech, yew, box and hawthorn are nowadays often regarded as 'large garden' or 'old-fashioned' hedges, which is a pity because some of these traditional hedging plants can become a real feature in a garden of almost any size if you are prepared to train and clip them properly.

Making a feature of your hedge

If you want a hedge to be proud of, and one that will stand out from the run-of-the-mill hedges found in most gardens, go for a thick, dense, 'classic' one. Other, less formal, hedges have an important role to play however. And it is a good idea to introduce a variety of hedges into the overall design of your garden – many flowering and informal hedges are very effective *within* the garden. It is not necessary to confine them to the boundary. Yew (*Taxus baccata*) and box (*Buxus sempervirens*), in particular, can look superb defining an area within the garden – perhaps even as a framework for a Dutch garden (see page 207).

Hedges do not have to be tall to be interesting or admired. The dwarf box edging of a knot garden or *parterre*, and the dwarf yew edging to some of the more formal styles of flower beds, are magnificent examples of miniature hedges.

If planting a new hedge, think of the possibilities of including a bay (*Laurus nobilis*) to provide a suitable niche for a garden seat, or as background to a piece of statuary. A white ornament looks superb against the dark green of yew and, if placed on a plinth within the arms of a bay created for the purpose, it can make a splendid focal point.

Hedges can make excellent bases for topiary pieces, but bear in mind that you may need to modify the profile of the hedge to suit. How to make a tapering hedge, which is broad at the base and narrow at the top, is set out below. However, your cockerel or peacock may look better sitting on a flat-topped hedge.

Preparation and planting

It is spacing, as well as clipping, that determines the height and shape of a hedge. The stately beech (*Fagus sylvatica*) is a forest tree if grown in isolation and without undue competition; it is a compact hedging plant if spaced 450mm (1½ft) apart.

The table on traditional hedging plants (see page 220) sets out recommended spacing, although this can, of course, be varied slightly without causing too many problems.

You have only one chance to get the soil right, so it is worth going to some trouble to make sure you have the correct conditions for growth.

Because weeds are extremely difficult to disentangle and eradicate from the base of a hedge – weed competition will do much to restrict early growth and may cause the hedge to become bare at the base – in the past it was common to cultivate and keep hoeing the area for several months before planting to make sure the ground was 'clean'. Modern herbicides (weedkillers) make this practice unnecessary.

If you use a weedkiller, choose a non-persistent one. If the ground is infested with difficult perennial weeds, choose a weedkiller that is also translocated into the roots. Always read the instructions carefully before deciding which one to use.

If the weeds are mainly annuals, you may be able to control them by digging them in and, at the same time, removing any noticeable perennial roots.

A good hedging plant should be small (see box on page 220), but the trench should be wide. Although it will *look* very wide, it is worth digging a strip 900mm (3ft) wide, which should be kept weed-free after planting.

Double-dig the strip and cultivate to the depth of about 500mm (20in), keeping the topsoil at the surface. Work in as much manure or garden compost as you can spare. Traditionally, this was worked into the bottom spit (lower 250mm/10in), but we now have evidence that it is best spread throughout the cultivated depth.

Rake the ground level and sprinkle a balanced general fertilizer over the surface at about 100g (4oz) to a 900mm (3ft) run.

Container-grown plants can be planted at any time, provided the ground is not frozen or waterlogged. Bare-root or balled plants are best planted either in October or November or in late February or March. Planting distances depend on the plant.

A single row of plants should be perfectly adequate. A double row is more difficult to weed.

How big?

Resist the temptation to buy large plants. Smaller ones are not only cheaper; ultimately, they are also likely to overtake larger ones because they transplant more readily than older plants. More importantly, a small plant means that you can train it from an early stage, which results in a fuller, more clothed base.

Even the reputedly slow-growing yew (*Taxus baccata*) should make a hedge about 1.8m (6ft) high and over 900mm (3ft) wide at the base in about nine years from plants 300mm (1ft) high. Starting with plants four times this height may only produce a hedge perhaps less than 300mm (1ft) higher and broader – and at much greater cost.

Training

After planting, remove the tip of the leading shoot from all the plants, and cut to an even height (use a garden line, stretched between posts, to ensure that they are trimmed to the same height). This will encourage bushiness and will help to

How to plant

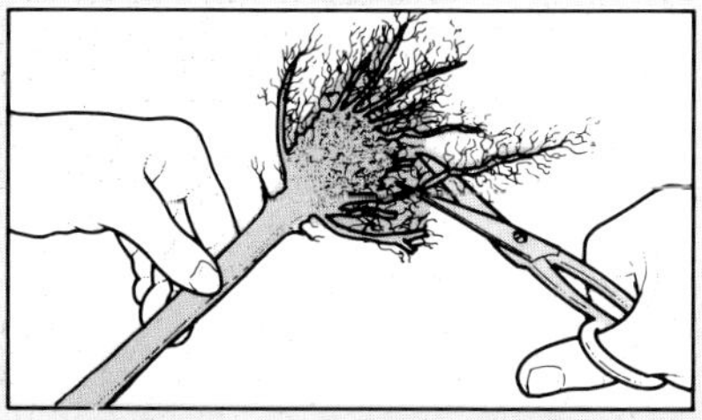

1. *Allow one or two weeks for soil to settle before immersing bare-root plants in water for a few hours prior to planting. Cleanly cut off damaged or over-long roots.*

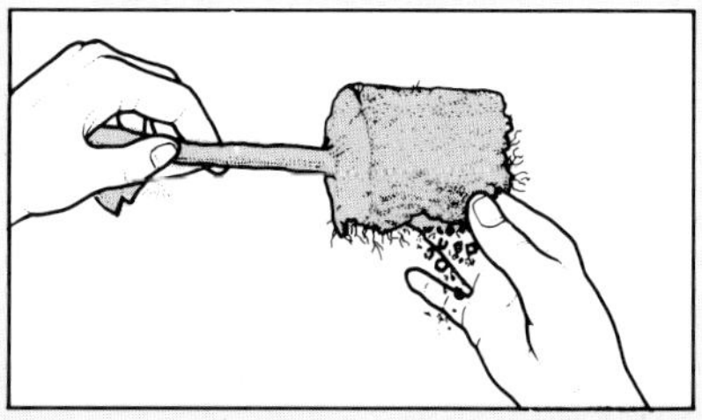

2. *If using container-grown plants, tease out a few roots from the root-ball to encourage rooting outwards.*

3. *Mark the row with string; dig holes large enough to comfortably accommodate roots, making sure the plants are planted to same depth as before by matching old soil-marks on the stems.*

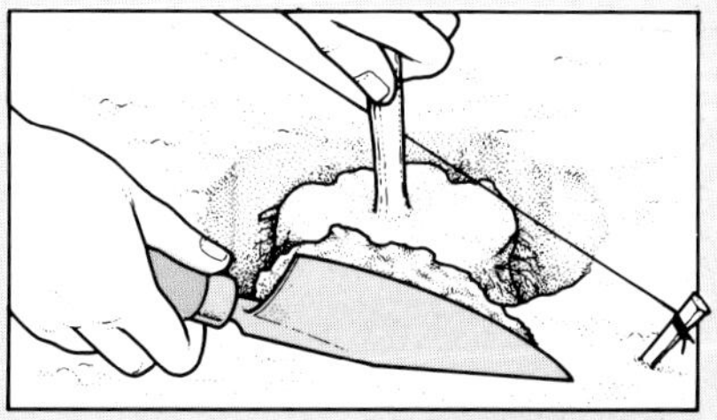

4. *Backfill the holes and firm the soil. Water thoroughly unless rain is imminent.*

produce a uniform height from an early stage.

At the end of the first summer after planting, trim the shoots to an even height, again using a line as a guide.

It is now time to start shaping the sides, too. Tip back sideshoots to form parallel lines, and taper slightly towards the top (this is known as the 'batter').

The batter is one of the hallmarks of a good hedge. The broad base and narrow top will make a pleasing shape, but it also has practical advantages. It lets in more light both to the ground beside the hedge and, or course, to the hedge itself. Generally, the plant is likely to be well clothed at its base, and with a good batter there is less risk of snow damage because it is more likely to fall off instead of weighing down the upper branches. A batter can make all the difference between compact, even growth, and a lanky, stalky hedge.

Producing a batter

The finished hedge should ideally have a batter of about 50mm (2in) in every 300mm (1ft).

Aim to prune for the batter at an early stage – it will be more difficult to achieve later.

It is worth making a couple of wooden frames to achieve the right profile. A typical frame is illustrated below. Assuming you eventually want a hedge 600mm (2ft) across at the bottom, and 300mm (1ft) at the top, to a height of 900mm (3ft), the dimensions would be as shown, but these must be adapted to suit the individual hedge.

The exact profile will also depend on the effect to be achieved – two slightly different profiles are shown below.

Knock nails into the edge of the profile frames so that you can stretch strings between the frames at key points. These will serve as useful cutting guides during the formative years.

Scallops and other decorative effects are difficult to achieve, and need a lot of care and attention to maintain. Take the hedge up to the lowest point in the finished design, avoiding a pronounced batter,

Knightshayes Court in Devon, England, is famous for its topiary and yew hedges. This picture shows part of one of the old crenellated yew hedges. The scale here is large, but a similar effect would work in a small garden of more modest proportions.

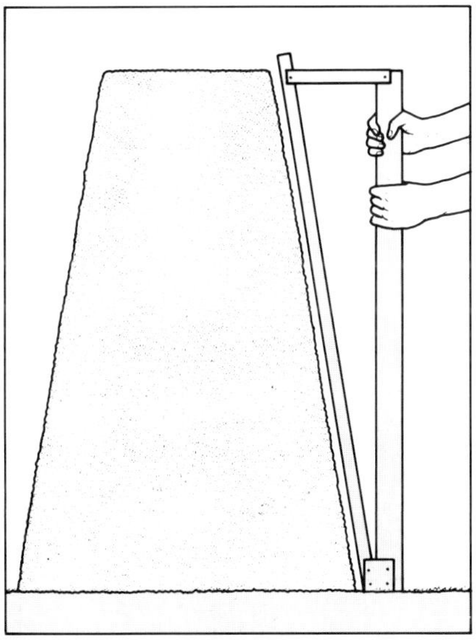

Clipping a batter. A simple frame which would give a batter of 50mm (2in) in every 300mm (1ft). Stretch strings between two frames to give a cutting guide.

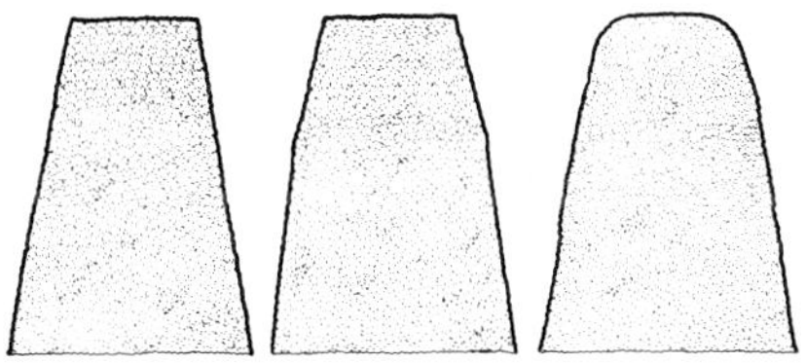

Three types of batter.

otherwise the combination of steeply sloping sides and wavy top can look disconcerting. It will take several years to achieve a dense hedge at the base line. You then extend the hedge to form either turrets or scallops as set out below.

Turrets, or the raised sections of a crenellated hedge, are relatively easy to achieve. Carefully measure the hedge and mark off the areas to be extended by inserting canes at the relevant points. Leave the shoots untrimmed where you want the hedge to extend, but top these areas when they are a few inches higher than the main hedge. The following year let them extend another few inches; by crenellating gradually the hedge will remain dense and solid.

Scallops need much more skill and a good eye to achieve satisfactory results. Perhaps the easiest way to acquire the desired effect is to use canes as guides when the hedge needs trimming. Insert a cane into the hedge every 300-600mm (1-2ft), each one with the top marked at, say, 75mm (3in) intervals. Stretch some string along the baseline of the top of the hedge, so that the canes are aligned, and by eye alone extend the slope from one cane to the next at the desired incline. This will have to be done in stages. Once a few inches of height have been gained the rest of the hedge will have to be trimmed flat, but each time you trim the slope can be extended a little more. Whatever you do, do not let the hedge run up to its full height and then hack into it to produce the slope. Disastrous results will follow.

Once the desired scallop or turret shape has been achieved, it will be relatively easy to trim to the required shape by eye, *provided* the hedge has increased in height slowly and is dense and thick.

Suitable plants

There are hundreds of plants that could be used successfully for hedging, but only a few that are especially good for a formal hedge. These plants respond well to close clipping and can be shaped with relative ease. They are listed below, together with recommended planting distances and suggested height to be reached eventually for a formal hedge.

Plants suitable for hedging

Name	Planting distance	Suggested final height	Number of cuts a year [1]	Remarks
Buxus sempervirens (box)	450mm (1½ft)	600-1200mm (2-4ft)	1 (mid or late summer)	There are many varieties. 'Handworthensis' is one of the best for tall or medium hedges.
Buxus sempervirens 'Suffruticosa' (dwarf box)	230mm (9in)	300-450mm (1-1½ft)	1 (mid or late summer)	Be sure to choose this variety for a dwarf hedge.
Fagus sylvatica (beech)	450mm (1½ft)	1.5-2.4m (5-8ft)	1 (late summer)	Good screen, but not for close, formal clipping.
Ligustrum ovalifolium (privet)	300-450mm (1-1½ft)	900-1200mm (3-4ft)	Monthly, late spring to late summer	For a golden variety, try *L. o.* 'Aureum'.
Lonicera nitida (shrubby honeysuckle)	300-450mm (1-1½ft)	600-1200mm (2-4ft)	Monthly, late spring to late summer	'Fertilis' is the variety to look for, though the ordinary species can be used. 'Baggesen's Gold' is a golden form.
Taxus baccata (yew)	500mm (20in)	1.2-1.8m (4-6ft)	1 (late summer)	There are many forms. 'Elegantissima' is good for hedges.
Thuja plicata 'Atrovirens'	500mm (20in)	1.2-1.8m (4-6ft)	1 (late summer)	'Atrovirens' is the one most suitable for hedges. *Thuja* is not suitable for elaborate clipping or for topiary.

[1] Once hedge established and shape formed.

Forming an arch

Although seldom seen nowadays, arches and openings used to be very popular. They are practical and may well provide the main interest to a garden. It is true that forming an arch with plants takes years to develop and also requires a great deal of patience to cultivate, but in almost all cases, the end result is worth waiting for!

Even a simple arch can form a useful purpose as a gateway which will give a sense of direction and purpose to an area. The arch should lead to a focal point or into another 'outdoor room'. It is a very good idea to take the hedge up over the garden gate to form an archway through which to enter the garden (or to lead from one part to another) if you really want to make the hedge a feature of the garden. Note that an arch sticking up in the middle of nowhere, which you can easily walk around, will seldom be effective. It is therefore best to consider the practical aspects of an arch first, before anything else. An arch tends to look more imposing together with a gate, but, as garden gates are nowhere near as popular as they used to be, this bit of 'dressing' can be omitted.

How to build an arch

Tie together long twigs at the end of the hedge, either side of the opening, possibly supported with canes until sufficient height has been gained to consider bridging the gap.

If the span is wide, or the width of the hedge slender, build a light, wooden framework 25mm × 25mm (1in × 1in). As the arch will take many years to form, a framework made from thick wire may be less obtrusive.

Traditionally, tarred string was used for tying in the shoots to the wires until the branches met and intertwined, but any modern rot-resistant tying material can be used without any harmful effects on the plants.

Do not hesitate to clip straggly or untidy shoots while the arch is forming. Clipping will encourage denser growth and sturdier plants.

Archways will take years to form – especially ones on this scale – but the impact is worth the training and waiting.

Index

Acknowledgements

Swallow Books gratefully acknowledge the assistance given to them in the production of *The Book of Home Restoration* by the following people and organizations. We apologize to anyone we may have omitted to mention.

Acquisitions Fireplaces Ltd of London 134 BL & BR, 135 BL & BR; Berger Paints 80 L & R, 81; The Bridgeman Art Library 13, 26, 40L, 40R, 45, 51, 52, 54, 70, 115; The British Tourist Authority 105L, 111, 113, 129, 201; Classic Furniture Ltd 105R; Cuprinol 36, 66R; Elon Tiles 155, 157; Sally & Richard Greenhill 200R; Lyn Le Grice Stencil Design (SB) St Buryan Cornwall TR19 6HG 89, 90; The Iris Hardwick Library of Photographs 204, 206, 207R, 210, 211, 215B, 221; Magnet & Southerns 123T; Peter McHoy 186, 190R, 191, 207L, 208, 209, 213, 215T, 217, 219; Museum of English Rurlal Life 30, 168, 187; Myford Limited 19; The National Trust Photographic Library 28, 102, 146, 162, 176; Osborne & Little 42, 84; Timothy Plant 85; John Prizeman 182, 190L; Paul Quail 119, 122, 123B, 126T, 127; Rentokil 149 T & B; Ronseal 57, 58, 60, L & R, 61, 66L, 67, 69, 153; Rustins 62, 64; Sanderson 74, 75, 78, 79, 82, 92, 93, 99, 100, 101, 145; Scottish Tourist Board 131, 181; Jessica Strang 166; Swiss National Tourist Office 73, 194; Topham 8, 18; Trannies/Liz Eddison, 126B, 130, 188, 192; Nick Eddison 179, Richard Steeds 198; Vigers 151; EWA/ Gary Chowitz 118, Steve Colby 109, Michael Dunne 38B, Clive Helm 38T, 138, 142, Frank Herholot 86, Ann Kelly 103, Tom Leighton 6, 83, 87, Neil Lorimer 136, 160, Jay Patrick 184, Spike Powell 2, 135T, Jerry Tubby 29, 139; D Wickens 170, 172, 173; Anna Wyner 158;

T: Top B: Bottom M: Middle L: Left R: Right